Wang Gungwu
EDUCATOR & SCHOLAR

Wang Gungwu
EDUCATOR & SCHOLAR

Editors

Zheng Yongnian
East Asian Institute, National University of Singapore, Singapore

Phua Kok Khoo
Institute for Advanced Studies, Nanyang Technological University, Singapore

World Scientific

NEW JERSEY · LONDON · SINGAPORE · BEIJING · SHANGHAI · HONG KONG · TAIPEI · CHENNAI

Published by

World Scientific Publishing Co. Pte. Ltd.
5 Toh Tuck Link, Singapore 596224
USA office: 27 Warren Street, Suite 401-402, Hackensack, NJ 07601
UK office: 57 Shelton Street, Covent Garden, London WC2H 9HE

Library of Congress Cataloging-in-Publication Data
Wang, Gungwu, author.
 Wang Gungwu, educator & scholar / Wang Gungwu ; editors, Zheng Yongnian, East Asian Institute, National University of Singapore, Singapore, Phua Kok Khoo, World Scientific Publishing Company, Singapore.
   pages cm
  ISBN 978-9814436625 -- ISBN 978-9814439930 (pbk)
 1. Education, Higher--East Asia. 2. Education, Higher--Pacific Area. 3. Educational change--East Asia. 4. Educational change--Pacific Area. 5. Wang, Gungwu. I. Zheng, Yongnian, editor of compilation. II. Phua, K. K., editor of compilation. III. Title. IV. Title: Wang Gungwu, educator and scholar.
  LA1143.W36 2013+
  378.5--dc23

                                                             2012035456

British Library Cataloguing-in-Publication Data
A catalogue record for this book is available from the British Library.

Copyright © 2013 by World Scientific Publishing Co. Pte. Ltd.

All rights reserved. This book, or parts thereof, may not be reproduced in any form or by any means, electronic or mechanical, including photocopying, recording or any information storage and retrieval system now known or to be invented, without written permission from the Publisher.

For photocopying of material in this volume, please pay a copying fee through the Copyright Clearance Center, Inc., 222 Rosewood Drive, Danvers, MA 01923, USA. In this case permission to photocopy is not required from the publisher.

In-house Editor: DONG Lixi

Typeset by Stallion Press
Email: enquiries@stallionpress.com

Printed in Singapore.

Preface

Zheng Yongnian and Phua Kok Khoo

It is hard for us to find the right words to describe Wang Gungwu, an eminent individual with many interesting facets and stellar achievements. He is best known to all as an established academic or scholar. Yet, he has also distinguished himself as a leader in various institutions that he has led or continues to head. He has further been recognised for his exemplary public service. Many individuals, organisations and even governments have sought his wise counsel and insights on not only issues related to Asia but also developments in other parts of the world. To those who have interacted with him, they are struck by not only his breadth and depth of knowledge but also his utmost humility and gentlemanly manners, akin to that of a scholar-gentleman or "*junzi*" in Mandarin. On a lighter and no less important note, Margaret, his wife of 57 years and who is the pillar in his life, has described their life together as rich and fulfilling in an earlier interview with the East Asian Institute. She further added that they have a very good marriage and they both enjoy each other's company.

Thus, in preparing a commemorative book on Wang Gungwu, we run the risk of failing to adequately account for his contributions. This task is even more difficult as Wang continues to make an impact on matters relating to the various appointments he presently holds as well as the numerous lectures and presentations that he still commits himself to.

In Singapore, Wang is concurrently the chairman of three institutions, namely the East Asian Institute, the Institute of Southeast Asian Studies and the Lee Kuan Yew School of Public Policy. In addition, he is a member of 11 other boards and institutions in Singapore and over 30 boards of overseas institutions and international journals. Given his global presence and influence as an educator and scholar, a book on Wang and his extensive contributions in education, especially higher education, is long overdue. We would rather subject ourselves to being criticised for not doing enough than for not doing anything at all.

History, as historians would like to describe it, is full of unexpected twists and turns. Wang himself has reminisced that he never expected himself to be a historian. He was more interested in literature in his youth. His father was a literary type and he grew up with a fondness for literary things. And to him, history in school was never very interesting. It was all about the British Empire. This did not quite inspire him because it was someone else's history. Even his choice of history at university was really quite accidental. The English professor, whom he admired, had returned to England. The Economics professor was not very interesting. Fortunately, the History professor was a lively fellow called C N Parkinson whom Wang signed up for in his honours year. The rest we could say is history.

But this historical twist did not just affect Wang's choice of subject in his honours year. Other unexpected developments permeated the life of Wang, especially his formative years. He was born in Surabaya, Indonesia in 1930. The Great Depression soon forced Wang's family to leave Surabaya and move to Ipoh, Perak by the end of 1931. Just as he completed Standard 5 (the equivalent of primary 5 in Singapore) in 1941, World War II disrupted his studies. After the war, his family moved to Nanjing, China. He was accepted into the National Central University of Nanjing in 1947 where he studied foreign languages. Not long after, the Civil War forced the closure of the university and he returned to Ipoh at the end of 1948. Malaya was then under a state of emergency declared by the British government against the Malayan Communist Party.

In 1949, Wang enrolled at the University of Malaya to study English literature, history and economics. He obtained his honours in 1953 and master's a year later. He applied for graduate study at the School of Oriental and African Studies in London in 1954 and graduated with a PhD in mediaeval history in 1957. Thereafter, he returned to the University of Malaya where in a short span of time he became lecturer (in 1959), senior lecturer (in 1961), dean of the Faculty of Arts (in 1962), and then professor of History and head of department (in 1963). From 1968 to 1986, he was professor and head of the Department of Far Eastern History, and director of Research School of Pacific Studies at the Australian National University, Canberra. He was appointed vice-chancellor (president) of the University of Hong Kong from 1986 to 1995. In 1995, former Singapore Deputy Prime Minister Goh Keng Swee wrote to him and invited him to Singapore to take over the chairmanship of the Institute of East Asian Political Economy, the predecessor of the East Asian Institute. When the East Asian Institute was formed, Wang was appointed director and also faculty professor in the Faculty of Arts and Social Sciences at the National University of Singapore (NUS) from 1997 to 2007. He became chairman of the East Asian Institute in 2007.

Wang's resilience could be seen in the face of sudden and big adjustments, demonstrating at the same time an uncanny ability to seize opportunities that presented themselves. More importantly, he created opportunities to excel through his sheer intellect and unflinching commitment to academic research and writing. Most inspiring of all, his love for research, writing and history is contagious; unknowingly, he has converted several aspiring research scholars in disciplines like economics and politics to history and he seems to derive boundless energy from these tasks. He is an excellent role model.

This book focusses on Wang as an educator and scholar. It is organised into three parts. The first section highlights the writings of Wang in the field of higher education. There are 24 selected articles written by him from 1971 during his stint with the Australian National University, to 2008 when he was with the East Asian Institute. In these articles, Wang shares his perspectives on a range of topics from the relationship between the university and community (both of which are not monolithic); the issue of funding for universities; the role of universities in Asia as global institutions; the idea of universal standards of excellence in education in the Asia-Pacific region; the need for national education to take into account the value of the scientific tradition; the state of social science study in Asia; the shifting paradigms and their impact on research and writing; the role of university in shaping modernity in Asia; to the efforts of the Chinese in pursuing higher education in China. Many of the points and ideas in his essays have a particular resonance today as universities grapple with the multidimensional and complex issues of change, modernity, relevance, sustainability, creativity and innovation.

Closer to home, and of immediate interest to those at NUS is Wang's commemorative essay on the centennial celebrations of NUS in 2005 and his address on the occasion of the East Asian Institute's move from the Kent Ridge campus to the Bukit Timah campus of NUS in 2007. In these two papers, Wang shares his personal experiences and insights on the two institutions which he has been and is an integral part of. In addition, readers will find Wang's several shorter articles which he wrote for *Times Higher Education Supplement* (known today as the *Times Higher Education* that focusses on issues related to higher education) equally illuminating and interesting.

The second section introduces a selection of over 50 books written and edited or co-edited by Wang as well as those written in honour of him. Each book is accompanied by a short description of its contents, and where relevant, comments by other renowned scholars on the particular book. The selected books cover a wide array of topics including the Five Dynasties (that is based on Wang's PhD thesis submitted in 1957); Chinese diaspora and overseas Chinese; Chinese culture, history and civilisation; Chinese trade; maritime China; China's ideological battles; the Chinese Communist Party; China's political economy; China's reform; China's external relations; China and the new international order; Chinese world order; migration; nation-building; Hong Kong; Malaya; Malaysia; and the Iraq War. The books listed are arranged in alphabetical order from the earliest published to the latest for the easy reference of readers.

The third section provides a detailed chronology of Wang's life from his birth to the present day. It shows not only the tumultuous and challenging times that Wang has experienced but also historic and memorable moments such as the visit by a delegation of historians, including Wang, and China specialists from the Australian National University to China in 1973 just after Australia and China established diplomatic ties. This was Wang's first visit to China in 26 years. He last visited China in 1947 when he sat for the entrance examination to the National Central University in Nanjing. Another historic moment was when Wang, as vice-chancellor of the University of Hong Kong (HKU), had to steer HKU through the ramifications of its part in the Tiananmen demonstrations of 1989. Before the crackdown, Hong Kong students, including those from HKU, marched in the city centre streets to show their solidarity and raise funds for Chinese students in Tiananmen. Some HKU students even travelled to China to show their support.

Beyond his academic achievements, the chronology also showcases Wang's contribution to public service when he was in Australia, Hong Kong and Singapore. As chairman of the Australia-China Council from 1984 to

1986, Wang helped to promote mutual understanding and foster people-to-people relations between Australia and China. As executive councillor of the Executive Council of the Hong Kong government from 1990 to 1992 (before the handover), Wang was involved in an intense period of negotiations between London and Beijing over issues such as electoral timetables and the new airport at Chek Lap Kok. In recognition of his contributions, Wang was awarded the Commander of the Order of the British Empire by Governor David Wilson in Hong Kong in November 1992. In 2004, Wang was appointed Singapore coordinator for the Network of East Asian Think-Tanks, an organisation that brings together thinkers from ASEAN, China, Japan and Korea to brainstorm ideas to promote closer cooperation among these 13 countries. He was awarded the Public Service Medal by the Singapore government in 2004 and a second medal in 2008.

This book was conceived more than three years ago. Initial preparations focussed on compiling a detailed chronology and list of publications by Wang. Focus then shifted to selecting and editing his articles. The process took longer than expected, a testimony to the voluminous works and wide-ranging achievements of Wang. With Wang's kind permission, we have timed the publication of this book to coincide with the 15th anniversary of the East Asian Institute. This is to recognise Wang's instrumental role in establishing and laying a strong foundation for the institute that we see today. As current chairman of the institute, he continues to be a huge source of inspiration for academic excellence and public service.

On a final note, we would like to thank the dedicated staff of EAI for their unstinting involvement in preparing this book. Special mention goes to Jessica Loon and Ho Wei Ling for their painstaking and meticulous editing work, including checking and verifying sources as well as liaising with the publisher World Scientific Publishing. We would also like to thank Lye Liang Fook for lending his drafting expertise to this exercise. In addition, Lim Chee Kia, Catherine Chong Siew Keng, Zhu Jinjing, Courtney Fu Rong and Pan Rongfang have helped to compile the relevant facts and publications. Furthermore, Lam Peng Er and Yew Chiew Ping have assisted in their proofreading efforts. Our thanks also go to the various external publishers for granting us permission to reprint the writings of Wang.

Last but not least, we would like to express our most sincere appreciation to the Lee Foundation for generously sponsoring the production of this book.

July 2012

About the Editors

Professor ZHENG Yongnian is director of the East Asian Institute (EAI) at the National University of Singapore. He received his BA and MA degrees from Beijing University, and his PhD from Princeton University. He was a recipient of Social Science Research Council-MacArthur Foundation Fellowship (1995–1997) and John D and Catherine T MacArthur Foundation Fellowship (2003–2004). He was Professor and founding Research Director of the China Policy Institute of the University of Nottingham in the United Kingdom. Professor Zheng is the editor of Series on Contemporary China (World Scientific Publishing), China Policy Series (Routledge), *China: An International Journal* and *East Asian Policy*. His research interests include both China's domestic transformation and its external relations. His papers have appeared in journals such as *Comparative Political Studies*, *Political Science Quarterly* and *China Quarterly*. He is also the author and editor of numerous books. Besides his research work, Professor Zheng has also been an academic activist. He served as a consultant to United Nations Development Programme on China's rural development and democracy. In addition, he has been a columnist for *Xin Bao* (*Hong Kong Economic Journal*, Hong Kong) and *Lianhe Zaobao* (Singapore) for many years, writing numerous commentaries on China's domestic and international affairs.

Professor PHUA Kok Khoo obtained his PhD in Mathematical Physics from the University of Birmingham in 1970. He was awarded the Institute of Physics Singapore (IPS) President's Award by the IPS Council in 2006. He is a fellow at the American Physical Society, the founding director of the Institute for Advanced Studies at Nanyang Technological University, an adjunct professor at the National University of Singapore, and honorary professor in many universities in China. He is also chairman of the World Scientific Publishing Company, chairman of the Tan Kah Kee Foundation, vice-chairman of the Tan Kah Kee International Society, and president of the Singapore China Friendship Association and Singapore China Business Association. Professor Phua's research interests are in theoretical high energy physics, science education and science policies. He has published many papers on scientific research in internationally refereed journals and comments on scientific research and higher education in Singapore national newspapers *Lianhe Zaobao* and *The Strait Times*. For nearly 40 years, Professor Phua has dedicated himself to strengthening scientific research in Asia and promoting physics education, higher education and scholarly exchanges at the international level.

Contents

Preface   v

About the Editors   xi

Part I   Wang Gungwu on Higher Education   1

1	The University and the Community	3
2	National Education and the Scientific Tradition	27
3	Who Should Pay for Universities?	43
4	A Very Peculiar Business	59
5	The University as a Global Institution	63
6	The Asian Renaissance	71
7	Cities Light Torch of Excellence	75
8	Lessons Closer to Home	79

9	The Asia-Pacific: Region and Universalism in Higher Education	83
10	The Modern University in Australia and Asia	99
11	Social Science and Asia	109
12	Shifting Paradigms and Asian Perspectives: Implications for Research and Teaching	129
13	The Classics and the East Asian Entrepreneur	139
14	Universities and Modernity for Asia	145
15	New Interest in Old Powers	155
16	Change and Adaptation: NUS at 100	159
17	The Chinese Pursuit of Higher Education	181
18	New University, Three Generations: China, Malaya, Singapore 1949–2007	197
19	Versailles' Chinese Legacy	209
20	Commonwealth Universities in Eastern Asia	213
21	You've Come a Long Way	217
22	Academic Blind Spot in Asia	221
23	English Rules the Waves	225
24	Rise of Anglo-Chinese	229

Part II Wang Gungwu and His Works — **233**

Part III Chronology of Wang Gungwu — **315**

Index — **397**

PART I

Wang Gungwu on Higher Education

1

The University and the Community

Keynote Address

The subject of higher education in Asia has attracted a great deal of attention during the past decade. Some of this attention has consisted of somewhat unwelcome publicity; some of it has been most constructive. The Association of Southeast Asian Institutions of Higher Learning has given the subject constructive attention for several years and should be congratulated for organising this Second Workshop on Higher Education. I am greatly honoured by the invitation to speak about some of the recent developments in Asia affecting those of us teaching and studying in universities.

This is a revised version of the keynote lecture delivered at the Second Asian Workshop on Higher Education, organised under the auspices of the Association of Southeast Asian Institutions of Higher Learning (6 to 15 December 1971). It was published in *Proceedings, Second Asian Workshop on Higher Education*, edited by Rayson L Huang (Singapore: Nanyang University, 1971), pp. 17–29. Reproduced with the kind permission of the Association of Southeast Asian Institutions of Higher Learning.

The theme for the Workshop, "The University and the Community", raises many kinds of issues and has been considered from many angles by many different people. On the surface, it would appear that many pious things have already been said about this subject. Are we just going to re-examine some of the well-worn observations? On the other hand, much of what has been said has been said in different contexts and under different conditions. In Asia we are changing so fast that we cannot simply accept what was said a generation or two back, or even what was said some years ago. It is obviously not enough to re-examine old themes. We must expect changes to have taken place and must be prepared to identify these changes.

The Workshop has chosen four areas for discussion and we should examine the topics in terms of the principles involved and the conditions which are applicable in Asia today. The four areas cover academic standards; relevance; rigidity and immobility within the university and the community; and the question of consensus between the university and the community. These topics will be examined in various seminar sessions and case studies papers will be presented. I shall explore some of the assumptions both university and community leaders make concerning the future of our societies in Asia and the role of universities in that future.

Perhaps the most basic assumption in all new Asian countries is that *change* is necessary. This is so often said that it is beginning to become something of a pious cliché. It would certainly not be remarkable to refer to this idea of change were it not for the fact that most Asian societies never emphasised it in the past and never before has the whole of Asia faced so much change in so short a time. If only for this reason alone, there is the need to affirm that our viewpoint about the university and the community should be made in the context of rapid and thorough change of many of our greatest traditions and institutions. These changes form a more complex background than it appears on the surface. We also have to consider how each country is trying to change in its own way and at its own speed. And depending on the speed and direction of change, its universities will be expected to play different roles. Equally complex are the various efforts in each country to determine what to change and the order of the changes to follow so that what the community (and perhaps the university as well) wants to preserve should be preserved.

Obviously, when both universities and communities change, it is possible for communities to be changing faster than universities or for universities to be changing more rapidly than their communities. It is even possible to have them changing in different directions and at uneven and disjointed rates. At one time, the universities appear new, progressive, far advanced and even revolutionary, compared to the sluggish, tradition-bound communities. At other times, we find the communities, once awakened, move forward steadily and picking up momentum. Then it would be the universities which appear to slow down and stop, or even appear to be putting the brakes on the community itself. And not least, there could be situations where some universities and some sections of a community are moving or changing at a far faster pace than others in the same country and also the situation where the rate of change in one country and its universities causes anxiety among its neighbours and their universities. All these conditions may produce tensions and conflicts between communities, between universities, and particularly relevant to this Workshop, between universities and the communities they operate in.

These changing conditions have been widely discussed and we have to be conscientiously careful in our deliberations. There are many circumstances in which universities are potentially, if not actually, in conflict with their communities and it would be futile to pretend that such tensions and conflicts do not exist.

Another major assumption concerns the ideal relationship between the university and the community. It is often assumed that only harmonious relationships are ideal. This is probably rather naive. The more fruitful relationship may well be one which is taut and tense, with the university and the community frequently acting and reacting upon each other. But there is a growing consensus of opinion not only in Asia but throughout the world that the two should be, if not one and inseparable, at least closely integrated. Only in this way can both university and community benefit from the pressures of change and the availability of skilled human resources. So widely is this felt now that there are very few who would explicitly deny the importance of this close relationship. The debate is now generally on how this relationship can be the most efficient and constructive, what the ideal proximity is between university and community and who should decide on the nature of that relationship. The significance of these debates is indubitable, and our gathering together at the Workshop underlines the hope that such debates be fruitful and the results more widely applicable.

But the fact is that these debates have been long-drawn and encrusted with many misunderstandings. Some of the debates have concentrated on the ideal of the university and innumerable disagreements have arisen.

Other debates have centred on the needs of the community and the university's responsibilities to serve those needs, which remain difficult to resolve largely because of the high public expectation on universities in the short run and the lack of distinction between immediate and long-term community needs. There is a need to sort out ideas about two key points in the debate if we are to make any progress in understanding. The first concerns the current image of the university and the second concerns the concept of the community.

First, the image of the university. The university is not to be construed as a body of people (both staff and students) united in all its effort and speaking always with one voice. There is no such thing. The term "university" is shorthand for a wide range of activities directed towards acquiring and imparting knowledge under conditions which permit these activities to take place successfully. There are many varieties of universities. At the First Workshop on Higher Education held in Hong Kong in 1969, I spoke about the background of the existing universities in Asia. Many of them are colonial or sectarian in origin, others are aggressively modernising or nationalistic, and still others are mainly conservative about indigenous traditions. But all of them, whether given a choice, have had to meet the challenge of a rapidly changing Asia, particularly in the years after the Second World War.

It is easy to satirise some of these universities, either as poor imitations of European universities and parodies of the American ones, or as heroic but struggling do-it-yourself local variants. Either way, they are easy targets for criticism. If they remain colonial or sectarian, they are serving outside masters and foreign goals and therefore quite irrelevant if not actually subversive. If they are modernising, they may still be too slow for the community's needs or they are pushing fiercely in directions which the community is not prepared to go. If they are nationalistic, they may be seen as conceiving their goals too narrowly and ignoring the experience of others. And if they are conservative, they may be blamed for all that is going wrong in the country.

The university is a convenient scapegoat in many countries, and any kind of outcry against it would not be surprising. This is true not merely in Asia. The outcries against universities in Europe, America and Australia are, in fact, much fiercer than any that have been heard in most of the new countries in Southeast Asia and East Asia. And those Western universities are changing and responding to criticism probably more rapidly and more imaginatively than any of the universities in Asia, although some of them are ancient and conservative universities like Oxford, Paris and Harvard. What our universities should be worried about is not the fact that they are being attacked but that they are being attacked on the basis of an image which is largely negative.

Two examples of the extreme views are still currently held. The first emphasises that the university is not doing what the community wants. Two kinds of arguments are used for the view that the university exists to fulfill the community's demands: firstly, that this is the truly democratic way as the university must serve the people and respond to their needs. This can be described as the moral and political argument. The other argument emphasises the money angle — the "pay-the-piper-and-call-the-tune" argument — which is particularly persuasive among those who value money more than education. The image of the university invariably doing what the community wants is superficially attractive to those who know nothing of what a university can, in fact, best do and have never given any thought to what a university should do. They also oversimplify the idea of a community as a single entity which always knows what it wants and fail to see the part the university plays in helping the community to know and find out what it wants.

The second extreme, long-held view sees the university as an ivory tower — expensive and isolated from the community. Such a view has often been attributed to academics who regard themselves as superior beings whose work should not be debased by mundane and practical considerations. My own impression is that such academics are rare in Asia, and indeed in the whole world, and even those few who still hold this view are usually intelligent enough to recognise that it is indefensible or to accept that it is too unpopular to be defended and therefore keep the view to themselves. More commonly, the accusation that universities are ivory towers come from the same critics who want universities to rise to the community's every demand. Frankly, that particular horse being flogged is now dead. I know of no university in the world which is not trying to respond to its own communities, although each may do so in a different way and for varying reasons — sometimes from conviction, more often because of financial and public pressure. The degree of responsiveness and effectiveness of serving community's needs may also vary, but this has little connection with the university being a tower or being as smooth as ivory. Again, we return to the question of what the university can best do, of what the community is and who determines what the community wants.

One can suggest a more positive image of what most Asian universities today try to shape. This image takes into account the complexity of the relationship between university and community and identifies the four main layers at which this relationship is meaningful.

Firstly, there is the level at which the university tries to work closely with the government, providing it with information, advanced analyses, even expert personnel, and trains skilled young men and women to run the government's many administrative and research organs.

Secondly, there is the level at which the university accepts briefs to conduct specific research on behalf of some segments of the community, whether they are capitalist entrepreneurs, trade unions, social welfare or religious or educational groups and other kinds of voluntary associations.

Thirdly, there is the level at which the university initiates research and teaching on disciplines which it thinks are important and acts independently to direct attention to problems which it expects to arise in the future.

Fourthly, there is the level at which the university examines the ends and means set up by the government and claimed on behalf of the community, and establishes standards of quality and excellence in the fields of its competence.

For the first two levels, the relationship to the community is more obvious and the critics of the university are usually silent even though the university may not actually help the government and community organisations very successfully. It is often thought that it should suffice that the university has tried and showed that it is willing to be responsive. It is the third and fourth levels where the university takes the initiative that have been harder for government and community leaders to understand. Here is also where the university itself is sometimes to blame, especially when it takes these two levels of activity for granted and makes little effort to explain why these are vital responsibilities for the university. Besides, the university sometimes does make mistakes. It may be mistaken about the future value of the research and teaching that have been initiated. It may make mistakes about the selection of staff to do the research and teaching. It may even appear to be incompetent in the criticisms its staff and students make about the government's and community's goals and methods. But the mistakes notwithstanding, the right and duty to initiate such teaching and research, the idealism needed to take risks in order to anticipate future problems, and the readiness to offer moral and intellectual leadership and to criticise independently and responsibly the community it serves are an integral part of university's relations with the community. Without this right, this idealism, this leadership, the university can only work with its body and limbs, possibly with part of its brains but certainly without its heart.

I have been treating the university and the community as separate entities for the purpose of clarification and analysis. The university consists of people who work, teach and study in the institution, and who act and think in terms of what they believe their university stands for. While a university may claim to be a community on its own, these people are also members of the community as a whole, or of different sections of the community. As such, they also reflect many of the conflicts, anxieties and hopes of their communities. Indeed, broadly speaking, much that has been said of the university could be mirrored in the community. It is important, and at times painful, to ponder on the nature of the community a university is expected to serve. In many cases, universities are paralleled by similar kinds of communities and community elites which the universities, in fact, had helped to produce in the first place. We find that communities and their elites also vary from poor imitations and parodies of the West to the heroic but struggling do-it-yourself types. Indeed there are various kinds of communities in Asia today. Understanding the relationship between university and community, the tension between the two and the necessity to make such tension positive and creative goes beyond simply assessing the various universities, and certainly involves deeper analysis of the types of communities in existence and the concept of community.

The concept of "community" describes distinctive groups of people presumed to have characteristics recognisably different from one another. Most commonly, it is loosely used to signify an idea which in turn is often interpreted with the same meaning as the nation. This is most misleading. The idea of community is derived from one of the basic units of human organisation and, in one of its earliest and purest forms, it is the small village community. In such a community, its members are attributed the highest social cohesion — they work and play together and ideally, they enjoy themselves and suffer as one community. In this sense, the community is one which evolved organically over a long period of time and is characterised by its dependence upon extended kinship, shared activity and experience, and strong values which the whole community accepts. Beyond the village, the sense of community can exist in towns and cities, and in larger areas and regions where people share and are committed to the same set of cultural values. We can, at one level, talk of local, rural and urban communities, but we can also, at another level, stretch the concept to include larger communities like the Ummat Islam, the Hindu, Buddhist and Christian communities, the combination of Confucianism, Buddhism and Taoism which produced the Chinese community and other combinations which produced the Japanese, Korean, and Vietnamese communities. But the concept of nation is new in Asia and the attempt by any country to build a national community is fraught with great difficulties. For one thing, it presumes to combine different units of sociocultural forces and significance into new political entities. For another, it involves pushing existing and often minority communities together and forcing them to coalesce within new and often artificial boundaries. Naturally there are great tension and almost permanent conditions of potential conflict. It is in this context that the university finds it difficult to know which community it is to serve.

I shall begin with the proposition that all countries in Asia have meaningful local and minority communities, but few, if any, have built their national communities yet. The biggest challenge to the idea of a national community is that the Western and modern idea of nation, which is used as the model for Asia, is based on different principles — principles of free association among the people which, if pursued to their logical conclusion, would greatly dilute any sense of community. What Western nations have succeeded in building are modern *societies* which emphasise the activities of individuals and the primacy of voluntary and contractual relationships. These relationships are fluid and flexible and may be frequently renegotiated, readjusted and revitalised. If we in Asia want to build our nations, we must be clear if the model fits what we have in mind, or it is something else altogether that can somehow give us a new political unity and security without losing our sense of community. This leads us to ask if we expect our universities to emphasise the aspects of modernisation which create new societies of a largely contractual kind or whether we want our universities to teach a little technology but really help our community leaders to construct the new Asian type of nation based on community pressures and moral suasion. If the former, are we realistic in believing that we can preserve our sense of community? If the latter, are universities as we know them suitable instruments for creating that kind of community, or would we need a new kind of university altogether?

Broadly speaking, most Asian universities are modelled on those in the West and are geared to creating modern societies while most Asian countries consist of rural and urban, majority and minority communities in search of the yet unattained national community. Hence, any discussion of the university and the community in Asia today brings us to serious contradictions that have exacerbated the tension between many existing universities and the governments which speak for the various kinds of communities in Asia. Thus, before we can speak of the future national community which many Asian nations claim they want, we must look at the constituent parts of that future community and determine if the university has any significant relationship with them.

I shall briefly consider the local communities and colleges and universities which are supposed to cater for a region or for a number of rural and urban communities. These communities are usually thought to be too small and insular to perceive the boundaries of the larger community and are really too inefficient on their own or too poor to develop their resources. The university is then expected not only to support these communities but also to provide a bridge between them and the future national community. In this bridging position, the university is invariably faced with tension, and even conflicts, as it tries to find ways of serving small local groups and the national leadership at the same time. When communities have yet to be integrated, and the outcome is uncertain and must take time, the university cannot simply be an obedient servant. There will be many important decisions to take. Will the university have the initiative to act and judge what it can and cannot do?

Then there are countries in Asia where local communities are linked with questions of tribal, religious and "racial" differences and important minority groups, making it all the more difficult to build the future national community. With these problems, most governments face the difficult choice of using more force to bring about rapid integration at the expense of minority rights or of employing techniques of compromise to permit the free growth of minority communities within clearly defined limits. Is there a role for the university to play in an area where even governments run into great difficulties? If the university is to be responsive to the needs of the community, we may well ask, to *which* community? Or, how much to the majority community and how much to the minority communities? Also, should there be universities for minority groups? These questions alert us to a fundamental problem: is a university still a university if it favours one type of community over another, or the larger over the smaller, or the national interest over different community aspirations? Should a university be allowed the initiative to determine on its own the extent to which, by reflecting the country's various peoples and cultures, it is acting in the country's highest interest?

Given the fact that local and minority communities are still meaningful in Asia today, we note that national leaders are often ambiguous themselves about the kind of nation they want to build. They want to build a nation and also to preserve the sense of community: they want to avoid the kind of modernisation which might bring social fragmentation in its wake. They want, therefore, to establish a strong central government which can act and speak for the national community which they hope to create. In this context, where does the university stand? It is certainly expected to work for the government to help it create the larger national community out of the local and minority communities. The idea of the university and the community in Asia then has become increasingly a question of the university and the government which represents the politicised sectors of the various communities. In this way, the university has become a political institution, and the pressure to politicise it further and make it an instrument of government as well (if it is not already one) is likely to increase. But, as long as local and minority communities also look to the university for help to survive, intolerable conflicts for the university are created. It is therefore necessary to re-examine some of the implications of the apparently simple statement that the university must serve the community and be responsive to its needs. We must take into account the fact that as all rural-urban, majority-minority communities are being politicised, the university's most important responsibility today may be to recognise that it has to be political itself and try to understand what being political means for the university.

It should be emphasised that being political does not mean mere awareness of party politics or the processes of government, nor does it mean that the lecture theatre should become a political forum. Being political invokes a deeper sense of commitment and participation which involves the sharing and clarifying of political rights and duties, the making of value judgments, the willingness to act on academic principles both inside and outside the university and, most of all, the readiness to take responsibility for its actions.

There are at least three basic structures in which most Asian universities operate. Firstly, I describe these universities in countries where they reflect the national purpose as well as others which serve local and minority communities as non-political mixed structures. This type of university structure is found in Japan where national unity is not a serious problem, and in India and the Philippines where the creation of the future national community has not been seen as either urgent or immediately practicable. Such structure can also be found to some extent in Indonesia where strong regional forces and the isolation of some local and minority communities make it necessary for the central government to accept the mixed structure. But few Asian countries can really afford this mixed form due to the high cost and high demand for scarce skilled resources, and most of all, the ubiquitous fear that local and minority universities will encourage divisive elements in their countries. Apart from Japan which is exceptional because it is already a fully developed country, it is probable that this structure in the other three countries will be dominated by the central governments and be gradually politicised.

Secondly, universities are seen as political structures in countries where they are expected primarily to help create the future national community, but may also respond to existing local and minority community needs as long as they do not conflict with national goals. Some obvious examples are countries like Ceylon, Malaysia and Singapore. But in their volatile political conditions, even this tolerance of local-minority needs meets with real difficulties. For one thing, this semi-mixed structure requires considerable initiative on the part of the universities themselves. For another, it requires a higher degree of political consensus between the universities and the governments concerned. Given the conditions where governments are reluctant to entrust universities with latitude to take initiative, and where universities themselves may in fact not be equipped to make such sensitive and delicate decisions on their own, there is an urgent need that universities be politicised so that governments need not take them over altogether.

Thirdly, the universities described as bureaucratic structures are common in countries where universities are totally controlled by central governments and are used as instruments for national integration and for speeding up the modernisation process. This control by government is far from a new idea. Traditional Asia has always favoured conformity with the major tenets of the community, and kings and priests, local Brahmins, gurus, scholar-gentry, and even samurai, all played their role in controlling the education of the elites. What is different is that the new conformity is entirely secular and the control more total. Modern governments argue that so much is at stake that they must control all initiatives, including initiatives in teaching and research which universities have claimed to be their preserve.

Here, one may distinguish between communist countries which believe in total control as a matter of ideology and utopian principle and fascist ones which glory in absolute power as an end in itself. One may also distinguish these two from those countries which seem to increase and tighten their hold on universities gradually and claim to be doing so in the name of survival, in order to prevent wastage and to increase efficiency. Universities working under totalitarian systems tend to be totally subservient to the ruling elites and relevant government ministries and departments. What we should all be concerned with is universities in countries that are still trying to mobilise resources for modernisation with the minimum use of force. These are countries which still believe in varying degrees of private initiative, whether on behalf of local and minority communities or of universities, but whose governments increasingly find such initiatives inefficient and irksome and even obstructive. The tendency then is to whittle away at private initiatives which do not directly help a rather narrowly conceived nation-building process.

Of special concern are countries which may well have begun with the first or second kinds of structures, but are tempted to turn to the third type of structure and resort to holding direct control of their universities on the grounds that the universities constituted at present fail to provide bold and intelligent initiatives and do not reflect the political realities in their countries. While direct control appears to be the simplest and most satisfactory solution, I question the assumption that bureaucratic control may make for more efficient universities. I suggest that, whether the total control is justified in terms of ideology or absolutist power or as a necessary evil, the result is similar. The university becomes an administrative organ, obedient and pliant from above, but is unable to respond to any community as it is, in fact, politically dead.

In sum, the university here does not have *the* integrated national community to work for but it is expected to help create such a community out of the various kinds of local and minority communities. At the same time, the university is also expected to be modern and to modernise without undermining the traditional sense of community. Under these conditions, the university itself must be clear about what it can and cannot do and make this widely known. It does not have political and economic power as the government does, but it can educate most of the men and women who will exercise that power. Hence it must understand the principles and goals of its own government, even though it is not a branch of the government. The university cannot directly plan for the future as a government can; neither can it read the future. But it is equipped to examine long-term possibilities and probabilities. Hence it can and should demand the best and latest data to work with, including data which it must collect itself, over and above those which the government or community can provide.

The university must not pretend that it can solve all problems by intellectual effort alone. It must, however, insist that intellectual and academic integrity is essential so that it can evaluate the quality of a wide range of scientific and cultural values as no other institutions can. The university also must not pretend that it is the government's best critic or that it is the only conscience of the people. The university has too much to do in research and teaching to merely play the critic or to endlessly worry about what conscience means. But it has the capacity to test propositions, assertions and propaganda, and should speak out against false conclusions and wrong analyses fearlessly. This is the university's conscience, its commitment to the truth as far as it can be known, and it has the duty to try its hardest to make sure that its conclusions are right.

Finally, the university must believe in itself. If it does, then its first duty is to survive as a university. This does not mean that it should bow to the government's slightest command. Nor do I mean that it should build higher walls and arm itself to the teeth against threats to its autonomy. Neither means survival, and in Asia today, they would more likely lead to certain death. A university must win the right to survive by being alert, responsive and political. I suggest that, for the university to survive in this way, it must aim to forge the best possible relationship with whoever represents and acts for the communities of the country. The university owes it to the values of academic excellence and courageous criticism to give itself the best circumstances to accomplish its function. A university wins confidence and trust by continually proving that it is a part of any community and is prepared to confide in that community. Only then can the university have the prerogative to judge and criticise the community it is committed to serve. A community, on the other hand, has the right to know what the university is doing and has achieved, and if the university can show that it is responsible, creative and fearless despite the difficult conditions under which it has to work, then the community in turn has the duty to accord the university every support.

I repeat the university is under attack. I shall end by paraphrasing the challenge issued by the Prime Minister of Singapore, Mr Lee Kuan Yew, in another context some years ago and ask, "Are there enough universities in Asia to save the university?"

The University and the Community

Closing Comments

The Second Workshop on Higher Education organised by the Association of Southeast Asian Institutions of Higher Learning has been primarily an inside-the-university affair. Almost all of us, participants at the Workshop, have spoken in terms of self-examination. Some have had more direct experience of working with the government or for the community than others, but essentially we shared our views as teachers, administrators and scholars working within universities and looking out at the community. Those with direct experience of government and community have been

---

This is a revised version of the closing lecture delivered at the Second Asian Workshop on Higher Education, organised under the auspices of the Association of Southeast Asian Institutions of Higher Learning (6 to 15 December 1971). It was published in *Proceedings, Second Asian Workshop on Higher Education*, edited by Rayson L Huang (Singapore: Nanyang University, 1971), pp. 111–120. Reproduced with the kind permission of the Association of Southeast Asian Institutions of Higher Learning.

appreciative of the experience and have shown us the good that has done them; but even those who have not had much similar experience seem to have convinced themselves that much more can be done outside the university. It would be interesting to know what the community outside would think of the theme of this Workshop. If we had articulate representatives of the government and the community attending the Workshop, what would they say of our efforts to talk our universities into having greater involvement with the community? Will they say, as my Australian friends say approvingly, "Good on you, mate", or will they say, "This is too little and too late", or will they now begin to wonder, given the present structures and staff of universities, can universities ever really help the community directly? If they should wonder in this way, they may well say, "Let the universities stick to what they can do best and not thrash about in areas outside their competence."

We can probably deduce the answers for some universities but I have the impression that there will be further misunderstanding and confusion if the universities are left to their discretion to determine what the community needs when these universities are not yet well equipped and have not been accustomed to engage with communities. The community representatives would observe that the university representatives are eager to have their universities serve their communities more openly and devotedly. It is generally agreed that universities in Asia have not been, with very few exceptions, doing enough or doing the right things. Where universities have been more successful, it is because they succeeded in a number of specific ways and under specific conditions. The most spectacular example is university staff becoming political leaders and participating in the running of the country. They are seconded to man part of the government, dedicate themselves to the country's power and wealth and actively consolidate their many communities into an ideal national community. Slightly less spectacular but no less important for the communities are examples of governments that choose their top planners and administrators from university staff who have not been tainted by party politics but who have the expertise and are committed to the goals of the government. It is clear, however, that the aforementioned examples are atypical special cases and happen only to one or two universities in very few countries. There is thus little evidence that they can serve as an exemplary model for other universities and communities.

More commonly, such relations existent between university and community are far from spectacular and it is by no means clear that either the university or the community really wants relations to be that spectacular. The main demands of the community and the main functions that universities believe they are competent in accomplishing include educating youths of the community for the community, providing analytical assessment of the community to promote community growth, and providing extension education opportunities to working adults. These seem to be the modest but agreeable minimum direct relationship between university and community. Beyond this, opinions begin to diverge. Some community leaders and some university staff and students want universities to change their orientation altogether and develop new attitudes towards participating in community life — that is, each member of the university doing his best in his own special field as well as in his capacity as citizen and intellectual. Others are less demanding and would allow some staff and students to concentrate on extending knowledge to levels not previously reached, but urge them to apply their knowledge and intellect for their community positively and self-consciously. There is nothing extraordinary in the debate about how much can or should be done. What would be of interest to the community representatives would be the degrees of agreement among the university representatives that raising the awareness of universities of their responsibilities to the community is imperative. At the same time, the community representatives would have been appalled by the numerous examples of university's culpability in the intellectual arrogance of its staff, in its resistance or slowness to change its attitudes towards the idea of serving the community, and in the pettiness, the drabness, even the pathos, of internal university politics.

But on the whole, community representatives would find that, although it has taken universities a long time to re-examine themselves, it becomes obvious that many universities are now prepared to ask fundamental questions about themselves. Most of us, the university representatives, emphasised the success and failure of our universities as key to universities. The main drift of the observations was that the university must reform itself before it can either serve or lead the community. But what to reform and how to reform? There seems on the surface many kinds of generalisations about universities. But essentially the starting point of all universities is teaching — what to teach, how to teach, how much research to keep teaching alive and what facilities are available to enhance the teaching. Essentially, all universities comprise three vital sectors — the administration, academic staff and students. Although the proportions may differ and the relative power of each of the three groups may vary considerably, it was extraordinary the extent universities are alike in staff-student problems, administration-faculty problems, and most of all, in the problems of cooperation, dissent, rivalry and personalities among academic staff.

What was striking about our universities today, however, was the attitudinal shift from the 1950s when universities at the time were more confident of themselves and tended to believe that inadequate funds and facilities were factors that prevented them from bringing excellence to the institutions. Funds and facilities still remain vital today, but the emphasis now seems to be more on university structures and on motivating universities to make distinctive contributions that justify their existence. In other words, there has been a shift from the position when the university said that it knew what to do, that it was well organised to do the job and just needed the funds for staff recruitment as well as equipment and book acquisition so that the community would voluntarily enrol its students to be educated in the institution. It is important to remind ourselves of this earlier period when the university felt it had the right to dictate the terms under which it worked, and then to examine ourselves today with that perspective in mind. This is not in order to enjoy an orgy of denunciation of the "bad old days" or of nostalgia about the "good old days". That would be too pathetic and obviously absurd. It is important that we should measure the extent to which the position of the university has changed during the past decade or so in order to cope with rapid change — a phenomenon that all communities in Asia had concurred with.

In reviewing the achievement and failure of universities in Asia over the past decade or two, we would recognise that, apart from a few exceptions mainly in Japan, Asian universities have not been the symbols of excellence they had claimed to be. The attempts to strive for international excellence have been met with frustration and universities have attributed this to the shortage of resources and the lack of appreciation by their communities. Few new discoveries, original solutions and striking ideas have come from Asian universities partly because they were starved of funds and overloaded with undergraduate teaching, and partly because they started decades, if not hundreds of years, behind the great universities in the world. But if we look more closely at this phenomenon, we would recognise that a major factor in this failure has been the aloofness of the universities from their environment.

This aloofness had many facets, but it stemmed mainly from a crucial misreading of the nature and functions of those major universities in the

West on which many of the Asian universities were modelled. It was noted that those major Western universities prided themselves on their aloofness and claimed to have done their best work by being left alone, by riding above the urgent needs of their communities in search of the important universal principles that determined all existence and the meaningfulness of life itself. What was often not understood was that those universities had begun quite differently. They had initially concentrated on power and influence in their respective communities, they had produced the ruling elites of both Church and State and carefully cultivated a rapport with their elites. Ultimately, they were integral parts of the governing structures in their respective countries. By modern standards, not all Western universities can be said to have been responsive to the community, but in their own terms, they were highly responsive to the community of the ruling class which mattered. They therefore took an active part in providing leaders for the community and these leaders in turn took great pride in the universities which nurtured them. The rapport and the continuity of rapport provided the strong framework in which these universities were given the money and resources, and the freedom and power to do their work apparently undisturbed by the immediate problems around them. It was out of this freedom and power that these universities produced their traditions of scientific inquiry and intellectual leadership.

The great universities of the West developed their kinds of structures and earned their greatness over a long period of time by retaining the confidence of their governments and vital sections of their communities. Asian universities, however, modelled themselves upon those universities in their late mature and elitist form and many thought that the confidence of government and community would and should come automatically. They admired the structure which they had borrowed from the West for the achievements they thought that these structures produced. They thought that by reproducing these structures and defending the ramparts against the philistinism around them, they too would succeed in Asia as brilliantly as the originals had done in Europe and America. They obviously believed that it was all a matter of the mind, the superior mind which discovers truth, and it followed that their governments and communities had the duty to keep that mind supplied with money and facilities indefinitely.

I believe that institutions taking for granted that they were already excellent by being called universities and by having the same structures as the great universities was the fatal flaw in many of the universities in Asia. Thus there were false starts, false pretences, a self-deceiving nominalism which few were able to overcome. The shift in emphasis between the Asian university in the 1950s and the Asian university today comes from having many of these pretences exposed. There have been fresh attempts to establish a rapport with government and community leaders, and a recognition that unless they did so, they would be taken over and restructured forcibly from outside. Some have already been restructured from outside. Others were indeed ordered to reform because some governments and communities were no longer willing to wait for the rigid universities to do so themselves. It is against this background that we should see many of the reorganisations which have been initiated from within universities. It has been indeed heartening to see some universities trying to save themselves from becoming sick traditional institutions by trying energetically to regain new direction, purpose and strength.

Organisers of the Workshop had picked the right theme to make the discussion worthwhile, offering fresh awareness of the university's part in the community. The university is not doing the community a favour when it looks to the community today (the community is disappointed with what might be described as the tokenism which underlies much of what some universities claim to do for the community!); the university turns to the community now in order to save its own life. I believe it is thus important for the university to know what the community means and the rapid changes in Asia, and put the context in perspective.

The strength of the great universities of the past had been built upon the close relationship between the university and those in power. There had certainly been a comfortable understanding between the ruling elites and the universities which produced those elites. In most countries of Asia, there has been the same problem of arriving at an understanding between those in power and those who run the universities. It would, however, be too simple to think that universities today would be fine and strong again if a new rapport could be built up between them and those of their graduates who control their governments. The historical conditions have changed. The modern Asian ruling elites do not base their power on inherited birthright, nor do they have the compact solidarity of a traditional ruling caste. Their right to lead derives from new sources of authority and strength, varying from administrative skills, entrepreneurship and academic merit to the ability to command the numbers whether in their armies or at the polls, and also from the combination of qualities which produced the professional revolutionary and the disciplined ideological parties. In all cases, these elites no longer have the relatively simple task of dealing with passive and backward peasant communities; nor do they have the opportunity to lead their communities gradually over several centuries to accept the secular, sceptical and scientific attitudes which produced our modern world. Instead, all at once, the ruling elites find themselves far too few in number and the jobs to be done much too complex. At the same time, they are aware that the speed of change is increasing, that larger sections of the communities are restive and demanding, and that the concept of elitism itself is out of fashion and on the defensive.

It is therefore not enough for the university to learn the lesson that it should get along with those in power, with the government, and serve as one of the key organs for controlling the communities below; nor is it enough to reject the model of the great Western universities and seek a largely Asian form. The main features of rapid change are common to all parts of the world. The difficulty is that some parts are better equipped to deal with the pace of change while institutions in Asia still lack some of the foundations which allow them to change without too much traumatic effect. Thus, for example, the universities in Asia are geared towards producing better trained elites for countries with democratic pretensions. Also, the rhetoric of popular will has spread widely and quickly while the universities are still struggling with older problems of manoeuvring between rival and competing elites. The universities now discover that they are somewhat out of step with all these changes and the meritocracy they produce is already facing the choice of manipulating various kinds of democracies or of being fiercely authoritarian.

Our talk of archaic structures and the need to reform them reflect the most critical problems in Asia of authority and consensus confronting both governments and communities today. Governments are being challenged and opposed, communities are polarised between rich and poor, young and old, radicals and conservatives, more dramatically than Asian countries have ever known before. And whether the universities like it or not, similar problems have collected around them. They no longer consist of faculty and students from more or less the same class who shared or were promised the same privileges, and acted as a select community of knowledgeable people united in defence of its rights from both the governments and communities outside. Instead, many of them have become microcosms of modern governments and sectors of their communities, and this has never really happened to universities before, certainly not in Asia.

It is in this context that the search for authority through knowledge and specialist skills, and the search for consensus through speaking the same academic language and discovering the same universal principles, may not be sufficient in themselves. As microcosms reflecting the deep contradictions outside their walls, universities are no longer free to neglect those contradictions. They have to examine themselves as much as they have to examine what they reflect. How governments and communities approach problems of authority and consensus between themselves is completely relevant to how the universities can restore authority and regain consensus within themselves among faculty, among students and between faculty and students. Also, hopefully, how universities recreate their own respective communities and how they become responsive to rapid change may be of use as examples for both government and community outside.

What I have suggested is that universities structured by and for ruling elites may not be able to meet the needs of self-conscious and democratising communities, and merely modifying and adjusting the structures from within may also be futile. The time may have come for universities to acknowledge that they cannot do their own restructuring by themselves. They are facing so many challenges simultaneously that it is probably foolish to pretend that they know the best approach and that they can do it alone. Before we can think about the university serving and offering leadership to the community, we must admit that universities have become as complex as the communities they are part of and cannot solve their structural problems without the help and cooperation of their governments and their communities. If we emphasise too much the peculiarities of each university, we may truly get bogged down in administrative paralysis as well as academic isolationism.

Furthermore, the phenomenon of rapid change is no longer limited to any one country or any single region. It is Asian and it is global. Communities are no longer alone and nations, too, are no longer alone. We must surely guard against giving too much emphasis to the peculiarities of each country's universities. It may be virtuous to do-it-yourself, but it certainly takes too long and too many trials and errors for most communities to afford. We know what we want for our universities and there is considerable consensus on what should be done, which has largely come from the perception of common experience, recognition of our own problems in other universities, and renewal of purpose when we compare notes with our colleagues from different countries. We can end our deliberations with fresh faith in our commonality, reaffirming that the general has been distilled from many particulars and we study the general in search of solutions for the particular. This is what universities do very well.

I do not know whether any new kind of university will emerge in Asia or how many kinds of universities will have to be evolved to deal with communities undergoing rapid change. Many universities have succeeded in adapting themselves to the immediate demands of economic and technological change and should continue to do so with little real difficulty. These universities can collect and analyse the relevant data, recommend measures to improve existing methods and have the confidence to judge good or bad policy. There should be no great anxiety on this score. Some universities may be sluggish and others more efficient, but the former can be streamlined and the latter further tuned up for greater readiness to meet future changes.

But those are not the fundamental problems some of our communities have been facing. What is fundamental is the social and psychological health of our communities which have been driven to rapid change at rather short notice. The questions, for which the answers have yet to be found, stem mainly from the pressures upon our communities to participate in that change *in toto*, from the great force being applied to our communities to abandon deep-rooted mental attitudes, and from those aspects of the scientific method which have emphasised the materialistic and the cerebral and made us afraid of passing value judgements on matters which concern us deeply and persistently. Such questions have been repeatedly asked before, and they are well-known questions raised for strikingly new situations. There was remarkable agreement about where the universities have succeeded least and the areas where the most need to be done, and what the university's greater responsibility towards its community should be. This is the responsibility to change ourselves for a new age without losing our sense of community.

Most universities have failed us on this score, not because they have paid too much attention to the arts and humanities as many critics claim, nor because they have dedicated too little attention. Where they have failed most notably has been the lack of emphasis on relevance and the lack of awareness of rapid change. Without relevance and awareness of change, the study of the arts cannot rise above the mere training of guides for stately tour of a fine museum. There will be little fire and no imagination unless the universities can show that it is valuable, even necessary, as guiding principles for our thought and intellectual stimuli. If universities fail to project a vision of ourselves as useful and constructive men and women in the future community, then the danger is that our humanity will slowly wither away.

More so than ever before, the community embraces the university and the university is embedded in the community. More so than ever, this is true everywhere. If the university and the community can live creatively together anywhere, they can live creatively here in Asia too.

2
National Education and the Scientific Tradition

The subject of my lecture, "National Education and the Scientific Tradition", came about because I recall Ruth Wong's work for national education, first for Malaya, later Malaysia and then Singapore, and because her teaching of mathematics symbolises the key to modern science. It is science education that has given us, during the past century or so, the universalist ideals that guide the idea of excellence in education. Science education has also done much both in laying the foundation of national education and enabling new generations of Asians to internalise the scientific standards that are considered to be applicable universally.

Education for groups of elites has long been available in most societies. Education for all, however, has come only during the 20th

---

This is a revised version of the Ruth Wong Lecture delivered on 26 November 1996 at the Institute of Southeast Asian Studies, Singapore. It was published in *the Australian Educational Researcher*, vol. 24, no. 1 (1997), pp. 49–62. Reproduced with the kind permission from Springer Science + Business Media B.V.

century, first in developed countries and then as an ideal for the rest. It is harder to agree on the criteria to judge excellence. There is elite excellence, that is, quality for the very few, and there is, with different criteria of excellence, all-round quality education for the many. For the former, the fact that brilliant individuals can be found in the population of every country does not tell much about a country. As for the latter, all-round quality education is a major gauge of a country's development, which depends on how much a country can afford and is willing to commit into provision of education. Funding is essential to deliver good-quality education to everyone. Only affluent countries can provide access to consistently good educational facilities and working conditions for their teachers, and attract brilliant individuals from less affluent countries to their centres of excellence.

Since the end of the Cold War, there have been extensive efforts to define a new world order or new ways of explaining the world. For many, the "end-of-history" school of thought is one viewpoint that trumpets the ultimate triumph of capitalism and liberal democracy. This view would expect the West to dominate. If the world were to be described as a pyramid, the United States would be seen by some as the top third of the pyramid. An Asia-Pacific that includes the United States, and other "Western" extensions like Japan, Canada and Australasia, could then look forward to being near the top of the pyramid because of the powerful pull of the Americans. That could also mean, however, the top third will dictate the standards of excellence to the rest.

An alternate view focusses on the "clash of civilisations" and offers quite a different perspective. The West is depicted as being on the defensive. The universalism that it claims to represent is no longer valid. Its civilisation (or civilisations, if Samuel Huntington is right to consider Eastern Europe and Latin America separately) has been challenged by at least two rivals, representing the Islamic and the East Asian "Confucian" civilisations, which may combine to end the past two centuries of Western dominance. If this is true, both the West and the potential enemies of Western dominance are to be found in the emerging Asia-Pacific region. Is the region, therefore, destined to be an arena for future conflict between countries that are expected to represent the two opposing sides? National ideals of education, under such circumstances, are likely to be submerged to cope with the ensuing tensions. If such conflict is imminent, there would be no universal criteria of what is excellent and what is not.

There are, of course, more optimistic approaches that look at the world as ultimately a common humanity and therefore one diverse whole, whether it be seen as a universal civilisation, a global village, or a series of interlocking and interdependent regions. Thus, even in the absence of an obvious world order, the Asia-Pacific region has the potential to be considered as one which overlaps with others through complex networks, but contributes to the overall integration of a one-world modern civilisation. Such approaches, portrayed as naïve or implausible, or as illusory images obscuring the reality of Western dominance, have recently been questioned. Or, they may mislead Western civilisation to overreach itself and go the destructive way of some earlier civilisations which were overambitious and self-deluding. All the same, the positive and universalist approaches are far from obsolete and still deserve attention in the context of educational excellence.

This is possible chiefly because, underlying the claims of universalism for the past two centuries, the triumphs of modern science have indeed established a control over the imagination of peoples globally. The impact of modern science on modern education, including national education in various countries and societies, is truly a remarkable development. It would be a mistake to treat advances in science as a peculiar, or even uniquely Western achievement. Similarly, it is erroneous to regard scientific advances as being detached from the modern West and their results and theories accepted in each country without consideration of the cultural baggage that made science possible in the first place. It would be difficult to point to examples of rapid progress in any Asian country during the past decades and not recognise how much they were the product of modern science and technology.

We are all familiar with the origins of modern science in Renaissance Europe and the development of mathematical and experimental methods that followed. The great thinkers and scientists after Newton and Descartes, through Watt and Stevenson, Lavoisier and Pasteur, Darwin and Einstein, are too well known to detain us here. They deserve the world's admiration and their place in history is assured. The scientific tradition I want to discuss, however, is not confined to the great scientists and their splendid contributions to humankind. What I want to concentrate on is the idea that modern science could only have transpired with the cumulative boost of earlier scientific traditions, which were found in several civilisations. I would emphasise that knowledge of these traditions is necessary for a balanced and rounded understanding of the value of science in Asia.

The early traditions I refer to are the four better-known civilisations of the Greeks, Chinese, Muslims and Christians. Each of these civilisations enjoyed a period of flowering followed by withering and stagnation, which stunted the leap to modern science. The truly important question is not why none of these civilisations led to the growth of modern science: the marvel is how modern science emerged at all in Western Europe in the 17th century. But this is not the question I want to delve into. It is important to recognise that modern science did not spring up as fully formed and without attribution to earlier achievements. The geniuses who brought humankind modern science belonged to cultures and societies that had been through many phases of scientific enquiry. Some cultures had run out of steam or ideas. In some cases, their talented scholars had been thwarted by powers beyond their control. Science was man-made — it could soar to the heavens because of human will; but it could be aborted, also because of human will.

The extraordinary achievements of the Greeks have been widely acknowledged because key concepts of modern science have been traced back to their inspiration. Such recognition confirms that the origins of modern science owe much to an earlier tradition. Similarly, there have been arguments in favour of even earlier traditions of mathematics, astronomy, medicine and technology in Babylonia and Egypt, of which we can find echoes in the traditions of Hindu Indian and Greek science. When we say that these traditions shared some ideas in common which did not lead much further at the time, this does not denigrate the attainments of the ancient peoples. Their efforts did have cumulative effects on civilisational growth, and therefore their contributions should be entitled their rightful place.

The same can be said for the Chinese, Muslims and Christians. The Chinese had concerns with mathematics, astronomy and medicine, which received considerable stimulus from the West and from South Asia. But the Chinese also developed their own methods, especially in certain areas of mathematics and technology. The Muslims and Christians could be analysed and classified together because they came from the same religious tradition and, for some time in the Middle Ages, had some attitudes towards science in common. The Muslims, however, appreciated Greek science earlier. At the height of Muslim power, from the ninth to the 12th centuries, their mathematicians and astronomers were some of the most sophisticated of that age. But these men were expected to give precedence to their theological needs, and the theocratic states they lived in tended to confine their studies and discoveries to what served the faith and not beyond.

The mediaeval Christians, however, became active in scientific enquiry much later, from the 12th to 15th centuries, and extended their interest to a wider range of fields. Important help was received by the development of autonomous centres of learning during this period. Such institutions were given a small degree of legal protection for scholars to engage in enquiries over and above the concerns of the Church, such as in areas like calculations about stars and planets, medicine, anatomy and alchemy. Just prior to the astronomical breakthroughs of Copernicus and Galileo, several key universities had been pushing at the edges of knowledge with the assurance of a degree of patronage. However, Copernicus' revolutionary discovery, which challenged some fundamental ideas the Church had grown accustomed to, was unacceptable to the Church.

For each of the four groups of civilisations, scientific tradition advanced them only thus far and did not lead to the scientific revolution which occurred in the 17th century. The reasons are complex. There were religious inhibitions about certain secular enquiries and these led to the intervention of theological or bureaucratic states. In some cases, it was the lack of recognition, accompanied by contrary inducements to turn intellectual efforts towards moral, spiritual or more practical matters, which deterred scientific enquiry. In other cases, there were actual prohibitions against the pursuit of certain sensitive questions in the eyes of clerics or political leaders. And not least, there were no clear economic incentives for discovery and invention, least of all, the forms of protection for free enquiry and property rights which would encourage scholars to share knowledge in order to speed up progress. Only by making discoveries and inventions could mankind accumulate their experiences for the benefit of later generations, thus enabling each generation to be better prepared to make further discoveries.

Seventeenth-century Europe saw the coming together of many strands of scientific thinking, combined with economic and political conditions, which favoured the innovative and creative scholars to turn them to their advantage. It is essential to understand how that happened and remind ourselves of the circumstances which made modern science possible, universal, and thus capable of continued growth throughout the world. This is, however, inadequate. Although earlier scientific traditions were inhibited and met with too many obstacles blocking modern breakthrough, we should not dismiss them as unworthy of our concern. On the contrary, it is time to pay careful attention to the earlier scientific traditions.

Firstly, if we neglect the origins of modern science, we would fail to appreciate what a successful revolution that was and take science and even modernity for granted, thus not understanding how truly remarkable the human mind is. Secondly, only by reminding ourselves of the complex and positive factors in earlier traditions can we understand the roles they played and thus grasp the way modern progress has been made. Knowing the kinds of social conditions that either impeded or accelerated advances in science can help us ensure that favourable conditions are maintained for future developments. Thirdly and not least, it is vital that we, as Asians, do not view modern science as something that sprang out of Western Europe without any antecedents. Otherwise, we may assume that there is nothing in other traditions that could be called scientific, or associated with the development of modern science. Such a view would shut off our ability to appreciate how, all over Asia today, modern science is being studied successfully with relative ease, and how important it is that the modern scientific tradition is not isolated from earlier knowledge traditions in this part of the world. Nothing can be gained by alienating the modern mind from its deep roots in earlier human achievements.

The education scene in Singapore is an ideal case to elaborate these points further. Singapore is a microcosm of Western and several Asian traditions. Its national education has made splendid progress in the teaching of science and technology as well as the practical application. It is, at the same time, conscious of the need to remember the links of its various communities to their cultural roots. Perhaps, Singapore has not done enough to remind the younger generation that each of the cultures had an earlier scientific tradition that is relevant to their present responses to modern science. If this knowledge that modern science came out of the traditions of many peoples is promulgated, our students would realise that science is compatible with the ideas and institutions that support our society's moral and spiritual needs.

I shall illustrate this further. The Muslims and the Christians may be aware that their traditions had made contributions to the rediscovery of Greek science, after the fall of Constantinople in 1452, and to the rapid development of new mathematical skills. Similarly, one might also note the contributions of Hindu scholarship to Muslim discoveries in mathematics, astronomy and medicine. As for the Chinese, much attention has been focussed on certain technologies — notably printing, the magnetic compass and the invention of gunpowder — which enabled modern science to flourish and spread. A background knowledge of earlier discoveries and inventions is thus a valuable starting point to examine those scientific traditions which in themselves did not lead to modern science but, in combination and over long period of time, enriched the intellectual environment that made modern science possible. From that broader understanding, there could derive explanations as to how different individuals and peoples today are receiving the fruits of science and mastering the problems of modernity. The way they seek to transform their societies partially or fully, and make scientific knowledge a part of their own modern heritage is itself one of the marvels of the 20th century.

I shall not try to cover all aspects of this fascinating story. Because of its dramatic impact on recent developments in Asia, the response of "Confucian" civilisation in China, Japan and Korea to the acquisition of the scientific method is of particular interest. As three-quarters of the population in Singapore is of Chinese descent and can relate to "Confucian" civilisation, I shall focus on how some Chinese regarded scientific tradition. The point to underline is that the Chinese experience of modern science this past century can be attributed to that tradition. A similar probe into the very different Hindu, Christian and Muslim earlier experiences with science would be equally illuminating.

For the past decades, China's advances in science have been very impressive. Many people now take for granted that the Chinese should excel in science because of the remarkable achievements of its ancient civilisation. But there are others who, bearing in mind that their earlier inventions had not led them to science, are surprised that the Chinese took to the scientific method so readily when presented eventually with the fruits of modern science.

During the 20th century, the Chinese scientists rediscovered a scientific tradition for China. This was in the context of a multitude of contributions to scientific progress, the recognition that varieties of ancient or mediaeval science, premodern or proto-modern science, had flowed into the mighty river of modern science. This does not mean that Chinese civilisation could be described as a scientific one, but it allowed the Chinese to say that they were no less scientific than the West was before Galileo and Newton.

There are many Chinese equivalents for the word "science" in its broadest sense of "truth" or "knowledge", but none is related to the development of modern science. If we confine ourselves to science as methodology, there was no word in the Chinese language that would describe the way of determining truth. The phrase that has the closest meaning would be *gewu*, to discover everything we can about something. The phrase also conveyed a philosophical ideal, which was valuable to scholars who did their utmost to establish the accuracy of documents and empirical observations. Dating and editing of ancient texts, as well as deriving the precise meaning of words and concepts were particularly useful. But these were not applied to the practical skills that the Chinese acquired or to the technological advances which the Chinese made through the centuries.

The separation between *gewu* and Chinese technical ingenuity meant that technology was never recognised as a source of knowledge that addressed more fundamental questions in life. Thus, when Chinese scholars first encountered the idea that Western wealth and power were the results of modern science, and then grasped the scientific methods and research that expedited the Industrial Revolution and remade the world, they thought that their own civilisation was deeply defective. Many therefore turned against their own traditions and cultivated an obsession with science that was close to being fervently religious, or at least seeing it as a substitute for religion, a kind of scientism.

By the beginning of the 20th century, there was general acceptance among the Chinese intelligentsia that it was essential for China to master modern science. Their position was that mere technological imitation was not enough. The Chinese intelligentsia and their followers were convinced that China had quickly to show readiness and willingness to learn more from the West. What was not agreed upon was what to learn and how much to learn. The period of acceptance lasted from the turn of the 20th century to the 1950s. It was subject to intense debate followed by hardening of positions, not so much about the importance of science as about the nature of Chinese society and civilisation. Just before the May Fourth Movement in 1919, most educated Chinese were still confident that the ethical principles which provided the foundations of Chinese civilisation were sound. Learning science to strengthen China was necessary but it was no threat to the core of the ancient and glorious

Chinese civilisation. After 1920, following intense debates at many levels of Chinese society, the position was reversed. In order to save China, the narrow and outdated moral and political traditions had to be replaced by scientific thought and modern methodologies, even if this led to the discarding of most conventional wisdom.

This included the idea that neo-Confucian ideas and practices — which needed thorough reform at the least, and for the revolutionaries, they were better thrown out altogether — were obstacles to progress. But there was also a deep underlying contradiction in that position. The talk about national salvation stressed the need for advanced science and technology and a deeper understanding of the values which made science so effective and Western countries rich and powerful. At the same time, it also required a rejuvenation of the Chinese people, of their pride in national identity. The Chinese should not deny their heritage of a once great civilisation.

I shall take a few examples from China and Southeast Asia to illustrate this. I shall first mention Yan Fu in China at the end of the 19th century. He had studied chemistry, physics and mathematics in England and then introduced not only the ideas of Darwin, Thomas Huxley, Herbert Spencer but also those of Adam Smith, Montesquieu and John Stuart Mill, among many others. Yan Fu, who knew the latest developments in Western science and social sciences, also believed that Western knowledge could coexist with the humanist and moral values of traditional Chinese culture. Others who learnt their science indirectly through Japan, notably Zhang Ping-lin and Liang Qichao, were equally influential in calling for a new spirit of scholarship. But they too thought that the scientific civilisation of the West could be complementary to the moral civilisation of China. In fact, after watching what happened to Europe at the end of World War I, Liang Qichao went further and publicly denounced the materialistic civilisation that led to such destruction and slaughter.

Of their contemporaries in Southeast Asia, I shall mention the examples of Gu Hongming, Lim Boon Keng and Wu Lien-teh. They were remarkable men who had studied scientific subjects abroad but continued to appreciate the rich cultural heritage of China. Gu Hongming (1857–1928) was thoroughly soaked in a classical Scottish education, including a good grounding in science and mathematics that enabled him to obtain an engineering degree in Germany. He was a good example of a culturally deracinated overseas Chinese — he descended from several generations of traders who had settled in Penang — whose scientific education led him back to classical Chinese culture. Despite his early training in the sciences, he argued strenuouly against adopting "the intensely materialistic civilisation of modern Europe".

Lim Boon Keng (1869–1957) grew up in Singapore and would be better known to Singaporeans. Also educated in Edinburgh, with the essential scientific knowledge to enable him to become a medical practitioner, he had a brilliant career in Singapore before taking up the presidency of Amoy (Xiamen) University in 1922. He was a moderniser who wanted his students to have a good science education. Nevertheless, he was convinced of the value of Confucianism and supported efforts to preserve that tradition. Unfortunately, he had the misfortune of being the target of one of the sharpest critics of the age, the famous writer Lu Xun, who mocked him for being an arch-conservative. Since Lu Xun's writings are significantly better known, Lim Boon Keng has gone down in history not as the keen supporter of science education that he actually was but as the diehard defender of a dying faith, a reputation which he did not deserve. On the contrary, it might well be said that what Lim Boon Keng did for Amoy University was a lot more constructive than Lu Xun's calls to reject the past.

Wu Lien-teh (1879–1960), also born in Penang like Gu Hongming and Lim Boon Keng, was another Queen's Scholar from the Straits Settlements. He studied medicine in Cambridge and became world-famous as a plague fighter in China and a pioneer in medical research. He was indisputably a modern scientist who turned his knowledge to optimal practical application. Less well-known was his contribution to the first modern study of the history of Chinese medicine. In the midst of his scientific research, he continued to pay close attention to the medical traditions of China. He was thus a pioneer also in China's efforts to consider that tradition as worthy to parallel the modern medicine that he so ably advanced. Till this day, the two traditions have remained closely related in China, and this reminds us that the achievements of the past could be richly helpful in national education today.

There are, of course, many more examples of learned and influential men who had studied scientific subjects abroad and returned to China to warn against undervaluing the social and political underpinnings of the Chinese civilisation. It is remarkable how they initiated a series of intellectual and academic debates about science and civilisation which led to great political and ideological passion. The debates coincided with a period of disunity and civil war and with desperate efforts by patriotic youth to forge a strong national movement to bring about the unification of China. Western ideas were sifted through in search of suitable formulas that would help solve China's problems. The scientists were in the forefront of the debates, notably, the new American-trained generation from the Science Society founded by Ren Hongjun, Ding Wenjiang and Zhu Kezhen. Together, they led the call for extensive and better science education in all Chinese universities.

Non-scientists, for example, Chen Duxiu and Hu Shih, were equally inspired. They were particularly influential and their lives were illustrative of the politicisation of the debate. Both of them had a strong classical education, but this did not stand in the way of their fervent wish to witness the development of science and democracy in China. Although they parted ways — Chen Duxiu was diverted by the revolutionary ideologies of Marxism and communism, while Hu Shih remained the liberal humanist — they continued to support the spread of scientific method into all aspects of learning and education. They both contributed to the excitement among the youth who advocated: Young China must be creative, socially responsible, and must adopt a scientific approach to everything!

One of them, the young philosopher Fung Yu-lan, asked the famous question: why did modern science not develop in China after the brilliant start of its civilisation? He wrote an article, entitled "Why China has no Science — An Interpretation of the History and Consequences of Chinese Philosophy", in 1922 while he was still studying at Columbia University. He asked in the context of his concern that the lack of science in China was the key reason why China was weak and backward.

The debates of the 1920s ended with victory for modern science against Chinese traditional values. Scientism won the day and science became sacred, something of a holy cow. This was a pyrrhic victory. The politicisation of science as a measure of progressiveness had appropriated the intellectual discourse about a subject that was much more complex, that is, the nature of traditional civilisation and how it could promote rather than hinder the process of modernisation. Thereafter, everything that was opposed to the received traditions was seen as scientific and progressive. All else was backward. This view continued into the 1930s and 1940s among the most active and aggressive polemicists who, directly or indirectly, supported the view that only Marxism and the Chinese Communist Party embodied the scientific approach in its socialism and dialectical materialism. It was thereafter but an easy step to paint everything as either black or white. This was done by equating all that was scientific and progressive with Marxism-Leninism, and all that was reactionary, backward, feudal-traditional and unscientific with the government that was trying to crush the communists.

The politicised polarisation became uncritically accepted among most of the patriotic and the rebellious young during the 1930s and 1940s. An illuminating example is Chen Li-fu's *Sheng chih yuan-li* ("The Philosophy of Life"), which was one of the compulsory texts for first-year university students in the 1940s. Chen, a former minister of education of the Nationalist government, was a mining engineer trained in the United States. He tried hard to marry modern scientific ideas and methods to what he considered was well worth preserving in Chinese civilisation. His book, which argued that there was no contradiction between tradition and science, and that Chinese civilisation was compatible with the development of a modern scientific country, was rejected because of his political background rather than the validity of the argument.

In short, for more than two decades, those who clamoured the loudest for science as a basis for national education started with the premise that there had never been any science worth speaking of in Chinese civilisation. Even defenders of the ancient Chinese civilisation who described the glories of its material culture and the intellectual brilliance and artistic ingenuity of the Chinese people made no strong claims for the existence of a scientific tradition of any kind.

As an historian, I am aware that traditional Chinese civilisation has been seen as hindering the progress of its practical geniuses to modern science. Traditional Chinese civilisation extolled a philosophy that was holistic and organic, one that placed great emphasis on the absolute authoritarianism of both the family and state systems. Severe limits were placed on knowledge transmission, making it virtually impossible for any knowledge collaboration, except among family members (or among some tightly controlled guilds). Otherwise, all new knowledge that the state did not know about would have been suspect. If anyone possessed useful knowledge which they did not offer to the court would have been seen as either heterodox and therefore condemned, or dangerous and even treacherous.

In such a culture, anything like technology transfer in the modern sense would have been impossible. The examination-based bureaucracy looked down on the practical discoveries of artisans and craftsmen, and there was little chance of the kinds of interaction which induced the officials to be creative themselves. It is not surprising that in such an environment, there developed something that can be described as scientific inertia or stagnation.

During the past five decades, there has been a manifold increase in the quantity of Chinese texts and artefacts related to early science that scholars in and outside China had found and reexamined. Most scholars would be familiar with the remarkable work of Joseph Needham and his colleagues. Needham's *Science and Civilisation in China* — with 16 volumes published to date and several more volumes pending publication — has put the subject on the map throughout the scientific world. There were numerous Chinese scholars who made it possible for him to tell the world of China's earlier achievements. In the copious texts that have been translated and interpreted, there are found solutions in mathematics, astronomical observations and calculations, the magnetic compass, agricultural tools and techniques, alchemical "experiments", the discovery of gunpowder, the development of printing, and mechanisms in the "heavenly clock". These were remarkable scientific discoveries by any standards. Many of these have been accepted to a greater or lesser extent to corroborate the idea that China might have been able to develop modern science if other circumstances had been more favourable.

This has led to many Chinese rediscovering their science. The question has aroused the interest of many scientists, philosophers and historians of science as well as sociologists of knowledge. The literature on this subject is large and still growing. I shall mention a few examples. We still do not know enough about all facets of early science and the conceptual framework in which some scientific and technological developments had taken place. Despite this, what we do know shows the scientific mind at work. There may be doubts whether China ever had a science civilisation, but even the critics endorse the need to ask why achievements enumerated in recent studies, especially the aforementioned discoveries, did not lead to modern science. They do think it useful to sift out the nuances in China's material culture so that we can better understand China's present response to modern science.

Scientists themselves, of course, do not always agree. For example, two physicists, both originally from China, totally disagree with each other about whether there had been any science in early China. The first is Qian Wenyuan, a physicist from the People's Republic of China. He does not share the Marxist assumptions about the "universality of science" prior to Newtonian physics. He believes that the technical inventions of the Chinese did not add up to anything that is recognisable as science as we know it. The cultural inertia in Chinese civilisation totally inhibited the kind of experimentation, initiative and creativity that modern science needs.

In contrast, Chen Cheng-i, who left China as a young man and had been educated in Taiwan and the United States, holds a starkly different view. He argues that scientific thought in traditional China deserves much more careful research. While Chen stops short of claiming that China had a science civilisation before modern times, he does suggest that Qian's views are too Eurocentric, that Qian had not asked the right questions of the many sources used. Chen has therefore set out to prove that the ancient Chinese thought more scientifically than we have given them credit for. The contrast between the two scientists brings out the danger of defining science anachronistically, or too narrowly. If it is done anachronistically, we could identify almost any rational argument as potentially scientific. If it is done too narrowly, then we could easily conclude that nothing deserves the name of science until the age of Galileo and Newton. Some interesting research has also been done by sociologists and economic historians, including some who argue that the rise of capitalism and the bourgeois class formed a unique driving force in the rapid advances in science and technology in the West. Without capitalism, there would have been limits to what could be achieved. But technological ingenuity was not enough for either capitalism and the Industrial Revolution or the rise of modern science. Another study contrasts the legal and educational institutions of China and the Islamic world with those of the West, highlighting the beginnings of legal protection for some universities of Western Europe long before Copernicus. Such protection against both Church and State was essential if independent inquiries were to be pursued. This was conceptually impossible in China even during the relatively tolerant Song dynasty, least of all during the much more restrictive Ming and Qing dynasties. And without such protection of the efforts of scientists to pursue their researches freely and fearlessly, modern science could not have been born.

The question remains: given that China now produces some of the most talented scientists in the world, how could it achieve that if there had never been a scientific tradition in the past? We know that Chinese civilisation suffered immensely during the century of foreign threat, military defeat, and political decline from the mid-19th century to the mid-20th century. After 1949, there has been a new confidence in Beijing that China was finally being guided by science and technical advancement. Many writings now speak of three or four thousand years of China's glorious scientific and cultural achievements. In itself, the boast is not significant. What makes it interesting is that, for most of the hundred years before 1949, Chinese scholars had thought the opposite. It is, therefore, probably no accident that there has been renewed interest in the earlier Chinese view about modern science, the idea of "Chinese learning as foundation and Western learning for application" that was so cogently stated by Zhang Zhidong about a hundred years ago. This had put the emphasis on modern science offering new methods, or new means of mastering the secrets of advanced technology in order to gain national wealth and power. That approach would be compatible with many other scientific traditions, certainly with those of the Christians, Hindus, and Muslims as well.

This brings me back to national education in the context of promodern scientific traditions. The Chinese example deserves attention. Their efforts to identify a scientific tradition and provide Chinese civilisation an added dimension that links it with the outside world have given young Chinese scientists new confidence that their world of science has a broad and distinguished pedigree. In today's world, national education must do more than prepare future generations by attending only to the present and the immediate past, or to the local and the neighbouring region. The nations of the West are successful because they have recognised the contributions of history, including history well outside their own region, to their growth as representatives of a scientific civilisation. New nations in Asia should learn from that, especially when there are scientific traditions of their own to explore and bring into present stages of development.

If national education fails to include the sense of range and depth in several scientific traditions, I foresee at least two scenarios for societies in Asia that give great precedence to science, however understandable that may be. One, the universality of modern science in our education will strengthen the assumption that the Western heritage alone had brought it about. It will follow that all sense of the past, and in the end, of the future as well, would be dominated by that single world view. Secondly, the impact of scientific knowledge that is regarded as outside the framework of the living cultures which still have moral and spiritual meaning is likely to produce an imperfect and partial learning of modern science. Given the tremendous potential for modern science to uplift standards of living and add to the quality of life, national education needs to give it full rein. But if national education did not appreciate the fact that other cultures have scientific traditions, it will not integrate modern science with the rich moral and spiritual life which people do need and which the traditions provide. I do not know what Ruth Wong would say to these thoughts, but I imagine she would agree that any science education which fails to recognise that science, no less than modern society, has a distinguished past which we need to know about more fully, would be seriously incomplete.

3

Who Should Pay for Universities?

"Who Should Pay for Universities?" is of course very much a question in many people's minds today, not only in Singapore but also almost in every country in the world. I offer some random thoughts on a subject of increasing concern.

The question of education funding, and especially higher education, seems to have aroused keen interest in China for much of the last century, more dramatically than in other parts of the world. The founding of Xiamen University, the private university totally funded by Mr Tan Kah Kee, is a case in point. I first heard about his bold initiative from my father through whom I met several graduates of Xiamen University. They told me about how Xiamen University started, the kinds of problems it faced,

---

This is a revised text of the transcript of a talk given at a seminar on "Entrepreneurship and Education" to mark the 20th anniversary of the Tan Kah Kee Foundation held on 6 September 2002. An earlier version was published in *The Tan Kah Kee Spirit Today*, edited by K K Phua, Hew Choy Sin and Ong Choon Nam, Singapore: Tan Kah Kee Foundation and Tan Kah Kee International Society, 2003, pp. 45–73.

and how the students coped with studying in a university that was constantly struggling for funds throughout most of its first 16 years, from 1921 to 1937.

The university was established by Mr Tan Kah Kee, the entrepreneur and philanthropist who made his fortune in British Malaya. Despite Mr Tan's generosity, the university's alumni I met told me that, even in days when costs were lower and universities smaller, a university was really too expensive for any one person or any one group of private philanthropists to support. Indeed, that point was strongly stressed when its graduates talked with regret about the university's inability to fulfill its potential because it was never adequately funded.

Of course, there could have been other outcomes. Had it been possible for Mr Tan to use a better business model for the university, for example, by not using his capital but only his income, he might have survived the economic downturns of the 1920s and thus also the Depression that followed. Had the British colonial government been more sympathetic to his philanthropic cause, had there been a strong national Chinese state or a more prosperous provincial government in Fujian, had the rubber industry been better regulated, had he found other Hokkien or non-Hokkien rich partners to share his vision, one can go on.

There were many factors that undermined his vision of a great university. In other environments, one can think of the success of Stanford University and others that also started with one man's dream. I can also think of Li Ka-shing's blueprint for Shantou University. Mr Li learnt from Mr Tan's mistakes and devised a business model that combines Xiamen and Stanford lessons and his university is still doing well. And when we look around, it is possible to imagine that, if Bill Gates or Warren Buffet were to found a private university, their chances of success today are much better than that for Mr Tan in the 1920s. Nevertheless, I think the best universities are not heroic enterprises but should be the responsibility of multiple stakeholders that include all key sectors of the state and the community, including industry, the professions, the body of dedicated teachers and scholars and all who care for the values of a progressive civilisation.

When I started my university education in China in 1947, at the National Central University in Nanjing, the point about university funding came to mind again. I was at the university for about a year and a half and returned to Malaya before the People's Liberation Army arrived on the northern shore of the Yangtze River. Despite my short stint there, I was privileged to be in a national university of the Republic of China and the largest one in China at that time. With a population of over 400 million, it was surprising that the country's largest university, one offering courses and degrees covering the whole spectrum of faculties and departments, had only 4,000 students. Clearly, the universities of China could not cope with the demand for higher education in the country. When I learnt how most of the public universities were fully funded from state coffers, I could understand why there were so few universities and why they were all so small. The country was very poor and had been suffering from decades of civil war as well as the 1937–1945 Japanese invasion.

The National Central University was first established in Nanjing but was moved to Chongqing during the war. I joined it after it returned from Chongqing and was part of the first batch of freshmen admitted to its home campus. What struck me most was that the university was fully funded by the central government. When compared with what I knew from my conversations with graduates of Xiamen University, the contrast between a government-funded and a privately funded university was indeed great. Xiamen University struggled as a privately funded institution until it could not support itself any longer. So Mr Tan Kah Kee made a gift of the university to the central government and invited the government to take over the running of it. This made an enormous difference to the university's later development.

I did not know the details then and only understood more about university funding later. What was remarkable was that everything at the Central University was paid for by the state. The university was fully residential, all 4,000 students staying in campus dormitories. None of us paid anything for our studies. I had a scholarship and there were no tuition fees. Three meals a day were provided free in our hostels all year round. We were given a little spending money although it was not much help. The inflation rate in China was so high that there was no point counting money as banknotes were wrapped in bundles and transactions were made by guessing each bundle's weight. We were also given one set of summer clothes and another set for the winter. The hostels were pretty bare but it was adequate for us to survive the freezing cold winter.

That contrast between a public and a private university remained in my memory for a long time. After I returned from China, I went to the University of Malaya when it was founded in Singapore in 1949. The University of Malaya was not fully funded and we had to pay fees, but the fees were highly subsidised. The policy was to keep the fees very low.

A few of us had scholarships but basically the system was based on the idea that education should be highly subsidised. After the University of Malaya where I studied for five years, I went to London on a scholarship. As far as I know, the School of Oriental and African Studies that I went to at the University of London was also heavily subsidised by the British government.

In 1957, I returned to teach at the University of Malaya, first in Singapore, and then in Kuala Lumpur when it was still one university with two campuses. When it was later separated into two separate universities, I stayed on in Kuala Lumpur. Again, that university was almost fully funded by the government. Fees were highly subsidised, and students were required to pay only a very small amount for tuition and other student fees. Both the University of Malaya and the University of London were not fully residential, so the cost burden was less than that in China where national universities were invariably residential at that time.

The Chinese policy that universities should be fully residential and everything completely paid for by the government continued after the communists took over in 1949. That policy has been slightly modified only very recently. In fact, most universities in China, certainly the major ones, are still run on that basis. For China, the tradition that the government pays the expenses of the major universities established by the centre has been consistent for at least a century.

Mr Tan Kah Kee, however, took the initiative to fund a university in his home province, Fujian. Why did he need to do that? It was quite clear that there were too few universities in China. In 1898, the imperial government of the Qing dynasty began to build its first modern university in Beijing, the *Jingshi Daxuetang* (the Metropolitan University) that became Peking University. This was followed by others in Nanjing, Tianjin and some of the provinces. They were partly in response to the fact that private colleges were being set up by foreign missionaries offering modern education as in the West. Most of them were Americans, but among them were also British, French, German and other missionaries. They set up private colleges that normally started off as secondary schools, and many prepared students to go on to university education in the United States and Europe. The Chinese government gave permission for these colleges to exist, especially in the treaty ports such as Shanghai and Guangzhou and eventually in Beijing as well. It was aware that they were private institutions paid for mainly by the missions in the United States or by Catholic missions in France and some Lutheran and other state missions from Germany. Following Kang Youwei's Hundred Days Reform in 1898, the imperial government finally realised that there was a great need for modern higher education, something that it had been reluctant to support.

When I began to look at the imperial government's policy towards higher education, I was surprised to discover that education had been a more or less a private affair throughout Chinese history. This puzzled me because the Chinese people have been known to value education. They have always stressed that education was important and should be respected, and everyone was taught to be respectful to scholars. So it had not occurred to me that even basic education had never been supported by the central government. It was taken for granted that education be provided by people who could afford to get private tutors or scholars to teach their children and to set up private classes. All serious study was focussed on preparing for official examinations. State-appointed officials conducted the local, the provincial, and certainly the imperial examinations, and these and related costs were paid for out of pubic monies. But the cost of educating the young was basically private. Occasionally, local and provincial communities did offer help, but the government did not fund education or even preparation for the examinations.

After the imperial examination, there was a high-level in-service training academy where the best of the *jinshi* (advanced scholars) were recruited into the *Hanlinyuan* (College of Letters) to provide tuition to the emperor's children as well as specialised training for officials to become the highest mandarins in the country. But that was more a preparation for higher government service rather than higher education as we understand it.

I was amazed to discover that there was never any money spent by the imperial government for education and could not find any satisfactory explanation for this policy. From miscellaneous sources, for example, various memorials and memoirs by the mandarins and their essays and letters, we know that education was pivotal to getting into higher office. A mandarin in high office was so well rewarded that education was regarded as a kind of investment. This was something that could be taken on by individuals, families or local communities, so there was no need for the imperial government to pay for that.

Indeed, the essence of a traditional society was that the rulers were not expected to do much for it. It is only the modern state that has taken on many responsibilities for the society. This is a completely new concept.

If we were to ask "who paid for universities?" in the feudal European states, we would have found that there were a few private donors, such as kings, princes, aristocrats, and very often the church, and sometimes the professionals, who paid for higher education or advanced training. The medical professions supported medical education; the legal professions encouraged the study of law. Professional societies and various craft guilds provided funding for apprenticeships for people to become doctors, lawyers and a variety of technicians. And there were seminaries established by church authorities to prepare people to become priests. None of the monies for these institutions came from government. There was, in effect, no such a thing as state responsibility for education. Some of the famous colleges, for example, of Oxford and Cambridge, were supported by kings and aristocrats and other private donors, using their own money for their own special reasons, but the funding did not come out of state coffers.

In continental Europe, the idea that the state should pay for universities came out of the social and cultural revolution that occurred in several countries. Although this also occurred in England, it did not happen to the same degree. The states in Europe began to take over the cost of education following a series of major developments: the Reformation against the Catholic Church, the competition among churches, and eventually the French Revolution against monarchies. The separation of church and state was a major factor that led to the state taking over responsibilities like higher education. This was because the state did not want the church to have anything to do with it. The state wanted to create, out of the Enlightenment Project of the late 18th century, institutions that it could sponsor and support and ultimately also to shape and control.

The motives were varied but essentially it was to break the control that the church had over higher education and allow secular, humanist and scientific authorities to take over. During the 19th century, as each state accepted this responsibility, there was an increasing awareness that the countries needed graduates in science and technology. The Germans led the way to develop the research-based university. There was increasing awareness of the need for human capital of high quality and that the state should do more to ensure that this capital be enriched by universities to serve modern needs.

Thus the idea that the state should pay for higher education was very recent. It took nearly a hundred years before that idea spread to Asia. The early universities in India, like those of Calcutta, Madras and Bombay, were legacies of colonial universities. There, the British Empire in India did not believe that the state should pay for education, but merely help to subsidise it. The first Asian universities to have been completely supported by the state were those in Japan. This began with Tokyo Imperial University, and later Kyoto Imperial University. The Japanese modelled them on those in Germany. German universities, which were based in each of the various states before there was a united Germany, were fully funded by the respective states. It became very competitive among the states to recognise that universities could produce the kind of people that brought economic wealth; they could increase the profile of the state and make better-quality officials to serve the state. The Japanese were greatly impressed. But, like the Chinese, there was in Japan a tradition of private funding for education, so private universities like Waseda University and Keio University were also established not long after the imperial universities. That balance was achieved early and has served the country well.

In England, changes also began to take place to the Oxford and Cambridge model. Municipal responsibility for funding a university, for example the University of London, took off at the beginning of the 19th century. This was also supported by important segments of the population for a variety of institutions of advanced training, including the medical and legal professions and later the engineering and other technical professions. In other words, there was in England a mixture of state, public and private institutions, but state funding of universities was influenced by developments on the European continent and became increasingly important.

In Europe, the competition between states to produce better universities and better-educated graduates to serve their states became serious. In Asia, Japan adapted this to their needs and it is the main reason for the country's rapid economic development in the late 19th and the early 20th century. The Japanese responsiveness and foresight to recognise that the state had to play an integral role in educating and training the workforce needed by the state or society was critical. It enabled the country to modernise and industrialise quickly and thus keep up with the Western world.

I have noted elsewhere that the Japanese universities were not the first European-type university in Asia. The first was established in the Philippines, the University of Santo Tomas founded by the Dominican order in the 17th century. There were also other orders that had small colleges, often no more than seminaries for training priests. In that way, higher education was church-funded from the start. They were not like the modern secular universities of the 19th century, but more like mediaeval universities of Europe. Largely because of that, it had no influence on Asian educational development. Thus, it is true to say that the first modern university in Asia was that of Tokyo, and that was completely state-funded. And both Tokyo University and Kyoto University remain two of the best universities in Asia today.

That is the background to Tan Kah Kee's exceptional philanthropy in education. Tan Kah Kee made his fortune in the rubber industry; he returned to China several times to found primary, secondary and technical schools. He noted that there were very few universities in the country and no full-fledged university in Fujian. There was a missionary college in Fuzhou, and there were a couple of other private missionary colleges, some of which were meant for training teachers. For other provinces, there were mostly provincially funded colleges and many new missionary-based colleges located in other major cities.

Tan Kah Kee was shocked that Fujian — a large province with over 20 million people — did not have a university. He soon realised that the only way to set up a university in Fujian was to do it himself. He did not start with the university; he had started first with schools. Innovative in a whole range of ways in his educational philanthropy, Tan Kah Kee built up schools gradually, culminating in his endowment of Xiamen University. When he lost most of his fortune in the Great Depression, his friends and relatives tried to help but in the end they could not manage to meet the rising costs that modern universities needed. The Depression affected businesses everywhere in China and Southeast Asia, and the personal fortunes of the Southeast Asian Chinese were much diminished. Supporting the university thus became much harder. Finally in 1937, Tan Kah Kee gave up.

Throughout that period, the man who was the vice-chancellor was also from Singapore — Dr Lim Boon Keng. He made many sacrifices, giving up his medical career and his business interests in Singapore to do what his friend Tan Kah Kee asked him to do, and took up the presidency of Xiamen University. He struggled for 16 years right to the end, trying to raise funds and implement a number of policies to build the university he wanted. But he found it extremely difficult without adequate funding.

I was moved to read some of the Xiamen University accounts of what happened, in particular about Lim Boon Keng's efforts. He often travelled with Tan Kah Kee, trying to canvass for funds throughout

Southeast Asia, especially among the Hokkien population because after all, the university is in Fujian province. They were rarely successful and Tan Kah Kee was more than a little disappointed. But Lim Boon Keng kept on working very hard. As an entirely private university, there was little else he could do. He also respected Tan Kah Kee's wish to keep tuition and other fees low so that students from ordinary families could go to the university. This was an additional burden, as he also had to raise money for scholarships for the poorer students.

Today, universities face new problems of growth and funding. Singapore and Commonwealth universities in the United Kingdom, Australia, as well as others in Europe and elsewhere are looking around at new models to meet growing popular demands for university education. Unlike in the past, they are ready to look at the successes among universities in America.

The history of how universities grew all over the United States makes interesting reading. There were two main strands in their development. The earliest colleges were private colleges, funded mostly by various Protestant churches, and later the Catholic Church, with little public funding of any kind. Public institutions only came about after the American Revolution when the 13 colonies became federal American states. In short, during the colonial period, there was no policy of public funding for higher education. It was the local communities and their churches, together with some generous philanthropists, that enabled the small colleges to grow.

During the 19th century, the idea was advanced that the state should take on more responsibility to help more people get an education and that this was good for the country. Once that was introduced, it gained ground quickly. In every state where the government could afford it, land grants were offered for colleges to be built and public funds were used to back the systematic development of the institutions. Other kinds of grants were also made to these colleges and eventually large public universities sprang up in every state.

This tradition of providing higher education to as many people as possible was very different from the elitist traditions of Europe. What was important in the American example was that private colleges came first, with state colleges to follow, and both coexisted everywhere. Through such coexistence, more people had access to college education and the public and the private were never treated differently. Both were respected and, ultimately, even private universities drew on public funds when the cost of higher education rose significantly after the Second World War.

As a result, unlike elsewhere, some of the best universities in the United States today are private universities. During the last 50 years or so, the United States has developed many very good state universities as well. But the majority of these were founded to perform a service for the community and have not been expected to aspire for the excellence that some of the private universities have been focussed on achieving.

This is the broad picture and in that context, let me ask the question again, "Who should pay for universities?" Clearly, the answers have been different at different points of time.

There are many other factors to take into account. For example, conditions in a city-state like Singapore are very different from most others. The city has no other resources except human resources. Hong Kong is also in a similar position as the former colony also has only human resources. When I went to the University of Hong Kong, my first concern, which was also the university's concern, was whether it was producing graduates with the necessary skills for Hong Kong. How could we nurture our graduates' capacity to maximise their innate talents to serve and promote the economy of Hong Kong and provide the social cohesion that Hong Kong needs? These are values that the community would expect their university graduates to cultivate.

Singapore has the same concerns. Without natural resources, the need for human skills, talents and creativity that are produced for the city-state is overwhelmingly important, thus higher education has become a matter of tremendous concern. It is rightly a matter of major investment for the government of Singapore. Obviously, the state would wish to be fully involved in helping to determine how the institutions develop.

Compared to most other countries, the government in Singapore has had, and continues to have, an exceptional role to play in the running of its universities. Singapore simply does not have the conditions to do what large countries like the United States can do to achieve the balance between public and private higher education. The difference is stark between a country with mainly human resources and one with an enormous store of natural resources. There is, therefore, no question of Singapore copying the US model. All the same, in order to obtain what is best for Singapore, there are specific lessons that some parts of Singapore universities can learn from their counterparts in the United States. It is interesting to see how this learning is proceeding in recent decisions made for its universities.

There are, however, other concerns about how much the state should pay for higher education that are worth noting. I was at the Australian National University from 1968 to 1986 before I went to Hong Kong. During that time, I saw the Labour Party when it came to power under Mr Gough Whitlam make a major policy change, that is, to make universities free. All students could go to universities without having to pay tuition fees. That decision was to become one of the reasons why large numbers of students from Southeast Asia, not least from Singapore and Malaysia, turned to Australia to study. They did not have to pay the high fees asked for in the United Kingdom, or in America where it was even more expensive. The Labour government's policy change was an idealistic one. Mr Whitlam was a socialist who looked at the experience of other socialist countries, notably those in Western Europe, but also countries like the Soviet Union, China and those in Eastern Europe, where the state paid for education so that more students could go to university.

The consequences, of course, were predictable. Mr Whitlam believed that, if the state paid for higher education, even the poorest students in the country would have a chance to have a university education. He thought everyone would be inspired to go to university. After about 15 years, a review was done on the policy and the results of this review showed that the policy did not produce the desired results. The reality was that the rich and the middle class were given free education for their children while the number of the poor who benefited was small and those who graduated even smaller. My family was a beneficiary of the policy because our three children went to university without having to pay for tuition. Was that right? It would have been acceptable if the country could afford it and could fund it indefinitely. But it was wrong because the government could not afford it, certainly not if it also wanted each of the state's universities to maintain high standards. As time went on, the burden of providing free education for universities became too heavy even for a relatively well-to-do country like Australia.

Before long, the universities were asked to take in full-fee paying students from overseas. All international students from Singapore, Malaysia and elsewhere had to pay full fees to study in Australia. The universities later reintroduced lower fees for local students but it was politically difficult to raise the fees any further. Even to this day, the struggle is still going on between the government and the students and academic staff of the universities about how much fees local students should pay. Of course, universities are collecting fees now and they are using many new devices to get over the problem created by the Labour government about 30 years ago. There is, however, a limit to how many more full-fee paying overseas students can be admitted without starting to lower academic standards. But the universities have little choice as long as the central or state governments were giving them less money while costs continue to rise.

Another issue comes from the move by the government to push the universities to corporatise and seek outside help when they are running into financial difficulties. The University of Melbourne was brave to take the route of setting up a private university parallel to that of the University of Melbourne. At a time when full-fee paying overseas students were a major source of university revenue and Australian students did not have to pay full fees, setting up a private university where both overseas and Australian students would pay full fees seemed an attractive solution. But it is not one that many places can afford.

A third issue, also painful for any government, is to identify different classes of universities and fund them accordingly. In America, the many types and different classes of universities and colleges had evolved gradually over time through trial and error. Accreditation of education quality, faculty quality and research quality reviews were introduced to ensure that standards did not fall. Efforts were made through ranking and other reports to help parents and students distinguish between the better universities, the ordinary ones and the weaker ones. But in Australia, where universities are state-funded, with only three small private universities, such methods of differentiation are much harder to implement. The alternative, that the state apportions more money to research universities and less to those that concentrate on teaching, has not been welcomed and has already caused considerable loss of morale.

The situation will arise when the state cannot afford to fully fund all its universities equally. More than two decades ago, all the polytechnics in Britain were converted to universities. Overnight the number of universities increased from 50 to more than a hundred. Problems similar to those in Australia quickly came to the surface in Britain. The government could not afford to fund the universities equally and all kinds of pressure were put on them to cut costs and recruit private and full-fee paying students, to go out and canvass for donations, to secure contracts and seek collaborations with business enterprises.

From the above, the idea that small states should focus on public universities and larger states being encouraged to turn to having more private universities does not seem right. When a city like Hong Kong and a city-state like Singapore are without other resources, it is totally justified for the state to pay for higher education because human capital is the major resource. But for larger well-developed countries to take on the burden of financing all higher education only to find that they cannot afford it, that would have a destructive impact on the quality of education. That phenomenon is already apparent in Australia and is increasingly causing concern in the United Kingdom. The quality control that universities had once been well known for cannot be the same now because the respective governments do not have the money to make their universities really good. If this continues, it would expose further the mistake of doing what is socially correct by taking on full responsibility for higher education, and then reducing funding because the public purse is unable to carry that burden. Such a policy would create further social, economic and political problems for the governments concerned.

Let me draw two conclusions from the examples mentioned. There are situations when the government simply has to pay for higher education, when such a policy is obviously essential. The government clearly must know what its best interests are and is prepared to use its powers to achieve its goals. When it has to bring out what is best in its people to maximise its human resources, then it must give the universities the kind of nourishment that would enable them to flourish.

But if any government is forced to spread its funding thinly to all its universities, that would lead to impoverishment all round. The quality of education provided would be uncertain and good universities will have much to lose. This would lead to other losses, not only loss of credibility but also loss of the capacity to control quality that employers, academics, students and their parents could have worked out for themselves. When quality assurance and control are no longer in the hands of the university stakeholders because the state makes promises that it cannot deliver, that would be the worst of two worlds.

From the many experiences surveyed, I am persuaded that the American experience points in the right direction. This is not because I think other countries can imitate what the United States does with equal success. For example, I certainly do not think that the US model can be applied to Singapore because this is a totally different kind of state. But to answer the question as to who should pay for universities, I think the kind of balance achieved in the United States has merit. It accepts the fact that there are differences in the natural ability of people in any society and that only a certain percentage of those people have the capacity to be inventive and creative for a knowledge-based economy. The country has invested richly in them and provided them with the very best opportunities to develop their talents fully. Certainly, good general education should be provided to everyone in order to establish a stable and productive society. But those who want to acquire additional or professional skills for themselves should be expected to contribute to their own education.

It may be difficult for the American experience to be influential in countries like China or the former Soviet Union where education has long been structured to prepare for a rigid series of public examinations. It is hard to reconcile that with the fine balance that enables Americans to obtain their higher education through the state system or the private system, or a mixture of the two.

But this US system has now become so expensive that it is beyond the reach of most countries. Thus, we see countries like Australia, also belonging to the Commonwealth system of which Singapore's universities are also a part, and the United Kingdom as well, taking into account what has been developed in the United States and only picking what they can learn from and afford. As the European Continental system where the state pays for everything has also found, it is very difficult to change to the fluid and flexible system that the United States has evolved over three centuries. It is significant that Australia and the United Kingdom are considering implementing changes to their well-established structures. This is in recognition that the principle of the state paying for higher education for most of its population is unsustainable. Not even the United States can afford to fund everyone if they want at the same time to provide the best quality university education to their ablest citizens.

Coming back to the question of who should pay for universities, I repeat that a small city-state like Singapore should, and should be able to, pay. It would at the same time expect different parts of its communities to contribute to that investment. The citizens agreed that the quality of education is vital if the country is to make use of its best human resources. A measure of that success is when a general consensus about education can be reached.

In larger countries like that of China, it is unclear how funding policies will work out in the long run. It is fascinating to see that the Chinese have accepted the idea that universities must source for some of their funds. They have also accepted the idea that private universities can contribute to China's needs and have allowed several new ones to be founded. But from what is known so far, some of these private universities in China have encountered financial difficulties and many have not being able to sustain quality. It is still uncertain if private universities will work well, but at least the Chinese have acknowledged that no state can afford to provide good education for every one of its citizens from public funding alone. Although I am confident that the Chinese will readjust to a mixed public and private university system, I do not know how long it will take for them to provide adequate resources to make most of their universities really good.

Simply turning to, or depending on the support of, private enterprise is not the answer. The private universities in the United States depend a great deal on their successful graduates. Their alumni have been exceptionally loyal and many have gone out of their way to devise ways of attracting donations and securing lucrative contracts for their alma maters. In addition, in a dynamic and thriving economy, various organs of the state are able to complement and supplement such funding when necessary to ensure that the institutions produce the skilled talents desired. So going private does not mean 100-per-cent private, and being public does not mean 100-per-cent public, that is the way the American universities have evolved. What have been impressive are the flexibility the system has achieved and the balance of interests its people have arrived at.

I wish to emphasise that it is not necessary to copy what the Americans have done. Ultimately, the important considerations are to know the conditions of one's own society and identify what it really needs and what it can afford to do. A country's leaders should be consulting their people about what kinds of enterprise and creativity are needed to help the country deal with new challenges. The state has to provide leadership here, but it should expect inputs from the private sector and the community in general. There should not be too much dependence on private enterprises to support higher education. Business inputs and outcomes are primarily short-term and profit-oriented, and the priorities of higher education require long-term goals that benefit the whole society.

Therefore, looking at any of the institutions around us, the answer to the question of "who should pay for universities?" should not be determined by any specific model but a mix of models, by taking a leaf from other universities' experiences and adapting key features to best serve each country's and each university's needs. This kind of realistic assessment of what is possible has to be done between the state and those in the society who are deeply concerned about the issue. Such collaborative sharing of ideas should be the basis to seek the solutions that educators want.

In short, there is no simple answer to the question: who should pay for universities? I cannot see any simple formula. A wide range of experiences have shown that there is no alternative to the broad cooperation worked out between the universities and the government departments concerned, the active participation of private enterprises and the commitment of key community groups. There should be much more consultation and discussion about the ultimate goals of what higher education should be. As we recall the great contributions of Tan Kah Kee to establish Xiamen University on his own a century ago and compare the conditions under which he set forth to do that with the conditions prevalent today, we can be thankful that he was bold and visionary and made the commitment he did. Although what he attempted to do is less possible today, he remains nevertheless an inspiration to the generations of donors and educators who have been contributing generously to universities ever since.

4

A Very Peculiar Business

More universities in Asia of late have turned to headhunters in search of a new vice-chancellor or president. If the university is serious about being an international institution, the qualities listed for the kind of head it needs today read increasingly like those for a chief executive of a multinational corporation. Some universities go further and ask that the person they want should not only be entrepreneurial but also be a scholar with a fine international reputation.

The chairman of one such search committee, who had been the head of the public service commission in his own country, confessed to me that his brief led him to feel that he was expected to find a cross between a Nobel Prize winner and the chief executive of General Motors. He was obviously exaggerating, but only partly because he thought the university was unrealistic. His concern was whether the combination of chief executive and scholar was really what universities need.

This article was first published in the 9 March 2001 issue of the *Times Higher Education Supplement*. Reproduced with the kind permission of *Times Higher Education* magazine.

In recent years, there has been a tendency for vice-chancellors and university presidents to be feted if they were compared to chief executives of large corporations. Indeed, many universities have become so large that they could well be better run by people who work, and are paid, like chief executives. The problem is how to adapt corporate methods of leadership and control to the scholarly structures and educational needs of universities.

It is true that some professional schools and technological colleges by themselves would have little trouble going all the way with the style and rhetoric of corporations. This fact reminds us that universities originated in the Middle Ages as professional training centres, notably in theology, medicine and law, and the modern world has now added that of business to this worldly list.

In the face of such a revival of professional priorities, the professors and lecturers who subscribe to Cardinal Newman's idea of the university have had to become a little defensive. Those who teach in humanities and science faculties that offer a broader education, and intangible values such as thinking pursuits and critical skills, may argue that they try to reproduce themselves to keep the academic fires burning. But they have a hard time explaining to management consultants what they produce and how their productivity might be measured. It is, therefore, easier for chief executive-type heads of institutions to belittle their efforts, neglect their needs or even ignore them.

It no longer surprises me to hear that a department of classics or even modern languages has been closed in the face of rationalisation; or that a department of philosophy or physics has to give way to save funds for worthy and more practical courses such as environmental or media communications studies.

Living in Asia and comparing its new universities with the older ones I visited in Europe has made me wonder at the speed at which many Asian universities have adopted the language and aspirations of a chief executive-led organisation. The great faith they used to have in historic, ivy-clad institutions has retreated before the advent of the super-administered ones, including some covered in ivy, that now flourish in North America. If one of these new Asian universities is told that it would have to count on student fees and loyal donors if it were to thrive, its vice-chancellor, president or rector would be quick to toe the line. Before long, he or she would realise that most of the departments and their teaching staff do not fit well in the new scenario. The university head then has the choice of treating these academic colleagues as square pegs in round holes, or as exceptions for which different criteria have to be found.

This is the moment of truth for the average chief executive. If he or she sees them as square pegs, this is because he or she believes that round holes are the norm and what he or she has to do is to shave the corners and make them round. If he or she is prepared to think of them as exceptional, he or she is in danger of compromising corporate principles that maximise efficiency. This is an especially difficult choice if he or she is someone from the academia who has merely read about modern chief executives and admired their vigorous style.

Clearly, the chief executives of single industries are not the best examples to follow. Universities are too variegated in the kinds of graduates they produce to be compared to the highly focussed production line. They are more like smaller versions of multi-industry conglomerates that need different approaches for different sectors of their organisations. In addition, they are expected to survive in a highly competitive international marketplace of ideas and practices.

In Asia, there are few scholars with exceptional administrative talents and even fewer who know much about multi-faceted corporations. To create a climate of high expectations about their adaptability while nursing hopes for quick results is a recipe for disappointment. To avoid this, the choices are stark. The university could aim low and find a head who would treat the university as a single-industry organisation. An efficient norm is quickly identified and all parts of the university are made to conform to optimise efficiency. If this is not feasible, the university might simply proclaim that the corporate rhetoric is in place and then muddle through. The least viable choice in the business atmosphere in Asia today is to try to prove that the university has the right and duty to find its own way of managing the unusual people, both staff and students, it has to have within its campus.

5

The University as a Global Institution

There is one institution which embodies most of modern culture that matters today and promises to provide some of the enduring ingredients for a genuine global culture in the 21st century. This is the university. It is a microcosm of complex and changing societies; at the same time, its store of talent and knowledge has the capacity to reshape the world.

The modern university is barely 200 years old; the vast majority came into being during this century and the numbers are still growing. In its modern form, this institution had been introduced into Asia during the second half of the 19th century and it has taken root well. Today the university has spread in every direction and its origins are recognisable

---

This lecture was first presented at the First Richard A Harvill Conference on Higher Education on the theme "The University of the Future", at University of Arizona held on 23 November 1992. Published in *The Universities of the Future: Roles in the Changing World Order*, Tucson, Arizona 2003, pp. 45–73. Reproduced with the kind permission of University of Arizona.

wherever it is found. All of them include the core elements of cultural transmission, political elitism and professional autonomy. Underlying them is the quest for wisdom and ultimately for the intellectual excellence that modern societies need to ensure progress.

As one of the tests of the global nature of the institution, we could look at the universities in Asia. Many of them were established parallel to traditional religious education centres and classical academies that trained people for public and communal service. The modern university focussed on knowledge not already available. What made the early ones remarkable was the way they demonstrated quickly that they were open and flexible in expanding into new disciplines and professions. They acquired and transmitted new knowledge efficiently and thrived on international linkages with similar institutions elsewhere.

I shall focus on four themes in a comparative survey of Asian universities.

From Periphery to Centre

The university was first introduced on the peripheries of ancient civilisations: the coastal cities of Bombay, Calcutta and Madras and cities like Tokyo and Kyoto. Eventually China followed suit, partly by converting traditional institutions into public universities and partly by allowing Christian missionary societies to build private ones. Thailand and the colonies in Southeast Asia started a little later, with a variety of models to follow: the French, the British, the Dutch and the American. For the Philippines, one could include the Spanish universities, but their early ones were more traditional Catholic than modern secular institutions.

The University of Hong Kong, is a good example. It was built on the edge of two contrasting worlds, both a colonial university and a peripheral Chinese one. From the beginning, it was a bridge between modern professional education and Chinese values and was intended to attract students from the Chinese mainland. It symbolised the uneasy birth of the modern university in the East, trying to serve two masters: the expansionist West and a defensive East in search of ways to strengthen its threatened value systems.

Much of that unease disappeared after the Second World War. The Japanese universities had proved their value to their country and become confident centres of nationalist and progressive ideas. This was similar in

China, except that Chinese students had absorbed radical ideas at universities, including those founded by Western missionaries, that had become centres of dissent if not outright opposition to the government. The speed at which these universities became transmitters of the latest ideas was astonishing. Notwithstanding the fact that much of what was introduced was half-learnt and poorly digested, the intellectual force engendered in the universities was both refreshing and destabilising.

This phenomenon was further stimulated by the rapid expansion of universities in the Americas, Europe and Australasia. The university became an institution that every country had to have; in fact, the more universities there were, the more likely, so the social scientists began to proclaim, the rapid development of a modern economy.

Unity in Diversity

This takes me to my second theme: unity in diversity. The new institutions have followed different models and taken many shapes. There are times when one could say that there is so much diversity that one may well question whether the name of university should be applied to them at all.

But, in most cases, the diversity in origins, in appearance, in quality, in ideological dispositions, is superficial or temporary. Everywhere, beneath the formal structures and the official declarations of purpose and goals, there are comparable mixes of staff and students. Degrees of control over thought, teaching and research may vary, from the light touch of almost total freedom to the heavy hand of almost complete regulation. But behind the different managerial styles, we would find much that is positive and central to the ideal of the university.

There would be, common to each institution, the desire to learn and the urge to teach; the respect of keen and curious students for their teachers and the love and appreciation of teachers for their best and brightest students. Even the key relationships between academic staff and administration may have fundamental similarities. There is certainly the same kind of debate and struggle for teaching and research funding, the same demand for enhanced scholarly links between institutions at home and abroad.

Some recent examples are illuminating. When we meet Russian and East European scholars today removing their ideological cloaks, we find them not only totally recognisable as the products and the backbone of universities, but also dedicated to the same cause of learning, seeking creativity and originality. In addition, we have just seen the extraordinary decade when Chinese universities, after having been isolated from outside institutions for 30 years, restored their old ties with them with the minimum of fuss and discomfort. There was nothing more moving than to see foreign academics and their Chinese friends meeting anxiously only to discover that they still have so much in common that they could collaborate and together guide their respective students to the highest levels of scholarly achievement.

Propensity for Free Trade in Knowledge and Ideas

This propensity, my third theme, was a great step towards the concept of the universal academy. In the field of education, I consider this credo to be one of the three most important advances in history. I place it beside the idea of examinations for a meritocracy and the ideal of a basic education for all, without any discrimination on the grounds of race, class, religion and gender. But, unlike the other two, this free trade of ideas is peculiar to the university, an institution that has become the major repository and reservoir of knowledge and research talent.

Indeed, when the university espoused this ideal, it laid the foundations for it to become a global institution. The idea of free trade in knowledge has helped the university to transcend the national, racial and religious boundaries that constrain intellectual initiative. This has been possible because the great universities had insisted on open access to the fruits of research and scholarship, the academic freedom to teach without interference and the right to publish and disseminate knowledge in a borderless world.

This right has not been easy to establish, nor is it always easy to defend. It certainly cannot be taken for granted. Indeed, one of the wonders of the modern world is how this mystique of free trade in ideas was transplanted to regions which had always subscribed to their very opposite. In Asia, the powerful believed that all knowledge should be held in monopoly. Emperors, kings, princes, chiefs, priests and all those who had access to knowledge, especially practical and valuable knowledge that produced wealth and power, wanted no one else but themselves to enjoy that knowledge. In China, there were numerous examples, documented in that great work by Joseph Needham on *Science and Civilisation in China*, of inventors and technical geniuses who made discoveries that were eventually lost because they were never transmitted. Some of them disappeared as family secrets; others became imperial secrets for fear that they might empower the rebellious and the ambitious. The lack of laws that protected private property and patent rights contributed to these losses, but even more important was the tradition that denied people the right to unorthodox knowledge.

This idea is still being tested. But for China, the will to preserve the right to free trade in ideas enjoyed by the rest of the modern world has remained remarkably strong. No scholar I know would deny the benefits of access to new knowledge. I have yet to meet a teacher or student in China who did not believe that academic freedom that permits the free exchange of knowledge is what every university should have. This leads me to believe that this propensity is one of the key features in a university that has contributed immeasurably to making the university a global institution.

Alternative Visions

The phrase, alternative visions, is barely adequate to cover all the things my fourth theme has to encompass. The starting point is that universities stagnate when they are mere transmitters of given knowledge and they flourish when they seek the new knowledge that they were established to produce. But for this modern institution, that is not all. As a global institution not prohibited by national and other artificial borders from generating new ideas, it is well positioned to set new agendas and scenarios for progress and world civilisation.

For any one university, such goals would put it clearly out of its depth. But then I am not talking about any single example, or even any group or national network of universities, but about the university as a global institution. This means that we should not be content with recounting its glorious successes or marvelling at its resilience in any one place or over any period of time, but also examine the record to tease out its potential for the future.

The record shows that the university has been changing over the centuries and changing ever faster during the past decades. From my own perspective, these changes have been mainly for the better, but I recognise that there are many who would argue that some of the changes are distinctly for the worse and that some of the most precious values of the traditional universities have been abandoned. There have been of late more essays with titles like "Universities in transition", "Universities in crisis", and headlines like "More cuts in university funding", "Less money for research", "Academics to be more accountable", to suggest that the university has become a globally wasteful, complacent and, surprisingly, even intolerant institution.

Whatever truth holds in these titles and headlines, what strike me are the range and vehemence of the vigorous debates that are going on about the nature of the university in not only the rich and developed countries, but also the insecure and impoverished developing world of Asia and Africa. Taken separately and fought within the confines of each campus or even each country, there seem to be a preponderance of desperate and despairing tones in the various contrasting calls for defence and restoration of established values or for radical surgery or for massive new funding. But the overall picture remains for me one of growth, not of size and numbers, but of the determination to be better at serving the needs of the time.

What are these needs? Each country and its leadership will have its priorities for its respective universities; each university will try to work out what it has to do to serve those priorities and save itself. But the needs of the time for the university as a global institution must include the need to understand and explain the process of globalisation that is taking place around us. That process has speeded up in recent decades. Where it is leading us greatly depends on there being more global institutions to help delineate and project the future. And there are many more such institutions today, ranging from international agencies and professional associations to multinationals and financial organs.

The university is but one such global institution, but it is unique in that it is the only one that exists to educate and train those who are responsible for organising all the others. The great paradox is that it does its global job despite the fact that it is dependent on the support largely of local, national and even exclusive business and professional interests. What gives this global institution its exceptional quality is that it has been historically structured for some parts of it to tackle current problems while other parts remain above the fray. It is this quality that gives the university the capacity to provide alternative visions to what is immediately desirable and urgently needed. By this, I mean it can embody present drives and urges while mapping out possible and probable scenarios of the future, including agendas that have not been encompassed by accepted wisdom or even existing knowledge.

I am not suggesting that the phrase alternative visions adequately conveys what the global institution of the university can contribute to the world's future. What I see is no less than an institution that is already interlocking, through its mastery of enhanced communications technology and new knowledge networks, whole new generations of the people which it has educated to determine the future of the world. The present uncertainties of each university or even each country's universities need to be placed in this broader perspective.

It does seem rather feeble to end by calling for an act of faith in an institution that prides itself on being rational and scientific, but I believe that the record of the university in all its manifestations through history, and especially in surviving the acid tests provided by modern history, gives us reason to be faithful. It is a global institution that I commend to all of you.

6

The Asian Renaissance

I note that James Boswell died 200 years ago and Robert Burns followed a year later. This leads me to reflect on something that I have always found interesting: the Scottish renaissance of the 18th century that produced such outstanding men as David Hume and Adam Smith. Even more noteworthy is the question, why did these Scots suddenly do so well? Was it the Act of Union of 1707? Was it the peace that the Union brought across the border?

One suggestion was that it was the Scotland Act of 1696 which "enforced previous legislation setting up a school in every parish". The quality of education in Scotland was exceptional, and that was probably what made the difference.

My thoughts turn to the place of education in Asia, especially in the areas that had been parts of European empires. Was there "a school in every parish" by the beginning of the 20th century? Probably in Ceylon (Sri Lanka), parts of British India, and the Straits Settlements. Burma and

---

This article was first published in the 14 August 1995 issue of the *Times Higher Education Supplement*. Reproduced with the kind permission of *Times Higher Education* magazine.

the Malay States had to wait longer, but the Philippines under the Americans and Cochin-China under the French were not far behind. By the time of independence, all the former colonies in Southeast Asia were building schools at a very fast rate.

During the 1950s, apart from Singapore and Malaysia remaining active in the British Commonwealth education system and the Philippines maintaining close connections with the United States, Southeast Asia's direct ties with former imperial powers were largely broken. But for the three countries which kept their lines open, the advances in education were quite spectacular, as were those in parts of South Asia.

There have been claims for an Asian "renaissance". How far can they be related to progress in education? Writers, scholars and scientists are normally the most prominent direct beneficiaries of education.

For Southeast Asia, the list of those who have made an impact on the rest of the world is small but growing. In contrast, the political figures have been larger than life. In the English-speaking world, such men as Rizal, Quezon, Tunku Abdul Rahman, Lee Kuan Yew and Dr Mahathir might not have been of the stature of Gandhi and Nehru, but they were well-educated in modern schools and universities, and the "technology transfers" in their public careers were remarkable. Some were also considerable intellects.

Others like Aung San had learnt little from the British, though U Nu was a careful student of British ways; Sukarno and Ho Chi Minh picked what they needed from the West, the former desultorily and the latter with deadly purpose, but they really became great because of their direct opposition to what colonial systems had to offer. Perhaps Prince Sihanouk can claim to have thrived because of his metropolitan education. Thus, political leaders tend to dominate in Southeast Asia. They owed less to formal education, but were really heroic figures created by the opportunities of their times.

The story in South Asia, of course, is somewhat different. It saw the establishment of the earliest modern universities in the three great cities of Calcutta, Bombay and Madras. The stress from the start was on cultural and philosophical education, and the splendid achievements reflect these beginnings.

From Ram Mohan Roy to Tagore, from Vivekenanda, Radhakrishnan, Satyajit Ray to Salman Rushdie, South Asia's renaissance came early, was well-sustained and has continued vigorously to the present.

What about Thailand, China and Japan, countries which were never colonised? Here the contrasts are great. In Japan, education was given the strongest possible emphasis and official support, and there were far more writers, scholars, scientists, and engineers than politicians among the great achievers. By learning systematically and directly from European institutions, the Japanese mastered the latest advances in learning at a spectacular speed. They were also quick to turn their newfound knowledge to practical use. Their national renaissance could be said to have been "hard" in comparison with that of India's, which might be described as being of a "softer" variety.

Neither the Chinese nor the Thais could match what the Japanese did in education. Both were constrained during the first half of the 20th century by circumstances beyond their control. The Thais still lacked a strong national identity and remained very insecure in between the British and French empires. The Chinese were overwhelmed by military humiliations and civil wars. For most of the past 150 years, their education system developed despite the lack of a consistent policy. But because they had the numbers and they opened themselves to modern ideas and practices through Shanghai, the most cosmopolitan city in Asia, they did produce their share of brilliant individual writers, scholars and scientists.

They had begun well, with intellectuals like Kang Youwei, Liang Qichao, Zhang Binglin, followed by Lu Hsun, Hu Shih and others, but their best scientists seemed to have done better outside. China never had the peace and political order for its educated people to sustain their achievements or allow them to contribute more to the country. Like many of the Southeast Asian countries, it was the politicians and military figures who dominated all developments: from Tseng Kuo-fan, Li Hung-chang, Sun Yat-sen, Chiang Kai-shek, Mao Zedong, Zhou Enlai to Deng Xiaoping, and their rise to greatness had less to do with education than the tenor of their times.

The two colonies of Japan — Korea and Taiwan — fared poorly. Only when they were free to turn to tertiary education in the United States in the 1950s did they join the race. But the long line of scholars, scientists, writers and film-makers produced in the two countries in less than four decades is spectacular. Nothing in postcolonial Southeast Asia can match their numbers.

What do we make of all this? There is little doubt that, unlike the 18th century Scots who had their renaissance when they numbered about one million, we are dealing here with much larger populations.

Nevertheless, it would appear that, in Asia, numbers do count, not in absolute terms, but relative to those who received modern education. Also, how many schools and universities did each country have, say, in 1950? Not surprisingly, with a few exceptions, there is a positive correlation between population size and quality of education, and the local and national renaissance that is later claimed.

What is less clear is how important was the contribution from the indigenous traditions. The East and South Asian experiences suggest that these could help prepare the response to the Western challenge. For Southeast Asia, there is the added question of whether the colonies fared worse. Did it matter how long they were colonies for, and which great powers they were colonies of? Did those under the British do better than those under the French, the Dutch, the Japanese or the Americans? It is noteworthy that, after the 1950s, there has been a rapid spread of schools, colleges and universities everywhere.

The keen response to increased tertiary opportunities abroad, especially to the United States, has clearly had a significant impact on intellectual development. For the postcolonial decades, looking to the United States may be like the Scots looking to England 300 years ago. If that is so, perhaps an historic Asian renaissance will not be long coming.

7

Cities Light Torch of Excellence

One of the most remarkable developments in the 20th century is the way modern education has become accepted as the norm throughout the world. Those who regularly attend meetings on education would be encouraged to believe that we are heading towards one-world universalism and that it is only a matter of time before the unity of mankind will make the world a peaceful and safer place.

There are reservations about this optimistic view. The resurgence of nationalism emphasises the immediate needs of states, in which leaders guard against any kind of cosmopolitanism that would dilute the national spirit. Universalist standards in education would work against that goal. At the same time, the growing importance of cities in the global economy encourages a kind of international metropolitanism. Cities tend to lead the way in universalist education. One of the reasons for this is that they are the sites for most universities.

This article was first published in the 25 November 1996 issue of the *Times Higher Education Supplement*. Reproduced with the kind permission of *Times Higher Education* magazine.

Universities not only produce educated and skilled personnel, but also leaders of the community. Some of their students may be activist and rebellious, but they are also likely to be creative and constructive in preparing for a civil society. Their understanding of issues such as the environment and ecology, class and welfare, minority rights, cultural and political pluralism, and their outward world view not only make many of them able civil servants and business executives, but also leaders of non-governmental organisations.

In the Asia-Pacific region, universalism in education has been strongly endorsed in the cities, especially in the universities. This is despite the fact that national leaders know how much it is based on Western ideals. Although many Western intellectuals are questioning the future of universities in their countries, the region itself has not so far joined in the chorus of doubt. It remains confident that universities have a vital role to play. Why is that?

The universalist ideals of the Enlightenment brought to the rest of the world by the modern university have been used to determine the way modern education was shaped in most countries. It was the university that first embodied the idea of educational excellence. On top of the high standards of technical and professional skills needed for the Industrial Revolution, universities also added the ideals enunciated by philosophers and religious leaders for cultural, moral and intellectual quality.

The scepticism about the future of the modern university in the West, if anything, confirms the continual quest for excellence. The measures of excellence may be subject to change, but the efforts to refine them are still widely respected. This is particularly true where science and technology are concerned. It was always doubtful whether the measures that touched on culture and value systems would be readily transferable. The tension between concepts like "region" and "universalism" stems from competing cultural values. For example, countries in Asia may each claim distinctive needs that challenge the validity of universal ideals. Each may insist on the superiority of its Confucian, Islamic, Hindu, or Buddhist value systems and resist the idea that their cultures could eventually be replaced by the excellence of the modern and the secular. Here is where the university comes in. Most are expected to serve their countries' expanding needs. Their international experience in the past five decades shows a sharp contrast between being restrictive and being open.

Two examples would suffice to illustrate this. Most universities in the postcolonial world have retained their cultural and economic links with their metropolis; the English-speaking and the French-speaking areas are the obvious ones. The Association of Commonwealth Universities enabled a particular model of university to be widely established in former British territories. The countries that remain in the system are not uniformly enthusiastic about following the British models, but habits are hard to change and ties remain strong. This suggests that the universalist claims of modern knowledge have been accepted. Without an external reference point about quality, it is feared the universities will sink into provinciality and irrelevance.

Although alternative models from the United States are gaining influence, a common rhetoric about excellence is still shared among the Commonwealth universities. In contrast, educational institutions in Asia that were products of the Cold War have not worked together. Ideological and practical concerns had divided those leaning towards the West from those linked to the Soviet bloc and those who claimed to be neutralist. Their access to development aid for educational institutions opened them up to some universalistic standards of excellence.

But the apparent existence of common political ideals was not enough for a shared sense of educational excellence to emerge. There were a number of reasons for this. First, the United States consciously tilted towards the Atlantic. Although US education influence in Asia grew rapidly in the Philippines, Japan, South Korea and Taiwan, the main penetration in universities has been in medicine, the natural sciences and technology. In the arts and social sciences, the impact was cerebral and instrumental, but never held moral and emotive authority.

Second, Japan could have played the role of bridge, but it had recently been an enemy and could only be an ally as a junior partner. Also, differences in cultural outlook have restricted the use of US standards of excellence in non-science fields of learning. There have been calls in Japan for internationalisation and foreign students have been welcomed. But the openness has so far been limited to science and technology.

The third reason is more hopeful: the Cold War produced the divide between the peripheral states of East Asia (mainly the island states plus South Korea and Thailand) and the hinterlands of China, North Korea and parts of the Southeast Asian mainland (Cambodia and Laos). This ideological divide had a profound impact on cultural and educational exchange, even though it can be argued that science and technology standards remained comparable on both sides.

Thus comparable standards of excellence in universities based on a common political ideology did not get very far. Now that the political divide has been removed, the new openness should enable similar standards of excellence to be extended from the periphery to the reforming hinterland states like the People's Republic of China and Vietnam, and eventually Burma.

The experience confirms that universities are most dynamic when they are as open as the modern cities that connect the global system of liberal capitalism.

Japan and the "four tigers" in East Asia not only drew the United States deeply into the region's economy, their cities and universities also ensured that universalist standards, beginning with science and technology, made a lasting impact on their cultures and societies.

8

Lessons Closer to Home

The Bangkok gathering of the heads of Asian and European governments in early March 1996 was unusual.

It took one regional grouping, the Association of Southeast Asian Nations (ASEAN), to bring another, the European Union, to a meeting that would have been inconceivable a few years ago. Yet when it happened, there were no great expressions of surprise. It was almost as if it was just another one of those conferences allowing a select number of the rich and the not so rich countries to talk about how to make even more money.

But it was more than a by-product of the Asia-Pacific Economic Cooperation Forum, or a preview of the World Trade Organisation meeting planned for Singapore. It was a truly historic occasion for some of the countries represented, one cluster of former colonial nations meeting with some of the metropolitan powers that had ruled them for centuries.

This article was first published in the 18 March 1996 issue of the *Times Higher Education Supplement*. Reproduced with the kind permission of *Times Higher Education* magazine.

There were references to cultural and educational exchanges, which were to be expected. There is nothing new here. Technology transfers through tertiary education have been the most important and fruitful relationship between former colonies and their former masters.

What is less appreciated by the countries in each of the two regions is that there have been efforts at cooperation among universities within each region for decades. Is there something here that regions can learn from each other?

About 40 years ago, six universities in the Southeast Asian region came together to form the Association of Southeast Asian Institutions of Higher Learning (ASAIHL). They represented Thailand, Indonesia, the Philippines, Malaysia-Singapore, Vietnam and Hong Kong.

Today, the ASAIHL has a membership of more than 150 institutions, and has associate members from countries outside the region, like Australia, Japan, the United States, Canada and New Zealand. The core members are still those within Southeast Asia. They meet every two years and organise academic lectures and seminars on a large variety of themes relevant to current research and teaching problems. Staff exchanges are regularly arranged, and support for graduate students is provided through scholarships and travel grants from time to time.

But, despite the best intentions, there has been little success in enabling undergraduates to move freely around the region. It has been much easier for students to go to universities in North America, Western Europe and Australasia. The major difficulties within the region, it is said, have come from two sources: the incompatibility of admission criteria and curricular structures, and linguistic differences under nation-building conditions.

One other might be added: governments, parents and the students themselves have preferred, with a few exceptions, the older established universities of the West to the struggling new ones in the neighbourhood.

Members of the ASAIHL were very enthusiastic to try to resolve these difficulties during the first two decades. They were defeated, especially by some larger factors: political tensions accompanying decolonisation, communist rebellions in several countries and a regional war such as that in Vietnam.

It became clear that students who wish to study abroad found it easier and more worthwhile to do so outside the region altogether. It is now the universities from the West who come to the region to try to loosen up the structures, criteria and even the language requirements. And each year this is happening on a larger scale.

Does the Asia-Europe summit in Bangkok have anything to offer tertiary education that would ease the situation within the region? The European countries have a long tradition of wandering scholars and some countries have positively encouraged peripatetic students.

Since the end of the Second World War, there have been systematic efforts to ensure that bright young students have the opportunity to study and obtain degrees outside their countries but within the region. Is their experience relevant in Southeast Asia?

There are several difficulties the two regions have in common. There are numerous admission criteria and curricular structures; there are even more linguistic barriers. But Europe has proved that when universities and the governments that support them are really keen, no obstacles can stand in the way of progress for long.

They have, however, at least two clear advantages over the Asian region. European governments, on the whole, regard the universities within their own region as comparable.

While exchanges are not encouraged simply for their own sake, reciprocity has not been difficult to arrange when wanted, despite linguistic and cultural differences. In addition, they have been willing to set aside funds to build European institutions for both undergraduate and graduate students in preparation for ever closer relations among themselves.

One might also say that there is no perception that universities outside the region have academic and technological superiority over their own, nor is there any great social pressure for governments, parents and students to look elsewhere for tertiary training.

There is no reason to believe that what the Europeans have achieved in intra-regional tertiary education is applicable to the ASAIHL or the ASEAN region. But it seems important, now that the heads of governments of both regions have discussed educational exchanges, that attention be given to what can be done to revive some enthusiasm for intra-regional exchanges among Asian countries themselves.

Unlike 40 years ago, or even 20 years ago, there is peace and growing prosperity in the region. Most Asian governments can now afford to push for such exchanges, and there are good reasons to believe that the products of these exchanges would enhance the quality of graduates available to serve the community. If it is done within the region with confidence, it would make future inter-regional exchanges even more meaningful.

9

The Asia-Pacific: Region and Universalism in Higher Education

Education for a small group of elites has been available in most societies for centuries. Education for all, however, has come only during the 20th century, first in the developed countries and as a distant ideal for the rest of the world. As for excellence, it is hard to agree on the criteria by which to judge. There is the elite excellence, that is, quality for the rare few, and there is, with different criteria of excellence, the all-round quality education for the many. For the former, it can be said that brilliant individuals can be found in every country but the rarefied few are not representative and do not tell much about the characteristics of a region. As for the latter, all-round quality is normally a function of a country's economic and cultural development. Delivering good quality education to

---

This keynote address was first delivered on 13 September 1996 on the occasion of the Education Victoria 1996 Conference, held in Melbourne, Australia.

everyone requires substantial budget. Only rich countries can provide access to consistently good educational facilities and working conditions for their teachers. Furthermore, they can attract brilliant individuals from the poorer countries to their centres of excellence and thus ensure that these centres remain excellent.

What Regionalism Means in Asia-Pacific

It would be easy to point to a city or a nation where excellence in education is the goal and where centres of excellence have been established. But a region? In a cluster of rich cities and nations forming a region, there is no doubt that the sum of its parts would enable that region to claim to be one of excellence. Western Europe is clearly one such region; North America is another. Not long ago, the Soviet Union and its satellites could claim the potential to be the third one in excellence. Australia and New Zealand, on the one hand, and Japan on the other, might be seen as successful extensions of the larger Euro-American region, often referred to as "the West". That West is not a region. For more than a hundred years, we needed a different metaphor to describe its dominant position. If we were to describe the world as a pyramid, the West would be at the top third of that pyramid.

Since the end of the Cold War, among many efforts to define a new world order or new ways of explaining the world, the "end of history" school of thought would tend to confirm that metaphor. The West is the top third of the pyramid, with the United States as the top third of that. If so, an Asia-Pacific that includes the United States and other "Western" extensions like Canada and Australasia could look forward to being near the top because of the powerful pull of the Americans. An alternative view that focusses on the "clash of civilisations" and argues that such a clash is now inevitable offers quite a different perspective. The West is depicted now as being on the defensive. Its civilisation has been challenged by at least two rivals, representing the Islamic and the East Asian "Confucian" civilisations. Thus both the West and potential enemies of Western dominance are to be found in the Asia-Pacific. If this is true, is the region destined to be an arena for future conflict between countries that are expected to represent the two opposing sides?

There are, of course, other global approaches which look at the world as ultimately human, and therefore one diverse whole, whether it be seen as a universal civilisation, a global village, or a series of interlocking and interdependent regions. In a context when there is no obvious world order, the Asia-Pacific today could be regarded as potentially one of those regions, overlapping with others in complex networks, but contributing to the overall integration of a one-world modern civilisation. These optimistic approaches have recently been questioned and portrayed as naive or impossible. But they are far from impractical and deserve close attention if we are to speak of a region of educational excellence.

In the midst of these conflicting pictures about the world, we obviously need to look hard at the idea of the Asia-Pacific as any kind of region. Is it a region arising out of insecurity, essential for the intense competition that faces its members, or merely the product of a splendid imagination or an uncontainable optimism? The kind of region it becomes may determine what kind of centre of educational excellence can be produced, or whether it would ever become such a centre. In other words, who decides what is excellent — those who insist on following some universally accepted standards? Or those rich and powerful members who dictate to the others what should be the region's primary interests? Or local and national leaders in quest of wealth and power for their own countries? If the answers to these questions are not clear and not generally accepted, the Asia-Pacific may end up as another "talk shop". Without a common goal and the will to work towards it, it will be very difficult to produce any centres of educational excellence.

In fact, the idea of some kind of regionalism is not new to Asia. The 1950s was a criss-crossing of plans and organisations with attempts at a regional focus. The discussions which accompanied them are relevant to the future development of the Asia-Pacific. I would suggest that an approach through universal ideals in higher education would provide the leverage to prod the region towards educational excellence. As outlined here, these are some thoughts as to why this approach might be helpful.

One of the most remarkable developments in the 20th century is the way modern education has become accepted as the norm throughout the world. This has encouraged those who believe in one-world universalism, in internationalism, in globalisation, to feel that we are now heading in the right direction. For them, it is only a matter of time before the unity of mankind will emerge to make the world peaceful and safe.

There are reservations about this optimistic view. Many studies show the new importance of cities in the global economy. Others, however, stress the resurgence of nation-statism. The former suggests that a kind of international metropolitanism, in which cities lead the way in universalist education, would enable their political and economic elites to bring about greater integration of peoples and cultures. The resurgence of nationalism, however, points the other way, and emphasises the immediate needs of the nation-states. Nationalist leaders would guard against any kind of cosmopolitanism that would dilute the national spirit, and they would worry about the effects of universalist standards in education. There are reasons to believe that these two separate developments, in cities and between nations, need not be in conflict and may even be related. Given the power and speed of modern communications, they could be complementary and reinforce one another in seeking progress.

But let me concentrate on the region, on the idea of universal standards of excellence in education in a region. Regionalism has been with us for several decades. The most outstanding example is the evolution of the European Community. There are surely lessons for educators in the Asia-Pacific. In the context of a future centre of educational excellence, I believe the relevant theme to examine is the history of universalism in education which Western Europe has stood for and projected to the world for centuries.

The Universalism Phenomenon

First, a brief account of this modern phenomenon of universalism. Where education in concerned, its main thrust has been secular and positivist, especially in its emphasis on the scientific method in all forms of inquiry. Secular education, for better or worse, is now the norm in secondary education. The impetus for it, however, started with the modern university which really became a universal phenomenon through its successful transplantation to every corner of the globe. With the ideals of the Englightenment strongly reinforced by the Industrial Revolution and the French Revolution, totally new demands were made of the traditional universities in Europe. It was the transformation of these universities early in the 19th century in Western Europe, starting in Berlin and moving westwards to the United States, that created the conditions for a completely new approach towards education. Following that, the growth of tertiary education played a direct part in two major systems — firstly, the system that shaped the syllabus of the elitist secondary schools which were expected to prepare students for the universities, and secondly, the system that helped to train the teachers and also promote the research necessary to ensure better understanding of the educational needs of future generations.

The tertiary system of the 19th century in Western Europe is the starting point of the educational revolution that promised universalism of knowledge. By this, I refer to the optimism that sprang from the confidence that the methods of science would answer all knowable questions. Away from matters of faith, custom and cultural heritage of each segment of humanity, the mind, through rational, logical discourse and scientific experiment, would eventually find the answers. That indeed would have been the key to progress, as marked by a universal civilisation.

This confidence was strengthened by further successes during the first half of the 20th century when the modern university became the symbol of educational progress everywhere. In the Asia-Pacific region, the outreach, largely through colonialism, started early, during the second half of the 19th century — for example, into British India (the Universities of Calcutta, Bombay and Madras) and into Australia (the Universities of Sydney, Melbourne and Adelaide). A little later, a most significant development occurred. This was the establishment of modern universities at the initiative of Asian people themselves. It began in Japan, notably with the founding of the imperial universities of Tokyo and Kyoto and the private universities, Keio University and Waseda University. They represented the first breakthrough of Western civilisation into the East made voluntarily by indigenous elites, and they were to have momentous consequences.

The top-down effect of elite universities on changes to the whole education system of Japan is now well known. Indeed, more than in the West, the Japanese have retained the policy of allowing the tertiary system to set the standards of the secondary schools. This was largely true of India as well. As colleges and universities proliferated, largely on the model of the first three universities, namely Calcutta, Bombay and Madras, in India, they deeply influenced secondary education well into the 20th century.

The successful transplantation of this institution — the modern secular university — outside the West within a century of its appearance in Europe itself is a truly remarkable story. The next great step was taken by China at the end of the 19th century and the beginning of the 20th century. China did this both by establishing public universities in Beijing, Nanjing, Shanghai and major provincial capitals and by allowing missionary organisations to build their private colleges around the country. Their models came from many sources such as France, Britain and Germany, and from Japan and the United States. In Thailand, the only independent country in Southeast Asia at the time, Chulalongkorn University was founded on continental models early in the 20th century, the same time when the British established the University of Hong Kong. The British went further with the University of Rangoon and also colleges in Singapore. Similarly, the Americans introduced modern universities, both public and private institutions, into the Philippines. The French and the Dutch were slower and more technically and professionally oriented, but all the colonial powers had, on the eve of decolonisation, laid the foundations of modern tertiary education in their respective territories.

To complete this account of extension and growth, I refer you to the explosion in tertiary education throughout the region during the past 40 years. It was led by post-war Japan which followed the model of the United States in rapidly expanding its university education. China first followed the Soviet model and expanded more slowly, but since the early 1980s, there has been a fivefold increase in the number of colleges and universities. Australasia also moved slowly at first but university expansion speeded up considerably during the past two decades.

Furthermore, the Japanese economic miracle was testament to education as one of the fundamental pillars of modern wealth, and this set the pace of educational expansion throughout the region. This was particularly true of the postcolonial new nations, in not only South and Southeast Asia, but also the former Japanese colonies of Korea (South) and Taiwan. From a few dozen universities at the end of the Pacific War in 1945, there were several hundreds by the 1960s and more than two thousand in 1990. In almost all cases, the modern secular university as evolved in the West was the classic model for the new institutions. What should interest us now is how the transplanted institutions have, or have not, brought excellence to the region and whether the region can now generate quality education itself and become a centre of excellence in its own right.

The universalist ideals of the Enlightenment brought to the rest of the world by the modern university were used to determine the way modern education should be shaped in most countries. It was the university that first embodied the idea of educational excellence. On top of the high standards of technical and professional skills needed for the industrial revolution, the universities also added the ideals for cultural, moral and intellectual quality enunciated by Cardinal Newman. However imperfectly the universities actually carried out these ideals in practice, the combination of skills and personal distinction they possess remained the basis for the continuous quest for excellence that all universities have claimed to endorse.

One obvious point has to be made. The measures of educational excellence were developed in Western Europe and extended and further refined in the United States. Where science and technology were concerned, these measures were fully accepted in Eastern Europe, and then in Japan and China and parts of the British Empire. It was always doubtful whether other measures of excellence which touched on culture and value systems would be so readily transferable. We need to look firstly at the tension between concepts like "region" and "universalism", and secondly, the seemingly competing cultural values within each region. For example, regions like Southeast Asia and East Asia each claims distinctive needs which challenge the validity of universal ideals that emerged in the West. Or, each of those regions may insist on the superiority of its Confucian, Islamic, Hindu, or Buddhist value systems and resist the idea that their respective cultures could eventually be replaced by the excellence of the modern and the secular.

The university comes in at this juncture. The simple fact is that most universities are built in or near cities and have, with the rise of the nation-states, been expected to serve the expanding needs of their countries. As these countries find it important to group their common interests in regional terms, there are new reference points for the quest of excellence. Thus, to see what is in store for the Asia-Pacific, we need to look at the earlier experiments with regional concepts and the efforts to relate the region or regions to universalist ideals.

The Four Approaches to Standards of Excellence

It would be difficult to do justice to the plethora of proposals and debates concerning education in specific regions during the past five decades. What follows is but a very brief introduction to four of the approaches to define and raise standards which I believe are relevant and need closer attention.

(i) Firstly, metropolitan powers in the postcolonial world tried to retain their cultural and economic links with Asia for higher education. Most notably, they were the English-speaking countries that formed part of the Commonwealth of Nations and the predominantly French-speaking areas in Africa as well as Vietnam. The Association of Commonwealth Universities, whose Asian members are largely in South Asia, is an admirable organisation that enabled a particular model of university to be widely established in former British territories. The speedy growth in the number of universities was due largely to the assumption that the original models, mostly from the United Kingdom, were of proven excellence and therefore, of universal validity. The standards defining what was excellent were thought to be self-evident, and experts from the metropolis and their chosen agents quickly installed replicas based on a set of agreed goals. If there were reservations about the universality of those goals, they were not expressed, so that no delay came in the path of getting the institutions established.

There had been an early rejection of the model in Burma. But the consequences for Burmese universities in the past decades seemed to confirm that the decision was a mistake. Without an external benchmark on quality, it is easy to sink into provinciality and irrelevance. For other countries, confidence in the original models is not uniformly enthusiastic but remains strong, suggesting that universalism of knowledge is accepted within this kind of postcolonial regionalism. Although there are alternative models from North America, a common rhetoric about British excellence is still shared among the Commonwealth universities in the region.

(ii) Secondly, the educational institutions that were products of the Cold War did not work together towards regional centre of excellence. The so-called Third World was divided ideologically into three or more regions. During the decades of the US-Soviet divide, the greater part of Asia was under the educational influence of the English-speaking world, increasingly represented by the United Sates. In this context, Eastern Asia may be seen as part of the same littoral of the Western Pacific that includes Australia and New Zealand, and thus bears features of a region almost like a counterpart of Western Europe looking to the United States.

But this apparent similarity was not enough for a regional sense of educational excellence to emerge. A number of reasons contributed to that. Firstly, the balance of power in the United States was consciously tilted towards the Atlantic for security reasons, and also because European institutions represented the origins of American civilisation. Although American educational influence in Asia grew rapidly from the 1950s to the 1980s, notably in the Philippines, Japan, South Korea and Taiwan, the major penetration of influence in universities has been in medicine, the natural sciences and technological disciplines. In cultural and social sciences, the impact was cerebral and instrumental, but it never attained the moral and emotive authority that Western and Western-trained scholars had expected. Only in Australasia did the American approach to cultural education begin to replace some of the earlier European models. In short, standards of excellence in East and Southeast Asian countries were limited to the scientific fields.

Secondly, Japan would have been vital to the new region, but it was the enemy during the Pacific War. Although it was willing to receive material assistance to revive its economy and to defend itself against the eastward expansion of Russia, Japan could only be an ally as a junior partner. Differences in cultural outlook greatly restricted the use of American standards of excellence in Japan in non-science fields and this was reflected in the education enterprise. Japan had for some time felt the pressure to cultivate its own environment of excellence. There were calls within the country for internationalisation, and foreign students have been welcome. Not surprisingly, the Japanese were sceptical about the extent to which their education system as a whole should be exposed to American ideas of quality. There was strong opposition to the adoption of Western cultural principles. Japan prefers that its educational criteria remain unique. It prefers to serve as a bridge for technology transfer, and maintains its neutrality on being Western or Asian. If this continues, a key component for the creation of a region of excellence would be missing.

The third reason is the divide caused by the Cold War between the peripheral states of East Asia (mainly the island states plus South Korea and Thailand) and the hinterlands of China, North Korea and parts of the Southeast Asian mainland. This ideological divide had a profound impact on the standards of educational excellence even though it can be argued that science and technology standards remained comparable on both sides of the bamboo curtain throughout the years of conflict and rivalry. With the political divide now removed, obstacles in perpetuating similar standards of excellence from the periphery to the reforming hinterland states like the People's Republic of China and Vietnam (and eventually Burma, Cambodia and Laos) seemed to be fewer on the surface. China has led the way by sending tens of thousands of their brightest students to study in North America, Western Europe and Australasia. Although a majority of them have not returned, those who did have made a difference to the quality of research and technological excellence. When more of them finally return, the impact is likely to be even greater. As with most countries in Eastern Asia, evidence has so far suggested that the idea of having common standards will be limited to areas of science and technology.

As explained above, comparable standards of excellence based on a common political ideology could not get very far. The idea of educational excellence was present, but it was developed in a highly competitive, threatening and even deadly environment for about three decades (1950s –1970s). Nevertheless, it was a dynamic situation, and profound changes were taking place. The economic miracle led by Japan and the four Tigers in East Asia drew North America more deeply into the Asia-Pacific. This in turn increased Australia's confidence to take new initiatives in Asia, culminating in the skilful conceptualisation of the Asia-Pacific Economic Cooperation (the APEC Forum) among some rather sceptical neighbours. The impact of this development on a possible future centre of educational excellence in this newly discovered region will be briefly discussed before the conclusion.

The following third and fourth approaches provide the background to a regional sense of comparable standards which are also relevant to our thinking about the future.

(iii) The third takes us back to an earlier educational regionalism in Southeast Asia that was directly concerned with excellence. This came from a local effort represented by the Association of Southeast Asian Institutions of Higher Learning (ASAIHL) which started in 1956 with only six members, namely the University of Indonesia, University of the Philippines, Chulalongkorn University, the University of Hong Kong, National University of Vietnam and the University of Malaya (in Singapore at the time). From a modest beginning, it has slowly grown into an organisation of some 200 members and associate members, including more than a score of Australian universities. Perhaps not purely by coincidence, most of these members are also member economies of the APEC.

Of special interest is that the six founding member universities represented at least five different tertiary systems: the North American, the French, the Dutch, the British (Malaya and Hong Kong) and the special example of Chulalongkorn University which was inspired by a mixture of German, Swiss, British and French traditions. What ASAIHL sought to do was not only to encourage new generations of scholars and students to be more region-minded, but also to develop common ideals of educational excellence among institutions by regular staff and student exchanges and through mutual help with teaching and research programmes. The six universities believed that they could learn from what appeared then to be different standards of excellence.

The Association of Southeast Asian Institutions of Higher Learning remained non-governmental and its funds were limited to contributions made by its members. It organised regular meetings and created small practical groupings for institutional support. At the level of staff and postgraduate student exchanges, there were successes. Whereas in the area of undergraduate exchanges, the association made little headway. The reasons for the failure are important for future reference. Differences in the medium of instruction, for example, Bahasa Indonesia at the University of Indonesia, Thai at Chulalongkorn University, and English at the University of Hong Kong and University of Malaya, made for some difficulties, but the curricula and accreditation criteria were greater obstacles. Also, for understandable reasons at the time, the ASAIHL organisation was reluctant to depend on government channels of communication. The reality, however, was that the new region of Southeast Asia did not have sufficient commonalities yet for non-official efforts to flourish. It needed much more time to mature.

In the meantime (some ten years after the ASAIHL), the establishment of the Association of Southeast Asian Nations (ASEAN) opened up other lines of communications. The respective ministers of education set up their own cooperative efforts. While these were initially channels for sharing experiences, and learning from each other's policies and experiments, they consequently led to the growth of common ideas on how to achieve educational excellence. Over time, the various heritages of the colonial past were blurred, and a sense of what the region might be able to accomplish began to emerge. And, if we were to focus on measurable areas of excellence like those of science and technology, we can agree that a great deal of progress has been made.

It should, nevertheless, be noted how slowly this cooperation had taken place. The regional identity of ASEAN is still fluid as more members have been invited to join the association. What the new members have brought to educational ideals and standards will have to be fitted in over time. For example, Vietnam and Myanmar have developed so differently from the core members of ASEAN that a great deal of rethinking will have to be done if regional educational programmes are to have any coherence in the future. It would be too easy to say that education in the core states achieved standards of excellence comparable to those of the developed world, while education in the new member countries is far below par. Even if the scope of collaboration is limited to the areas of science and technology, cooperation within the region requires new approaches to overcome the vast differences that still remain among its member states.

(iv) In contrast to regional efforts, there were countervailing pressures to globalise and universalise the goals of education. These lead to the fourth approach to comparability of standards. Pressures had begun as universal organisations like UNESCO and other United Nations agencies and, in the area of higher education, organisations such as the International Association of Universities stepped up their efforts. They recognised the practical need for some kinds of regional groups to facilitate action. It was clear that regional forces were growing, and many countries and their educational institutions really preferred to develop within smaller groupings, where they indeed did better under more intimate conditions. But the longer-term goal of these universal organisations was to achieve — what many academic and educational leaders believed in — a world of relatively equal countries and peoples. It was therefore their duty to try to overcome regional differences wherever possible.

One way of doing this was offering help to all countries to achieve comparable standards at all levels of education. That was probably utopian because even in the most developed countries of the West, not all educational institutions were equally good. Quite obviously, the raising of standards could not be done all at once. For many, starting the implementation from the top with higher education and tertiary training seemed to be the most direct and effective way. The best-established institutions in the world in each field could be identified and serve as ultimate models for the developing countries. In the meantime, students from all over Asia and elsewhere are sent to study at these institutions and upon their return, they can play a role to raise the educational standards at home.

This ideal was extremely expensive to pay for. Organisations that favoured universalism could not afford to do it, and expected the developed countries in Western Europe and North America to carry the burden. Most of them were willing, but the demand for quality education was so great that these in turn could not meet the rising costs on their own. Increasingly, the task was left to the open international market. Here would be the test of what developing countries really want and could afford. But, other things not being equal, this market was not a true indicator of demand and supply. The range of institutions was great even in the richest countries in the West, and educational standards in much admired countries like the United States range from world's best to ordinary and mediocre. Some countries, and also the richer families, could afford much more than others. They could pick and choose to send their children, their students and staff, to the very best institutions at whatever fee; others would have to be content with the more affordable and less glamorous, if not the obviously less good. All the same, the openness of even such unequal market helped to offer universalism in higher education to more and more people and to dilute the opposite tendency of centrifugal forces dividing the world into regions. The market propagated the principle that excellence has to be paid for and that excellence knows no regional identity. The developing countries would have to calculate their priorities carefully if they wish to buy educational excellence. Given the overwhelming evidence that good education and better training help directly in speeding up economic development, as demonstrated in East Asia, this should be money well spent. It is money that countries must find if they want to transform their disadvantaged conditions. If this educational market system continues, then a region cannot itself be a centre of educational excellence. It can be an integral part of a global system, where excellence is universally acknowledged, or it can serve as a convenience, a lay-by or stopover stage, on the way to an ultimate universalism.

I would like to relate Asia-Pacific's future as a region to the Asia-Pacific Economic Cooperation forum in which Australia played such a large part in initiating. Although I am not wildly optimistic about the region acting in concert to bring the received ideals of educational excellence to all its members, I do recognise one major advantage. There is now an acceptance of English as an international language. This certainly makes communication and mutual comprehension much easier, and a great deal can be done to enable common standards to operate wherever possible. Every effort should be made to build on this.

But there remain the great cultural differences among the APEC countries. I have mentioned that five civilisations are inextricably involved in shaping the human resources. The respective criteria of what makes a moral and spiritually healthy person are rooted in historic religions, and although modified to suit some universal standards of modernity, their core values demand respect, if not absolute adherence. At times, these values pull in several directions.

It is not only differences in religion that separate people's ideas about educational excellence. Even at secular levels, definitions of excellence also vary a great deal. For example, the ideal of useful citizenry, the importance of creativity in life, the reach and effectiveness of the law, the depth and spectrum of freedoms and rights, and the attitudes towards order and authority. Although universalism in higher education points the way to an eventual convergence of some of these ideals, it is not clear if that could be more easily achieved by setting them in regional terms. The universal may need global involvement for its realisation.

Also, there are, within the APEC, obvious gaps in economic and technological development that profoundly influence the attainments in educational excellence. These differences too are not peculiar to any region. Sharing experiences within a region will certainly help but narrowing those gaps cannot be done by the region alone, even though the APEC may be able to count the United States as a powerful member. The knowledge explosion introduces much dross and irrelevancies. The task of sifting out what is essential has always been daunting and the material resources needed to do so are massive. The US and Australasian commitments might go a long way to help, but it is also increasingly clear that global contribution is vital.

Finally, the great advances in science and technology that enabled education to be universal have also reduced the size of the world. It has not only shrunk the distances between natural regions, but has also made it possible to imagine a gigantic and not so natural region like the Asia-Pacific. Also, it has enabled many institutions in the region to establish themselves as bearers of the universalist ideals in education. They are at the moment still rather spread out, and tend to look away from the region in order to sustain their efforts to achieve excellence. But a freshly inspired Asia-Pacific should be able to draw the institutions together more consciously to tackle new educational ideals.

The region's institutions of higher education are committed to seek the best they can afford. But even the best is not immutable. Past experience suggests that regional inputs have enriched ideals of universalism by offering insights as to what standards of excellence should be like in the future. Many colleges and universities have had considerable experience in focussing on specific regional problems. A practical start would be to set them a distinctive agenda for educational cooperation. If they could be brought into the new APEC framework, that would help to educate generations to consolidate the future identity of the Asia-Pacific, and help develop common ideals of educational excellence within it.

10

The Modern University in Australia and Asia

After some 50 years of studying and working in universities in various countries and territories, I have come to believe that the modern university embodies most of modern culture that matters today and promises to provide some of the enduring ingredients for a genuine global culture in the 21st century. The university I know from my experience is a microcosm of complex and changing societies. Its collective store of talent and knowledge has the capacity to shape the world. It therefore always gives me great pleasure to write on this great institution.

The lecture was first delivered on 1 October 1997 on the occasion of the Menzies Oration on Higher Education at the University of Melbourne in Australia. Published in *The Modern University in Australia and Asia*, The Menzies Oration on Higher Education, University of Melbourne, 22 pages. Reproduced with the kind permission of the University of Melbourne.

The Heritage

The modern university is barely 200 years old. The University of Melbourne may be said to be an early example that has evolved from British foundations to one adapted to local conditions. Thousands of universities have been established in the 19th and 20th centuries, the vast majority during the past half-century. And the numbers are still growing. In Asia, the growth in response to the nation-building needs in former colonies has been particularly impressive. Students and scholars have always sought to learn from great universities but the relatively recent surge in the number of students seeking a higher education is unprecedented. The desire for higher education has caused hundreds of thousands of students, mainly from Asia, to travel all over the world to seek a university education. The effect of such intermingling of cultures on the emerging global culture is mind-boggling. And when one considers the demands made on the modern university — from producing mandarins to run the bureaucracy, engineers, business managers, research scientists, a host of professionals, and generally graduates who are expected to be the leaders of the future — it is astonishing that it has succeeded so well in its relatively short history.

What is the secret of the university's success? Its roots in Europe were clearly derived from the mediaeval institutions that fathered early ideas about professional autonomy and intellectual independence from both church and state. The original role of transmitting traditional values and training political elites had also been prominent in other civilisations, notably in different parts of Asia. But nowhere in Asia did there appear the ideas of autonomy and independence that marked the modern European universities.

These ideas were revolutionary at the time. But even today, no state is entirely comfortable with them, and Australia is no exception. In some parts of Asia, they are strongly disliked, and yet there is a recognition that they are necessary for the advancement of knowledge and for national development. Over time, these ideas of autonomy and independence have earned the respect of intellectual leaders everywhere, including in Asia. As these ideas deepened and expanded into all areas of teaching and research, they have had a profound influence on the university's evolution in modern times.

Accompanying this development has been the institution's protean character. This had first been tested successfully in Western Europe, and led to further experiments and adaptations in the Americas. Eventually, through colonial rule in the European empires in Asia and Africa, the versatile modern university was exported throughout the world. It is this capacity to adapt and change wherever they are established that was noteworthy.

This modern institution was introduced into Asia not long after the establishment of this university. It was the same impulse that led the same British worthies to build the first universities in India. In the case of Japan, however, it was the Japanese who took the initiative. That they did so enthusiastically partly explains the country's rapid modernisation. We should ponder on the fact that the first great universities of Japan came soon after those of Australia and were, by the turn of the century, better funded and more nationally appreciated than those in Australia.

The way universities in Asia had taken root in vastly different circumstances and among communities which prided themselves on their very different cultures provides the test of its inherent universal nature. The early ones were established parallel to traditional religious education centres and classical academies that trained people for public service. As modern institutions, they focussed on knowledge that was not already available, especially science and technology. They demonstrated that, by being open and receptive, they could shake off not only their dependence on tradition but also their reliance on the original models in Europe. Many have joined the international cohort of universities not merely as consumers but also as contributors.

Little noticed at the time, the new universities marched to different drums, drums of many sizes that played to multiple rhythms. At the beginning, most of the universities seemed to have had a simple task, to build bridges between two contrasting worlds, one colonial and the other traditional, and between modern professional education and local values. This modern ideal often placed them uneasily between the rich progressive West and a defensive orientalist Asia that was searching for ways to strengthen its threatened value systems.

But much of that unease disappeared after the Second World War. The Japanese universities had led the way to prove their value and had become confident centres of nationalist and progressive ideas. In China, the students absorbed radical ideas at universities, which had become centres of dissent if not outright opposition to the government. The speed at which these universities became transmitters of the latest ideas as well as the severest critics of hoary traditions was astonishing. Notwithstanding the fact that much that was introduced was often half-learnt and poorly digested, the intellectual force engendered in all the modern universities was unprecedented.

This phenomenon was further stimulated by the rapid expansion of universities everywhere, not least in the Americas, Europe and Australasia themselves. The university became an institution that every country had to have; in fact, the more universities there were, the more likely the rapid development of a modern economy. Given the great diversity in origin, in appearance, in quality and in ideological dispositions, one could well ask whether the name "university" should be applied to them all.

But, despite the different degrees of control over thought, over methods of teaching and research, and in managerial style, the similarities remain beneath the formal structures and the official declarations of purpose and goals. Staff and students all share a common desire to learn and the urge to teach. There is often the same kind of debate and struggle for teaching and research funding, and the same demand for enhanced scholarly links between institutions at home and abroad.

Some examples of contrasting backgrounds were most illuminating and reassuring. I met Russian scholars who had removed their 70-year-old ideological cloaks to reveal themselves to be not only totally recognisable as the products of universities, but also dedicated to the same cause of learning, to seeking creativity and originality. Similarly with Chinese scholars from the China mainland. The Chinese universities have not been isolated by Leninism-Stalinism for as long. But when their scholars began to restore their ties with their American and European counterparts in the 1980s, they did so with minimal fuss. There was nothing more moving than to see Western, especially the American, academics and their Chinese friends meeting anxiously only to discover that they still had much in common. They quickly found that they could collaborate in research and guide their students together to the highest levels of scholarly achievement. And although the Australian academics had not shared the same kind of intimate relationship with the Chinese as the Americans had, the Chinese embraced the Australian university as an institution they fully understood.

Another feature that represents the key towards the universal academy is the free trade in knowledge and ideas that universities stand for. This credo is one of the three most important advances in the history of education. The other two advances are the idea of examinations as a means of ensuring a meritocracy, and the anti-elitist ideal of a basic education for all, without any discrimination on the grounds of race, class, religion and gender.

I have had the privilege of reading about the University of Melbourne's initiative in Universitas 21. I was naturally delighted to see both the University of Hong Kong and the National University of Singapore included in this enterprise. The objective to assist its 20 members to become global universities and advance their plans of internationalisation was particularly interesting. One of its most important requirements would be that each university commits itself to the free trade in knowledge and ideas. One cannot emphasise enough how this commitment has helped universities to transcend all national, racial and religious boundaries that constrain intellectual efforts. This has been possible because the university ideal guarantees open access to the fruits of research and scholarship, the academic freedom to teach without interference and the right to publish and disseminate knowledge in a borderless world.

This intellectual freedom has not been easy to establish. Nor is it always easy to defend. It certainly cannot be taken for granted. Indeed, one of the wonders of the modern world is how this ideal of free trade in ideas was transplanted to regions which had always subscribed to the very extreme opposite. For thousands of years in the Asia region, the powerful believed that all knowledge should be held in monopoly. Emperors, kings, princes, chiefs, priests and all those who had access to knowledge, especially practical and valuable knowledge that produced wealth and power, wanted no one else but themselves to enjoy that knowledge. The lack of laws that protected private property and intellectual rights resulted in great losses to knowledge, but even more important was the tradition that denied people the access of knowledge, particularly if it was deemed to have been unorthodox.

Most people are aware that there are no guarantees for this freedom. But one may not be aware that Asian scholars have embraced the idea with enthusiasm and no country has been able to deny them this freedom for long. The will among scholars to preserve that right to free trade in ideas has become remarkably strong. No scholar I know would deny the benefits of access to new knowledge. I have yet to meet a teacher or student in Asia who did not believe that academic freedom is what every university should have. Even in repressive countries, where the tension between state and university is extreme, the state has to keep the universities open.

On the other hand, one should not get too sanguine for all universities. Some will be universities only in name for years to come. But observing around the Asia region, it is believed that the propensity to free trade in ideas and knowledge is one of the key features essential for universities if they are to continue to play their progressive role in the world.

The Challenge

What is the challenge for the future? The University of Melbourne's commitment to cultural diversity is a strong indicator. Its recognition that culture is dynamic and constantly changing and that diversity is marked by the existence of many traditions, beliefs, values and practices, is most inspiring. The search for alternative cultural visions in our era of rapid change is thus identified as one of the most important ways for universities to meet future challenges.

It had been shown that universities stagnate when they are mere transmitters of given knowledge and flourish when they seek the new knowledge that they were established to produce. Records had also shown that, over the decades, contrary to popular belief that universities are "ivory towers", the university has never been slow to change in order to deal with new circumstances. It has had to answer critics who argue that changes are distinctly for the worse and that the most precious values of the university are being abandoned. But it has also had to deal with ominous commentaries with topics like "Universities in transition", "Universities in crisis", and headlines like "More cuts in university funding", "Less money for research", "Academics to be more accountable", and so on. When these lead political and community leaders suggest that universities are wasteful and complacent organisations, they are challenging the universities to disprove that.

To that, whatever the truth in these arguments and headlines, the range and vehemence of the vigorous debates going on about the nature of the university were astonishing. This is true in not only developed countries like Australia, but also the insecure and impoverished developing ones among its Asian neighbours.

Of course, if these debates were to be taken separately and fought only within the confines of each campus or even each country, there may well be a preponderance of desperate and despairing tones. If taken together, however, the overall picture around the world remains one of growth, not simply of size and numbers, but of the determination to make universities better at serving the needs of our time.

What are these needs? Each country and its leadership will have different priorities for their respective universities, and each university will try to work out what it has to do to serve those priorities. But one of the more important needs of the time must include explaining the processes of economic, technological and cultural globalisation and its impact on national borders, and equipping people with knowledge and skills to deal with those processes.

The university is unique in that it is the only institution that exists to educate and train those who are responsible for organising all other modern institutions. The great paradox is that it does its job for the world despite the fact that it is dependent on the support largely of local, national and even exclusive business and professional interests. What gives this institution its exceptional quality is that it is structured to tackle current problems as well as remain above the fray. It is this quality that makes it possible to provide alternative visions to what is immediately desirable and urgently needed. It can embody present drives and urges while mapping out possible and probable scenarios of the future, including agendas that have not been encompassed by accepted wisdom or existing knowledge.

Some Australian universities have taken the lead to respond to the changes that will be increasingly important in the next century. I refer to Australia's awakening to its position as a Western outpost on the edge of several Asian civilisations. Unlike most of Europe and the Americas, which are secure centres in themselves, Australia has long been perceived as being on the distant periphery. This has not deterred Australians from creating their own traditions out of those they had brought with them. But when the great distances left them no longer secure, both politically and economically, the response of the universities showed how ready they were to adapt and change whenever necessary.

I was privileged to have come to Australia some 30 years ago at the turning-point of that change. The University of Melbourne was quick to join other leading institutions in Australia to recognise the urgent need to transform attitudes towards Asia. From modest beginnings, which followed British classical approaches, to ancient civilisations, which were a variety of orientalism on a small scale, the emphasis quickly became one of more direct concerns for the deep-rooted civilisations in the region.

Australian universities were quick to realise that these civilisations were being newly revived by the impact of modernity. This realisation led to bold efforts to induce young Australians to immerse themselves in the study of the different value systems at their doorstep. This is an ongoing and demanding task. But by embarking on it early, it has prepared the country well for what will turn out to be the major trend of civilisational exchanges of the next century.

In this reorientation towards a rapidly modernising Asia, there are questions to be asked. Should Australian universities continue to support classical studies in order to deepen their understanding of what has survived today? Should they follow the United States in stressing the strategic and defence concerns of the country? Or should they also stride boldly to confront the vital issue of proximate coexistence as acceptable partners of their counterparts in Asia? The debate on whether the best course to take may comprise all three continues. Will that better prepare new generations of Australians to come to grips with the civilisations in the neighbourhood, civilisations that openly question what they perceive to be the dominance of Western values?

And why is there this questioning today? To the modernisers in Asia, there is a resurgence of forces which they see as "feudal" political structures, traditional institutions, "mediaeval" value systems, and reactionary mindsets. These forces are unwilling to accept a world with a dominant civilisation that had come through physical conquest and economic and technological superiority. At the same time, leaders in Asia recognise that modern power had also built new knowledge. Thus, most of them studied what the West had to offer, especially the rapid advances in science and technology. In this way, they have prepared themselves to defend their own cultures and societies from becoming mere artefacts of the past or furnishings of other people's museums. Hence this explains the importance they hold of their own modern universities.

Australia is part of the dominant culture of the West that has concerned many Asian leaders. In their eyes there are at least three other great civilisations. Islam in all its manifestations in Asia and Africa deserves to be understood and heard. The traditions of Hinduism and Buddhism in parts of South and Southeast Asia remain strong. And the Confucian heritage found largely in Eastern Asia has won renewed attention. There obviously can be no peace if the current dominant civilisation and these three very different ones should be at one another's throats.

However, at the same time, there is now a growing global culture that cuts across all the different civilisations as mentioned.

The 21st century will see many complex layers of interrelationships. At one level, the elite layers of the powerful, the rich, the educated, the professional and middle classes, will find no difficulty with the civilisation of shared scientific values acquired through modern education, especially higher education. Their cosmopolitan nature would ensure that they could be enlarged, modified, and even transformed without reference to any single country or its national culture. This is already happening all over Asia, and it does not seem to matter to what civilisation these elites might claim to belong. The only constraint on these values becoming more prominent is the fact that the vast majority of the people are yet to share in them.

At another level, where basic technical and managerial skills mark the modern "civilisational competence" of people, there is also much more sharing across national borders than is commonly realised. To mention only a few examples, like the skills related to manufacturing, whether of motor cars or television sets, to film-making, piloting fighter planes, or computer programming, the speed at which these skills have been taught to new generations all over Asia is astounding. Within a generation, millions of young people have become the equals of their counterparts in the West and can now communicate freely — and electronically — about almost any subject they like. Then there is the phenomenon of the consumer. All over Asia, the penetration of popular music and dance, fashion and design, the print and electronic media, and the spread of major brand names, is deep. Whether or not this can be described as civilisational is immaterial. It will go on growing and the reach, global.

In the evolution of this multilayered phenomenon, universities in Australia have a role in providing alternative visions. The temptation to say it is too hard to cope with so many major civilisations in the Asia region, some of them possibly hostile, would have to be resisted. The foundations laid down during the past decades since the 1950s have provided a good start. Although questions are now being asked as to whether research centres in each university are receiving the kinds of financial support they need, their edge over most universities in Asia will remain undisputed for a while. But it should be noted that many neighbouring universities have made considerable progress in science and technology, in improving and upgrading their universities. The gaps are closing.

Students who had come to study in Australia from developing countries in Asia have been returning in large numbers and have transformed their own universities to serve their communities more directly. They now expect the status of their institutions to be recognised and respected.

The great challenge for the modern university is not where cultural convergence has already occurred or is occurring, but where differences in value systems will remain. For this, teaching and research in the humanities and social sciences will be even more important. Enough had been said to show modern universities are likely to remain strong and adaptable. The experience of cultural adjustment between those in Australia and Asia over the past half century confirms why the university is one of the first truly global institutions in the world.

11

Social Science and Asia

This paper is largely a story of the cultural impact of modern Europe on Asia. It examines the way Asian scholars have organised knowledge and how the pursuit of knowledge today has been transformed by what they have shared with their European counterparts. I begin with the following observations. The first two are factual and not controversial, but I state them here simply to contrast them with the third. The first observation is that most Asians at the turn of the 20th century thought of their classical traditions of knowledge mainly as received wisdom essential for spiritual and aesthetic development, and these may be grouped together under the label of the humanities. They had no difficulty with that notion and were confident that, under this new label, they would continue to be creative and could learn new ideas from the West when they wanted to. The second is that the advent of the natural sciences from Europe was welcomed in most parts of Asia where it was accepted as transformative and important. They may not have understood the word "science" always in the same way, but have accepted that it is a progressive set of methodologies that

---

This article, written in 1998, has never been published before.

would benefit all who mastered them and individual scientists have had little difficulty being innovative in their work. The third observation, however, is not self-evident. That is, social science has been formally received into the structures of most universities in Asia, but there remains considerable uncertainty about their applicability and value. As a result, creativity in this area is more problematical.

The three observations aforementioned should not be surprising. It may be argued that the situation is not that different elsewhere. In the West, classical texts that were dominant in most of the major universities until early in the 20th century now form a distinct part of the humanities. Natural science came to challenge that dominance successfully in two stages. It did so through its proven value in support of older medical knowledge, and then its value was further reinforced after proving its practical value in technology and this went on to reshape all modern material developments. After the Second World War, this dominance of scientific knowledge has become the widely accepted test of useful truths. As for social science, after it broke out of classical philosophy and having gained richly from the application of scientific methods, it has begun to overshadow the humanities. But there remains doubt about how reliable social science is as guides to action and whether it can be a source for the wisdom that people still need.

Scholars in Asia seem to be moving in the same direction in marginalising their classical knowledge and are not that far behind where attitudes towards natural science are concerned. It is only in social science that there is still resistance except where some specific disciplines have contributed directly to practical professions, for example, in the areas of legal, business and public administration. There is still doubt about whether social science can be value-free science and whether it can stimulate the kind of creativity that we have learnt to expect from the humanities in the past and in natural science today. I shall explore this doubt by looking at aspects of shared histories between Europe and Asia and focus on the conditions under which creativity in social science has been possible.

Stages of Knowledge Evolution

Although not especially fashionable to analyse this topic today, I have located social science somewhere between the humanities and natural science and tried not to be more exact in making distinctions. There are overlaps created by individual scholars, who, for example, would like fields such as economics to be as precise as mathematics and the physical sciences. And there are other scholars in fields such as psychology and linguistics whose work comes close to the life sciences. Yet other scholars of ancient and mediaeval history as well as archaeologists reason and speculate in ways not unlike those of geologists, even of astronomers. And indeed there are also many social scientists whose skills are no different from philosophers and historians, and who use literary and artistic materials just as naturally as those who would call themselves scholars in the humanities. As we know, in real life, none of these disciplinary boundaries found in universities are clear-cut and exclusive. Thus, in the categories that I use, I have approached the subject as an historian and have employed a chronological base for identifying the stages of evolution. First, the stage when traditional knowledge was the core of the humanities. This was followed by the stage when natural science became as important and began to influence all knowledge. Finally, there emerged the disciplines related to them both which sought to carve out what was distinguishable as social science.

The historical approach recognises that the humanities in Asia were challenged by Western learning during the years of colonial dominance. For the first period of culture contact down to the end of the 19th century, there was no feeling that Western knowledge could displace received knowledge and wisdoms in any way. European scholars were themselves respectful of tradition and the Asian elites were confident that their traditions were strong, even while they became genuinely curious about the different ways the Europeans were organising their knowledge. The only sign that this confidence would not remain for long came when certain areas of technological superiority was shown to be linked with the development of natural science, first in medicine and civil engineering projects and then in contributions to agriculture. Eventually, Asian leaders recognised that scientific thought in itself brought new dimensions to knowledge that their traditions could not match. The first clear and lasting breakthrough in Asia may be dated from the establishment by the British of the universities in Calcutta, Bombay and Madras, where alternative ways of studying literature, philosophy and the arts were introduced. But the most impressive changes were found in subjects like physics, chemistry and biology and the developments which laid the foundations of an alternative modern medicine.

The great revolution in practical knowledge, however, occurred when the Japanese began systematically to learn the technologies of the West. The first to realise that the Western challenge to their modified Confucian state ideology was very serious, the Japanese set out to learn the secret of European power and wealth. They had decided that the primary cause of China's and Japan's weakness was the lack of a scientific approach towards technology, and therefore, they sent their brightest students to Britain, France and Germany to study with the best scientists there. Within a generation, the Japanese can be said to have mastered all fields of modern technology. They even went so far as to acquire the same expansionist ambitions and behave as the Western powers did in Asia.

In China, the transformation was not entirely voluntary. By the end of the 19th century, a number of small American missionary colleges were established in the treaty ports of China as the effort to Christianise the Chinese began in earnest. The French, the British and then the Germans followed with their institutions of learning. But by the early 20th century, it became clear that Christianity was not getting very far, but the excitement at what science could offer to the development of the country grew rapidly. In the 1920s, the conversion to at least the rhetoric of science was complete. Natural science became not only an essential feature of the whole education system but the very justification for a modernist revolution and the challenge of scientific socialism. This was social science entering China as the engine of change. The impact of that scientific transformation has had a mixed success but, even among those least educated in natural science, lip service was paid to everything that could be described as scientific.

I shall not dwell on the partial and peripheral developments of scientific knowledge in Southeast Asia during the colonial or semi-colonial period. Suffice it to say that the overall picture was one of commercial exploitation by the colonisers with little input of European ideas and values. The earliest colleges and universities in Asia built by the Catholic church in the Philippines were modelled on theological institutions in Spain and they did have a profound impact on the religious lives of the native peoples. Catholicism replaced the simpler indigenous faiths so that the peoples could not even appeal to a classical tradition of their own afterwards. They had to await a second round of colonisation under the Americans before the question of modern science was systematically introduced. But, when that occurred, the adoption of an American frame of reference for secular knowledge was quickly internalised by the

Filipino elites. No other part of the Southeast Asian region enjoyed the rapid adoption of modern scientific standards as thoroughly as it did in the exceptional case of the Philippines. For the rest, when Western learning was belatedly introduced through the tentative establishment of tertiary institutions, the impact was similar to that in East and South Asia. Received traditional knowledge remained confidential or was protected, and natural science was considered wondrous and readily accepted. Again, only the social science fields were looked at with varying degrees of suspicion.

Nevertheless, it is clear that most of Asia and Europe have had a shared history in their experience of the diversification and enrichment of modern knowledge, even in the more controversial fields of social science. Here I shall focus on social science. Its relative newness and the doubts about, and resistance to, various kinds of social science, has remained. I shall explore this phenomenon by suggesting that, unlike in the humanities, the concepts and models being applied in Asia today are largely intellectually derivative and are fed largely by academic work done in Western universities. They consist of concepts teased out by European and American scholars and then applied to Asia. Their use is still very new and underdeveloped, and in some cases, probably artificial, so it is premature to speak of Asian perspectives at this point. But in so far as they are having an impact on social change and the future growth of knowledge in Asia, they need to be noted.

Changing Political Climates

The greatest impact of social science in Asia among the elites, who read original works produced in translation, was made by the writings of Adam Smith and David Ricardo, Auguste Comte and Herbert Spencer, Karl Marx and Friedrich Engels, Sigmund Freud, and more recently, John Maynard Keynes, Max Weber and Karl Popper, and even Milton Friedman in some circles today. But it is not clear how far the new paradigms have penetrated beyond the best universities. The high degree of creativity among these thinkers and scholars has been most inspiring. But it is interesting to note that there are no equivalent advances among social scientists who live and work in Asia. Unlike in natural science or in literature, with Nobel Prizes being awarded to Asians in the 20th century, it was not until 1998 that Amartya Sen became the first person in economics to receive that degree of recognition, and he has not been working in an Asian institution for a long time. I shall focus on Amartya Sen later when I talk about how Asians have fared with social science creativity.

I suggest that the creativity that has produced paradigm shifts in Europe and the West has come largely from academic and intellectual activity, much of it associated with the universities. That is to say, it has been the product of cerebral responses to social and cultural changes over time, and scholars have been creative in the context of a larger picture of universal science and progress, with modern civilisation as the main driving force in history. In Asia, especially in the newer nations over the past half century, that creativity even in the universities has been more influenced by contemporary political and economic developments. It is useful to distinguish between responses to academic advances emerging from major scholarly centres in the West and responses to situational changes that have been experienced in Asia itself. I shall look at these responses through a few examples of creativity involving Asia and scholars of Asian origin and then through the way major Asian universities are tackling the problem of social science today.

There have been many kinds of creativity in social science over the past few decades. Some of the striking developments in the West have elicited Asian responses and influenced many Asian scholarly writings. Of these, a few have been inspired by Asian experiences while others have been the work of scholars of Asian origin. I shall not deal in detail here the well-known work by Western social scientists who have made theoretical contributions through their outstanding research on various parts of Asia, for example, Gunnar Myrdal in economics, Clifford Geertz in anthropology and Benedict Anderson in political science. I suggest, however, that much new work in social science among scholars in Asia has been responses to situational changes that have impacted on their countries while, on the whole, the bulk of the research that led to innovative theories in the West, including that done by Asians who work in Western universities, may be described as knowledge-driven.

In Asia, the most striking situational change reflected in social science scholarship is the shift from colonial interpretations of contemporary local developments to anti-colonial revisionism (under conditions of decolonisation), often most successfully debated in historical terms. The best examples are often deeply influenced by calls to model new Asian states after European nation-states and the reactions against them. The efforts at revisionism were varied and took many forms. For example, the response to historical change began as being very obvious, taking the form of crude rejections of the set of imperial premises and the insistence on a new set of nationalist premises. Everything represented by the colonial scholars was therefore suspect. It had to be challenged or reinterpreted in terms of newly discovered national interests. This was so self-evident for the protagonists that no logical arguments were necessary. It was enough to say that the circumstances have changed, and old assumptions no longer applied. Strong emotions were often involved and the consequences had considerable impact on the education of a new generation of intellectuals. This nationalist phase is now largely over in the scholarly research in most Asian countries because the best scholars find the negative reactions increasingly limiting and less intellectually satisfactory. But politicians and governments still often resort to this model and, in some cases, still insist on this orthodoxy approach in the way they use historical interpretations.

A second set of examples is still linked with the modern nation-state and thus related to the postcolonial perspective. This represents a shift from classical humanistic value systems to modern social science models or paradigms influenced by the successful nation-states models of the West. This has been a wrenching experience for older scholars who believe in continuities in the study of their past, especially those of India bearing the Hindu-Buddhist heritage, those who believe in the sense of "ummat", or community, of the Islamic world, and even among the more secular scholars from countries of Confucian persuasion. For them, the classical approaches are valid and the nation-state framework is both a challenge and a source of intellectual tension. The more deep-rooted the classical tradition is, the greater the resistance to approaches which assume a national norm. This tension will remain as long as there are social science disciplines which continue to take the nation-state as a starting point in research.

Another interesting variation in Asia of this challenge comes from two branches of Western scholarship which tend to dispute the nation-state framework. I refer to the scholarly contest between liberal social science and Marxist science. For Asia, we can detect the pressures to shift from one to the other — firstly, the trend to choose Marxist science over liberal social science, and more recently, the need for some to abandon Marxist approaches and shift back to liberal premises. Major protagonists of the two opposing positions had fought one another fiercely in Europe for decades, from the late 19th century down to the middle of the 20th century. The experience was more vicarious in Asia, and there was a tendency among some to follow the political twists and turns in the Soviet Union. The Cold War led many more scholars to accept Marxist paradigms and reinterpret all their traditions in Marxist terms, notably in Japan, China and Vietnam, as well as in some scholarly circles in South and Southeast Asia. Although most older scholars were forced to do so in countries that were taken over by communist parties, younger scholars tended to find the Marxist framework both revolutionary and exciting, especially when this meant that they could totally reject their respective heritages and still remain respectable. The reinterpretations that were made using new terminologies were impressive because they seemed internally consistent and did not leave much room for doubt.

More recently, in China (even more strikingly in Central and Eastern Europe, in countries like the former East Germany, Hungary, Poland, the Czech and Slovak Republics), the reverse movement to liberal social science has occurred. Many scholars have turned away from Marxist science to a whole range of new social scientific paradigms taken directly from a triumphant West (notably the United States). In China, many of these new paradigms are yet to be fully digested. Others have been modified and further developed, notably among a younger generation of scholars, often together with their counterparts in Hong Kong and Taiwan. Major academic battles are still going on among groups that might be described as "new liberals", or "restoration nationalists", or neo-Marxists (that is, excluding Leninists, Stalinists and Maoists). Marxist scholars who had not been forced by governments and political conditions to adopt Marxist analyses in all matters, as in Japan and India, for example, are in a different position. Few of them held extreme and exclusive views in the first place. Thus, if there was any revisionism, it has been less dramatic. But I would suggest that, although the Marxist paradigm was initially brought into Asia from the West, it has been adapted and modified, and even domesticated, in countries like China and Vietnam. In this way, it has been integrated into the philosophical foundations of both countries and given a national tenor. Thus, a local or Asian perspective here might sustain the neo-Marxist paradigm long after it has lost its vitality in the West.

Yet another example, somewhat further away from the modern nation-state framework but not free from its influences, is that of culture as a national phenomenon and as an explanatory agent in social science.

In Asian tradition, cultural explanations for almost any kind of social and value change were preeminent. In comparison, the strong trend away from cultural explanation towards the elimination of culture among some Western social scientists today has been disconcerting. We can observe some efforts to give due weight to cultural factors in the study of politics and economics. In Asia, the preferred explanation for any event tends to be holistic and therefore inevitably involves religious and ethical values as a necessary background to all economic and political changes. Modern social scientists, notably among economists, are suspicious of all cultural explanations. A paradigm of value-free or culture-free scientific premises has been trying to overcome this cultural bias for several decades. But I suspect that, in Asia, this may be a genuine case of a shifting paradigm, moving back and forth between positions that seem to be ambiguous, or positions that want it both ways.

In each of the examples above, Asian thinkers are reacting and adapting to their changing political environments or to the social science debates prevailing in the West. They seem hard pressed to be independently creative. This is quite unlike in the humanities where scholars and artists have retained the initiative. They deeply understand their own traditions and can use Western theories, methods and insights to seek fresh interpretations and emerge with new cultural developments. Nor can the social science scholars compare with their natural science counterparts in Asia who work in fields like medicine and engineering. Whenever conditions allow for experiment and innovation in the applied branches of their disciplines, as may be found in some universities in the larger countries like Japan, China and India, the natural scientists have shown ability to be as creative as scholars in the West. The impression that Asian social scientists are driven by situational changes rather than being inspired by their own impetus for innovative thinking may be unfair and misleading. But it would be true to say that creativity has been constrained by the different working conditions in Asian universities. This is striking when compared with the kind of creativity found among many scholars of Asian origins working in the West. The following brief examples illustrate some key aspects of the phenomenon.

Creativity of Asian Origins

I mentioned earlier Amartya Sen, the Nobel Prize winner. I now focus on him and the work of a number of scholars of Asian origins whom I have chosen here to represent different kinds of working experiences and creativity in social science. Amartya Sen was deeply influenced by having been born and educated in Asia, and then spent most of his working life in Europe and the United States. The others also have similar experiences in sharing histories, as many Asian and Western scholars now do. To make some comparisons, we could look at two examples of people of Asian origins who have achieved world appreciation through working in the West or specifically with Western categories of analysis. I refer to Ranajit Guha and Kenichi Ohmae. Like Amartya Sen, they built their experiences and observations of Asia into their theoretical concerns and this has stimulated new formulations. For purposes of contrast, we could look at the examples of Edward Said and Francis Fukuyama. Said is only marginally Asian, being a Palestinian who grew up in Egypt and then studied and worked in America. In the case of Fukuyama, he was educated entirely in America and only his family background is Japanese Asian. I include them here to remind us of the kind of knowledge continuum between Asia and the West which we are familiar with in natural science and which may now be emerging in social science. It is a continuum which has incubated creativity. How important is this as a function of shared history?

Amartya Sen

Amartya Sen's kind of creativity is in a class of its own. It drew on sophisticated layers of economic and social theory and integrated them with the basic realities of India which none of the theoreticians would have known. Perhaps this is the creativity that every social scientist in Asia would like to be able to show. The direct impact of Amartya Sen's work on the reassessment of the problems of poverty in the world is already obvious, as seen in the latest World Bank report on poverty. It illustrates his success in questioning the received wisdom about the nature of poverty and the wealth creation solutions found in economic theories worked out in Europe and North America. By drawing deeply from what he understood from growing up amongst, and studying, the poorest people of India, he brought about a marriage of theory and practice which is exemplary. It is an inspiring case of creativity in the highest sense. He was not the first to appreciate the cultural and material differences between Britain (or the West) and India. A number of British colonial administrators had done field research since the later years of the 19th century, and some Indian scholars who used Marxist analytical concepts have long claimed that the most meaningful ideas come from the interaction of theory and practice. We also had the example of Gunnar Myrdal's *Asian Drama* a generation earlier which had considerable influence on social theory for a while. It is too early to say if Sen's contributions will be followed by greater practical success than that of Myrdal, but the fact of his originality cannot be denied. He has set standards of creativity for economists and other social scientists to measure themselves against. Asia at last has a role model in social science to match those in the humanities and the natural sciences.

Ranajit Guha

A different kind of creativity may be found in the case of Ranajit Guha, also originally from India. He, too, has spent long years away from his home in Bengal, first in Europe and then in Australia and now back in Europe again. He was the activist and ideological historian who did not choose to remain in academia but ventured out to battle for the causes he supported in the Cold War world. He had begun with a deep understanding of Marxist social philosophy and steadily applied some of its concepts to modern Indian history. But, despite his commitment to an internationalist cause, he did not allow himself to be bound by the Marxist framework. Instead, he creatively modified the class analysis he started out with to initiate a postcolonial approach to historical records. In this way, he came to identify the range of subaltern relationships that had enabled the British to govern India with relative success. He demonstrated the efficacy of his approach decisively, thus inspiring a generation of scholars to use subaltern studies as an original way of explaining everything from Indian nationalism and democracy to the structure and culture of modern caste politics. Although it was his studies in the West and his use of Marxist ideas that provided the main stimuli for his work, his early life experiences in India and his explorations of indigenous historical data were the springboards for his inventiveness. So far, the study of subaltern groups in other Asian or African postcolonial societies has not developed, but the potential for a major theoretical input into contemporary history is there. His is a case of delving into a period of shared history to sift out new insights on modern society.

Edward Said

You may well ask if this is not simply a continuation, or another face, of the creative debate that sprang more directly from Western academia and found considerable resonance in Asia. This after all is the expected consequence of introducing Western learning into any Asian education system. It takes me to the renowned example of Edward Said. His Orientalism, and the postcolonial perspectives that it aroused, have been spectacularly provocative to the academic world of both social science and the humanities. This was an effort to shift Western scholars from their habitual views about Asia (and the wider Islamic world) as "the Orient" to attitudes that would admit to having started with condescending and manipulative assumptions about colonised Asia. His was certainly a more direct contribution to postmodern cultural studies than that of Ranajit Guha. Orientalism has the support of devoted friends and also made strong enemies, but the shift he tried to make to the Western mindset has not got very far with either Europeans or Americans. Instead, the rich debate has attracted many Asians working in the West who have spoken on behalf of Asia against Western arrogance. But, unlike the followers of Ranajit Guha, Edward Said's creative contributions to theory have not inspired those social scientists who work primarily in Asia itself. I believe this is because Said's views were really internal critiques from someone within the Mediterranean world of Christians, Muslims and Jews. Despite the numerous references to colonial policies in the rest of Asia, his new theoretical formulations have drawn little from the social and historical phenomena found within southern and eastern Asia. In any case, Said does not claim to be a social scientist. He reached his creative heights through literary and humanistic inquiry that owed little to the kind of social science that had inspired someone like Ranajit Guha. Thus, although what Said observed and exposed has excited many social scientists in Asia, his creativity is of a different dimension from that of Amartya Sen and Ranajit Guha.

Francis Fukuyama

Another example of creativity is also illuminating. I refer to that of Francis Fukuyama, whose triumphant proclamation of "the end of history" has aroused so much controversy. Although of Japanese descent, his contributions to vigorous debate has little to do with his roots from the eastern end of the Asian continent. He is American-born and educated, and specialises in European political philosophy, drawing from the larger canvas of world history to study the struggle for supremacy between the Soviet Union and the United States during the Cold War. In this way, his training was deeply rooted in the 19th century origins of social science itself, the sort of intellectual transition which Wolf Lepenies wrote so brilliantly about in his book, *Die Drei Kulturen,* or *Between literature and science.* From that background, Fukuyama responded to the end of the Cold War by describing it in terms of the victory of capitalism over communism. Most Asians today who had experienced the Cold War with different perspectives from that of Fukuyama would find that "the end of history" thesis does not match their understanding of their own histories. But they are nevertheless likely to be inspired by this kind of pursuit of larger truths through social science.

Fukuyama's further ventures into the place of Asia in global history have been even more stimulating. For example, his theoretical treatment of the concept of trust in Japan and Germany, and by extension, that in China, Britain, United States and other parts of the West, certainly takes us deeply into shared histories and shows how effectively the sharing of such histories has triggered powerful social and economic changes in disparate parts of the world. Although his analyses and comparisons have attracted a number of rebuttals, they nevertheless demonstrate the explanatory power of social science in Asian societies today. I make no claims to the long-term validity of Fukuyama's theories, but there is no doubt that they illustrate the kind of creativity that is normally expected in the West, one that is inspired by crossing several social science disciplines and not so much by taking geographical and cultural differences into account. He nevertheless provides a good example of how an American scholar of Asian descent can enrich social science as vividly as other Asian Americans have done in the humanities and natural sciences. The useful thoughts developed from his forays into Japanese and Chinese behaviour have been acknowledged in Asia itself and cannot be easily dismissed.

Kenichi Ohmae

The fifth example represents a creativity which is very different again. I have already mentioned the exceptional case of Kenichi Ohmae. Here is someone who came not from the portals of academia but from years of working in the corporate world. He trained as a nuclear engineer before joining the great multinational consultant company, McKinsey, one of the most dynamic of its kind in the world. His is not a profound creativity but a practical and no less influential one. As a Japanese, he dedicated much of his working life to explaining corporate Japan through his company outlets, including writings which took on a global dimension. From a series of essays to his two best-known books, he employed the paradigm of "the borderless world" and "the end of the nation state". He repeatedly and effectively used all parts of the media to represent what he saw as a decisive shift away from the sovereign state model. This was the model copied from the West that has dominated Asia for the past century. The force of his arguments made the ideas sound newer than they were. Drawing on the spectacular advances in communications technology, and the reality of the globalisation of commerce, industry and finance, the case he made was persuasive to many. The ideas were also extensions of modernisation theory and marked the progress from the earlier rhetoric of interdependence. They could also be described as direct offshoots of an older "One World" paradigm that we have heard of in the last few decades. And this in turn can be traced back to the Enlightenment project launched from Europe at the end of the 18th century. I refer to the body of ideas that served as the underlying basis of much of the modern quest for secular knowledge. Ken Ohmae benefited directly from his shared experience of working with an international group committed to the use of social science to advance corporate growth. By immersing himself in this way, he tapped the creativity that social science can stimulate and did so in the tough business world within Asia itself. For Asians now persuaded of the dynamic power of entrepreneurship, this is the kind of creativity they appreciate. Whether or not it is central to the disciplines of social science, its manifestations suggest that it is in the world of business where social science creativity may be best tested. It may be here that social science will find its best future in Asia.

Variously "Asian" Creativity

The five examples demonstrate different kinds of creativity. The backgrounds of the five men show varying degrees of the shared histories that the modern West has had with a modernising Asia. The sharing was achieved in different ways but what they had in common was that it came from shared educational and intellectual histories. If we were to take Amartya Sen, the economist as someone closest to the kind of inquiry that seeks to adapt the methods of natural science to the study of society, then Edward Said would be furthest from him. The other three may be seen to occupy different positions in between. But the philosophical Francis Fukuyama was too positive and optimistic to be truly creative as a social scientist. The historically oriented Ranajit Guha, on the other hand, can satisfy both: those with a social conscience and those who would like their theories founded strictly on empirical, in the case historical, data. As for Ken Ohmae, his is a lower order of creativity but one that resonates more strongly among the young generation of Asians who see social science as most valuable when pursued for practical ends.

In summary, all five have shared histories with their Western academic or corporate colleagues, but each started from a different geographical or intellectual location. If we were to suppose that they are all variously "Asian" in some ways, we cannot explain their responses to social science phenomena by referring to what they know about the peoples of Asia. We would need to consider the histories they had each shared with Asians and Westerners alike. Amartya Sen and Ranajit Guha come closest to sharing a past, having both been born in Bengal during the late colonial era, and spent their youth in the same part of the country. But their ways parted after that and they have shared little ever since. As for the others, there are greater variations. These range from the Western practices in Japan that Ken Ohmae shared with corporate colleagues who are unmistakably Japanese to the other end of Asia where Edward Said left the edge of Asia to represent the "Orient" to his sceptical American colleagues. And out of geographical range of any of the other four is Francis Fukuyama. As the son of Japanese immigrants, Fukuyama steeped himself early and deeply in a Western life of ideas.

The tenuous use of "Asian" that allows me to refer to them here is not meant to imply that that is what they have in common. The commonality lies in the ability they all share to write creatively about man in modern and modernising societies, and in the broad area between the humanities and the natural sciences. Beyond that, the experiences they represent on their respective creative journeys have, as far as I can see, only one clear condition in common. They were all products of modern universities, major institutions which had similar mixes of humanities, social science and natural science choices. As undergraduates and as graduate students, they also shared a common heritage with their teachers and fellow students and were soaked in the same kind of knowledge framework.

The Fact of Unshared Histories

There are, of course, many more creative ideas in the social sciences that have no Asian connection but have received warm responses around most of Asia. For purposes of comparison, I shall take three well-known examples to point to contradictions that come from the fact of unshared histories. The most recent is the stimulating paradigm of "the clash of civilisations" and the heated debate which that aroused. It marked a significant turnaround away from the prevalent position in 19th century Europe. This had identified civilisation as one and that of the West, and expected all other cultures, big or small, ultimately to be measured against that single civilisational standard. There is a paradox here. Although many Asian scholars are critical of the idea that civilisations will clash, many others are at the same time fascinated by this acknowledgement of other civilisations in the best tradition of Arnold Toynbee. Samuel Huntington seems to have recognised a plurality of civilisations, as Toynbee did, and used the idea of a clash between civilisations as a new paradigm in the field of international relations and strategic security. What is intriguing is that earlier generations of Asian thinkers, steeped in their own classical traditions and confident of the longevity of these traditions, would have had no difficulty with the image of civilisations struggling to assert superiority. Their perspectives about clashes between civilisations would have received little attention at the time, except from those who were equally traditional in approach. Or they might have been mocked by those who thought that Asian civilisations could challenge Western civilisation was nothing more than wishful thinking. It is, of course, doubtful if this creative restatement of clashes in the future by Huntington derived from shared histories, or that it will produce lasting analytical results. But it is a symptom of modern social science scholarship that, when a Western academic shows doubt about the ultimate supremacy of Western civilisation, it drew so much response in Asia.

The second example is one of knowledge-driven creativity, and it comes from the intertwining of natural and social sciences in the cumulative case made for conservation, for saving the environment, and for societies to pursue sustainable economic growth. From its beginnings in the early 1960s with Rachel Carson's *Silent Spring* to some three decades later, social scientists in Asia had left the matter as mainly a natural sciences concern. The best part of the debates had been among biological scientists. A creative response from social science was late in coming even in the West but, in Asia, social scientists did even less and simply waited for their Western counterparts to deal with the consequences before taking the issues on board. There was in this case no shared history to speak of, only sequential responses as each stage of development was proved to be appropriate. Almost in the same way, contemporary Asian social scientists have rarely sought creative solutions to the epidemic of HIV infections and the spread of AIDS. Although not actually in denial, as some government ministers and bureaucrats have been, no social science faculty in Asia's higher education has distinguished itself by leading the way to deal with the obvious threats to all the people in their countries.

My third example is the paradigm that is most akin to postmodernism. I refer to the shift from unisex (male) analysis to gender studies. Sociologically speaking, there is growing political correctness on this subject in some parts of Asia, but gender studies have just come to be taken seriously in only a small number of communities. With increasing numbers of women, and some enlightened men, entering the field, the prospects for the future are good. But gender studies are still at a very early stage. To engender Asian perspectives here, a lot more work would need to be done to counter the resistance that may be found in most Asian societies. The paradox here is striking. For example, in contrast to the fierce struggles that Western women fought for their legal and political rights, most women in Asia were, at least nominally, given political rights and a steady increase in financial and legal status, either through the transfer of colonial power to an independent regime, or through rational argument. In some cases, it is astonishing how insecurely women took to their newly offered status of equality and how quietly they awaited further improvements in their political positions. This is clearly a core issue in social science for Asian women, yet all creativity has come from the generations of battlers in the West, while the field remains quite underdeveloped among most social scientists in Asia.

The Challenge of Social Science in Asia

I shall end with some comments on the experience common to most of the examples mentioned earlier, that is, the exposure to tertiary education. Social science creativity is dependent on educational and intellectual environment. On the ground, in various parts of Asia which do share histories to some degree with the West, the stages of development vary a great deal. It is true that the university is now ubiquitous. These modern secular institutions in Asia are modelled directly on their Western counterparts. They began with two main models: (a) elitist European state-funded universities which stress secondary school and first degree education; (b) popular American public and private universities of which a large component stresses the quality of their postgraduate/professional schools. The former recognises that longer-term needs are critical. Therefore, the key question is how to produce leaders for the country and in which academic disciplines. The debate for years was whether the liberal arts produced better-rounded people for leadership, or whether knowledge of science and technology and professional school education better trained the kind of leaders that rapidly changing societies need.

Most importantly, the question became one of asking how we are to stimulate creativity and encourage innovation? Can it be taught or learnt? Ultimately, the need was for more freedom to encourage new ideas. How are we to reconcile this desire for creativity with the training in sharply defined academic disciplines? Is creativity and innovation possible within received traditions? Or is the Western/modern experience essential for future progress? In short, what kind of university education could make the difference?

It is everywhere clear that there are considerable differences in performance and priorities within Asian universities. But the trend has been clear for several decades. The fields of natural sciences and the professional schools of medicine were expected to lead the way, but eventually schools of law and engineering also took prominent places in Asian society. They were all new in their modern forms, but students were still expected to know their own societies and cultures and the question was, how much humanities and social sciences were needed to supplement their education? Most academic leaders took the view that, for Asia's future to be distinctive, the humanities had to be strengthened so that the heritage of traditional learning, notably religion and ethics, literature, history and fine arts, could be protected and revived. This was to be challenged again and again, with humanities losing out to science and medicine, and then to engineering. It became increasingly difficult for humanities to make their work relevant and interesting unless they were useful to the professional schools.

As for social science, the response in Asia was a belated one. Most countries did not have full-fledged universities until the end of the Second World War. When the rapid expansion of tertiary education came, greater emphasis was given to the professional schools with relatively few that acknowledged distinct faculties or colleges of social science. Where they have gained recognition, it was linked closely to the way each society was politically organised. For Asian universities to have more impact on how their societies develop in the future, it would be important to consider how social science theories and methodologies are treated. Are they seen as universally applicable and thus vigorously applied to the study of Asian societies? Or is there a tendency to reject such laws and methodologies as derivations from Western social patterns and have them discounted when adapting them to the study of Asian societies? Or should they consciously use social science from the West as guides or hypotheses in order to stimulate fresh understanding of Asian societies through uncovering new theories and methodologies and, in this way, ultimately enrich the fields of social science themselves?

This is a major challenge for social science in Asia. We have seen, in examples like Edward Said and Francis Fukuyama, that Asians born and settled in the West can make an impact in social science through fields like literature and philosophy. For areas more central to social science, we find men like Amartya Sen and Ranajit Guha, who clearly show that great creativity has been possible by scholars staying long in the West. And a distinct kind of creativity within Asia has been possible, as in the case of Ken Ohmae, but that had come out of working professionally within a dynamic Western system. If they, and the latter three in particular, inspire future social scientists to make similar achievements within Asia, that would help us answer the questions that I have posed. The evidence so far is that the fields are still relatively new, the academic conditions and research agendas in most Asian countries are yet to be encouraging, and the best brains in Asia are being pushed by circumstances towards the natural sciences and the professional schools more determinedly than in the West. Thus, not too much can be expected for some time. But, given the five examples of shared histories and the variety of creativity described earlier, there is no reason to doubt that the capacity of Asians to learn and translate social science to suit their needs when the time comes would be very strong.

12

Shifting Paradigms and Asian Perspectives: Implications for Research and Teaching

I do not have a strict definition for paradigms. When I was young, we used models, or patterns, even world views, to convey what the physical scientists called paradigms. But I would recognise the examples of shifts in the way we studied the humanities and social sciences as comparable to paradigmatic shifts and I shall treat them as such here. My own starting point is that of a multidisciplinary historian, who comes from the humanities side and uses the methodologies of the social scientists when deemed appropriate and helpful. Also, I am fascinated by the uses of the

---

This lecture was delivered at the National University of Singapore Centre for Advanced Studies' launch of the Centre's books and research papers on 2 November 1998. Published in *Shifting Paradigms and Asian Perespectives: Implications for Research and Teaching*, Research Paper Series no. 10, Centre for Advanced Studies, NUS, 22 pages. Reproduced with the kind permission of the Centre for Advanced Studies, NUS.

past by scholars in other disciplines, as well as by the histories of other disciplines themselves, especially in the context of the sociology of knowledge.

One general point of contrast: in universities in Western Europe, North America and Australasia, paradigm shifts come more from academic and intellectual activity, or cerebral responses to social and cultural changes over time, taking in the larger picture in the context of universal science and progress, and of modern civilisation, as the main driving force in history.

In Asia, especially in the newer nations over the past half century, paradigm shifts are more situational, and much more influenced by contemporary political and economic developments. Thus, we might distinguish between responses to academic shifts emerging from the major scholarly centres in the West and those responses to situational changes (which sometimes produce paradigm shifts) that have been experienced in Asia itself.

I have seen many shifts in my time, more accurately, many kinds of shifts. Where they have clearly elicited Asian responses and influenced many Asian scholarly writings, the following paradigmatic shifts are striking. In each case, it would not be difficult to show how they have influenced research and teaching. I have chosen ten examples, some of which are more like scientific paradigms than others, but all representing potential discontinuities in research and teaching.

But I would like to distinguish between those which I consider situational and those which may be described as knowledge-driven. Of the ten examples, the following four belong to the category of situational shifts.

Situational shifts

(i) The shift from colonial interpretations to the anti-colonial (decolonisation).

These have aroused xenophobic behaviour and calls for modelling new Asian states on European "nation-states". Revisionism of all kinds is one of the forms that they all took. The response to historical change began as being very obvious, manifesting even crude rejections of one set of premises and fierce insistence on another set of premises. For example, everything represented by the colonial scholars must be challenged, or reinterpreted in terms of newly discovered national interests. This is so self-evident that no logical arguments were necessary. It was enough to say that the circumstances have changed, and old assumptions no longer applied. Strong emotions were often involved. In effect, this was a paradigmatic shift that had considerable impact on research and teaching in many Asian universities.

But that phase occurs largely in scholarly research in most Asian countries. The best scholars find the paradigm increasingly limiting and less intellectually satisfactory. But politicians and governments still often resort to this model, and in some cases, still insist on this "orthodoxy" in teaching at school levels, if not at college levels.

(ii) The shift from classical/traditional assumptions to modern/Western new paradigms, especially in the study of the past.

This has been a wrenching experience for two or more generations of Asian scholars. The struggle still continues, especially among the older scholars in the guru traditions of India (bearing the Hindu-Buddhist heritage), the Islamic world, and countries of the Confucian persuasion. It is still a source of intellectual tension: the more deep-rooted the classical tradition, the greater the resistance to new paradigms. I do not wish to dwell on this, as it is more common among scholars working in the fields of early and ancient history, literature and philosophy than among social scientists. Indeed, this is the clearest divide between humanities and social science scholars today. Strictly speaking and almost by definition, researchers and teachers of the modern disciplines of the social sciences do not move in this direction — that is, from classical to modern. Some social scientists, on the other hand, have moved the other way. They would do so if and when they discover the strengths and merits of classical scholarship regarding premodern subjects. Some learn to appreciate the older paradigms as admirably suited to the elucidation of such subjects.

On the whole, the forward direction towards modern models and methods in scholarship is regarded as progressive and is still in the mainstream direction. The emphasis on continuity and tradition of scholarly pursuits still survives in the humanities, but the reverse direction of moving back to classical paradigms would always be exceptional in the social sciences. In effect, from the point of view of social scientists, this paradigm from the traditional to the modern can be described not as shifting, but as already wholly shifted.

(iii) The shift from liberal social science to Marxist "science" and the shift back.

Major protagonists of the opposing positions fought one another fiercely in Europe for decades, from the late 19th century down to the middle of the 20th century. In Asia, however, political changes following the formation of the Soviet Union and the beginning of the Cold War led many scholars to accept Marxist paradigms and reinterpret all their traditions in Marxist terms. Although most older scholars were forced to do so in countries which were taken over by communist parties, younger scholars tended to find the Marxist framework both revolutionary and exciting, especially when this meant that they could totally reject their respective heritages and still remain respectable. This was especially true in China, Japan, and also in Korea and Vietnam; to some extent, in Myanmar and India as well. When this happened, teaching and research were subjected to reinterpretation in the new categories. The categories were internally consistent and did not allow for any questioning of the key premises.

More recently, in China (even more conspicuous in Central and Eastern Europe like the former East Germany, Hungary, Poland, the Czech and Slovak Republics), the reverse has occurred, that is, with scholars turning away from Marxist "science" to a whole range of new social scientific paradigms taken directly from a triumphant West (notably the United States). In China, many of these new paradigms are yet to be fully digested. Others have been modified and further developed in Taiwan and Hong Kong. How this will affect teaching and research has yet to be evaluated. There is evidence to suggest that nothing is conclusive as yet. Major academic battles are still going on among groups that might be described as "new liberals", or "restoration nationalists", or neo-Marxists (that is, excluding the Leninists, Stalinists and Maoists). This must have considerable influence on how subjects in the arts and social sciences are being taught and how research in these fields is still being constrained.

Marxist scholars who had not been forced by governments and political conditions to adopt Marxist analyses of all matters, as in Japan and India, for example, are in a different position. Few of them held extreme and exclusive views in the first place. Thus, if there is any revisionism, it has been less dramatic. But I would venture to suggest that, although the Marxist paradigm was initially brought into Asia from the West, it has been adapted and modified, and even domesticated, in countries like China and Vietnam. In this way, it has been integrated into the philosophical foundations of both countries. Thus, the local or Asian perspectives here might sustain the paradigm long after it has lost its vitality in the West.

(iv) The fourth shift is one from the pre-eminence of cultural explanation to the elimination of culture in the social sciences, and the continuous struggle to return to cultural factors in the study of politics and economics. Together with the three aforementioned shifts, it can be related to the underlying struggle among culturalists and anti-culturalists in the social sciences.

In Asia, the preferred explanation of any event tends to be *holistic* and therefore inevitably involves religious and ethical values as a necessary background to all economic and political changes. Modern social scientists, notably among economists, are suspicious of all cultural explanations. A paradigm of value-free or culture-free, scientific premises has been trying to overcome this cultural bias for several decades. But I suspect that, in Asia, this may be a genuine case of a *shifting* paradigm, moving back and forth between positions that seem to be ambiguous, or positions that assert both ways.

Knowledge-driven shifts brought to Asia

I shall turn to what I believe are knowledge-driven paradigms that may or may not have been inspired by changing political and economic conditions in the modern Western world. I shall briefly explain these paradigms which, where Asia is concerned, are largely intellectually derivative and are fed largely by academic work done in Western universities. They consist of concepts teased out by European and American scholars and then applied to Asia. In short, the use of these concepts is still very new and underdeveloped, and in some cases, probably artificial, so it may be premature to speak of Asian perspectives at this point. But in so far as they are having an impact on teaching and research in Asian universities, they need to be noted. It is too early to say how many of these examples of new paradigms — five of the six examples to be described in brief — will eventually take root in Asia. Examples that have caught the most attention of late are listed as follows.

(v) As distinct from the postcolonial paradigm that was generated partly in Asia, there are paradigms of postmodernism that sprang out of challenges to received scholarship in the West. They range from those that are all-encompassing in conception, which throw doubt on almost every premise in post-Enlightenment learning, to those which are more modest and specifically targeted at major weaknesses in knowledge production. These studies, especially those in literary and cultural studies, have been applied to local conditions with different degrees of success. But as long as they are stimulatingly keen, new research and are producing fresh results, they are likely to remain influential in teaching as well.

(vi) One major example of a paradigm shift which is akin to postmodernism is the shift from unisex (male) analysis to gender studies. Sociologically speaking, there is growing political correctness on this subject in some parts of Asia, but gender studies are still peripheral to mainstream teaching and research in most Asian universities. But with increasing numbers of women, and some enlightened men, entering the field, the prospects for the future are good. But gender studies are still at a nascent stage. For there to be Asian perspectives in Asia, a lot more work would need to be done to counter the resistance that may be found in most Asian societies.

(vii) Another paradigm that has sprung from Western academia but has found resonance in Asia is that of orientalism. This is an attempt to shift Western scholars from their habitual views about the Orient to one that acknowledges their superior and distorting starting points. The paradigm has had both its devoted friends and vicious enemies, and the shift has probably been halted. The rich debate that followed has, however, often joined forces with postmodernism, especially by Asians who work in the West and speak on behalf of Asia against the Western premises and the cultural arrogance that underlies some of those premises. This paradigm shift has not run its full course. But so far there is no specific Asian perspective discerned here.

The next two examples are recently claimed as paradigm shifts, and may be seen as responses to the three as mentioned earlier. They may have already attracted scholars in Asia to pursue them further and adapt to Asian perspectives, but have yet to produce a corpus of literature. These shifts are: "end of history", "clash of civilisations" and "the borderless world".

(viii) "End of history" (Francis Fukuyama). This shift has followed what is seen as the triumph of capitalism over communism after the fall of the Soviet Union and the end of the Cold War. Most Asians, I believe, would find that it does not mesh with their recent historical experiences. But it is still on the table and should not be dismissed.

(ix) "Clash of civilisations" (Samuel P Huntington). This marks a significant shift from the point of view of those in the West who, for the past century or so, have believed that there is only one civilisation. All else are different cultures, big or small, which ultimately have to be measured against that single civilisational standard. Many Asian scholars are critical of Huntington, but are, at the same time, fascinated by this new paradigm in the field of international relations that acknowledges a plurality of civilisations. Again, it is too early to say if the shift will really take place, but the controversy is producing new research and will influence teaching.

(x) Finally, the last example, "the borderless world" paradigm from Kenneth Ohmae, represents the latest shift from the sovereign nation-state model that has dominated Asia for the past century. It sounds very new, drawing upon the spectacular advances in technology and the reality of globalisation of commerce, industry and finance. It is also an extension of modernisation theory and the phenomenon of interdependence. But, when taken together with "end of history" and "clash of civilisations", I believe they are all direct offshoots of an older paradigm, what might be called the "One World" paradigm. This is, of course, descended from the larger Enlightenment Project that goes back to the end of the 18th century, and is the underlying basis of much of the modern quest for knowledge.

This is a vast subject and the ramifications are great. I shall focus only on a small aspect of this to illustrate how Asian perspectives are shaped by such a knowledge-derived paradigm. I shall use the case of emigration and assimilation, which are both good examples of the use of modern concepts, in the study of traditional and transitional Asia, especially on Southeast Asia. The concepts are drawn mainly from studies in European and American societies and then applied to local societies in Asia, and both have had a great impact on research and writing all over Asia.

(a) The shift from emigration as aberration to emigration as normal. This is especially true for China, Japan, Korea and Hindu India, where it was once virtually taboo to leave one's shores to go and live among foreign peoples. Now that the phenomenon is treated as normal, the question of settlement and cultural maintenance has come to the fore. Thus,

(b) The shift from assimilation of migrants in nation-states to cultural pluralism in migrant states. The assimilation idea had come from two sources: the "nation-state" ideal with the emphasis on unity, solidarity and common values in citizenry; and the "melting pot" ideal of the migrant states, which assumes that all migrants will fully conform to the culture of the dominant majority. It is therefore easy to see assimilation as *natural* in the context of universalism, globalisation and oneness of human nature. In this context, stubborn cultural maintenance could be viewed as obstacles in the path of progress towards the grand ideal of a future of one world, one civilisation.

For decades, the paradigm of assimilation in new nation-states has been dominant. The expansion of the "borderless world" has helped political and social leaders re-examine the reality of cultural pluralism and challenge the dominant view that enforced national cohesion at the expense of cultural minorities is essential to progress. This larger paradigm may be described as one that is shifting, because the world is changing so fast that the policies of neither assimilation nor cultural pluralism have been fully accepted.

But, at least for some parts of Asia, there has been a retreat from assimilationist demands, especially those which have taken into account the experiences of migrant states like the United States, Canada and Australasia. The shift to multiculturalism is being resisted here and there, of course, and it is not clear whether that process will ultimately prevail. But the shift of emphasis has gained some Asian responses which are notable. The assimilationist ways that had been taken for granted as the model for the new states of Southeast Asia, for example, are being questioned. Here I note a situational response to a knowledge-derived paradigm.

I was particularly struck by the obvious failure of the assimilationist policy of Suharto's Indonesia. The assumption that there was a static Indonesian national culture to which all its citizens of Chinese descent must conform was false. The hope that such conformity would solve the problems of alienation for these Chinese proved to be tragically impossible. Can there now be a shift, from a situational paradigm that many Asians had taken to heart, to a knowledge-derived paradigm drawn from the work of scholars and intellectuals elsewhere?

I hope so, but I do not have an answer to this question. On the other hand, I have no doubt that shifting paradigms, whatever the source, and whether situational or knowledge-driven, have an important place in research and teaching. The real test of their value, however, is whether Asian perspectives can endorse, enrich or modify the paradigm, if not challenge its validity altogether. For that, it will take much serious, careful and sustained research for which universities like the National University of Singapore was established to stimulate and encourage. In conclusion, shifting paradigms benefit research and teaching, and Asian perspectives are necessary if we are to make a difference to the store of knowledge in the world.

Notes

My response to commentaries subsequent to the publication of the paper.

I agree with Professor Habib Khondker that the interaction between the "West" and Asia has intensified, and more account should be taken of this fact in our evaluation of contributions to knowledge. A great deal more hard work has to be done to relate, wherever possible, specific interactions to known examples of scholarly breakthroughs.

Professor N Sriram's optimism that the gap between the tertiary institutions in our region and those in North America and Europe will be reduced in the decades to come is commendable. For myself, I have long hoped for this.

I am greatly in sympathy with Professor Syed Farid Alatas' complaint that something like "cultural cringe" occurs in our downgrading of local journals. It is obvious that small countries, especially former colonies, are more prone to this than the larger more confident historical nations. Also, the contrast between students in B K Sarkar's times and those today may be ironic. It also reflects the freedom which elite students sometimes enjoyed under colonial and paternalistic academic structures. Academically ambitious students now are more exposed to the globalisation of intellectual challenges than those of British India.

As for Professor Mohd Shamsul Haque's warnings about the word "paradigm", I share his concern. I also plead guilty to the loose "portmanteau" way of using the word. He is right in pointing out that my list of "shifts" included those in traditions, in ideologies, in perspectives. My introductory remarks admit that I used words like models, patterns and world views before the word paradigm was picked up by social scientists. Given that I have grave doubts about the social sciences ever being truly scientific, and my reluctance to lose the word paradigm to the physical scientists and leave them with its exclusive use, I hope he can understand my attempt to have this one word to encompass all the "shifts" I talked about. I have no particular love for "paradigm" and would be grateful for another word that would do the job here.

13

The Classics and the East Asian Entrepreneur

The growing interest in the rapid development of the Four Tigers of East Asia — Taiwan, South Korea, Hong Kong and Singapore — has led many commentators to look for the common features in their culture and society. The link with Japan's "economic miracle" is unmistakable. The fact that three of the Tigers have largely Chinese populations is obviously significant. The spectacular performance of the People's Republic of China during the past decade, and the role of the ethnic Chinese in several potential Southeast Asian Tigers, have added further dimensions to the quest for a common factor. In terms of education, the question is whether there was a canon of books which entrepreneurs in these countries shared when they were young.

This article was first published, under the headline "Esteemed ancestors and good business", on 26 November 1993 in the Issue 1099 of the *Times Higher Education Supplement*. Reproduced with the kind permission of *Times Higher Education* magazine.

Historically, the Chinese, Koreans and Japanese (and, to a lesser extent, the Vietnamese as well) did share the language, Classical Chinese, and the doctrinal texts of Confucius. The best-known had been the Four Books, and the collections of moral aphorisms derived from the Confucian school of thought. There were also *The Book of History*, Sima Qian's *History* and the novel, *Romance of the Three Kingdoms*. There was poetry, especially the *300 Tang poems*. One could add the texts of Lao Zi and Zhuang Zi, and popular stories about Buddhist saints and Taoist Immortals.

It is possible to say that every literate person in China, Japan and the Four Tigers, would know of these books; and most students entering university would be familiar with their contents. But, unlike those at the beginning of the 20th century, very few students today would be able to recite from any of these works and even fewer would claim that any of these books had a decisive influence on their intellectual development.

The intriguing question is, how does familiarity with these books tie up with the success of Japanese, Koreans and Chinese as "economic animals", as entrepreneurs, or modern financiers, industrialists, and managers? It is as difficult to see a link here as it is to see one between familiarity with the Bible and Shakespeare in Britain and the rise of modern science and industrial capitalism. Nevertheless, many scholars believe that, if the Protestant ethic explains anything in modern economic history, so may the concept of a common Confucian ethic.

In the list of books mentioned earlier, apart from the texts and stories which pertain to Taoism and Buddhism, all the others are either central to Confucian education or are permeated with its values. One could make a good case for the Confucian ethic being the foundation of economic success among the East Asian people, except for the inconvenient fact that orthodox Confucians were dismissive about commerce and cynical about merchants as a class.

If we equate capitalism with private enterprise and the freedom of trade, then there is nothing in Confucianism which endorses that. On the other hand, if the secret of East Asian economic success is found in prosperity for the country, in increased productivity of the peasants and artisans (in modern terms, the agricultural and industrial sectors), and in state intervention only to ensure security and harmony, then the Confucian mandarin ideal could be important.

This is an authoritarian ideal which stressed that good government is found when the iron fist of rectitude and punishment is wrapped up in a velvet glove of Confucian moral rhetoric. The major Confucian texts promoted high standards of individual behaviour, of discipline and self-criticism, of industriousness and frugality — all personal qualities which capitalists of the Victorian England would find easy to appreciate. There was nothing in the texts which inhibited entrepreneurship, on behalf of one's family or one's country, which followed these standards. As long as wealth is seen to be honourable, the product of risk-taking, sacrifice and hard work, and not of dishonesty, crime and greed, it was regarded as esteemed.

In short, capitalism which respected authority, individual initiative which recognised the social boundaries, and even aggressive enterprise, as long it was on behalf of a higher cause like family and country, could find support in the classics.

It is doubtful, however, that the young East Asian students at universities who plan to go into business are conscious of the indirect contribution these Confucian classics can make to their careers. There are differences one can point to between Japanese and Koreans and the various kinds of Chinese. The Chinese, who are the direct bearers of the common heritage, deserve special attention here.

First, the young Chinese on the Chinese mainland. For a people who have always lived with the classics in one form or another, they look strangely adrift today. Not only are they bereft of the Marxist-Leninist and Maoist texts which their elders used to memorise, most of them have also become unconvinced of the whole received corpus of the Confucian, Buddhist and Taoist scriptures as well. The more freedom they now have to read the great books of the West and the classics of modern liberalism and capitalism, or to return to the ancient literature of China and the rest of Asia, the less certain they are of the respective value of such writings.

There are, of course, official exhortations to read Marx, Lenin and Mao, and encouragement to understand how to save the revolution by reading the recently published works of Deng Xiaoping. But times have changed. No one really expects any set of books to provide the answers. The entrepreneurship that is now allowed does not look to books for its inspiration.

The Chinese outside China are not better placed to help the Chinese inside with their reading. They are not agreeable with themselves as to which are the classics of ethics, philosophy, politics or economics. The young Chinese students at universities in Hong Kong, Taiwan, Singapore and elsewhere in Southeast Asia would claim to have many different sources of modern wisdom and knowledge. So would those Chinese studying in developed countries like the United States, Canada, Australia, Britain and others in Europe.

Their pluralism is likely to parallel that of their contemporaries of other ethnic backgrounds. Their normal choices would range from the Bible and Aristotle to the *I Ching* (The Book of Change), from Milton Friedman to Foucault and Rushdie. Some may seek their roots in a great Chinese work: possibly Lao Zi and Zhuang Zi (if they want to get away from Confucius), Tang poetry, novels of the Ming-Qing dynasties, or Lu Xun of the 20th century — it is a matter of *personal* choice.

Compared to the Chinese inside China, the offshore and overseas Chinese are more open and eclectic, possibly less bookish and idealistic. But there is little evidence to suggest that they are more, or less, entrepreneurial than their counterparts who have grown up under 40 years of communist rule. Modern education — whether with or without a canon of books — does not seem to have added to or subtracted from Chinese entrepreneurship.

The schools and universities have enabled anyone interested in business careers to read the necessary books, articles, or case analyses, to become economists, accountants, young executives in large companies, thus making potentially good managerial material. But no reading matter or training can be identified to have contributed to producing the kind of entrepreneurship for which the Chinese are renowned.

The traditional Chinese entrepreneur was encouraged by his family to take risks and be enterprising. He invested his profits in creating a business network with other family members and, through connections with local officials, ensured that it sustained the business down the generations. The family provided informal training through practice in the business itself. Through the strong element of trust within the family, the support for potential entrepreneurship was nurtured. Formal, classical education was only sought to enable members of the family to rub shoulders with influential mandarins, some ultimately to join their ranks, others at least to learn to negotiate with them.

The Chinese entrepreneur today ranges more widely. He is as bold as ever, and has a keener knowledge of global affairs. He respects the educated and is aware of modern technology, but can always pay the specialists to exploit it for him. But his entrepreneurship has not changed much. He values his family and such kinship networks that he can find. He seeks and selects from the widest possible sets of connections. His public persona is one of honesty and generosity. He may be a strong supporter of schools and universities, and even send his children to the best that he can find. But it is not in classical texts, nor in formal education, that we would find the secrets of his success.

14

Universities and Modernity for Asia

In my analysis of this critical issue of modernity for Asia and what universities can do to shape that modernity, I shall not deal with the nature and purpose of universities and their development over the centuries although, as an historian, I am immensely interested in how universities came to be what they are today and I believe their history tells us a lot about what they can and cannot do. I shall simply begin by saying that the modern university has evolved in recent times to become one of the major centres of innovation and discovery while retaining its historic task of transmitting tradition and knowledge through scholarly endeavour.

My emphasis on modernity leads me to ask, when did the university itself become modern? When did it begin to claim that it embodies the values of modernity? It is often assumed that the European university is synonymous with modernity. That is not true. The

---

This paper was first delivered at the 20th International Conference on Higher Education held in Universiti Kebangsaan Malaysia on 23 August 2008.

universities in Europe took a long while to become modernised and many universities were fortresses of conservatism until their countries became modern. We need to recognise that it was often external forces that led some universities to accept radical changes and that many universities to this day remain much better at transmitting and conserving than in advancing knowledge.

Modernity stems from the urge to change the ideas and practices of the past and the desire to find better ways of dealing with current and future problems. There have always been some human beings who have had that urge but the earliest institutions of higher education, whether in Europe or in Asia, were not created to allow admission of those people. On the contrary, people who were naturally unconventional and non-conformist were seldom welcome in the centres of learning that concentrated on training their students to respect tradition and where inculcating the wisdom of our fathers was the norm. In the past, we can find a few exceptional examples where someone with dissenting ideas was tolerated and even possibly encouraged for a while. But universities, on the whole, were not initially established for individuals who love to explore the edges of what is knowable.

In short, it was only when important changes had occurred outside the universities and these changes were recognised to be valuable and necessary to the well-being of state and society that some centres of learning began to review their work and allow their brightest scholars to experiment with new ideas and methodologies. One can point to examples like the oldest British universities, namely Oxford and Cambridge, which were slow to accept engineering studies as worthy of their attention until the 20th century and to consider allowing business schools in their midst until only recently. Eventually, these early universities did become convinced that their scholars should not only transmit past virtues but also lead the way to human progress. But serious transformations were not made until well into the 19th century and only followed the advances in geographical discovery and exploration and the rise of science, and the successes of capitalism and what has been called the Industrial Revolution. Many scholars have suggested that the first university that would fit our criteria of what is modern is the University of Berlin founded in 1810 by the reformist educator Wilhelm von Humboldt. It gave strong emphasis to the pursuit of new thinking and knowledge, especially in the natural sciences. It had the advantage of starting anew without the baggage of pre-Enlightenment theological concerns. The probing and thrusting approaches adopted by the thinkers and scientists working at the University of Berlin soon impressed other new universities that were established later in the century, notably among those in the United States.

All the same, it still took the rest of the century before the Berlin model became respectable, and it was not until after the end of the Second World War that governments and other institutions began to encourage universities to adopt increasingly rigorous standards of staff and student recruitment that centred on academic talent and merit. And it was only during the past decade that the model — newly modified and revamped in the United States — was universally applied to all universities in the world by a series of rankings in the so-called "league tables". Today, universities in many parts of the world feel the need to be measured in similar ways in order to gauge where they stand in the list of good universities. Following the remarkable growth in the number of universities around the world, there is suddenly the urgent need to know which are really good universities. This has become increasingly important because teacher-researcher and student mobility is now much greater and the best academics and students are no longer content with their own country's universities unless these can measure up to the best elsewhere. And it is now widely accepted that the criteria of excellence drawn largely on the standards employed in post-1945 developments favoured in the West are generally valid. The basic conditions are how modern the universities' research and teaching facilities are and how capable they are in attracting the best faculty and students.

The questions for universities in Asia are many, so I shall confine to the following questions that concern those universities that wish to confront issues of modernity: What kind of modernity should universities be committed to? Should they accept the dominant criteria identified in the developed West? How far should universities go to pursue the goal of modernity?

I need hardly remind you that the great majority of modern universities in Asia were established after 1945. But a quick look at some of those that were established earlier is instructive. For example, the Catholic Church which founded Asia's earliest college in 1611 was turned into a university. The University of Santo Tomas in Manila was established to train young men for the priesthood and the model was that of the traditional university in Spain. The question of modernity did not arise until the 20th century. On the other hand, the first universities in British India — in Calcutta, Madras and Bombay — founded in the middle of the 19th century were aimed at modernising India along British lines and the University of London was the direct model. They were followed soon after the turn of the 20th century by dozens of colleges and universities, including some that experimented with the merging of Indian and European ideas and values, most notably Tagore's university, the Visva Bharati University at Santiniketan. We can say that these early universities attained modernity if we agree that having several Nobel laureates among their alumni is relevant.

Similarly the Japanese looked to the West to free themselves from the Confucian traditions of education and their first four universities — Tokyo, Keio, Kyoto and Waseda — looked first to Europe and later to the United States. Again, several Nobel laureates took their first degrees at these early universities, marking a high level of modernity. The Chinese took longer to respond to the colleges that North American missionaries established in several Chinese cities during the last two decades of the 19th century. But when they finally did so at the turn of the century, all the institutions were designed to learn from the West, notably from the United States, Britain, France and Japan. Again, several Chinese Nobel laureates had studied under excellent teachers at these Chinese universities, including under the faculty who transplanted to National Taiwan University after 1949. As for the small colonial colleges and universities in Hong Kong, Burma, Indo-China, the Philippines, Korea, Taiwan, Singapore and the Netherlands East Indies, their purpose was to introduce modern languages and material culture to their students. For all of them, the goal was modernisation, especially to prepare students to provide services in the fields of medicine, science and engineering.

This brief reminder of developments before 1945 is to emphasise that the university in Asia was, from the start, introduced to help modernise the countries in which they were established. There is no question that newer universities have been built since then to achieve the same goals. And as secondary schools educate more of the young, the need to expand the universities and build many new ones became ever more urgent. It is time to ask and address the questions I mentioned earlier.

First, what kind of modernity should universities be committed to?

The earliest universities in Asia were concerned mainly to master the modernity of science and technology. The leaders who supported them were, on the whole, confident that the traditional values of their respective societies could stand up to the tests of modernity and that much of their heritage would survive if not even prosper with the fresh inputs of modern ideas and institutions. The Indian, Japanese and Chinese elites of the time came to welcome the challenge and were optimistic of a renaissance for their cultures. The formula was as follows: Sort out the good in tradition and the best of the modern, and great things will flow from that experience. Indeed, we can point to the many successes in universities all over Asia that everyone acknowledges are remarkable for their innovative approaches and their research results.

There is another hopeful note. It is from the universities established more than a century ago that most of our Asian Nobel laureates had their start in research-based education. As newer universities continue to make scholarly progress, could they also not expect the same in time? I am confident that they could. All the same, two factors must be taken into account. One is the depth and range of the global process of modernisation that universities face today. It is a modernity that is comprehensive with great outreach, and it seems to demand commitments that are deeper than what our predecessors confronted decades earlier. The other is that, not only will universities that want to be modern cost more, but also the desire of faculty and students to achieve higher goals will call for further investments of time and money. Do countries have the capacity and will to face these demands?

Clearly very few can afford to finance all universities to such high standards. If I am right, then those countries that cannot do that would have to make choices and be selective about what aspects of modernity should be given top priority. In the long run, global divisions of human and natural resources will seek to produce optimal and less wasteful results. But, already it is obvious that most individual nations cannot achieve such results by themselves. Adapting to globalisation is therefore necessary. This could be precarious if each nation is to face the complex demands of change alone. Clearly, there is the need for greater cooperation and pooling of limited resources — either by linking with the strongest universities wherever they may be, or by grouping regionally to consolidate limited resources. Of course, universities can do both if they really want to. The challenge then is for the interlinking universities to know what kinds of modernity they can effectively share.

This leads to my second question. Should universities in Asia today continue to accept the criteria of excellence identified in the developed West?

Remember that the earliest universities in India, Japan and China generally accepted the criteria that applied to science and technology, and many of them produced excellent results; in China's case, this was despite the fact that its revolutionary programmes derailed the growth trajectories of many universities, and made the road to modernity more difficult and uncertain for a quite a while. What proves to be noteworthy is that, after all that, the Chinese have returned to the key criteria of excellence, again in the natural sciences, back to the best practices that they have identified in the leading universities of the West, especially in the United States. Despite the sensitive political relations and disputes in residual ideological principles, universities in China and the West can now communicate with one another at almost all levels. That would seem to be the solution. We could just go on doing more of the same.

Except that nothing is quite the same. For example, the earliest universities did not go beyond the standards of mathematics and the natural sciences. And indeed, these are the areas where interchange of ideas and experimental results still flow most freely. Some scholars ventured forth into areas pertaining to political economy, but they could not always do so with conviction. As a result, they often failed to understand the complex nature of Western civilisation beyond the sciences. The consequences were that many Asians overestimated Western competence in some areas and underestimated the cultural values that underpinned modern scientific methods. An example of overestimation is the expectation that Western elites would understand the cultures of Asia and learn to respect them. A good example of underestimation is when many Asian leaders did not realise how important Western culture is to its modern successes — it is not merely machines and methodologies.

We can see how these issues are reflected in universities with the apparent retreat of the humanities and the rapid rise of the social sciences. How should we read that? Earlier generations, notably in China and India, believed that, through studying the humanities in universities, their cultural traditions would be enhanced. If there is indeed growing neglect of such studies today, cultural growth in both Asia and the West may both suffer. I do not, however, believe that there is imminent danger of that happening. Cultural interactions take time to fructify, and given the rise of popular cultures, such interactions are now occurring more outside universities than within. In the end, it is the intrinsic vigour of each culture that determines the kinds of culture that will prosper and those that will not. As long as universities continue to transmit heritage with critical attention to its uniqueness and are ready to accept new ideas, I am confident that humanities will remain a major source of cultural enrichment for all concerned.

What appears less clear is with the use of the social sciences. Here there are no counterparts in Asian traditions of knowledge. The social sciences represent the most modern, if also the least reliable, manifestation of scientific methodologies. They do not have the certainties of the natural sciences, nor do they provide the aesthetic and imaginative bridges of the humanities. They strive to offer approximations of reality but, more often than not, they leave the practitioners, the scholars and their students, stranded in disputation and confusion. Social science enquiries are often no more than efforts at philosophical and theoretical analyses with the artistry and beauty taken out.

Yet this is probably the most modern and original expression of the Western sensibility. That sensibility is something that universities and scholars in Japan, India and now China have found very difficult to explain to their local and national clients and communities. If what Asian social scientists produce remain nothing more than extensions of the outputs of Western universities, the practitioners may find themselves caught between accepting Western authority and facing growing scepticism among their own consumers. If that happens, the place of the social sciences in their universities will be their weakest link. This would be the area where dependence on external criteria of excellence could actually cripple the position of the modern university in Asia.

Perhaps one could ask, how far should universities go to pursue the goal of modernity?

I have suggested that, in the natural sciences, we can go for the furthest limits. The criteria here are clear and unlikely to change much. It is a question largely of investment in facilities and talent; the methods used to maximise results in these areas are well known, and deception and subjectivity would be difficult, and in any case, rare. Where talent is concerned, however, a university should be left to judge for itself. A good university is easy to recognise here. Its transparency in the use of objective criteria can ensure that it selects and uses talent fairly and effectively. In the humanities, there is more give and take. Cultures that are dynamic and alive tend to merge and interrelate, and ultimately enhance each other's real strengths. Dissonances may always be present but very few of such differences are irreconcilable. Ultimately, radically different cultures can coexist for long periods of time. And even if they do not move closer together despite continuous contact, there is usually little damage done to the people who teach these cultures or to those who set out to learn.

That is not so with the social sciences. Modern universities have been innovative here as they try to adapt the rules of scientific method in order to study human society and behaviour, and to analyse political and economic conflict and competition. Here Western social scientists work within their value systems, however hard they try to avoid any open display of them. The simple reason is that their societies live with implicit assumptions about what individuals want and value, and how individuals behave. Each society might carry variations but the underlying premises of how decisions might be made and changed are tied to the traditions that their societies had evolved over the centuries. In that context, their efforts to universalise social theories and policies are invariably subverted by habits of the mind, and the social and moral expectations they are rooted in.

This should not be misunderstood as any kind of denial of social science as a modern methodology. I admire what the social scientists have been able to achieve despite the vagaries of thought and action that characterise the thousands of individual decisions that determine social patterns. It is a slippery turf to work in and it is remarkable what some of the scholars have been able to do to influence events around the world. What remains troubling for universities in Asia that want to achieve such modernity is that there are no equivalent assumptions to help the transfer of hypotheses developed from phenomena in Europe or North America to Asian developments with any degree of confidence. As long as that is true, this is an area of contestation that universities must carefully examine if they wish to use social sciences to help bring modernity to Asia. The way social science in Asia has assumed that conditions in the West and Asia are comparable is beginning to wear thin. If the universities in Asia cannot handle the different underlying conditions, there will be areas of modernity that cannot be bridged across the East-West divide.

I shall conclude by saying that the hard question is whether there are universities in Asia in which the scholars and their students have the will to find new vitality in their own traditions to help them master the new tools of the social sciences. This is an area that can be most important for Asians in their quest for modernity. If they can harmonise the cultural underpinnings in Asian and European traditions, they can also help to shape a new modernity. That would be a major step towards making our quest for a universal humanity more achievable.

15

New Interest in Old Powers

A shift in the way Asians study Europe has changed for the first time in a century.

Encounters among officials, academics, artists and businessmen have confirmed the growing interest in Europe since the first Asia-Europe Meeting (ASEM) in Bangkok in March 1996.

Universities in Asia have been busy activating their European courses, from language and history to a wide range of social science questions about the European experience.

The earliest and most significant response to Europe came from the Japanese. The speed at which Japan sent its bright young men to Britain and Germany to master the secrets of wealth and power was breathtaking.

China followed close behind, but was far less systematic because the Manchu Qing dynasty fell and the new republic founded in 1911 was

---

This article was first published in the 20 September 1999 issue of the *Times Higher Education Supplement*. Reproduced with the kind permission of *Times Higher Education* magazine.

hijacked by warring generals. Divided China had no budget and even less vision, so students tended to go to the United States or Japan. A few went to Europe but it was obvious that not many had studied, as the Japanese did, with their national interest uppermost in their minds.

The only other country in Asia that was not colonised was Thailand. It followed parts of the Japanese model, but its interests were different. More concerned for the country's survival than for the strength to challenge Western power, Thai rulers preferred to send their brightest to France, Britain and Switzerland, rather than to Germany.

As for the rest of Asia under colonial rule, they predictably were allowed to send only a few students to the colleges of their European masters.

There were two exceptions. Higher-class Indians did get to Britain in significant numbers and they returned with a picture of Europe that only the British had. They in turn imparted the same image of British superiority and apartness to the elites of lesser colonies such as Ceylon and the Malay states. The other exception was the Philippines after the Americans took over from the Spanish. Its education was so transformed that Europe was seen entirely through US glasses.

Colonials of the Dutch and the French fared better, but it is still remarkable how little they knew about the rest of Europe outside the Netherlands and France. A few enterprising nationalists sought the larger picture as they wondered how their colonial powers were to be driven away. For this, they turned to alternative "Europeans", such as Britain, Germany and Russia. Failing that, they looked to Japan, an Asianised version of Europe.

These made up the broken pieces of the European heritage when decolonisation came after the end of the Second World War. Even less remained when Japan led the way by turning to the United States and China chose to side with the "European" heresies of the Soviet Union. Having to repair what survived of Europe after the war meant that the Europeans themselves had less to offer to those in Asia who were thirsting to learn from the West. Strong nationalists wanted to look for new sources of economic and technological development.

How then was Europe taught in courses at their new universities? At one level, the negative picture of Europe, whose people once thought they were superior, was sustained. But that was quickly replaced by a more abstract rendering of things progressive as coming from "the West".

This helped to displace colonial memories, and depending on political leanings, it allowed the United States and the Soviet Union to enter the education frameworks all over Asia without removing "Europe" from its historical position as the source of modern civilisation.

Many Western European countries have never really left the shores of Asia. They continue to be trading powers, and even while they are negotiating for their own security as a new regional bloc, they still tend to represent themselves as competing nations, albeit far less aggressively than in the past. In addition, Britain, France and Germany are still successfully projecting their cultural heritage in schools, colleges and universities wherever they are allowed to.

But except in the humanities — notably literature, philosophy, history and the fine arts — the Europeans have found it increasingly difficult to make a distinctive impact on Asian education. Too much of the heritage of progress is subsumed in a global Anglo-American body of knowledge and skills. Non-English-speaking Europe is fighting back as best it can, but its babel of voices has remained a handicap. For several decades in Asia, contemporary Europe is rarely seen as an example of scientific advancement.

With the reconfiguration of Asian-European linkages through ASEM, however, there is now a chance for old Europe to be replaced by a new Europe. This is not just because studying Europe has become fashionable.

What is new is the idea that the powers that had introduced almost all aspects of "modernity" and secular education into various parts of Asia still have something to teach. This is in the area of region-building in an era of global linkages. Suddenly, the efforts of the European Union to revive new kinds of European studies among Asian universities have begun to bear fruit. In a curiously modest and tentative way, Europe is returning to Asian tertiary education as a kind of "area studies". Thus, it begins with language, culture and history, and then the added issues of finance and economics, various unfinished social experiments and questions of political compromises. Can this challenge bring Asian students back to the new Europe?

16

Change and Adaptation: NUS at 100

A personal perspective

My former office[1] in a corner of Kent Ridge campus next to the Guild House has a sharp-angled view of the National University of Singapore (NUS) today. What I saw was a far cry from what the university looked like when I started as a freshman on the day the University of Malaya was founded at Bukit Timah in 1949. That has made me think often about the university and its future. I should begin with the reason why I agreed to write this commemorative essay. I stayed five years on the old Raffles College campus till 1954, so I can claim to have a perspective that come from the midpoint of NUS history, just about 50 years either way. But the

---

This essay was first published as "Inception, Origins, Contemplations: a Personal Perspective", in *Imagination, Openness & Courage: The National University of Singapore at 100*, Singapore: National University of Singapore, 2006, pp 1–31. Reproduced with the kind permission of National University of Singapore.

[1] The East Asian Institute was previously located at the Faculty of Arts and Social Sciences until 2007 when it was moved to its present site at the Bukit Timah campus, home to predecessors of NUS, namely Raffles College, the University of Malaya and the University of Singapore.

neat balance is illusory. I knew little about the first 50 years when the colleges, the King Edward VII College of Medicine from 1905 and Raffles College from 1928, were small and slow to grow, although I did get to hear some bright and fragmentary anecdotes. The university grew at a much quicker pace after that and is today among the biggest of its kind in the world. Although I was largely an observer from afar until 1996, my interest in NUS remained.

Let me begin with that midpoint in 1949. When I started as a freshman, three-quarters of my fellow students were from the two colleges. Except for the very few of the earliest graduates who were deceased, all those who received their licentiates and diplomas from the two colleges were still alive and active at the time. I particularly recall meeting Dr Chen Su Lan (who graduated in 1910 and was the first person named on the NUS Register of Graduates) who spoke affectionately of his medical teachers. Also, two of those who were awarded diplomas by Raffles College in 1931, were my teachers at Anderson School in Ipoh. Thus, I felt a sense of belonging to the then new university that was more than just freshman awe. Through me, it would seem a thread of continuity was linking the alumni of the two colleges together with generations of students to come. Altogether, 150 freshmen celebrated that Foundation Day. Not without a sense of self-importance, I felt that our class was to add fibres to a rope that would pull the university forward.

Like many others, I did graduate research elsewhere, at the University of London and the University of Cambridge. The two campuses were very different from the postcolonial university that Malaya was hoping to build. We were shown what we ought to aim for and what to avoid, and the models to be followed were etched on our minds. I, for one, confidently believed that I understood what the idea of a university meant. When I returned to teach in 1957, there were many more students and many of the junior academics were local. But, the most striking change was that the University of Malaya was about to be divided and some of us were asked to teach at the new campus in the new Federation of Malaya.

It was a new start that unexpectedly led me to work in three universities for the next 37 years. After Malaya, I went to the Australian National University (ANU) followed by the University of Hong Kong. This was not as promiscuous as it might appear. Underlying the differences in peoples, cultures and localities was a basic Commonwealth model of how to organise an institution of higher learning. Had I not twice had the chance to teach in the United Sates and also spent a research year in a quaint college in Oxford, I might have well believed that preserving the red-brick Commonwealth system was all that mattered. In fact, all three universities that I worked in were undergoing radical changes: the University of Malaya under the pressure of Malay nationalism, the ANU facing strident calls for egalitarianism and the University of Hong Kong caught between returning to the motherland and reaching out to the best universities in North America.

Thus, when I came to work in Singapore again in 1996, I was no longer an innocent where universities were concerned. Of course, I was never too far away. When I was in Kuala Lumpur, I was a regular visitor to Singapore. When Singapore was part of the new Federation of Malaysia, I was asked to chair the Curriculum Revision Committee of Nanyang University. For the first five months of 1965, I visited Singapore every few weeks and the committee submitted its report not long before the separation of Singapore that August. The committee was determined that Malaysia should have a strong third university. The last thing on its members' minds was that Nanyang University would eventually merge with the University of Singapore to become NUS.

I imagine I was not alone in this, but an independent Singapore had been inconceivable in my youth. When it actually happened, I watched that tiny state survive and grow from afar with increasing amazement. I was also fascinated by the twists and turns experienced by Singapore's universities during that transformative period. It is too early to judge whether the universities have been as successful as the city-state, but there is no question in my mind that they all tackled the many challenges they faced with a strange mixture of verve and stoic resilience. When I was in Canberra and subsequently in Hong Kong, I was farther away from and a less frequent visitor to Singapore. But I remained in touch with my fellow graduates and some of my students who stayed on to teach in Singapore. I was always happy to visit the campus whenever I came to Singapore and that averaged about twice every three years for some 28 years. For a few months in 1981, my dear friend Wong Lin Ken, then Raffles Professor of History, invited me to teach for a term. That was when I first got to know the then new Kent Ridge campus and those months rekindled my feeling of being part of the university again. Thereafter, my wife and I joined in several alumni reunions. We thus relived our student years of the early 1950s when Singapore's future was far less secure, when impending changes were dressed in uncertainty and when only students were optimistic enough to believe that the university would always be a beacon for progress and enlightenment.

Now that the university had gone past its 100th anniversary, the question is whether the university has reached a new maturity to cope with the rest of the 21s century. As I learned over the decades at the universities I worked in or visited, most of them have been forced to adjust to rapid changes. Whether they met each change head-on, fighting unwelcome changes thrust upon it or adapting to and benefiting from their impact, or they initiated the changes themselves, this has become something like the norm for universities today. In any case, being ready to change and being forced to change are new conditions. Some universities have lived through change for hundreds of years only to become stronger and more forward-looking. Others, on the other hand, have been content to go on in traditional ways when the world around them had changed and they have barely survived. A few simply lost their way because they could not innovate and compete with their more alert peers. But the pace of change has speeded up considerably in recent years and to respond quickly is now a much more challenging task.

Of course, no university can be sure how and what to change. Over the past hundred years, NUS has provided us with a good example of an institution that got some changes right and others wrong. But that it has changed beyond recognition makes its story worth telling again and again. That story has been told at several levels. The alumni and students have provided us with their nostalgic memories. Former faculty and administrators have written on behalf of the university or left us with their own accounts of what they had or had not done. And there is a wide range of records. At one end, there are the whole series of official documents that enabled the colleges and universities to become legal entities. These include the Carr Saunders Report that recommended the merger of two colleges in Singapore to form the University of Malaya in 1949. On the other, numerous accounts may be found in the local press in four languages, not to mention the student and alumni papers and magazines that date back to the beginning of the 20th century.

This essay has benefited from the many stories that different generations have already told, including the oral interviews that the NUS had arranged to do. One of the newer works of history has also been the most complete. This is the book by Edwin Lee and Tan Tai Yong, *Beyond Degrees: The Making of the National University of*

Singapore (1996). It provides the liveliest account yet of the development of the university from its two small colleges to one now ambitious to be a major international institution. That book is available for anyone who wants to follow the university's story. I shall take that as read and only focus on the NUS that struggled, and is struggling, to adapt to the changing conditions of Singapore, its neighbourhood and the world beyond.

It must be clear now how much a university man I am. I entered my first university at the age of 17 and have never left one ever since. This has made me believe that the modern university is an extraordinary institution and one of the most significant in a rapidly globalising world. No society can afford not to have one. Many countries have hundreds if not thousands. For this part of the world, the astonishing rise of the university has yet to be told. There was only a handful as late as the 1950s. Now it would seem that we could not build and expand them fast enough to meet demand. The key to a successful university, however, seems to me not to be its size or its longevity or its beautiful location, though each helps to support a dynamic campus. The ultimate test is the quality of its graduates and the scholarly tradition it generates. In order to do that, each university has to be open to new ideas and engage with all the forces, local, national and global, that can impact on its development.

The main theme of this essay is change and adaptation in Singapore and in the NUS. It will be in two parts. The first will deal with Singapore's social and political transformations and how the aspirations at each stage of its development shaped the growth of NUS. The second part will look at the university itself, the people in it and the education goals that helped it find its own identity. Inevitably, questions of how the university serves and represents different interested communities in and outside of Singapore will come up in each part.

Did Singapore always know what kind of university it should have? I doubt it. There was more than one Singapore. The colony trading port serving the region provided one kind of environment for any kind of education. The architects of decolonisation after 1945, however, had urgent needs and wanted a university that could service a stable state structure. Then came the sudden nationhood and the institution had to change course radically. Finally, the country's graduation to first world status requiring the nation to play a distinctive role in the global league led to different expectations again. I offer here my perspective of what all that means.

The Horizons of Different Singapores

The first Singapore

I am aware how little attention most Singaporeans today pay to questions of history. Apart from nostalgia, many may ask, what has the first Singapore before the Second World War got to do with the NUS? By today's standards, the two colleges never had enough money to provide the specialised teachers and laboratories that the students needed. The graduates received diplomas that were not recognised outside Malaya. The few who chose to serve the government would always be sub-professionals under young officials with degrees from Britain. What is there to be proud of? Would it not be more merciful to turn the page and concentrate on our glorious future?

A lack of a sense of history, in my view, could be fatal for any country. For better or worse, the success story that ultimately shaped a Singapore with few natural resources is linked to the history of its higher education. This is not simply because many of the post-war leaders had been students and alumni of the two colleges, although that alone is remarkable. More importantly, it is for us to understand three questions for this early period: Why two colleges and not a university? How did these two help lay the foundations of a viable plural society? To what extent were the small steps taken embedded in the state structure that independent Singapore built on?

Singapore today cannot be understood without recognising that it began its political life as the key city in the Straits Settlements, a British colony that actively sought to dominate a clutch of Malay States. Although this emerging Malaya was formed only at the tail end of imperial expansion, it was put together with immense confidence. It was a complex matrix that pushed aggressively towards a federal protectorate of four Malay States. By 1909, four years after it had built the first of the two colleges of Singapore, this subset of empire had added five more Malay States that each guarded its interests in a distinctive way. What would such an administrative mishmash need colleges for? There had not been anything like an institution of higher learning in this region. Riverine kings and opportunistic merchants of the day did not need one, nor did immigrant and transient workers who were struggling to find work. The British already controlled the largest maritime empire the world had ever known then. They had access to greater capital and labour markets than any other powers. Why would they invest their money to educate their workers to think and to question?

Even an empire at its apogee must face changing demands. Singapore and its appendages had experienced decades of rapid economic growth during the second half of the 19th century. The settled population now admired Western progress and the opportunities that modern ideas brought. English education would give them upward social mobility. There were more new schools and teachers were imported from Britain, India and Ceylon, and also from China. At the same time, British officials and businesses set higher standards of productivity. In the plural society that emerged, more families wanted professional training for their children. Thus the local-born — the well-established Straits Chinese, the Eurasians, the educated few from South Asia and the newly awakened Malay-Arab leadership that was then linked to the newly acquired networks of the Malay States — called for colleges and universities.

Why medicine? If colonial subjects were not those who aspired after power and authority in government, the medical profession offered status, respectable service and self-employment. It also appealed to those who had no respect or stomach for business. A medical college produced trained hands to serve an expanding British Malaya where the key tin industry, joined by a new rubber industry, spawned dozens of new entrepreneurs and brought in hundreds of thousands of workers. Here one sees the underlying pragmatism that has always guided the development of higher education. If so, why not law? Or engineering? Neither was offered for another 50 years. With law, the British thought it was premature to teach common law to people ignorant of the rule of law. As for engineering, it was enough to have trade schools and technical colleges. After all, even in Britain, the elitist universities were themselves reluctant to award engineering degrees.

Another refrain was also heard. Britain was unaffordable for most. A few could hope to attend universities in Madras, Calcutta or Bombay. Some began to look to Hong Kong where three fields of study were available, those of medicine, engineering and education. It is hard to imagine today how difficult it was before 1941 for students to go abroad to study. In the end, the colonial officials went further and agreed to establish Raffles College for the training of teachers in the arts and sciences. Like medicine, the numbers admitted were very few and the diplomas offered were worth nothing outside Malaya.

The colleges were never meant to meet the needs of the several communities in Malaya. Students were carefully selected partly on merit and also partly to ensure that the trained locals could really help the British to rule a mixed population. The colleges thus catered only to the few English schools in the colony and even fewer in the Malay States. No attention was paid to the future of students from the vernacular schools. The gap between them and the English schools had become obvious in the 1920s. In Singapore, it was only a matter of time before the graduates of the increasing numbers of Chinese high schools would ask for the same opportunities. In the Malay States, educated Malays would increasingly feel neglected. But the British persisted in their policy and this set the framework for ruling a plural society that became the hallmark for governing postcolonial Singapore. The British had not anticipated such an outcome, but their technocratic demands of the two colleges helped to lay the groundwork for post-war decolonisation. It became clear after 1945 that these early graduates were the people to whom they would have to leave their heritage.

The second Singapore

I see two phases in a second Singapore. The tutelage phase was when several groups of contenders for the succession to British power were getting ready to take over. This was followed by the control phase when a group of graduates of the two colleges and the university won the struggle to inherit British rule. But a number of choices were present in both phases. Would Singapore have to be an integral part of a Malay-led Malaysia? Could Singapore choose to be an essentially Chinese state? Was there a contradiction between the class-based divisions of non-communal politics and the ethnically based plural society formation that the British had shaped?

All three questions are relevant to the merging of the two colleges to become the University of Malaya, something that would not have happened if the Pacific War had ended differently. Speculation about other outcomes would not be helpful, but it is important to remember that the university began as part of the retreat from the empire. Once the British knew they had to go, they needed to ensure its future place in the post-imperial world. Who should be allowed to take over? Of the three questions mentioned, finding the right people to preserve the plural society formation was the clearly favoured path. This was the concern that determined the nature of the University of Malaya and was the central fact that explains the transition years of the two colleges from 1945 to 1949 and the turbulent years of the new university in the 1950s. They became the years readying people to manage independence in the framework of the Commonwealth. The older students who rejoined the colleges after the end of the war and the new generation of post-war school leavers were the chosen ones. British officials and teachers now expected these graduates to eventually fill the key positions when they left.

The British were still in control and this gave a keen advantage to those who shared their vision of a kind of multinational state. Of course, such a vision was contested by both the Malay- and Chinese-educated. Even among the graduates of the two colleges, there was no consensus. Those who recalled the grim stories of an alternative Japanese empire could not agree on what should follow with the British leaving. Some looked to the independence of India and others to the emergence of Melayu Raya together with peoples of the Netherlands East Indies who had been divided from the Malays of the peninsula for over a hundred years. But, for Singapore, the most difficult disconnect was among the Chinese. Among them were many who were educated in English schools but increasing numbers were educated in Chinese schools. For the former, the picture of British vulnerability was a terrible shock. It led them to rethink their future in the region after the British were gone. For the latter, many other emotional strands guided their lives. There was the trauma of racial discrimination in which Japanese fears of the Chinese anger against them led to killings and terror tactics and tested the loyalties of young and old within the Chinese community. There was the excitement of a revolution that would unite China and begin a new era. Hence the rise of rebellious sentiments directed against the return of the British and the intensified discrimination against them. In the field of education, what the Chinese really wanted was a university that represented their interests.

The fate of the second Singapore remained mainly in British hands for nearly 20 years after 1945. It is a measure of their forward thinking that they concentrated on developing, however belatedly, a postcolonial elite that would help them keep their global influence. It was not a vision they shared with most people in Singapore. It came from their sense of empire, one that would guarantee an effective system of open markets and free trade that the British themselves had done so much to establish. Their experiences in India and elsewhere had taught them that this was in their best long-term interests and that it was achievable through the dissemination of Western ideas, values and institutions. There was little time to lose and the Carr-Saunders Commission acted quickly. In Singapore, most of the graduates of the two colleges and the university could see that they had been given a decisive role to play in the next phase of the second Singapore.

There were many who could not reconcile the idea of education for nationhood with that of being trained to serve future British interests in Malaya. Life on campus became a curious amalgam. On one side, there were all the playful and creative things that undergraduates were wont to do. On the other, there were overt and covert political debates. The latter was not as fervent as might have been. An Emergency had been proclaimed under which dissent was seen as supporting the communist enemy. But, with growing skill, subversive books were being read and contrary ideas discussed. Student activities edged towards acceptable limits. A few followed some alumni into action groups that ended with various periods of detention. For the British, it was reassuring that only the minority took the path of class struggle. The rest were found to be promising material as future administrators, and the plural society solution was gaining ground. On the shoulders of new graduates would fall the task of keeping communal nationalism in check and having the new state successfully reject the appeal of communism.

In this second Singapore, the university that still served an increasingly independent Federation of Malaya (established since 1948) had to perform some contradictory tasks. On the one hand, the colony needed graduates who were secular and progressive, and committed to the plural society. On the other, it also expected its graduates to take on the task of nation-building of an independent Malaya. The inherent tensions were impossible for a single university to deal with. The national mission had at its core a Malayness for which the University of Malaya of the 1950s had little to offer. The students projected a plural society goal that the new leaders in Kuala Lumpur did not want. Dividing the university into two was inevitable under such conditions. Significantly, it was not simply a physical and rational division for the pursuit of academic compatibility and efficacy. The half that was left behind then had to change course to meet the demands of the second Singapore.

But what could this Singapore do? No one was confident that it could do it alone as an independent new nation-state. Its size and dependent economy would make it too vulnerable to both Malaya and Indonesia. The wisdom of the day was for Singapore to be rejoined to all the remaining parts of what the British still held in Southeast Asia. By so doing, Singapore's Chinese could also be contained from radical revolutionary ideas coming out of Mao Zedong's China and the spreading Cold War. The Chinese in the colony had already established their university in 1955, the Nanyang University. This was meant to meet the needs of the graduates of the numerous Chinese schools that were set up all over the Malay Archipelago. The communist victory in 1949 made it impossible for most of them to study in China. Although the British reluctantly agreed, this did not suit their plans at all. In addition, such a university was also against the interests of Malay nationalists who were set to build a new nation based on indigenous foundations.

The brief interlude in Malaysia led the second Singapore to another phase. Although mercifully brief, the interlude did have political repercussions for the two universities. Ejection from Malaysia meant that another set of questions had to be asked. What kind of new nation should Singapore's plural society become? If Malaysia, with just over half its population Malay, could seek to be a nation based on Malay special rights, could the Chinese majority in Singapore not claim something similar?

The times were not propitious for such a claim. Fear of communist China was widespread in the region. The new leaders of the government knew what the outcome for Singapore would be if they pursued that claim. The key contradiction was found in what Nanyang University stood for. An independent Singapore that was a Chinese mirror image of a Malay Malaysia was deemed not to be viable. Whatever admiration Singapore leaders might have had for the tough-minded and resilient spirit of Nanyang University, they chose to persist with the plural society way as embodied in the slogan of Malaysian Malaysia. Making that choice led them to prefer the University of Singapore model and to policies that ultimately forced the two universities to merge. That was done after a damaging confrontation that the leaders had to win if their particular vision of a plural society was to prevail. It was a striking case of university education becoming the battleground for the future shape of a nation.

The university was caught between an ideological war in the region and narrow ethnic and national ambitions both within and outside the country. It had to be protected from the terrorism of the Emergency years, the ethnic nightmares of the 1950s and the murderous riots of the 1960s. But this also produced a curious paradox in the 1970s. The threat of continuous politicisation on its campus was systematically removed. As the ruling People's Action Party gained fuller control over the levers of government, the university was directed to concentrate on producing graduates to serve the administrative and developmental state. The boundaries of a multicultural society were firmly drawn. Singapore turned away from active use of communal languages and cultures towards English, making it not only the official language, but also one that enables its people to reach out to the larger world on which Singapore's future depended.

Independent Singapore chose the Spartan route to success and fought its battle for survival by taking the first steps towards an engineering and business-centred culture. In particular, novel experiments in various industrial estates, notably in Jurong, demanded a different kind of university. Development priorities were changed with new emphasis given to new faculties of engineering and commerce, and a parallel growth of polytechnics. A definite bias towards improving the hardware needs of the nation led to a concomitant decline in what were considered the softer areas of knowledge. The most telling consequence of the new policy was the shift from a policy of placing the country's best students in the local university to one that sent the best students to institutions of excellence abroad.

In two respects, this was the continuation of past trends. From the start, there had been the elitism preferred by the British when the two colleges were established and during the first years of the University of Malaya. Now, deeply underlining the Confucian values that the government leaned towards was the meritocracy of the mandarinate. Together, they highlighted an academic elitism meant to enable certain qualities to be identified and given recognition early. For the NUS, however, this was the hardest blow to its hope of becoming the pinnacle of education in the country. The failure to attract the best Singapore students to study there inevitably projected a weakness it did not need. It was still far from being an outstanding university. The consequences for its international status as a university that most of the country's best students were discouraged from studying in were disabling. I still wonder if this was the necessary price the university simply had to pay for the third Singapore to be born.

The third Singapore

It is hard to date the rise of the third Singapore. Broadly it coincides with the time when Singapore began to be widely seen as a first world country.

This happened when Singapore was able to recover swiftly from the economic downturn of the mid-1980s. That exceptional capacity was confirmed when Singapore's resilience was tested, again with relative success, with the financial crisis of 1997–1998. The new changes that challenged the NUS were associated with Singapore's rise to first world status. The success story of the nation had thrust the university towards the threshold of global significance. By locating a series of well-funded scientific research institutes on the campus, the government placed the university among some of the best in Asia. In this way, the NUS had been associated with the frontline work of a number of practical fields that could match those in the better universities in the West. There had also been other pushes. There are now three universities and more institutions have been encouraged to come forth to ensure that this third Singapore can fulfil its ambitions.

For the teaching faculties of all these universities, they can be counted on to produce key personnel for the management of state and economy. They have all contributed systematically to Singapore's industrial growth. Certainly, it will be a long time before other institutions in Southeast Asia can match the NUS in resources and facilities and in its drawing power for students, academic teachers and researchers. The university could well be content with that achievement and choose simply to maintain that regional edge long into the future.

But there is another choice for the NUS, at once more demanding and more exciting. Beyond the quality markers that are linked to the country's image, this third Singapore aims to reach greater heights in several ways. In addition to being a Southeast Asian hub for multinationals, it seeks to become a useful if not indispensable connection to the two other regions of East and South Asia. In that way, the country could better ensure its future prosperity by being able to provide the necessary links for the major global networks. This new Singapore would expect the NUS to play its part in at least two ways, one immediate and the other more long-term. The first is to mark the NUS as the apex of a major and flourishing education industry, endorsing its brand-name undergraduate degree as one of excellent value. This is to be followed by a wider recognition that its master's degrees, notably in the business and engineering fields that the government has so fully encouraged, have high market value. Here Singapore has already gained the respect of students beyond the immediate Southeast Asian region. However, in other fields like the physical sciences, humanities and the social sciences, there are greater problems. This is partly because these fields have less mass appeal and partly because there is a perception that Singapore itself has paid them little attention. But there is growing awareness that the country has inherent strengths here. What it still needs to show is that these fields have comparative advantage because of not only Singapore's location but also a readiness to face a culturally more complex world.

The longer-term goals could build on the more immediate successes. This would require not merely some incremental changes. It would also be necessary for a research culture to emerge in Singapore. Already the country has made a commitment to compete internationally in areas that demand innovation and originality. Strong calls have been made for research centres to join the league of competitive institutions the world over to vie for the best possible students and itself produce some of Singapore's future talent. There have been admonitions for universities to position themselves in order to obtain the kinds of research grants that could attract and retain first-class academic faculty.

It is increasingly clear that, in order to lift any university beyond locality and region, an essential ingredient is to be always open to new ideas and people. Its staff and students would have been assured of the kind of freedom that has carried the great universities for long periods of time. Singapore has now decided that the education system would have to be structured to enable such an environment to prevail. It will take time for these conditions to be fulfilled and no one can guarantee that, as a result, fundamental advances to knowledge will be made. But it is encouraging that the third Singapore now understands that, without such conditions, scholarship would not flourish. Even so, a thorough change of mindset at all levels would be needed and this calls for all the social engineering skills that Singapore is known for.

Academic Transitions

I shall turn to the university itself. I have touched on the way the state and society of Singapore moulded the university to the shape they wanted. The practical details of adjusting curricula, expanding faculties and facilities, recruiting academic staff and retraining them if necessary are well known, and in the higher education system of the British Commonwealth, there are ready models provided that can be easily adapted to fit local forms. The uniformity was an asset that saved having to reinvent the wheel besides some transaction costs. An education industry complex centred in

London had evolved, ensuring that the right parts are almost always available somewhere in the Commonwealth for each member state to pick and choose, and adjust for a better fit. Although NUS dispensed with its official help early, the model was effective for several decades.

In short, using a ready-made network was an efficient way to gain international knowledge and master the ways that knowledge could be transmitted and discovered. But, in the end, the university has to face the challenges of a reawakening region and a globalising world. It has to become an institution that has its own distinct identity. In the course of achieving this identity, the university has woven in and out of the national and global networks that Singapore has constructed for the island nation. How successful has this work in progress been? This essay will not draw premature conclusions but will look at some of the questions that have regularly been asked about what we now already know, and then suggest how the university's past experiences might help it deal with what is yet unknown.

How long does it take to grow a university? In Singapore, it took 44 years to get two colleges upgraded to university status. It took another three name changes to become internationally known as Singapore's national university. What more needs to be done for the National University of Singapore to cross the country's borders and compete in the global knowledge industry? Another question, in what ways may a university and its graduates best serve the country? Among those who studied at the two constituent colleges, the Medical College and Raffles College, in the 1930s and the 1940s, there were already those who began to imagine a future postcolonial nation. They prepared themselves, together with new generations of students at the university founded in 1949, for the time when independence would come for British Malaya. But, for those in Singapore alone, it was only in 1965 that they were finally given a country to serve. By that time, there were two universities. The two had different beginnings and the new nation needed to have them share the same dream. For 30 years after that, higher education was kneaded and massaged as the nation-builders determined how it might help to shape and enrich the country. Since the 1990s, the National University of Singapore has sought to be the nation's pride beyond the country's borders. Is it ready? Is it really free to find its global level? Is that what it really wants?

From yet another perspective, how good has the university been for its students and alumni and how much better can it be? The colleges had a very slow start when only a few were admitted to the Medical College in 1905 and not many more entered Raffles College in 1928. By 1949, only about 600 students studied at the new University of Malaya. The graduates were expected to form the subcolonial elite that the British needed to help them administer its colony and protectorates. This in-built elitism ensured that the first graduates were given a heavy responsibility and would be in key positions to build the nation after first Malaya's independence in 1957. After Singapore became unexpectedly the newest nation in 1965, its leaders turned their attention to what the university could do for the country's future. In that context, its role was expected to change with every twist of the country's development. For one thing, the number of students rose at an increasingly faster pace. On the eve of its 100th anniversary, the student body at the Kent Ridge campus had well passed the figure of 30,000. This figure includes a large group of graduate students, many from overseas. How have they changed the university as an institution? Also, with the expansion, more of the academic staff not only have been trained abroad but are also not local-born. What has internationalisation done to campus life?

Ultimately, the basic questions are probably the same everywhere. What do we want a university for? To educate the best and bring out the best in everyone? To make the nation rich and strong? To stand proud with the world's most dynamic teaching and research institutions? But not everything depends on what a community wants and is willing and can afford to support, nor only on what a government decides for the nation's needs. The university needs room to innovate and seek out other sources to push its enterprises. What then is the record of the NUS in this regard?

Let us look inside the university at how it has adapted itself to academic challenges over the past decades. What an extraordinary leap it has been for the minimal conditions of the two colleges to translate into ambitions to become a university. The core change has come about at least in part because of the quality of the very small numbers of students that were selected for study. It is astonishing how those few men and women went on to first serve colonial needs and then lead a plural society to nationhood in two countries. We do need to be reminded how this pioneer group continued to debate for many years what kind of university the NUS should become. The stress, from the start, on close intensive training under demanding conditions had paid off. Until it became clear after 1941 that British rule, however tolerable it had been to some, would not last forever, the two colleges were bastions of purposeful preparation and a high degree of conformity to Western scientific and secular ways.

The first decade after the end of the Second World War was quite a different story. A Britain that could be defeated and the anti-Japanese guerillas emerging from the jungle convinced most people in Malaya that independence was only a matter of time. The graduates and students of the colleges were divided about the future and some then thought that the assumptions concerning the benefits of British rule that they had been taught were no longer valid. A few became active in challenging the colonial authorities and some of their younger supporters brought their views to the campus from 1946 to 1949. By the time the university was established, there were doubts whether the arts and social sciences offered by the colonial education was what the country needed.

In this context, the British university model proved resilient and adaptable. On the one hand, new academic staff had been carefully chosen to introduce the students to a postcolonial Asia in which future graduates would serve their new nations. This was well received. Most students could see that they had good patriotic careers ahead of them and all they had to do was to learn well and be ready to serve. On the other hand, a whole range of anti-colonial literature was available and many students responded to radical calls for a liberated and more equitable world. Although only a minority of them, inspired by alumni and a new breed of political activists, were vocal and organised, it was enough for British dominance in academic affairs to be questioned.

The University of Malaya was not a university in Britain or elsewhere in the peaceful dominions of the Commonwealth. Malaya came under Emergency rule in 1948. There was little freedom for any anti-British action or talk and the campus was no exception. Thus both staff and students experienced the first contradictions of decolonisation in higher education. The high ideals in their textbooks did not apply under hostile political conditions. An armed revolt accompanied by terrorism that targeted local peoples were not conducive to demands for liberalism. Among the students, there was political innocence but there was also cynicism. Most of all, the British officials and teachers wanted everyone to understand that they were there to restore order and to win back respect for Britain and the law. Until they were ready to hand over power to local leaders whom they could trust, they wanted the university to transmit as much of their modernising values, what they believed to be superior knowledge, to as many people as possible.

Once it was decided that Malaya was to become independent in 1957 and the war against the Malayan Communist Party was being won, a more liberal policy towards the university became possible. And with the British power gone soon afterwards, the emphasis shifted to both staff and students defending university autonomy against the rising nationalist authority. This became particularly so when the nationalist leaders sought to control the universities. It was not, however, a sustained struggle. The independent governments, first in Kuala Lumpur after 1957 and then in Singapore after 1965, had some of the senior foreign teachers replaced by their local colleagues in their administrative positions. But, at least in Singapore, there were no real changes to what was being taught. Physical and medical sciences subjects were generally strengthened by following the best practice standards established for the Commonwealth. The most radical differences came when the university's own graduates took charge and a senior cabinet minister took over the reins of the university. Nevertheless, even in the fields of the arts and social sciences, adjustments were more apparent than substantive. A powerful minister in control determined the shifts in emphasis and this did influence recruitment policies. But the courses of study remained largely aligned with those offered in other Commonwealth universities. Compared with the 1950s, however, the main dangers to national survival in the 1960s were different. Although the focus was less on communism, and it was understood that it had to move to growing concerns about ethnic and religious tensions both inside and outside the country, similar limits were placed, as in the 1950s, on student debates and actions. In this context, no relaxation of the constraints on academic freedom seemed possible and whatever had been effective during the Emergency years were retained.

There have been very few universities in the world where a cabinet minister would actually run a university. Indeed, a pattern of top-down decisions was set and this became the norm for decades. No doubt that adopting this way, changes were made more easily and much time was saved. But the price of centralism and a deep bureaucratisation on the campus was high. As this was accompanied by a policy that only encouraged research and teaching that directly benefited the nation, the impact on the nature of the university was profound. There were understandable grounds like the need for economy and to ensure that money spent always produced the desired results. In government and business, such a course of action is certainly reasonable and easy to justify. But the restraint this placed on the sense of adventure and enterprise among both staff and students was inimical to the ideals of a modern university.

There was a curious contradiction at the same time. The university was found wanting because its focus had become too local at a time when the needs of the nation were globalising fast. To respond to the latter, the country found that the local university was too limited in its mental horizon. Eventually it decided that it could not afford not to send the country's best students to study in appropriate universities abroad. The effect on this policy on the university's development was not surprising. The constraints on teaching outreach and research choices in turn made the university less attractive for the country's best scholars to want to return to the local university to teach. Instead, to meet the country's own current needs, the trend was to establish well-funded research institutes separate from the university and this was to become the norm. Given the circumstances, this was a forward-looking decision. It did create a more effective division of labour at the highest level of inventiveness, working on the assumption that greater efficiency could arise by asking the university to concentrate on teaching. But the result was that large sections of the university were deprived of the stimulation that active research invariably provides to its best teachers and students. It would be difficult for any university to gain peer respect in the larger academic world if such a policy continued. It is a measure of the dedication of some of the younger academics in the NUS that, despite these limitations over some two decades, they strove for excellence and sought to earn their rewards outside.

Since the 1990s, efforts have been made to reverse this discouraging practice. The goal is to revive the academic ambitions of the university and set it, wherever possible, on the road to emulate the best universities in the West, especially in the United States. The change of policy is to be applauded. The chosen goal is truly worthwhile, although the desire to achieve this as quickly as possible may undermine the morale of those who have given the university decades of loyal service in the older mould. Nevertheless, the move promises to bring exciting times to the campus. Indeed, with some hesitation and trepidation, the government is hoping to unleash the whole range of campus, alumni and community energies to enable a new kind of university to emerge. After a hundred years, the decision-makers rightly believe that the time has come for the university to exercise some creative academic rights.

Those who care for the university should not look back merely with regrets. They should survey the omissions of the past objectively in order to learn from them. They should also set off to make full use of the new opportunities that lie ahead. Any brief history of the NUS would register the ups and downs caused by internal political change and external economic and strategic pressures. But it would also mark the university's capacity to ride the threats and alarums with a dogged perseverance. The university is not renowned as an innovative institution, but it is well structured for reliable response whenever necessary. Recent policies have demanded changes to the older culture of acting only when told. There is a genuine call for the university to become what it long might have been — a dynamic site for new thinking and open and vigorous debate. The alumni who have waited long for their alma mater to return to that role can take heart that the university now sees itself as willing to compete internationally. It has so far only taken a few steps in that direction. But it cannot do it alone. There has to be fresh thinking in the community and both students and alumni would be in the best position to help the authorities to point the way.

Finally, now that the academic direction of NUS is set to achieve greater goals beyond Singapore's borders, it is time to take stock of the role it has played within the national community. Two features of that role are outstanding. The university has clearly played a major role in contributing to the leadership of the new professional classes that have helped to make Singapore a first world nation. There is wide recognition throughout the region and also elsewhere in the developed world that the university's maintenance of high standards of training has ensured that the country is served by doctors, teachers, lawyers and engineers of a consistently reliable quality. Other institutions, of course, have also helped but it is still the NUS which is expected to carry the responsibility of leading. This role can be sustained as long as the NUS acknowledges that the need to reach out globally is not going to be at the expense of the community within its borders.

Secondly, the university encapsulates the underlying values of the nation. I have already remarked on the extraordinary contributions of the small group of alumni who made the new nation possible in two countries. The same *esprit de corps* and coherent vision found in that generation of campus comrades also enabled Singapore to survive the first years of independence. What difference has that made to the formation of Singapore society? The core ideal that made the difference was the plural society that the British trading needs had determined for its colony. For a thriving international port and marketplace, there was really no alternative to the kind of harmony seeking openness that such a society must have. Whether planned or not and no matter what motives lay behind it, the two colleges captured the spirit of that plural society to some extent and anchored it in British (or Western) education and training. It was a secular and merit-based structure that appealed to the products of modern schools and ultimately won over the immigrant communities that chose to settle in Singapore. Indeed, it was the spirit behind that structure which made it difficult for Singapore to accept the ethnic-based foundations of the Malaysian constitution in the 1963–1965 years.

The development of the two halves of the original University of Malaya where I studied from 1949 to 1954 and taught in from 1957 to 1968 sharply illustrates the alternative roads taken. Behind the two halves was a nation-building purpose, but different nationalisms were at play. In comparison, the part that grew to become NUS remained committed to the founding concepts. Its students, staff and alumni have directly contributed to the nation's ideal to build a meritocratic Singapore. During the decades after independence, despite the distractions of other dissenting visions on campus, this ideal remained intact. And it reminds us to what extent the NUS has embodied in miniature the core values of a modern cosmopolitan city-state.

To some, this has come at a heavy price. A plural society recognises the coexistence of distinct communities, but the collective need for a greater consensus has dampened what may be seen as the primordial instincts of the main communities in the country. This has in some cases undermined the cultural roots of each ethnic group in order to defend the interests of a small and insecure nation in an uncertain world. It seems to me that this is an area where the university could do more. The anxiety to conform to global ways and be accepted by peer groups elsewhere could be overwhelming to the point that the university fails to support what is embedded in local communities. There is much lip service being paid to the multiple civilisational origins of the Singapore people. But it has seemed so much easier for the university to respond to competitive pressures elsewhere than to represent the cultural diversities that are found locally.

The plural society model expressed in the NUS has done well to strengthen the sense of national identity. There is now the possibility that this is succeeding too well at the expense of the very plurality that

Singapore prides itself to have. The university may, consciously or not, be contributing to the tendency to diminish the awareness of Singapore's rich social heritage. There is even a danger that the idea of being proud of one's heritage will become itself something more boasted of than really appreciated.

I believe that one of the roles of the university is to be the kind of institution that can remedy that trend. It can do more through its cultural and social courses and qualifications to provide a balance against the growing tendency to bend with the international winds. The ethnic communities here are now indigenous in Singapore. Their various associations have been officially encouraged to be more active to highlight a major insight. Only through a deep understanding of one's own culture can one begin to empathise with that of others. Only by regular contacts can the communities appreciate the value of the plural society's ideal. The NUS has embodied that ideal by successfully showing how that ideal can work at several levels of national progress. But, on the whole, for much of the past hundred years, the university has leaned in one direction only. It has chosen to conform with the Anglo-American standards as the inevitable core of modernity. However understandable that might have been at a crucial stage of the nation's formation, the time has come to re-examine the long-term validity of that course. As a state and society praised for its determination to plan ahead where its hardware needs are concerned, the challenge of this century is whether it can do the same for the country's software needs. The NUS would be one of the few places in Singapore where that balance could be openly demonstrated. It is my hope that its students, staff and alumni would join the forward planning and take up that challenge.

17

The Chinese Pursuit of Higher Education

Although I have benefited much from the British system of higher education all my life, I began as an unfinished product of the Chinese university system. My first university was one that belonged to a transitional phase in China's efforts to build modern universities. In 1947, I went to Nanjing, then the capital of Nationalist China, from British Malaya and sat for the entrance examination to the National Central University. Those were the last days of the Kuomintang regime. I was in my second year when the regime retreated from Nanjing, and in December 1948, the university closed and we were asked to return home. Thus I had to start my higher education afresh at the University of Malaya in Singapore. This was followed by three years in London in the mid-1950s. And I have remained in British-inspired Commonwealth universities ever since.

It was not until 1973 that I visited the Chinese mainland again, this time with my colleagues at the Australian National University (ANU),

---

This is a revised version of the Foundation Lecture delivered on the Foundation Day of the University of Manchester on 18 October 2006.

mostly historians and China specialists. For three weeks, we visited universities in the cities of Xi'an, Beijing, Nanjing and Shanghai, some of the best in the People's Republic of China. This was in the middle of the Cultural Revolution, and the universities had just reopened their doors to admit batches of students of worker-peasant-soldier origins. There were no public examinations and the teachers who taught them were not necessarily academics but those of proven revolutionary backgrounds. Those we met impressed upon us that their work was focussed on the communist classics and modern revolutionary history and only included those parts of the Chinese heritage that demonstrably supported their cause. All else was useless if not downright harmful.

For the next 33 years, I visited universities in various parts of China and observed the transformations that have occurred with both astonishment and admiration. The contrast between what we saw in 1973 and what is going on today is remarkable (for almost every development in China since the 1980s). I shall illustrate some changes from my most recent visit to the Xi'an Jiaotong University. This university was founded in Shanghai at the end of the 19th century to become the famous engineering university called Jiaotong (Communications) University. In 1956, it was moved to Xi'an for strategic reasons. Although located deep in the interior of the country without easy access to new industries or to the outside world when compared with universities in Beijing and Shanghai, its engineering faculties and departments still attract excellent students. They do advanced research comparable to that done in the best universities elsewhere. The Xi'an Jiaotong University is currently trying to overcome its narrow engineering focus to become a comprehensive university by adding the liberal arts, and popular fields like medicine, law and business to its faculties. In these areas, they still have some way to go. But the determination to expand is evident and no doubt, like many other specialist colleges and universities elsewhere in China, it will successfully integrate the new fields with its strategic core faculties.

The eagerness to build comprehensive universities confirms that the Chinese have returned to the models that they were following during the first half of the 20th century. They were diverted from that course after 1952 when the Beijing government chose to copy the education structures of the Soviet Union. The Chinese leaders now believe that the Soviet way had failed and expect the reforms introduced since the 1980s to bring them better results. Certainly, the access to higher education improved dramatically, especially since 1999 when enrolment figures into tertiary institutions doubled. A recent count reveals that there are at least 1,800 colleges and universities (including 300 private ones). Of these, about 80 of them are regarded as good and some 40 are recognised as research universities with significant numbers of doctoral-level students. The total number of students now exceeds 20 million, with the number of graduating students last year being over four million. The speed of growth has come from a deliberate plan to expand higher education as an industry that would contribute to the national economy by producing trained human capital and increasing consumption all-round. So quickly has the number of graduates increased that large numbers of them have difficulty finding jobs commensurate with their education. There are studies now examining whether this is a temporary phenomenon or whether it reflects serious structural problems in the system.

Needless to say, there are not enough resources to ensure that all these higher institutions are adequately funded. There have been cases of dysfunctional colleges and departments and dishonest and incompetent professors that throw doubt on their overall performance. Under the circumstances, it would have been surprising if it were otherwise. What seems important to me, however, is not to oversimplify achievements and failures. We should put current changes in the larger context of what Chinese people expect from higher education, what they went through to get to the present position, and what they ultimately want.

The Heritage

The Chinese people have had a distinctive approach towards education for over 2,000 years. During that time, higher education was unaffordable for most and literacy level was low. The upper classes, however, took education most seriously and became increasingly dependent on examination performance in order to attain and retain power, influence and even wealth. They thus made severe demands on their children to study assiduously until they could pass the imperial examinations and ensure their positions as mandarins or at least as respectable literati. In their minds, this was the ultimate in advanced education that combined the highest moral and sophisticated knowledge available with the quality skills that mandarins and gentlemen would need. This ideal of education began to loosen up at the beginning of the 20th century, but it remains unforgotten among educated Chinese and continues to be the strongest factor in their desire to build the best possible modern universities.

The elitist roots of all education in China have a long history. The literati classes justified that kind of education because they believed that the ideology devised and refined by generations of Confucian mandarins best served a stable agrarian society. As mandarins, they dominated dozens of dynasties and established a political system to ensure that ideal agrarian values would endure. This was why China's political culture was primarily couched in humane, moral and communitarian terms. Within that framework, every ambitious family pressed its young males to study hard to pass the required examinations, and this Confucian ideal became the basis for the meritocratic nature of bureaucracy. In practice, the selection processes varied from dynasty to dynasty and capable students and examinees did not always get recognised. But the idea that anyone from whatever background could be educated to serve his society remained strong from the 1st century BC. This was particularly true between the 7th and 9th centuries, when literati graduates replaced their well-born predecessors. For most of history thereafter, these men were entrusted to help the Son of Heaven govern China.

The connection between education and public office was thus very strong. Indeed, except for the higher ranks of the Buddhist and Taoist priesthood, no other profession down to the end of the 19th century required the kind of education that the state and the literati classes insisted on. For most ordinary people, high literacy was out of the question. It was enough if most men could learn to read simple Chinese for purposes of doing business, reading medical and religious texts, and perhaps also understanding government regulations and announcements. For others, the ability to count and calculate was perhaps more important. The training for these skills was locally provided, usually through apprenticeships and some private tutoring. Altogether, if we consider how important education was for public service, it is surprising how little the state did to finance education or to help the young to learn. There were no state-funded schools or tertiary institutions. Influential local families often arranged for the poorer children to be tutored and sometimes sponsored the brightest of them for further education, but literati and gentry families who could afford it were expected to provide the necessary education for their own children. As a result, there was a large gap between the quest for the best possible education and the worldly skills most people had to be content with.

From the point of view of the court and high mandarins, it was enough to conduct examinations. The privileges that followed graduation were so great that those incentives alone induced literati families to make their sons devote their youth to intense study. Among them were graduates who did not seek public office and dedicated themselves to teaching in private academies. Some high officials were scholarly and became very accomplished in philosophy, poetry, calligraphy and the fine arts as by-products of their classical studies. Thus, whether in service or not, literati contributions to the enrichment of high culture were considerable. But it is notable that there was no support to pursue scientific methods and ideas, or technological and business skills. As a result, the higher education they received did not prepare them for the challenge of European cultures that were aggressive in the pursuit of scientific and commercial progress. We know what happened to China largely because of that failure to learn.

Willingness to Change

I stress this here because that failure led not only to the disintegration of the Chinese system of government but also undermined efforts to build modern universities during the 20th century. The decision to end the imperial examinations system in 1904 meant that public service recruitment was in disarray. The first universities set up to replace that system followed the Japanese, and learnt from European and American models, but the Chinese had also studied the American missionary colleges introduced into China since the late 1880s as well as those built by the French, the British and the Germans. Finally, in the 1920s, it was decided that Chinese public institutions should be modelled after the best universities in the United States. But there were strong disagreements about how these institutions should be staffed and funded. The success of Peking University under the leadership of Cai Yuanpei was not matched in other institutions and the tensions between national and expatriate staff, and political conflicts among the Chinese, led to much confusion and paralysis. It did not help that bitter ideological differences, notably among the Kuomintang government, the opposition Communist Party and various liberal alliances, were reflected in the campuses. As a result, the foreign models did not sink deep roots in the community. Nevertheless, the possibilities the universities held out for the descendants of literati and new classes of urbanised people to advance themselves were great. Till this day, there is nostalgia for what might have been had China not been dominated by foreign powers and was allowed to develop its universities under peaceful conditions.

The Japanese war in the mid-1930s ended all efforts to provide systematic higher education, not least because the best institutions were forced to move into the interior with the minimum of resources. The heroic efforts of scholars and students to keep the teaching and research going under the most trying conditions were indeed admirable. They proved that a new spirit of intellectual enquiry had begun to prevail over the traditional links with public office. Increasingly, the ideal of higher education as a social good that served a developing nation was gaining acceptance. Of course, as resources were limited, the universities remained small. For example, the National Central University in Nanjing, as one of the favoured universities of the Nationalist regime, had the most complete range of faculties and departments and yet, as China's largest university, it only had a total of 4,000 students in 1948.

Nevertheless, in spite of wartime conditions, China's education culture was changing, and more people began to recognise the intrinsic value of acquiring new knowledge and educating young minds. With the end of the Second World War, expectations that universities could provide most of the advanced skills necessary to reconstruct a war-torn country were high. At the same time, students who were taught to have a critical mind of their own posed new sets of problems. The politics on campuses became greatly polarised; students (sometimes encouraged by staff) had become increasingly dissatisfied with the Nationalist regime, and the government found their activism troublesome. Most of the students were idealistic, if not a little naïve. Some of the brightest and liveliest were already members of the Communist Party dedicated to bring down by force the very government that provided them with education.

In short, the transformation of the ethos of higher education between the May Fourth Movement of 1919 and the victory of the Chinese Communist Party 30 years later led to a paradox. Students were exposed to liberal and egalitarian ideas within institutions that were still committed to elitism and privilege. The new learning spirit was bold, even courageous and heroic, but the change was incomplete, and was, in any case, quickly brought to an end. The modernising experiments before 1949 can now be read in the histories that have been written about Peking and Tsinghua universities and the wartime United Southwestern University (Xinan Lianda) in Kunming. There are also histories of National Central University in Nanjing, of Fudan and Jiaotong universities in Shanghai, and of Zhongshan or Sun Yat-sen University in Guangzhou that also illustrate the political ups and downs of those 30 years. These should be read in parallel with the histories of missionary institutions like Yenching (Protestant) and Furen (Catholic) in Beijing, and those in Shanghai like St John's (American), Tongji (German) and Aurora (French) and Jinling in Nanjing and Lingnan in Guangzhou (the last two were also started by American Protestant missionaries). These foreign-inspired institutions had led the way in shaping the modern Chinese university but most remained suspect because of their foreign origins.

Taken as a whole, the story of all these early universities can only arouse wonder and respect. The multiplicity of learning traditions drawn largely from Europe and America provided the Chinese with many choices and many individual Chinese benefited greatly from that variety. But, given the weak position of China's own educational institutions at the time and the uncertainty as to what rewards higher education would bring, that plurality of models also caused confusion and led the whole system to lack direction and confidence. Thus, despite the legendary achievements of a small number of brilliant individuals who did work comparable to the best scholarship done elsewhere, the glories of that period are often exaggerated. One can understand the nostalgia for the loss of a fine start that promised great things but, on the eve of the communist victory of 1949, the future of higher education was really precarious.

Double Reaction: from Mao to Deng

What were the expectations in 1949 when peace and stability followed the decisive victory of the Chinese Communist Party? We know that many well-known scholars moved to Taiwan, Hong Kong and beyond. Yet others, still at foreign universities in the West, chose not to return. These decisions weakened the depleted academic resources of the country. In addition, the new government in Beijing put pressure on those who remained to conform to the revolutionary ideals of the new regime. Exercises in re-education along ideological lines, often described as "brainwashing", were followed by a total changeover to copying what the Russians had done under Stalin. For those in the natural sciences and engineering who could apply their knowledge to urgent industrial and military needs, there were new opportunities, and those who were best qualified in these fields did do well. A large number of highly specialised technical and engineering colleges were established. Scarce resources were made available for them to help strengthen the country's defences and speed up the industrialisation desperately needed by the country.

The change from uncertainty to certainty was encouraging for some professions and there did appear a refreshing change from the demoralised condition of the universities in 1949. But it soon became clear that the priorities that enabled scientists and engineers to advance their work did not apply to the humanities and social sciences. All hopes for the latter were soon dashed when Mao Zedong launched a fierce campaign against intellectuals who had not accepted the national ideology wholeheartedly. The campaign, misleadingly called "Let the Hundred Flowers Bloom", decimated key sectors of the campus communities. Thousands of college-level teachers were found to have been politically incorrect or guilty of independent thinking, or were suspected of disloyalty to the central creeds of the Communist Party. They were removed from their duties and many were arrested and punished because they had sought respect for their personal autonomy or had shown signs of defiance.

How did all this affect the Chinese pursuit of higher education? One can argue that there was no fundamental change of attitude. Higher education was still an elite preserve and the privileges given to the successful scientists and engineers were in the best tradition of the Chinese mandarinate. Only the preferred fields of excellence had changed. Those who made it to the best schools had good chances to get into the best universities to study science and engineering and they were guaranteed rewards commensurate with their qualifications. If they were well trained in the communist classics as well, they could move up the echelons of power and responsibility. In short, ideological and technological elitism replaced the traditional elitism of the agrarian dynastic state.

Unexpectedly, the decade of the Cultural Revolution between 1966 and 1976 showed that even the science and technology elites were not spared, and the unfortunate ones were subjected to the destructiveness of Red Guard politics that Mao Zedong had encouraged. Afterwards, the important place of higher education was restored among those who knew what such education meant. When Deng Xiaoping became leader in 1978, in direct contrast to what Mao Zedong had done, formal nationwide entrance examinations were resumed. Academic staff who survived were encouraged to reconnect with Western universities to seek help from their old professors and fellow alumni to place their graduate students in some of the best universities. In most cases, these teachers got their students admitted and these first batches of students did exceedingly well. In addition, the thousands of high school students who gained entry into the best Chinese universities were also remarkably good. This showed that, despite the 10 years of deprivation, individual students had struggled to master linguistic and mathematical skills and had kept their minds alert. Between mindless politics and bitter living and working conditions, they had not stopped learning. They seemed to have readied themselves for the day when sanity would return and they could continue their formal studies again. Today, we have innumerable stories, novels, plays and films that capture the powerful spirit that enabled so many to scramble back to normalcy and embark on successful careers.

The transformations were not limited to that generation. Even more remarkable was the wider awakening among the ordinary people to the value of modern higher education. The opportunities opened up by the economic reforms in the 1980s linked universities once again to the best job opportunities the country could offer. All officials of Party and government were also encouraged to upgrade their qualifications. The pressure to reform the universities and have them matched with the best ones overseas grew stronger. On the one hand, some of the best graduates went overseas for their graduate education and did not return, at least partly because working and living conditions on Chinese campus were simply not good enough. On the other, the demand for undergraduate places soared so quickly that the elitist ideal became harder to sustain.

The national universities simply could not meet the new demand, and the turn towards local and private higher education was inevitable. It is difficult to increase enrolment in national universities as long as they have to provide residential accommodation for all staff and students. The Chinese know that this is not done in the best universities in the West but, despite the considerable cost, they have so far not been able to find a way out of that commitment. How much this is due to the desire to submit the best and brightest to nation-building discipline, or to protect them from distraction and exploitation outside campuses, or to simply subject them to social control is disputed. Whatever the reason, the policy limits their further growth. Hence there is need to promote a major education industry to meet the rising demand. The hasty preparations for this change have led to the rise of inferior and inadequately funded institutions. Again, like many other developments, the speed of transformation has been unprecedented. It took only a little over 10 years to go from a serious shortage of graduates in the early 1990s to the growing number of unemployed graduates today who may have to take any job they can find.

It is obvious that, at certain levels, all aspects of tertiary education appear be highly regulated. On the other hand, there is also much entrepreneurship at every level of teaching and learning that suggests how much a commodity such as education has become. By now, the pursuit has drawn fresh strength from three distinct urges. The first two remind us of what had inspired the traditional literati and is now manifested among the ablest graduates who have joined the dominant elites. They are, of course, now expressed through modern goals and globally comparable criteria. The first urge is obviously the most relevant. It is to master whatever is useful, advanced and progressive for the empowerment of China. Those who give the highest priority to this are modernisers who argue passionately about how best to achieve that goal quickly. They give the highest priority to science, technology and the market economy, and believe that the values generated from these will take the place of the values that were traditionally dominant. They think that, however beautiful the earlier values once were, they have outlived their usefulness. The future is in the hands of those who can harness the conflicting demands of the globalised world in the most efficient way possible. All else stands in the way of progress, and would inhibit China's desire to become wealthy and powerful again. This urge is strongest among the power holders who are most like those mandarins in the past who stressed the majesty and power of China's political system. In that way, they are true descendants of the Confucian literati, whose loyalty to the "Heavenly Mandate" has now been translated into preserving that of the Chinese Communist Party.

The second urge comes from a different emphasis in the literati tradition. It comes from the conviction that China's heritage of high culture was founded on the best that knowledge could provide. This thrust may be found today among those who seek continuity between modern and traditional knowledge. If that could be established, it would help them recover their faith in their heritage. They include ambitious thinkers and educationalists who moved from the liberal traditions of Western Europe and North America to support the collectivist heresies of Soviet Russia, and have now returned to the triumphant ways of the West. Throughout the changes in positions, however, they nursed hopes in, and never lost sight of, the deep structures of traditional ideals. Among many of them is the hope that somehow the new knowledge they are striving to get will enable them to rediscover the springs of excellence that once made Chinese civilisation great. In other words, they are uncomfortable with the idea that China should become like the nation-states of Europe that emerged after centuries of war and diplomacy. They have studied the states around them that were spawned by the 20th century decolonisation and do not accept that China is simply a larger example of those countries. What they believe is that China would not be worth much if it does not stand once again for an advanced civilisation. The pursuit of higher education is to enable generations of Chinese innovators and leaders to prepare for the time when a stable new society would carry the flag for a widely respected modern, scientific civilisation that they can call their own.

But there is also a third urge that is different from the first two, one that China has not known before the 20th century. This comes from the liberation of the *nong-gong-shang* (peasant-artisan-merchant) majorities that once constituted over 90 per cent of the population. It is the final result of the three revolutions during the past 100 years that released the latent talents of hundreds of millions of ordinary Chinese throughout the country. It is not surprising that these revolutions have thoroughly shaken up Chinese society. The three began with the call to nationalism by Sun Yat-sen a century ago that reached a climax following the Japanese invasions of the 1930s. This was when both nationalist and communist leaders implanted countrywide patriotism to save the country from foreign conquest. This was followed by the second revolution after 1949 and the upheavals that led to the total replacement of the ruling elites of China. Although that did little to uplift the quality of the universities except in the technical and scientific fields, it stimulated new ideals of social and economic equality and high expectations among those that had missed out in the past. Its climax was reached during the Cultural Revolution that overturned hierarchical structures that had survived the first two revolutions. Although damaging and disastrous to China's tradition, the struggles on behalf of continuous revolution actually laid the foundations for Deng Xiaoping's radical reforms that facilitated revolutionary changes to the whole of Chinese society. These reforms consolidated the hopes of ordinary peasants and workers who answered the earlier calls to revolution and have now found outlets for their talents. They lie behind the third urge in the pursuit of higher education. They are galvanising more and more people to exert themselves in support of modernisation, especially in response to the idea that socialism should make people richer and not poorer. It is an urge that is releasing the pent-up energies of millions at every level of society.

The impact of all three urges on higher education has not been immediate, and the decision to learn from the best universities in the West came slowly. But when it came, that fundamentally changed the academic ground rules. The most important spur to action was the direct link between popular higher education and better material prospects. This was quickly manifested in employment patterns by the 1990s. Although pressures on limited resources, especially at the personal level, are enormous, the new opportunities to study at higher levels have been widely welcomed. Millions more of the young thus seek better careers through education. Bottlenecks remain and the ambitions of most of those who began in humble circumstances are still unfulfilled. Nevertheless the commitment to redefine the purposes of higher education has been made and the social consequences of greater access are incalculable.

I am not certain whether the three urges will come together or lead to titanic struggles to determine which should be the dominant force in China's future. Very likely, as in the past, the first two might in the end coalesce to meet the challenge of the third. In speculating about the great challenge for the Chinese pursuit of higher education, I suggest that the deep structure in which educated elites led China to a higher civilisation will once again inspire the newly educated classes. That inspiration will not produce the desired results all that soon, but would have to be calibrated to take into account the relative positions of contending elites. The new kinds of political, economic, bureaucratic, professional and literati elites are assuming roles totally unknown in the past and it is not possible to predict how far they will work in unison. But as long as the desire to identify with viable parts of the heritage remains, and there are signs that new elites are prepared to do so, then the Western models chosen to guide the next phase of higher education development will not be ends in themselves.

Why do I think this is likely? I will retrace to what I call the three rejections in modern Chinese history. The first came from the denial by the Qing literati at the end of the 19th century that Western education could replace the Chinese cultural essence or substance. The second was the rejection of liberal American education by both Nationalists and Communists during the Republican years. The third, being the most recent, was a double rejection, first in 1949 by turning away from the West and then in the 1960s by rejecting the heretical West of Stalin. These three denials were not accidental or wilful displays of anger and frustrations. They remind us that the strong undertow of surviving values associated with China's civilisational deep structure cannot be avoided. This undertow is truly impressive. We note the radical reinterpretations of tradition by the last great Confucian scholars of the 20th century, and the efforts by young revolutionaries to "smash Confucius and sons", followed by the frontal and destructive attacks on all traditional cultural structures encouraged by Mao Zedong. Despite all these efforts sustained for more than 80 years, most Chinese have found that the deep structure of a great civilisation still resonates with them.

This is not to say that all Chinese are interested to help define a new civilisation that would one day grow out of the old. For most students, they go to universities with more practical goals like better training and more rewarding job opportunities in mind. However, the social changes are profound. Most students are freer than their earlier counterparts have ever been. Modern education has made gender equalities possible in unprecedented ways. Legal and political rights have been redefined and there is no turning back where people's hopes are concerned. The widespread availability of tertiary education has led to expectations of higher standards of performance from public officials, and ultimately, that the Party in power will have to be much more accountable. It may even lead to distinctive paths of democratisation, as long as these emerge from within and do not emulate those taken by Taiwan or South Korea or Japan and are not dictated by interventionist foreign powers. It would be easy to see the modern universities as representing a decisive break with the past, but there is ample evidence that the undertow of China's deep cultural structure remains strong. It is a force that induces the new elites to seek different directions for future change. At the least, and in ways reminiscent of earlier elites, they will emphasise the freedom to learn and better oneself as the literati had done; there will be more upward social mobility across a wider spectrum, and wherever possible, there will be greater participation in public affairs and this will contribute to the cause of China's recovery and revitalisation. The broad base from which the new elites have come should bring new generations of leaders closer to the ordinary people. They would then be more credible when they assert that the Chinese are capable of offering the world a distinctively modern civilisation.

There are signs that the new products of modern higher education are ambitious for such a development even if they cannot at this stage agree how they might articulate their goals. One symptom of that ambition is the urge to seek the highest attainments by first emulating and then matching the achievements of the best universities in the world, largely in the United States and Europe. It began with the efforts to place their students in the best universities and try to get them back to the Chinese universities. A few Chinese universities were selected to compete with the best elsewhere, and large sums of money for research and recruitment were invested. Some of this find expression in the desire to win Nobel Prizes. It also includes the monitoring of China's progress in the academic league table, with key universities primed to catch up with those at the top in the quickest possible time. Not unlike Mao Zedong's desire to catch up with Britain in steel production during the Great Leap Forward, there is a narrowly conceived element in this effort that could be amusing if it were not so serious.

The Chinese recognise that most Chinese universities are unlikely to catch up with the best for a long time. In the meantime, the pursuit could be a kind of sport that is both uplifting and challenging. But there is an emotional connection to the past that should not be ignored. China is neither a conventional empire nor a mere nation-state, and its century of effort to try to define itself has led its leaders to contortions that have left many people uncomfortable. But if history tells us anything, it would suggest that the Chinese would not want the enormous burdens of a global empire or the responsibilities of a sole superpower. They would not want to challenge the United States in terms of its hegemonic power but would be content if they could ensure that no external power would threaten China again. But the ideal that ultimately China would be nothing significant if it were not itself a major civilisation is still alive. The deep desire that such a civilisation should re-emerge remains strong. And to keep that as a goal requires that they converge their heritage with the best values in the modern world, ultimately to learn the best of those values in competition with the best in order to gain universal respect. Although some of them admire the United States military power, and others its political ideals, and yet others the efficiency of the capitalist economy, what all of them admire most is the cultural power that America (including its European roots) now enjoys. The Chinese acknowledge that the best of America is seen in the way its higher education is being widely emulated.

I shall summarise the Chinese view of this modern phenomenon by using one of their iconic metaphors. It is that of the famous Tang monk Xuan Zang who travelled to India "to bring back the sutras" (*qu jing*) in the 7th century. One could point to students going to colleges in America to be doing something similar. Of course, these students did not bring back the equivalent of religious sutras but something more worldly and scientific. But Xuan Zang and these students did have one thing in common. They won admiration by bringing back ideals and standards that were ultimately accepted by the Chinese people. I suggest that the new Chinese elites include many who would love to see a time when modern Chinese civilisation would attract others to China in the way they have paid tribute to the US universities. After Xuan Zang's return from India 1,300 years ago, Chinese civilisation integrated the best of externally inspired values with the best that it already had, and the amalgam went on to produce an even more distinctive civilisation that flourished for the next thousand years. It would not surprise me if the Chinese people would want to work together to make that happen again.

18

New University, Three Generations: China, Malaya, Singapore 1949–2007

The Bukit Timah campus of the National University of Singapore was where two generations of students grew up, and many went on to run the two countries of Malaysia and Singapore. Established in this campus in 1949 as a new university, the university was later renewed, and given a new name, in 1980.

I do not need to tell you what a university is, but I want to stress that each university meets a need and reflects the aspirations of a state or a people, or a section of the people. With a public university, it is usually the product of the agreed needs of state and society as a whole. The new university in 1949, the University of Malaya, was essentially a colonial

---

This address was first delivered on 8 July 2007 on the occasion of the official opening of the National University of Singapore Bukit Timah campus and the East Asian Institute's move from the Kent Ridge campus to the Bukit Timah campus. Published in s/pores: New Direction in Singapore Studies, vol. 1, issue 2.1, 2008, also accessible at <http://s-pores.com/2008/02/generations/>

university, one of several in the British Empire that were established on the eve of decolonisation. That it was an English-language university in a Malay world and was located in a city whose population was three-quarters Chinese made it distinctive. Thus the name of the university was a decisive statement. The university was to serve all the communities of British Malaya and represented a belated effort to prepare those communities for a future nation to be called Malaya. Two small points of note: the colonial government did not look backwards and call it the University of *British* Malaya but looked forward to a Malayan future. It did, however, tie the new university to the Commonwealth university system and that gave it an immediate legitimacy in a large family of universities.

Given that background, it is perhaps not too surprising that this new university experienced divisions and reinventions as the world around it began to change. The social and political complexities were great, so the university was probably doomed to divide but it avoided failure by reinventing itself whenever necessary to meet new needs.

The three generations in my title refer to the first two that lived through the period of divisions and early efforts at reinvention, and then the third generation that studied at the reinvented National University of Singapore and has been helping to retool and upgrade it ever since. For the first two generations, I shall talk about their distinctive features in terms of two images, "The China Presence" and "The Malaya Dream". For the third generation, I shall look to an image of "The Singapore Remaking". I should add that "The China Presence" and "The Malaya Dream" overlapped in the hearts of minds of the first two generations, but I shall try to talk about them separately.

I shall identify the first two generations of students and we are talking about those in a very small university, with a student pool of only about 650 in 1949 to increase to about 3,000 students 20 years later. Who were they? The first, those from the late 1940s to the early 1960s were largely products of the English-medium schools in British colonies and protectorates. Most were born locally but very few thought of themselves as members of a nation. The Malays were largely from the Malay States and the Straits Settlements, but some were proud of their origins in Sumatra, Java and elsewhere in the Malay Archipelago. But they were the minority among the students. The non-Malay majority was divided into varieties of Chinese, "Indians" (all those from South Asia today), and Eurasians. Among those who identified with "British Malaya" were the

Malays, the Eurasians, the Peranakan or Straits Chinese, and others of Chinese and South Asian descent who had lived there for two generations or more. The rest were varieties of migrants and sojourners. More than two-thirds of the students were not from the island of Singapore. Alongside this generation at the University of Malaya was the first generation of those who went to Nanyang University from 1956. They were the products of Chinese-medium schools in Malaya (including Singapore) as well as Indonesia and elsewhere.

The second generation went to university from the mid-1960s to 1980. Two events changed the demographics of the two universities. With the University of Malaya setting up a branch in Kuala Lumpur, most English-medium students from the Federation then went to Kuala Lumpur. Chinese-medium students went to Nanyang University or Nantah in Singapore. This meant that fewer Malay students went to Singapore and also meant that the total student body in Singapore was even more Chinese than before. The second event accentuated this change in a different way. I refer to the separation of Singapore from Malaysia in 1965. During the decade after that, the numbers from across the causeway dropped further, making up a very small proportion of the student numbers in Singapore thereafter. By the mid-1970s, it can be said that the two universities were Singapore universities and more than 80 per cent of all students were of Chinese descent. It is in this context that I talk of the overlapping images of the China Presence and the Malaya Dream and their residual features which had remained significant till the 1970s. Some may argue today that neither has quite disappeared and both images have survived in the memories of those who lived through the first two generations.

The China Presence

The China Presence was a strong one from the start. This is not surprising since the University of Malaya (MU) was located in Singapore where three-quarters of the population was Chinese. But that is not the reason why I highlight China here, nor is it because students of Chinese descent were the majority at MU. The China Presence was strong for three reasons.

First, most of these Chinese students were *huaqiao* (that is, Chinese temporarily living abroad) and claimed by the government of China as its nationals. In 1949, China was at the end of a deadly civil war in which the Chinese Communist Party (CCP) won. In fact, just a few days before the university was founded, Mao Zedong proclaimed that China had stood up on 1 October 1949. My impression is that most young Chinese both in China and outside felt some pride in hearing that. I do not know how many of the Chinese students on campus were Chinese nationals but what the idea of being Chinese meant at the time was not always clear. Those born in British Malaya were eligible to become British subjects or become Federal citizens of the then newly established Federation of Malaya, but it was several years later before the majority of Chinese in Malaya could identify legally with the new Federation. Malaya was, in any case, not yet independent — which occurred in 1957 — so strictly speaking, most Chinese were in a state of transition, and were still considered as some kind of colonial subjects or, if they lived in the Malay States, they were called British Protected Persons. In that situation, the Republic of China (Taiwan from 1949) and the People's Republic of China (the PRC), both then following the policy of *jus sanguines* (the law of descent), could stick to their policy of treating all those born of a Chinese father to be Chinese nationals. In short, at the time, any Chinese could apply for a Chinese passport. And, unless they were eligible for some other passports, even those who were local-borns could use Chinese passports if they needed one.

In contrast, other non-Malay students at MU in 1949 were mostly descended from immigrants from British territories like India, Ceylon, the Malay States, Sarawak and Sabah, and there were some Malays, Chinese and others who had come originally from the Dutch territories like Sumatra and Java. There were also Eurasians who could more readily identify with the British. Some were of part-Portuguese descent who could trace their families back to Malacca for some 400 years. Yet others were of part-Dutch Burgher descent who came some 200 years later, while the few of part-British descent were the most recent.

On campus, ethnic distinctions were kept superficial. As products of English-language schools throughout Malaya, most of the students had grown up with one another and, for most purposes, had habitually ironed out much of their cultural differences. But the shadow of communal politics was not far from where they were, and in Singapore, with its large Chinese majority, the spotlight invariably was on their responses in the context of the politics of China. To underline this further, the Chinese power struggle had been brought to British Malaya since the beginning of the 20th century and had been stimulated by at least two major factors: on the one hand, Chinese revolutionary nationalism (both of the Kuomintang (KMT) and the CCP) that was critical of British colonialism and imperialism; on the other, the extension of the Sino-Japanese war to Malaya from 1941 to 1945 that raised communal awareness to a degree much higher than ever in the past. It was this significantly contrasting heritage that both the British authorities and the Chinese students at MU had to deal with.

The second reason for the China Presence was more immediate. The Malayan Emergency since 1948 had taken its toll on lives and property. This was widely attributed to the Chinese who had founded the original Malayan communist movement in the 1930s. How they gained local support and were armed by the British to fight against the Japanese is a well-known story. But in 1948, the Malayan Communist Party (MCP) was in a state of war with the authorities in Malaya. In addition, there was another significant factor. In most parts of Malaya, Chinese schools outnumbered English schools by this time, although English schools produced more secondary school graduates who were eligible to study at MU. This had not mattered much as Chinese middle-school graduates could return to China to study at universities there. But with the communist victory in China in 1949, the government was suspicious of anyone who wanted to go to China and would not have allowed their return once they went. Thousands of Chinese middle-school graduates (not only in British Malaya but all over Southeast Asia) found themselves denied of the chance of higher education. This fact led to the spectacularly popular support for Nanyang University and cast a large shadow on the question of university education for the next three decades. This was the most enduring part of the China Presence.

The third reason was the PRC's decision to side with the Soviet Union by the end of 1949 and became the revolutionary vanguard for East Asia. I had just finished my first year of studies in mid-1950 when the Korean War began. For the following three years, Chinese hostility against the United States and its United Nations allies dominated local images of China. All over Southeast Asia, those images increased scepticism about the political loyalty of local Chinese. The impact on campus life at the University of Malaya was not immediately obvious, but it was known that students were divided on a wide range of subjects, for example, on neutralism and neocolonialism, as well as on the bitter struggle between the two main groups of Chinese, the Nationalists of the KMT and the Communists in charge in Beijing and fighting in Korea. The China factor increased the pressure on all community leaders to come together to build a Malaya that was free from Chinese and other communal politics.

Taken together, these faces of China and Chinese politics appeared somewhat menacing and the shadow of China touched the lives of most of the first generation of hopeful nation-builders, whether of Chinese descent or not.

The Malaya Dream

The second part of the university story, the Malaya Dream, was very much the case of "same bed, many dreams". The English schools all over Malaya, perhaps more of the government-funded ones that included students from all backgrounds rather than the mission schools (where very few students were Malay), consciously taught the students who came from different communal origins to play down their differences under the British flag. After the war, the shift was towards an awareness of a common destiny in a future Malayan nation. The bulk of the students at MU for the next two decades were steered towards thinking "Malayan" and indeed it was that futurist image that dominated many activities on campus.

Two questions had an influence on all debates. One was, did being anti-colonial and anti-imperialist make us part of a larger global discourse? The other was, how did anyone build a new nation from the many social groups that had been politically awakened by war, occupation and the diminution of British imperial power? In any case, what was this Malaya that we were taught to believe in? The name, University of Malaya, itself symbolised the future nation for the undergraduates of the first generation. But did they share the same dream? Very early, it was clear that the ideal of Malaya had to compete against other powerful calls, for example, the belief in the unity of Melayu Raya of the Malay Archipelago; or, among the Chinese, the fact of *Xin Zhongguo* (New China) that many found inspiring. Also there was Jai Hind, a call especially appealing to those who had sympathised with the Indian National Army. The question of what language was going to be the national language was a large disputed zone and some even tried to design new amalgams of the main languages in use. These were sensitive times. Under Emergency conditions in Malaya, most students had been taught to reject communal calls and generally to duck controversial issues, and focus on the positive features of the Malaya ideal. That was certainly so for most public activities where discussions would have to be couched in scholarly language and students were exhorted to be analytical and avoid anything that stirred high emotions. But, in small groups of the like-minded, there were more uninhibited appraisals of one another's political ambitions and interests. For example, among some groups, members would whisper to themselves that communal claims must come first. Let me mention two examples that captured the flavour of extreme positions: at one extreme, Malaya should be for the Malays of the whole archipelago and not only for the Malays of peninsular Tanah Melayu; and at another, the Chinese had fought the Japanese bravely. They were the toughest and most advanced people in the country and therefore, only they were strong enough to ensure that all the imperialists were driven out.

Against this was another set of ideologies, especially among those who believed in the class struggle. For them, only by uniting the workers could the dominant elites be put in their place and the poor be helped. This led to efforts to answer the question of whether the Malayan peoples were part of a larger revolutionary movement. Yes, they would say: the fight in Malaya was part of something bigger and only by joining in that Asia-wide struggle was there any chance of getting rid of the imperial masters. These extreme positions attracted police scrutiny. Over the years, several batches of students were arrested and some were jailed for long periods because of their links with banned organisations outside the campus. There was talk of secret cells of communist sympathisers, of "pinkos" or fellow travellers, and accusations against armchair socialists for whom it was all theory and no action. Among some, there was dissatisfaction with social, literary and scholarly clubs and a hankering for political clubs like those in British universities. Eventually, the university agreed to the setting up of the Socialist Club and this attracted many of the most idealistic. That was later followed by the Democratic Socialists who thought the Socialist Club was too left-wing. Nobody at the time seemed to have bothered with Conservatives and Liberals — neither was fashionable because they were either too mild or associated with those British who believed that the empire should strike back. But underlying the discussions and arguments, there was a serious concern for what kind of Malaya was feasible and desirable.

There were, in short, many dreams that made the Malaya project much blurred by the differences. The spectrum of causes that were actively supported ranged from Malay nationalism to a variety of Chinese, Indian and Eurasian explorations of identity that played with the idea of a multicultural nation. There were also those who were anxious about what it would be like after the British left, those who felt that such a mishmash of peoples were not ready to rule themselves. Yet others simply hoped for the best and kept their views to themselves. Among those who articulated their concerns, only the Malays felt that their nationalism had an indigenous legitimacy. The others acknowledged their immigrant origins and sought justification for their claims through rights of birth and settlement, something the British encouraged them to demand. Almost everyone was prepared to pledge his or her loyalty to some kind of Malayan nation. What was most striking, however, was that the debates were conducted in a common language, the English of their schools and the campus. This ensured that the protagonists understood one another well and they would not be communally labelled unless they wanted to draw particular attention to their cultural origins.

The Malaya Dream promised many things, but it did not pretend that it could simply imitate the states of Europe where the principle of nation was based, for the most part, on countries having one language, one religion and one history. The first generations knew that their Malaya would have several languages and religions and that its peoples had only shared a short period of history together. Thus, they saw the need for a different conception of national identity, something that could be achieved by developing a sense of common identity with everyone owing loyalty to an established state. That state, after the colonial power left, was one that would serve all people equally while it set out to build a future distinct nation.

In the meantime, the voices of hope, the idealism, the enthusiasm, the fierce emotions, the thousands of impractical ideas offered and the immense confidence that only young people can project coloured everything the students did for some two decades. Outside the campus, the atmosphere was tense. A war was going on, and two years after the university was founded, in 1951, Sir Henry Gurney, the highest civilian official in Malaya, was ambushed and killed by communist guerillas. On the streets of Singapore, labour unrest was politicised and turned against the British, and calls for merdeka and freedom were entwined with calls for social equality. For many, it did not seem possible for Singapore to attain independence on its own and only by joining Malaya could they be rid of colonial rule. But there were also doubts whether Singapore needed to be part of Malaya. The Malaya Dream was thus deconstructed several times over. But it remained at the core of the university's agenda even after the Kuala Lumpur division was established and the division in Singapore was renamed the University of Singapore. Most of the students were still engaged in asking what kind of dream could be ultimately realised. That provided for exciting debates among themselves and also when they confronted the new political leaders who were emerging in the decade after David Marshall dramatised the need for a timetable for Singapore's independence. These were the generations who were exhilarated by the thought that a new nation was being created. It was exciting to wonder what kind of political system could come out of the contested visions of political parties like the People's Action Party, the Labour Party, the Workers' Party and the Barisan Sosialis, to name a few. Although I was in Kuala Lumpur by the time the Malaysia solution was devised, I could see that it was the underlying Malaya Dream that was central in the students' imagination. The battle of Malaysian Malaysia was never far from that dream and Singapore's exit from Malaysia was deeply related to the failure to realise that dream in the Malaysia equation.

The Singapore Remaking

I now turn to the third generation and another new university, one that is totally absorbed in the remaking of Singapore. The National University of Singapore combined the University of Singapore with the Nanyang University and the decision, for better or worse, ended the unique experiment that the founders of Nantah had promised. This was the product of at least a decade of recovery and survival. In response to the immediate needs of a Singapore remaking, controls were tightened to fit new plans and meet targets that displaced older hopes. The focus was Singapore and the task of exorcising the China Presence and the Malaya Dream was both painful and reinvigorating.

This is a story that others could tell better. I spent some months visiting NUS soon after it moved to Kent Ridge and came back from time to time in different capacities in the 1980s and 1990s before coming to work on the campus in 1996. For a newer campus, its time is yet to come. One probably needs many more years for memories to be sweetened and for nostalgia to set in. As you can see, for me, it is this Bukit Timah campus that excites me and triggers memories of the beautiful moments and bitter fights that linger on in my mind. This was where we studied, made friends and hopefully courted our wives. As many of you know, I was one of the successful ones.

I have now spent some 10 years walking the corridors at Kent Ridge. I have been impressed by the variety of initiatives the students have taken to enliven their activities and stretch out beyond their classrooms. Their social concerns, their artistic urges, their drive for rich cultural performances, their entrepreneurial experiments and, from to time, their political curiosity surprise me. In particular, I am struck by how their reach has gone far beyond the borders of Singapore and the region, and how much less bound they are by the more specific nation-questioning realms of the two earlier generations. I can understand the make-up of this new university and empathise with the desire of the students for alternate paths of creativity and innovation. But I cannot put my finger on how and what they think about homecoming, either now or earlier on, and that is my excuse for keeping what I have to say very brief.

For this third generation of the new Singapore university, there is a fresh challenge that has gone beyond nation dreaming and nation-building. It is about how to see the local in global terms and how to bring the global into the local. Only in that way has that generation been able to overcome the confines of an island chained to uncertain hinterlands. There has not been any safety in size, no appeal to a deep history and culture of its own, and no reliable protection that a well-integrated region could give them. Any sense of security has come from forging multiple links between the local and the global, by ceaselessly networking the myriad vanguard institutions and wealth-making centres, and the organisations and associations that continue to drive the knowledge economy. More than ever, this generation still needs to be innovative and creative. The future looks very exciting indeed, but in quite different ways from what made this campus humming with life two generations back.

Concluding Thoughts

The China Presence cast a long shadow. At its core, it was about people's basic feelings drawn from their language, religion and customary practices that, in the postcolonial context, looked for freedom to continue, to gain self-respect, and to assert the difference. But, if their goals were successfully attained, the same feelings also impinged on other people's freedoms and threatened the social fabric on which the new nation wanted to build a fresh identity.

The Malaya Dream was in part to diminish the China Presence and remove all obstacles to a grand unity of the many peoples that lived in the Malaya that was about to be. Perhaps it was too much like an Anglo-Malay compromise to satisfy all the communities. Whether they liked it or not, the students in the new university were to be some of the agents of change to work out the new social contract. Its first two generations produced graduates who went on to run what turned out to be two countries. And most would look back with pride at what they eventually created. Theirs was a rational exercise aimed at curbing deep ethnic feelings. They acted with a sense of great urgency and shaped the minds to deal with the divisions that endangered the nation. For Singapore, they laid the foundations for social discipline accompanied by flexible thinking so that they could open the economy to the world.

For the third generation, neither being national nor regional could help secure the state's remaking. Only by connecting with the new forces of technology and international finance could a way out be found, powerful forces that no one had prepared for earlier on. Can the new university and the third generation ensure that the connections work? Singapore's efforts to expand its knowledge frontiers sounds exciting, but my memories are of a simpler era when we were merely trying to create a nation and not impress the globalised world.

19

Versailles' Chinese Legacy

Few universities just 100 years old can claim a major contribution to their country's historical transformation. Peking University, founded in 1898, had the distinction of doing just that in 1919, when only in its 20th year.

The Western imperial powers at the Versailles conference had agreed to let their ally, Japan, take over her special rights in the Chinese province of Shandong from the defeated enemy, Germany. China had also been an ally and had expected to get Shandong back from Germany. Its anger at the decision to let Japan have her war trophy was understandable.

Owing to the exceptional collection of liberal-minded professors at Peking University, some of the university's very bright students led demonstrations through the streets of Beijing, on 4 May 1919, to protest against what they considered a dastardly betrayal of their country.

This caught the tide of nationalist awakening and led to similar protests in every city. Ultimately, it became a movement associated with the rejection of Confucianism and superstitious religions, the *Baihua*

This article was first published in the 24 May 1999 issue of the *Times Higher Education Supplement*. Reproduced with the kind permission of *Times Higher Education* magazine.

(popular language) literature movement, the calls for new philosophy and scientism, and the foundation of the Chinese Communist Party.

Because it embraced modernising ideas and institutions, it came to be widely recognised as one that made a "cultural revolution" possible, on top of the republican revolution that Sun Yat-sen had started in 1911. The university, which backed most of the changes, has celebrated the May Fourth Movement whenever allowed.

In 1989, its students were preparing to celebrate the 70th anniversary when the popular, disgraced secretary-general of the Chinese Communist Party died suddenly. The demonstrations began early and May Fourth was celebrated by thousands of students joining the pro-democracy demonstrators in Tiananmen Square. Thirty days later, on 4 June 1989, the protests ended in tragedy, with dire consequences to the students, to Peking University and others, and to the country's international position.

In 1999, the urge to celebrate the 80th year was stronger than ever. Expectations were that the university would use the occasion to signal, at least, the restoration of its academic vitality and its liberal heritage. They were not disappointed. National leaders had decided to link the historic movement with the potential contributions of patriotic youth, and organised numerous celebrations, meetings and conferences in April. Peking University held a purely academic conference in early May, four days before the tragic bombing of the Chinese embassy in Belgrade. If the two had coincided, the whole conference would have been obliged to join in the protests with the kind of vigour expected.

The conference was a modest affair, with selected participants representing a wide range of institutions from China, Taiwan and Hong Kong, and 10 invited scholars, totalling 120. It achieved the objective of acknowledging the university's special claims and showing the government's careful support, but avoided the fierce enthusiasm that many might have expected.

It provided one of the correct messages that were sent out to those who had hoped for a more political occasion, some sort of a prelude to commemorate June Fourth in Tiananmen Square.

There were a number of papers on May Fourth protagonists who were not communists and even those who had been anti-communists. Several had been denigrated by the Communist Party both before and after 1949, for example, activists like Chen Duxiu and Hu Shih and some writers and philosophers who rejected Marxism or socialist literary criticism.

Some revisionism has been going on among more senior scholars for several years, but it was interesting that so many young Chinese scholars showed appreciation of "unapproved" people. In some papers, they revealed their excitement to have found so many young people — in the 1910s and 1920s — who had expressed modern ideas and clamoured for change.

Peking University has always claimed the right to lead the country in protest against corruption, injustice and political reaction. What is remarkable is that the national government in China is once again confident enough to recognise 4 May 1919, as a symbol of the willingness of China's young people to turn away from degenerate tradition and turn to modern values like freedom, democracy and science. By doing so, it has achieved three goals.

First, the Chinese leaders have identified the May Fourth Movement as a national concern. By encouraging all official centres to draw attention to its significance for young people, they have sought to appropriate for themselves its values. This should help them project a more sympathetic image on the eve of the 10th anniversary of Tiananmen Square.

Second, they have diffused the explosive character of student demonstrations by inviting many of them to the celebrations that have been officially organised. From pupils in kindergartens and primary schools to the older students in secondary and tertiary education, they have been selectively brought along to commemorate the positive and modernising features of an inspiring patriotic movement.

They have also allowed Peking University to organise a national and international conference as a scholarly event. They thus recognised the need to reassess the movement's place in history. They also made clear that the movement is no longer the elitist affair of the university and its privileged students, but something that the leaders now believe should, under their care, belong to all of the nation's young people.

20

Commonwealth Universities in Eastern Asia

Commonwealth universities have many identities today and this is no less so in Asia east of Calcutta, in Hong Kong, Malaysia, Singapore and Brunei. These new identities are the result of adaptation and change, of diversification and modernisation, during a period of over 40 years. But it is not all change. There are also great continuities that have provided the institutions with useful yardsticks to measure standards and progress. Perhaps the clearest way to distinguish past, present and future is to speak of the three phases of university building in the region.

The first is the "Empire" phase and consisted of three universities which were started before decolonisation began. These were the University of Hong Kong (1911), Rangoon University (1921) and the University of

---

This article was first published, under the headline "Far East looks to the future", on 13 August 1993 in the Issue 1084 of the *Times Higher Education Supplement*. Reproduced with the kind permission of *Times Higher Education* magazine.

Malaya (1949). Of these, Rangoon is no longer in the Commonwealth, and Malaya has essentially become two universities, with the original institution in Singapore now called the National University of Singapore and the one in Kuala Lumpur retaining the name of Malaya.

The "Commonwealth" phase which began in the 1950s had seen the rise of several new universities: one in Singapore (Nanyang University, 1956–1980, which from 1991, is known as Nanyang Technological University), seven in Malaysia (the University of Malaya since 1957; Universiti Sains Malaysia in 1969; Universiti Kebangsaan Malaysia in 1970; Universiti Putra Malaysia in 1971; Universiti Teknoloji Malaysia in 1972; International Islamic University Malaysia in 1983; and Universiti Utara Malaysia in 1984), two in Hong Kong (the Chinese University of Hong Kong in 1963 and the Hong Kong University of Science and Technology in 1991), and one in Brunei (Universiti Brunei Darussalam in 1985).

The third phase may be with us already — the phase of the international *English-speaking* university with markedly looser links with the Commonwealth. Formally, it will certainly be marked by the departure of Hong Kong from the Commonwealth in July 1997, but adjustments to global trends in higher education have been multiplying for at least two decades, not least within the region through the Association for Southeast Asian Institutions of Higher Learning (ASAIHL), which was founded in 1955. Through this organisation, Commonwealth university values intermingle with those originating in continental Europe and North America. The contacts have enabled comparisons between systems which have been of benefit to all their members.

It is important to know that the early "Empire" universities did adapt in order to meet new challenges in Hong Kong and Singapore, but their structures remain closest to the English red-brick universities after which they were modelled. This has provided some advantages in tapping British skills and experiences, but the connections have also inhibited local experimentation on the one hand and discouraged wider international teaching and research links on the other. During the past two decades, these inhibitions have diminished but changes have been slow and yet to be significant.

The post-1950 universities, however, were built to mixed demands and post-independence criteria. Most of those in Malaysia were begun by responding to nationalist needs and several were prepared to look to American universities for fresh ideas. Even in Hong Kong, which was

British territory then, the Chinese University of Hong Kong recruited Chinese academics trained outside the Commonwealth, notably from the United States. This, in turn, influenced the older University of Hong Kong to look further afield.

Future Challenges

The three major challenges for universities are to produce well-educated graduates out of the expanded numbers gaining access to the universities; to meet community and national needs; and to be modern institutions responsive to global changes. The challenges will not have equal place in the four different territories, nor in the various universities. But I would be surprised if the three challenges are not shared to a large extent by the majority of the academic staff teaching and doing research in each of the institutions.

Expansion in numbers began in Malaysia in the 1970s. Hong Kong has followed suit, especially after 1989. Singapore and Brunei have been more cautious, but the pressures for access are growing. Here the British elitist model has not been helpful and the universities have tended to look to North America and Australia for examples of how to ensure that more does not mean worse. Most of the institutions are more aware now of the need to revise teaching methods and criteria to cater for the large numbers on campus. Fortunately, the Commonwealth now provides a rich mixture of different kinds of universities from which the East Asian ones can learn. Academic conservatism, however, is widespread and it is unlikely that there will be radical departures. The most striking exception in the region is the University of Science and Technology in Hong Kong which has openly looked to the United States for help to get out of the Commonwealth mould.

Community and national needs can be met through course changes and the addition of new degrees and curricula. In most cases, this would not involve structural changes to the universities themselves. The challenge for universities in newly independent countries is mainly one of recruitment of academic staff of good quality and ensuring that the staff understand local cultural and political conditions and the changing world in which their respective countries seek progress and advancement.

This ties in with the third challenge, to be modern and responsive in a rapidly changing world. This is where organisations like the Association of Commonwealth Universities (ACU) do a valuable job. The ACU is one of the strongest of the global organisations that have been created to focus on the universal features of great universities. There is little doubt that those universities that have been served, and are regularly brought together, by the ACU have found the links valuable. The ACU has ensured that, while individual identities have been transformed, continuities remain to sustain a global sense of what universities stand for.

21

You've Come a Long Way

The Scottish renaissance of the 18th century was a remarkable development. Its original contributions to modern thought deserve the attention they have received. What is less well known is that the Scottish renaissance has also helped us understand something called provincialism.

For all their achievements, David Hume, Adam Smith, William Robertson, Robert Burns and James Boswell remained provincials from the point of view of London. They lived with that condition until they got used to it. Being reminded of this early form of English-language provincialism brings me to a contemporary manifestation of it that is of growing interest in Asia.

There is nothing new about provincialism itself. Every great culture, empire or large country with a dominant centre will have its provinces.

This article was first published in the 11 December 1995 issue of the *Times Higher Education Supplement*. Reproduced with the kind permission of *Times Higher Education* magazine.

If the culture is large enough, there may even be degrees of provincialism, distinguishing those nearest the centre from those further away. The Hindu-Buddhist idea of a mandala and the Chinese projection of a Middle Kingdom both imply the existence of concentric circles of the more or less civilised as defined by their distances from the core.

As far as provincialism is concerned in the British context, Scotland was only the beginning. The colonies in North America soon followed and, later, in the 19th century, the new provincials were those people who had emigrated to Australia and New Zealand. Indeed, there may be some people in Britain today who still regard these peoples as provincials.

Then, in a new application of the concept, peoples of different ethnic and cultural backgrounds came to be termed provincials. Where the British Empire was concerned, the first to qualify as some kind of provincial were the educated elites of British India and Ceylon (Sri Lanka) who admired the cultural values of the metropolitan country. They led the way in being accepted as provincials worthy of a place not far behind the Canadians and Australasians, and for a while, somewhat ahead of the rebellious and treasonable Americans who did not play cricket.

Thus an imperial provincialism spread to the non-white peoples of the empire. Elsewhere in Asia, the subjects of the Straits Settlements and the Malay States joined with those of the Caribbean and British territories in Africa and Oceania in qualifying for membership. When they met the standard, they were welcomed with tolerance, some condescension, and not a little affection. But the number of those people who were comfortable with such a reception was relatively small.

After independence, parts of British culture continued to be admired by the former colonials on every continent. In Asia, as Indians, Pakistanis, Sri Lankans, Malaysians and Singaporeans, many long remained provincials in British eyes, even though most British people no longer thought the concept appropriate. In any case, the Indians and other South Asians were too numerous and self-assured to care too much what the British thought of them.

This is less true of those in Malaysia and Singapore, where national identities are still new and there is still sensitivity about being patronised. What is remarkable is that this form of provincialism is not peculiar to Britain. It would seem that some United States politicians and commentators of late have come to look on the leaders of these two countries in rather familiar ways.

Why do I say that? Are Malaysians and Singaporeans now provincials in American eyes? This surely cannot be. I am reminded of some of the ways, especially during the 1950s, when British commentators had picked on Indian intellectuals, suggesting that they had grown too big for their boots. This was particularly so when Indian nationalist and anti-colonial writings were being reviewed in the British press. All that has now settled down, as various groups of South Asians have integrated their borrowed skills into the emergent national cultures of the region.

So where does the United States come in? As a superpower, and the only country worthy of that name since 1989, it may have claims to be the global centre of modern culture. Furthermore, through the dominance of English as a language of international intercourse, the United States could inherit the mantle of the empire where the sun never sets and see the whole English-speaking world as answerable to it.

Not to be forgotten is the American experience of having been provincials to the British, and then to the Western Europeans. With that background, it should not surprise us if the leading centre of Western culture today might expect to have provincials of their own and to see itself as responsible for setting standards of civilised behaviour.

For the Malaysians and Singaporeans, the United States cause today is that of human rights and democracy, a cause which the Malaysians and Singaporeans have stubbornly refused to come on board. On the contrary, they answer back and defend with something called Asian values. This seems to have been seen as something of an affront. And the right to speak of such contrary seems to have been questioned.

If this defence had come from Japanese or Indian leaders, would the United States have regarded them in a similar way? It seems unlikely as both those protagonists are big enough to have brushed all criticisms aside. What if the Indonesians or the Thais had spoken up? Again, that would be unlikely, because both these countries have strong indigenous traditions to argue from. And if the Filipinos had talked back, I suspect the Americans would have looked at their history and found that amusing.

Why then do the actions and words of Malaysia and Singapore arouse such ire among some well-connected Americans? The leaders of those two countries have many achievements to their name, and deserve the reputations they have earned. But they are seen as products of the English-language tutelage. Surely their education should have predisposed them to better appreciate Western values. It is thus likely that Americans perceive them as successful graduates of the core culture who are out there guarding the far-flung frontiers of civilisation and really should not be so misguided as to offer alternative Asian values. Instead, they should join the team on the periphery of an English-speaking heartland that has now been translated to the United States.

To come back to the example of Scotsmen in the eyes of London, it would be interesting to ask if the best-educated Malaysians and Singaporeans should be seen as the new provincials of a global English-language world. I am intrigued by the thought that only a new kind of education could rid us of this kind of provincialism. Perhaps the deliberate call for Asian values is part of the answer. But it will take a lot of fresh educational thinking and many original blueprints, a lot of voices in unison, and a lot of agreed agendas by much bigger powers with much greater resources, before that condition could be changed.

22

Academic Blind Spot in Asia

We are accustomed to the history of Orientalism in the West and its politically correct extension, the field of Asian studies. We are less aware, however, of the Asian efforts to study one another's societies and teach the subject in schools and universities. These efforts are, in any case, rarely described as Asian studies, for the simple reason that Asia is a European construct and Asians have discovered their "Asianness" only during the past century in reaction to being grouped as Orientals.

To be called Orientals reflects the fact that foreign cultures were being studied as the Other by Occidentals. It is different when scholars and students in Asia today turn consciously to study neighbouring countries and peoples as Asians. For most, this would be a new experience that identifies one's neighbours as fellow Asians.

It is time to ask how Asians are faring in the study of their neighbours as part of their discovery of Asia. How did scholars in Asia study the Other before the impact of Orientalism, and how are they doing it now?

This article was first published in the 8 June 1997 issue of the *Times Higher Education Supplement*. Reproduced with the kind permission of *Times Higher Education* magazine.

The first long-term example of this kind can be represented by Chinese scholarly writings on Indian Buddhism, which included knowledge of Indian states as well as worldly notes on Southeast Asian trading ports and kingdoms. The tradition began with imperial records about border states, a sort of Chinese Orientalism, which reached a climax with a series of studies before and after the Cheng Ho expeditions of the 15th century.

As for the Chinese Buddhist studies of the Other, they date back at least 1,600 years to Fa-hsien's *Record of the Buddhistic Kingdoms*. This was followed by the Japanese and Korean studies of Chinese Buddhism, and both groups were later to write profoundly on Confucianism.

Elsewhere in Asia, a new tradition began with Islam. Arab and Persian studies of the countries they traded with to their east were followed by books on India. And there were also the works in various languages that were spawned by the Mongol empire in Eurasia.

In Southeast Asia, too, several empires from Majapahit to Vietnam to Ayudhya left writings that reflected similar approaches to the study of the Other as exotic and dependent entities.

These earlier expressions of imperial Orientalism remind us that the awareness of the Other has both humble as well as arrogant beginnings.

The immediate antecedents of Asian studies in European and North American universities enjoyed an arrogant phase. And there is a residue of superiority in some of the approaches found today. But a more humble scientific attitude has evolved in the postcolonial period, and the study of Asia has diversified well beyond the classical and the ethnographic stage. In particular, the global expansion of the social science disciplines has left no part of Asia unstudied. The question is, how do Asians regard these studies and how far have they developed patterns for studying the Other that are peculiar to themselves?

This subject has intrigued a number of foundations, especially those that have supported Asian scholars in the arts and the social sciences to pursue their studies in Western Europe, North America, and on the edge of Asia, Australasia and the exceptional case of Japan. These scholars have much to offer Western and Japanese students but have also brought methodologies back to their own institutions. Over time, this has led to fruitful collaborations.

What had attracted attention then was the impression that, while scholars from each Asian country had established close relations with their counterparts in Western universities, relatively few had done the same with fellow scholars in Asia. To find out how true this is, and if this has longer-term significance, the president of the Asian Studies Association of Australia, Anthony Reid, was invited to chair a meeting to examine the state of Asian studies in Asia today.

The meeting, held at Hua Hin with Chulalongkorn University's Institute of Asian Studies as host, collected detailed information about each of the 16 territories covered. As one might expect, each country's teaching and research about itself is serious and sustained, but when it comes to the study of other countries or regions in Asia, the situation is quite different.

It is not surprising that the study of the Other varies from country to country. What is surprising is how few scholars in some countries study their immediate Asian neighbours at all. The reasons for this neglect are many. They include the obvious ones, such as shortage of money and research facilities and the historical distrust between governments concerned. No less important, however, is that many societies respect their scholars more if they keep close links with their teachers and colleagues in the West than if they work with other Asians. This is partly because the latter have little funding, and partly because exciting methodologies have come from the West.

As noted, Japan is an exception, not only because it has absorbed many Western scholarly practices, but also because it has had a long history of studying China as its Other for more than a thousand years. Switching from China to the West was a decision that transformed the country. It used Toyoshi (Oriental History) to cover what the West called Oriental, and employed similar attitudes towards the study of the Oriental Other. It is now the only Asian country that has continuously studied the history of the rest of Asia for more than 100 years.

China and South Korea have also established Asian studies, but economic and political constraints have limited their coverage. Elsewhere, with the exception of Hong Kong and Singapore, funding problems have been more severe, and local scholars often depend on sources outside Asia for funds to keep up their research work.

South and Southeast Asian countries are more prone to look to the West than to one another. Does it matter? For the present, probably not. But it does seem a shame that scholars who are more likely to understand their neighbours are lured away. It is probably because the near is too familiar and is not enough of the Other to stimulate intellectual interest. There is no relief from the same assortment of underdeveloped problems.

What is fresh and stimulating and worthy to be future models comes from the successful West. With the financial denouement[1] of the past year, this is likely to continue. Unless deliberate efforts are made to offer viable alternatives, the study by Asians of neighbouring Asian cultures may become even less appealing.

---

[1] Referring to the 1997–1998 Asian Financial Crisis.

23

English Rules the Waves

Thirty years ago, it would have been difficult to travel around Western Europe speaking only English. This is not true today. In fact, the standard of English among the educated in some of these countries is so good that it can match that of the best-educated native speakers.

Two recent trips, to Norway and to the Netherlands, confirmed this. I was frankly amazed at the quality of the English spoken by their university students. There is, however, no suggestion that this is a threat to the national languages of the two countries. So I am puzzled when language nationalists, notably in France, are defensive. With the European Union gaining acceptance, ever more Europeans have more than one second language and many have a few others in addition. The threat to national languages from the greater use of English must be more imaginary than real.

This article was first published in the 10 June 1996 issue of the *Times Higher Education Supplement*. Reproduced with the kind permission of *Times Higher Education* magazine.

In Asia, the willingness to learn European languages during the period of European supremacy gathered momentum during the early 20th century.

When Western political and military power retreated in the 1950s, that willingness was curtailed for a while and there was greater stress on the use and development of national languages.

Today, economic growth and national confidence have led to new attitudes towards the language of economic and technological potency.

Invariably, the language preferred has become English, partly because of the past extent of the British Empire in Asia, and partly because the successor to the British in global influence, the United States, also uses English. In all areas of science and economics, no other language now can be as useful. All the same, serious questions remain.

With the rapid economic development of Asia, are there enough people who have mastered English for national needs? Should there not be an alternative to English, or even a third-language competence, instead of total dependence on English for all cross-national transactions? Is there no room for an Asian language like Japanese, Chinese, or Malay (Bahasa Indonesia or Bahasa Malaysia), perhaps as the common third language?

In recent months, Malaysia has encouraged students to acquire higher standards of English and opened up international education opportunities on its own soil in an unprecedented way.

In China, the preferred second language is English, but more students are learning Japanese and there is once again encouragement to learn a long-neglected language — Russian!

In Vietnam, the French hope to regain their first foreign language status, and some Vietnamese leaders who had struggled with Russian or Chinese, and now face the pressures of English, are said to feel more comfortable with the idea of returning to the use of French.

It is well known that, in commercial cities like Bombay, Hong Kong, Tokyo, Shanghai, Bangkok, Kuala Lumpur, Jakarta and the city-state of Singapore, the demand for professionals with higher and yet higher standards of English is growing. Expatriates can be found to fill various gaps to some extent, but there is concern over the shortage of own-nationals to control this key instrument of international discourse.

In the hallways of chambers of commerce in every city, there is talk of the need for a whole army of English teachers to lift the standards in order to enable businesses to perform more efficiently and extensively.

There are interesting differences in the three regions of South, Southeast and East Asia. For South Asia, English is widely used, the quality of its English is high and there is no challenger. Also, there is no talk of threats to the various languages of India, Pakistan, Bangladesh or Sri Lanka.

In East Asia, English still has to compete with the national languages in areas like business and technology. And both the Japanese and the Chinese governments are seeking to make their languages invaluable for the region. Eventually, they hope that their respective languages will become widely accepted, especially in Southeast Asia.

There is no region in the world more complicated than Southeast Asia where religions, cultures and types of polities are concerned. A very practical solution to its linguistic variety has been for the countries of the Association of Southeast Asian Nations (ASEAN) — with its seven, and eventually 10, members — to use English for all official regional business. There is, therefore, no lack of incentives for everyone to learn English. On the contrary, in those places where English is most used, the perception is that English has gained at the expense of the native languages. This has not, however, led to hysterical calls to curb the use of English as had happened at an earlier phase of nationalism.

The rational response has been to improve the quality of all language teaching, and as the standards of education rise, to encourage the learning of other foreign languages, including the Asian ones like Japanese, Chinese and the two forms of Malay.

It is too early to predict the consequences of such developments. The experience of Europe should be relevant. As each nationalism becomes self-confident, the use of a common foreign language as a *lingua franca* becomes acceptable, and the learning of other foreign languages and cultures is regarded as normal.

This is especially true in areas of business and information technology, but increasingly, areas of ideas, institutions, culture and the arts will open up as possible components of a shared regional heritage. The gradual but steady growth of a common consciousness among the Southeast Asian countries has set a valuable example for the rest of Asia.

The role of an international English for advanced discourse could achieve, despite initial resistance, what it has done for Europe. In addition, it could also be a powerful catalyst to enable native languages to develop modern usages and thus seek new cultural expressions. Such a phenomenon, the beginnings of which are already visible, would deserve careful and sustained monitoring for years to come.

24

Rise of Anglo-Chinese

In this part of the world, it is commonplace to argue that English is important to the Chinese because of its usefulness in trade and finance. Anyone who is bilingual in Chinese and English can probably trade easily in most corners of the world. This, however, does not recognise the increasing social and cultural importance of English for Chinese people worldwide, the fact that English is the most widely used language of science and intellectual discourse today.

Before the mid-19th century, few Chinese knew a foreign language. The coastal traders of South China who traded in Southeast Asia probably found that the most useful language in the region was Malay, the parent language of Bahasa Indonesia and Bahasa Malaysia.

From the middle of the 19th century, China-coastal Chinese had more to do with the English and the Americans, both in Hong Kong and Shanghai. Also, the peasants and workers who went out as coolie labour to Western colonies were concentrated mainly in the British Empire, or

---

This article was first published in the 6 March 1995 issue of the *Times Higher Education Supplement*. Reproduced with the kind permission of *Times Higher Education* magazine.

there were those who went to California, Australia and Canada in search of gold. Within China itself, owing to the strong influence of British trade and American missionary education, the major foreign language of higher education during the first half of the 20th century was English.

Since 1949, emigrants have gone to the United States from mainland China; large numbers of students from Taiwan also went there. From the 1970s, they have been joined by migrants from Hong Kong and have also gone to Canada and Australia. Increasingly, the emigrants consisted of households, and not just students. Furthermore, there were thousands of Chinese re-migrants from regions like Southeast Asia, Korea and southern Africa who were admitted to these English-speaking countries.

For lack of a better term, I would call these people Anglo-Chinese. The term came into use in the Straits Settlements and Hong Kong during the second half of the 19th century and referred to Chinese who had received an English education and were using the language at least in their work. This term could now be applied to a better educated group who not only know English but are likely to be fluent in Chinese as well. Hong Kong and Singapore had been major sources of such Anglo-Chinese. Most of them travelled on British ships to North America, Australasia, West Indies, South Pacific as well as Southeast Asia. Today all Chinese fluent in English might be called Anglo-Chinese.

There are no accurate figures for such people. Of the 25 million[1] Chinese who live outside mainland China, Taiwan and Hong Kong, nearly half of them live in English-speaking countries, for example, the United States and Canada (about 2 million), the United Kingdom (250,000), Australia (250,000), New Zealand (35,000), West Indies (40,000), the South Pacific, including Fiji and Papua New Guinea (30,000); and, in Asia, Singapore (2.2 million). There are other countries where the ethnic Chinese are largely English-speaking like Malaysia (5.5 million) and the Philippines (about one million), parts of south and west Asia (200,000) and Africa (70,000). Altogether there are about 11.5 million Chinese overseas in English-speaking countries.

---

[1] This and the subsequent figures were presented as at the time of writing in 1995. Reliable figures for the number of ethnic Chinese who live outside mainland China are difficult to compile. As compiled from various statistical sources in 2011, there are nearly 40 million Chinese overseas outside mainland China; the United States and Canada (about 5.2 million), the United Kingdom (400,000), Australia (670,000), New Zealand (148,000), Singapore (2.7 million), Malaysia (7.1 million), the Philippines (1.1 million), Africa (500,000).

One could add more to these figures. My estimate is that up to 10 per cent of the rest (another one million) are literate in English, especially those on the European continent and various countries in Southeast Asia, as well as some parts of the Caribbean and Latin America. And if we count Hong Kong as outside the China region, we might add another 20 per cent of its population to the total, that is, at least another million who are competent in English.

What about the people in China? China's first foreign language is now English and the demand for fluency is growing. In theory, the majority of those who graduate from high schools know English. If only one per cent of the population is literate in English, as suggested by a recent estimate, that would be more than 10 million people, nearly as many as the total outside China.

If they travel or study abroad or emigrate, chances are most of them would turn to the English-speaking world. And if they seek relatives and friends among the Chinese already overseas, again the majority of them are likely to look to the English-speaking world. Furthermore, there are about a million *guiqiao*, or returned overseas Chinese, in China and a large proportion of them are related to ethnic Chinese in the English-speaking world.

All this has happened notwithstanding the ongoing contradictions in relations between China and the United Kingdom for more than a century and a half, and between China and the United States since the end of the Second World War. The love-hate relationship has not dampened the Chinese perception of the usefulness of the English language. Indeed, the better educated they are, the more they seem to value the language.

When Chinese coolies worked in foreign mines and plantations, they were easy victims of ill-treatment. Even the adventurous miners who flocked to the gold fields of North America and Australasia had to suffer from racial discrimination. Most of these miners were not known for their mastery of English.

But, at another level, many Chinese within China were targets for English-speaking missionaries. Such Chinese were also receiving aspects of Western secular education, and many went on to colleges and universities to receive advanced training in modern science and the humanities. In other words, beginning with the hope of spiritual conversion, English-speaking missionaries educated several generations of Chinese to a new scientific and political culture. This prepared the ground for thousands of students to study in the West, especially those who went to the United States, and developed the admiration of modern science and technology, which remains strong. Despite the tensions between China and the outside world, the foundations laid through education seem to have survived. The role of higher education among the widely dispersed Anglo-Chinese populations deserves closer attention. There has been a convergence of aspirations and activities among those who have shared modern tertiary education.

And as for the global market, Anglo-Chinese who are also bilingual have found it easy to participate in international trade. We need only to look at the growth of Hong Kong and Singapore as commercial and financial centres and their links with other Anglo-Chinese cities like London, Manila, San Francisco, New York, Toronto, Vancouver, Sydney and Melbourne. They also bridge the business worlds of the Chinese overseas and the multinationals.

Then there is the place of bilingual education in advancing science and technology. Such an education enables a large pool of Chinese talent to tie in easily with the great education centres in the West, while also acting as communication channels with mainland China and Taiwan.

And, not least, we note the growing social and cultural sophistication of a majority of the Anglo-Chinese through their knowledge of two civilisations. They have access to the best of Anglo-American culture, and through that, most of Western civilisation, as well as to both traditional and modern Chinese civilisation. This has been most marked in Hong Kong, but there are great possibilities in Singapore, where English is the main medium, and in Chinese cities like Taipei, Shanghai and Beijing. It is now past the time when these Anglo-Chinese were merely channels for Anglo-American values to China. They can now also offer channels for Chinese traditions and values to be appreciated by the English-speaking world and beyond.

PART II

Wang Gungwu and His Works

His Authored Works

The Nanhai Trade: The Early History of Chinese Trade in the South China Sea*

Kuala Lumper: Journal of the Malayan Branch of the
Royal Asiatic Society, volume XXXI, Part 2, June 1958
Singapore: Times Academic Press, 1998 (revised edition)
Singapore: Eastern Universities Press, 2003 (reprint)

南海貿易與南洋華人
Translated by Yao Nan 姚楠
Hong Kong: Chung-hua Book Co, 1988

The history of the China trade in Southeast Asia — known as Nanhai trade in ancient term — dates back to evidence of its first appearance in *Record of the Grand Historian* by Ssu-ma Ch'ien in the first century BC. The South China Sea, known as the second Silk Route, was the main route of the Asian east-west trade in goods and ideas. China's dealings with the West extended as far as India, Ceylon and even Persia at the time.

The exchange of goods and ideas between China and Southeast Asia had already taken place before the Europeans' arrival in the 16th century. The China trade and its lucrative returns provided the setting for rulers, explorers and buccaneers to pit themselves against one another, or to collude among themselves, to gain dominance and wealth in the Malay Archipelago.

This study examines various features and economic background of Nanhai trade, and the Chinese imperial and regional attitudes towards it. Three phases can be

---

*Wang's master's thesis in 1954. First published as a monograph issue of *Journal of Malayan Branch Royal Asiatic Society* in 1958. Chinese translation published in 1988.

distinguished in the Nanhai trade. The first phase lasted for about five centuries from 221 BC to AD 220, during which the commodities traded were largely precious items and luxurious goods such as jewels and perfumes as demanded by the Chinese courts and its royalists. Enter the second phase which lasted for almost two centuries during the Southern dynasties when Buddhism gained a stronghold in China, the merchandise transported by maritime trade then shifted from luxurious goods to "holy things" such as incense (gharu-wood), ivory or sandalwood statues, and glass vessels used for temple rituals. The third phase lasted more than three centuries, through the T'ang to the rise of the Sung dynasty, when trade in drugs and spices surpassed that of the precious items and "holy things" from the two phases.

Wang examines other aspects of the trade, which reflect as much of the politics and culture of China as of Southeast Asia. Interactions between the Chinese and the non-Chinese reveal the long-entrenched imperial attitude and cultural superiority of the Chinese. The role of eunuchs in maritime trade is also touched upon, with discussion on the inevitable corruption and greed tied to lucrative activities despite the glamour and glitter. "Tribute missions" sent by small kingdoms south of China such as the Yüeh, and the emerging maritime empire of Fu-nan to the Chinese empire were substantiated with historical data, and the complex nature of these missions and their motives provided depth to the analysis. Fascinating travelogues of different kinds of merchants, sailors and middlemen from various localities around the region add colours to the narrative in this book.

This book — an academically serious work yet enjoyable for leisure reading — is the definitive reference for students of the economic history of China and of Southeast Asia.

A Short History of the Nanyang Chinese
Singapore: Eastern Universities Press, 1959

南洋華人簡史
Translated and annotated by Chong Yit Sun 張亦善
Taipei: Shui-niu Book Co, 1969, 1988, 2002
Hong Kong: Chung-hua Book Co, 1988

The word "Nanyang", meaning "Southern Ocean", is used as an equivalent of more recent coinage, "Southeast Asia". From the perspective of a Nanyang Chinese, Wang Gungwu provides a brief historical study into the rise of Chinese commercial and political influence in Southeast Asia over the past centuries.

After the Tang and Sung dynasties, the South China Sea witnessed an increasing number of trading voyages of Chinese merchants via the "great highway". By the 13th century, the traders and seamen gained control of the carrying trade in the South China Sea. Unprecedented official voyages, representing a policy of state trading, began during the Yung-lo years at the start of the 15th century. However, the Ming ban on private trading and the arrival of the Europeans in the 16th century greatly depressed the activities of Chinese traders in the South China Sea. The 17th and 18th century saw for the first time the Nanyang Chinese playing a role in the politics of the Chinese empire in the loyalist resistance against the Manchus after the disintegration of Ming dynasty in 1644. In view of the growing importance of European influence in the region, the history of the Nanyang Chinese is not only linked with the imperial history of China and the politics of the Southeast Asian states, but also closely associated with the changes in the economy of Western Europe.

The activities of the Nanyang Chinese from the late 18th century to mid-19th century became complementary to the Europeans in the commerce of Southeast Asia until the "Opium War" in 1840. The British dominance in Asia in the 19th century and the establishment of colonial Hong Kong accelerated Chinese emigration to the Nanyang, and further led to a growing Chinese economic power in Southeast Asia. Most significantly, the anti-Manchu revolution in 1911 showed that never had the Nanyang Chinese such great influence in China. The closer ties between the Nanyang Chinese and their homeland are in the manifestation of their contribution to the Chinese government to aid China's development between 1911 and 1941. However, in the face of the Japanese atrocities after 1941 and post-World War II, "there is no political cohesion observable among the Chinese in the Nanyang".

The Structure of Power in North China during the Five Dynasties
Kuala Lumpur: University of Malaya Press, 1963 (reprinted in 1967)
Stanford, CA: Stanford University Press, 1967

"The author traces two main developments in power structure operating throughout the period... One development concerns the gradual restriction of the autonomy of the provincial governors...The second development was for the provincial founders of successive regimes to employ their own provincial military retainer organizations at the capital...Dr Wang's reconstruction of the principal developments in power structure over the Five Dynasties has made sense of a bewildering period, and provides a valuable historical introduction to the foundation of the Sung and the origins of Sung society."

— Donald McMullen
Journal of the Royal Asiatic Society of Great Britain and Ireland, no. 3/4 (October 1965), pp. 133–134

"Wang plunges into numerous primary sources and comes up with narrations hithertofore available only in Chinese, tabulations of significant data done for the first time in any language, and above all a revealing analysis of how the control measures and mechanism under the regional military rulers actually laid the foundation for some characteristic features of Sung government, in turn the model for later dynasties."

— James T C Liu
Pacific Affairs, vol. 38, no. 1 (Spring 1965), pp. 71–72

"[Wang] analyses the types of dissident officials and military officers involved in these rivalries, the extent of their powers and the part they played in disrupting the T'ang empire and making or breaking its short-lived successors. He shows that the experimental institutions and structure of state evolved by these governors of fortune should not be treated as makeshift arrangements, but that they form a definite part of the process that led to the re-creation of unified empire in 960."

— Michael Loewe
The English Historical Review, vol. 80, no. 317 (October 1965), p. 813

"[Wang] gives a detailed picture of the competing forces within the ruling minority and the antagonism between local military and court cliques. The result of the seemingly chaotic events is shown to be a gradual re-emergence of centralised power and a corresponding decline of provincial powers."

— Herbert Franke
Journal of the American Oriental Society, vol. 85, no. 3 (July–September 1965), pp. 429–430

"His viewpoint is that of a historian plus political scientist, not that of a sociologist or a cultural historian...Often, Wang's footnotes contain important information about events which allow insight into a number of other processes which could not be discussed in his book...[H]e has well succeeded in proving his main hypothesis that the rulers of the Five Dynasties, not the Sung, were the real creators of many innovations in the structure of government, especially in the structure of local government."

— Wolfram Eberhard
The Journal of Asian Studies, vol. 24, no. 3 (May 1965), pp. 498–500

"The essential elements of the story are the eradication of late T'ang eunuch power and the development of palace commissioners to fill the vacuum, the rise of literati bureaucrats to replace the disappearing aristocratic officialdom, and what Wang describes as the transformation of the system of military governorships into an aspect of the central authority, accompanied by a general reorganization of provincial administration."

— F W Mote
The American Historical Review, vol. 70, no. 2 (January 1965), pp. 465–467

"[Wang] shows that the relatively more open political system of the later T'ang failed to satisfy the ambitions of the new men of wealth or talent who were pushing their way upward. Some, like Huang Ch'ao, became rebels. Others found careers in the provinces with the military governors

or in professional military service...Wang shows persuasively that the governments which developed in this manner were adapting the institutions of the military governorships to the needs of a centralized state."

— Arthur F Wright
Bulletin of the School of Oriental and African Studies,
University of London, vol. 27, no. 2 (1964)

The work — originally Wang Gungwu's doctoral dissertation at the University of London — focusses on the intervening years between the T'ang (618–907) and Sung (960–1279) dynasties, or the Wu-tai period (Five Dynasties), which has often been disregarded or treated as a time of minor significance in the major context of China's history. The reason for this neglect is that in this period of division, there was no centre of authority and therefore no integral subject for study by the dynastic approach. In view of the great disunity and frequent dynastic changes in the transitional period, the problem of how the T'ang mandate was passed on to the Sung becomes intriguing.

The work is an attempt to answer the question by concentrating on the evolution of a new structure of power from the last years of the Huang Ch'ao rebellion (875–884), when the T'ang empire had all but disintegrated, to the Khitan invasion in 946–947. It explains some of the features of the period, the changes in political institutions and the ever-shifting decision of the many men in positions of power. Contrary to the traditional view, the changes during the Wu-tai period led to a central government which succeeded not because it rejected the *chieh-tu shih* system and returned to T'ang institutions but because it had incorporated the basic features of the *chieh-tu shih* system itself. The establishment of governmental structure, which is usually credited to T'ai-tsu, T'ai-tsung and their ministers, was in fact already introduced in the period under study. By 947, the court had become an enlarged *chieh-tu shih* establishment dominated by the emperor's army (*ya-chun*) and the palace commissioners (*ch'in-li*). From then on, the *chieh-tu shih* system was no longer a threat to central power; what remained of it became a part of imperial government itself.

China and the World since 1949: The Impact of Independence, Modernity and Revolution
New York: St Martin's Press, 1977
London: Palgrave Macmillan, 1977

"Wang Gungwu's book focuses on 'change,' and he has clearly set out to apply the historian's craft to the post-1949 period. In developing these themes [of independence, modernity, and revolution], the author consciously reacts against both the Stalinist sovietization model of Chinese change fashionable in the 1950s and the more recent tendency to emphasize the "Chineseness" of everything China has tried to do. Yet he does repeatedly and consistently stress the Chinese distinctiveness of these themes and the Chinese view in general."

— Guy Alitto
The American Historical Review, vol. 83, no. 4 (October 1978), pp. 1075–1076

"...it contains a wealth of interesting and seasoned perspectives on the meaning of the modern world for China and also on the meaning of China for the modern world."

— Victor C Falkenheim
International Journal, vol. 33, no. 4, (Autumn 1978), pp. 866–867

"Rarely is a study of Chinese politics or contemporary history conceived in a way that effectively links domestic development with China's foreign relations...For example, Wang demonstrates how the domestic problem of consolidating power in Tibet and carrying out socialist revolution there became linked to Peking's international relations with India."

— Peter Van Ness
The Journal of Asian Studies, vol. 39, no. 1 (November 1979), pp. 144–145

"Wang Gungwu's study is intended to demonstrate the continuing relevance of a broader historical approach to understanding Chinese perspectives on contemporary international relations. The belief that

> *various historical associations serve as an enduring and even pivotal 'filter' for elite values is a sensible and necessary idea. Toward this end, Gungwu argues that China's foreign relations since 1949 are best understood wthin the context of three recurring themes: 'the desire to assert independence, the problems of modernity, and the determination to make revolution'."*
>
> — Jonathan D Pollack
> Chinese Foreign Policy: Five Authors in search of an Interpretation, The Rand Paper Series, Santa Monica: Rand Corp, 1980

Published in 1977, this book is, during that time, the most up-to-date historical study of China since its establishment in 1949 to Mao's death in 1976. When the changes that took place in China were too drastic to be grasped by almost anyone, Wang Gungwu had organised his thoughts into a systematically historical analysis in which he looked at the events from three determinately important issues: the assertion of independence, the quest for modernity, and the need to keep alive the relevance of revolution.

China's struggle for independence goes beyond mere presupposition of sovereignty and freedom from interference. It is still a relatively foreign concept to the Chinese who have long been indoctrinated with China's geographical centrality and cultural superiority. Such ideas make the concept of independence irrelevant to a country which used to think that it is more independent, more equal vis-à-vis her neighbours, and hence freedom from interference had never been a concern for it than it was for others. How China struggles with striking a balance between its long-cherished self-identity and the new global power structure reality is the issue that Wang tries to address.

The quest for modernity seems such a platitude now that no further justification is necessary. The problem again lies at China's centrally superior self-positioning. Can modernity be equated with development? And for the case of Asia, is modernity merely synonymous with Westernisation? The Chinese were not so sure. In the words of Wang, "the Chinese did not have the idea of modernity and did not need it so long as they felt that their civilisation was superior". Hence, a survey was conducted in chapter two on how Chinese elites finally came to agree on what modernity meant for China, and the events that led to the crystallisation of ideas.

The revolution resulting in the birth of communist China is successful, but the mission is by no means accomplished. Revolution is far from being a completed enterprise, but seems more like an ever-going process. In fact, the book covered the way of life during the period. As a historian, Wang habitually traces back the idea to its very first introduction into China at the turn of the 20th century, and reconstructs the tortuous course it took among Chinese elites.

Through the lens of these three themes, this book is one of the first contemporary histories that study the changes that took place in China since 1949. Based on the limited data available then, Wang puts the changes into perspectives, and traces their origin back to China's very history and culture.

Community and Nation: Essays on Southeast Asia and the Chinese
Selected by Anthony Reid
Published for the Asian Studies Association of Australia
Singapore: Heinemann Educational Books (Asia), 1981

Community and Nation: China, Southeast Asia and Australia (New Edition)
Published for the Asian Studies Association of Australia St Leonard, New South Wales: Allen & Unwin, 1992

"'[T]he Chinese throughout Southeast Asia have at all times manifested three distinctive political groupings based on their commitments to politics in China, to the politics of the respective overseas communities, and to local politics whether indigenous, colonial or nationalist'. Wang Gungwu suggests here that no nationalist leader arose independently from among the Nanyang Chinese. His paper on 'Malaysia: Contending Elites' written after the riots of May 1969...provides an enlightening *analysis of the roots of the political tension arising from the conflicts between the Malay-educated, the Chinese-educated, and the English-educated elites."*

— Claudine Salmon
Journal of Southeast Asian Studies, vol. 15, no. 1 (March 1984), pp. 199–200

"For Sino-Southeast Asian relations, the author has extended his earlier interests in the Nanhai trade to China's tribute system, the rise and demise of early Ming contacts with Southeast Asia, and Sino-Malaccan relations. Drawing on all available Chinese sources on foreign relations and foreign countries, Wang has made substantial original contribution to the scholarship in this area."

— C F Yong
The Journal of Asian Studies, vol. 42, no. 3 (May 1983), pp. 734–736

"The overall title of the volume captures the common thread running through much of it; namely, the tension arising from a less than homogeneous Chinese presence in South-east Asia and the problems of adjustment involved in coming to terms with dominant political cultures...This collection of essays should appeal to a variety of intellectual tastes. They constitute a set of thoughtful commentaries and also sustain a sanguine note about the prospect of accommodation between the often discordant social forces of community and nation."

— Michael Leifer
The China Quarterly, no. 93 (March 1983), pp. 169–170

This book is a collection of 22 essays Wang Gungwu had written on Chinese in the region of Southeast Asia and Australia. Eleven essays are from an earlier collection in 1981, entitled *Community and Nation: Essays on Southeast Asia and the Chinese* (in the Asian Studies Association of Australia series on Southeast Asia). Of the eleven, three essays focus on early Sino-Southeast Asian relations. These essays provide valuable perspective on the formative years of the region before the Western penetration. Four other essays explore the key eras and critical issues of the Malay, Malayan and Malaysian history. The issues examined include Malayan nationalism, the roles of Malaysian elites, and Chinese politics in Malaya. The remaining four are articles on overseas Chinese in Malaya just before the process of nation-building began to kick in; and the contrasting, sometimes conflicting, picture of how the Chinese struggle with their emotional and political ties to their homeland. The tug of war between the identities of *huaqiao* (Chinese sojourners) and patriotic nationalists plays out in the heart of nearly all overseas Chinese.

Of the remaining 11 essays that make up the other half of the book, eight were published after 1981. Four essays pertain to Australia, covering the different aspects of its relations with neighbours in the region. Australia's relations with the four Asian economic dragons are discussed in the perspective of trade and cultural values; the vicissitudes of Sino-Japanese relationship and their implications for Australia are studied; and the Asian perceptions of Australia and how they may differ from the Australians is the focus in two essays. Two essays study the early history of Southeast Asia in the 9th and 14th centuries, and the regions' relations in the early Ming dynasty. Malacca, its first three rulers and the history of opening relations with China between 1403 and 1405, are discussed in detail in the final two essays.

The highlight of the collection is the inclusion of three writings by Wang that date back to his early career, namely "A Short History of the Nanyang Chinese", "A Short Introduction to Chinese Writing in Malaya", and "'Are Indonesian Chinese Unique?' Some Observations". The first essay is one of the author's earliest efforts to understand the Nanyang Chinese, and the latter two essays compare and contrast the Chinese of Indonesia and of Malaya-Singapore. Prepared in 1958 as broadcast talks, the first essay was out of print for a long time, and had been translated into Chinese and Japanese. Representing the early views and observations of a scholar in the 1950s, this essay is now transformed into a historical document, providing a glimpse into the Chinese communities in Southeast Asia in the mid-20th century.

東南亞與華人：王賡武教授論文選集
Southeast Asia and the Chinese
Translated by Yao Nan 姚楠
Beijing: China Friendship Publishing Company, 1986

This 12-essay collection marks the first publication on Wang Gungwu's work in Chinese history that become widely accessible in China's Chinese-language scholarship circle. Most of the papers featured are Wang's lifelong scholarship devotion, namely the interplay between Chinese civilisation and the outside

world, in particular the world of Southeast Asia. The papers are clear manifestations of his remarkable historical insights and scholarly acumen.

The seminal paper, "Early Ming's Relation with Southeast Asia: A Biographical Survey", is in fact a pioneering work on the theory of international politics from the perspective of the Chinese civilisation. The central issue in China's imperial relations with the external world, as defined implicitly by Wang, lies in the difficulty of situating China vis-à-vis the others. Historical discourse of international relations in ancient China revolves around the tensions between ever-changing real-world power relations and the infallible faith in the cultural hegemony/superiority of the Chinese civilisation. Based on historical evidences, Wang demonstrates convincingly that the apparent "universalist" attitude emanating from China's cultural superiority must be backed by military and political power. In fact, moral superiority cannot exist separately from creditable coercive forces.

The following three papers in the volume, "China and Southeast Asia: 1402–1424", "The Beginning of China's Relations with Melaka" and "The First Three Rulers of Melaka", all early works in Wang's graduate days, clearly manifest his basic trainings as a multilingual and cross-cultural historian and a young conscientious scholar. In the first two of these works, Wang drew his analysis from the primary Chinese sources, mostly the multi-volume *Ming Shilu* and the official histories to verify some of the most important historical sequence of events in early Sino-Malacca interactions. In the third paper, Wang scored a brilliant scholarly polemics against Winstedt, the then authority on early Malaya history, by establishing the existence of a second ruler in the early history of ruling house in Malacca sultanate. Wang's extensive use of extant Chinese sources, especially the *Ming Shilu*, is certainly more detailed than Malay and Portuguese sources. This finding is later accepted by Malaysian historical textbooks in their narratives of early modern history of Malaya.

The central theme of the other papers is the Chinese diaspora. Wang is one of the pioneering scholars who analysed the variegated social, economic and political lives of overseas Chinese community. He is particularly concerned with the diversity and dynamics in the socio-cultural identity of the migrant Chinese communities in Southeast Asia. He identified the clear distinctions between the migrants groups that are connected to China and share the nationalism in the mainland through common experience, and the majority of the Chinese migrants whose identity is essentially local rather than national and whose links to mainland is tenuous at best. His classification of overseas Chinese into three distinctive political groups — the China-centrists, the apolitical realists and the assimilated elites — has thence become a powerful tool in analysing the politics of overseas Chinese.

歷史的功能
The Use of History
Translated by Yao Nan 姚楠
Hong Kong: Chung-hua Book Company, 1990

The Use of History is a collection of Wang Gungwu's essays focussing on methodologies of historical research in the study of Chinese history, China's foreign relations, Chinese migration history and the history of overseas Chinese.

Wang identifies three purposes of studying history. The first use of history stems from the most basic need to preserve the group identity and to ensure survival. Second, history is useful knowledge for the practical and moral lessons it has for the present so that mankind can avoid repeating mistake and make progress. Drawing insight from the ancient Greeks who admitted that history was a kind of "philosophy teaching by example", Wang rationalises that history helps man comprehend his humanity and understand his destiny on earth, though this third use is not limited to spiritual concerns.

In Wang's analysis, there are three main techniques of presenting history. Narrative or stories, which include the epic, collection of didactic anecdotes, eyewitness accounts, chronicles and annals is one effective method that presents history with verity and accuracy. The second method of presenting history is through critical and analytical scholarship. Still at nascent stage, there is a great deal more to learn from and develop the scholarship not only by social scientists but also by the natural scientists. The third method of presenting history is through the form of propaganda, which is prevalently applied to arouse patriotic emotions and for proselytising among the non-believers or disbelievers, when historical data being used are imperfect and subject to different interpretations.

History, if applied constructively and with objectivity, can contribute to the success of nation-building. The past successes and failures of a country, the origins of its existing customs, laws and institutions, and the rationale of various decision-making are the lessons and historical basis of what people should be equipped to understand their country's place in the region and in the wider world.

China and the Chinese Overseas
Singapore: Times Academic Press, 1991
Singapore: Eastern Universities Press, 2003

"[...]Professor Wang is not afraid to 'think out loud', gently warning against chauvinism or prejudice, and encouraging all students of Chinese history to do the same. His special combination of Confucian dignity with twentieth-century realism, diplomacy and intellectual integrity provides a welcome model of principled scholarship."

— Michael R Godley
The Australian Journal of Chinese Affairs, no. 30 (July 1993), pp. 200–201

"Part I, 'Historical Perspectives' traces the history of Chinese migration, focusing upon particular types of immigrants (such as the Hokkien), migrant communities in Southeast Asia (principally the Malyan and Singaporean Chinese) and migration patterns...Part II, 'Contemporary Themes' concentrates on topics such as integration with the indigenous population, the sensitive issue of 'divided' loyalties and the different experiences of the ethnic Chinese in different parts of Southeast Asia."

— James Chin
China Information, vol. 12, no. 1 (Summer/Autumn 1997), pp. 280–282

This book is a collection of 16 essays, lectures and papers on the complex and perplexing issue of the true identity of overseas Chinese. The insights are drawn from two broad perspectives — historical and contemporary — which also form the part one and two of the book, respectively.

Chapter one examines four historical patterns of Chinese migration — the trader pattern, the coolie pattern, the sojourner pattern, and the descent of the re-migrant pattern — and focusses on the future direction in the research of the history of Chinese migration. Chapter two, "Southeast Asian *Huaqiao* in Chinese History-Writing", introduces the Chinese writings that had marked several important turning points both in the history of the Chinese communities and in the writing of history itself.

Chapter three studies the foreign relations of the Ming dynasty with Southeast Asia. It covers the court policies under different emperors towards the region, and the famous Cheng Ho naval expedition. "Merchants without Empires: the Hokkien Sojourning Communities" puts this group of overseas Chinese into historical perspective, singling out two regions, Manila and Nagasaki, for discussion. Chapter five is a comparative study of China's relationship with Southeast Asia during the Song, Yuan and Ming dynasties. Chapter six relates the "private" and "public" trade in Chinese history from before the fifth century to the 18th century, with the private-public distinction made with or without the Chinese court acknowledgement.

"Political Chinese: Their Contribution to Modern Southeast Asian History" sheds light on why overseas Chinese are in a state of flux today. This chapter looks into the past, and offers speculation for its transitional nature in the broader and larger continuous effort for stability. Chapter eight is a narrative of two historical figures, Lim Boon Keng and Lu Xun, who were influential during the 20th century in Singapore and China, and how their fate was tied to the exaltation and/or condemnation of Confucianism in Chinese societies in China and beyond. The last chapter in part one focusses on the Chinese in Singapore, and their transformation from immigrants to settlers.

Essays in part two take on a contemporary theme, starting with a discussion of the culture of Chinese merchants within and outside of China. "The Study of Chinese Identities in Southeast Asia" offers interesting findings substantiated with clear classification, flow charts and diagrams. Chapter 12 discusses the Chinese government's identification of "external China" as a new policy area, what this meant for China, and for overseas Chinese including those in Taiwan, Hong Kong and Macao.

Chapter 13 offers observations of the Chinese's perspective on overseas Chinese in south China, the homeland of most overseas Chinese. These were

Wang's observations during his trip to the four provinces in southern China. "Little Dragons on the Confucian Periphery" discusses the rising Asian economies besides China mainly from the cultural perspective, focussing on the Confucian heritage in these countries. Chapter 15 studies the education in overseas Chinese communities and settlements, the difficulties they face in juggling often more than one cultural tradition. The last essay analyses the Chinese communities in Malaysia, Thailand and the Philippines from different perspectives, that of the host governments, of China, and of the overseas Chinese themselves, in order to understand "what kind of minority" are the Chinese in these countries.

The Chineseness of China — Selected Essays
Hong Kong: Oxford University Press, 1991

"The collection deals with the history and civilization of China itself, and what we are treated to is a selection of views of Chinese culture through the professionally-trained eyes of one who has always belonged to but been detached from that culture."

— Hugh D R Baker
The China Quarterly, no. 137 (March 1994), pp. 270–271

"Wang brings as rich a range of experiences and resources to a discussion of Chinese historical and cultural identity as any one now writing. In this collection of his scholarly and occasional pieces we can begin to discern the distinctiveness of his point of view... Wang, to oversimplify, is in search of a modern China with which he can identify without wrenching ambivalence...I look forward to reading more of his efforts to make sense of the Chinese past and to discern a Chineseness in China with which he can identify without reservation."

— John E Wills, Jr
The China Journal, no. 35 (January 1996), pp. 214–216

Published between 1957 and 1990, the 15 essays collected in this volume provide a wide-ranging overview of Wang Gungwu's efforts — as a Chinese born and brought up outside China, but with deep roots in his culture — to learn about his motherland. The essays reflect his perception of how the Chinese view both their past and their present, and how these views have changed during the three decades since the first of these essays was written. Dedicated to his children, Shih-chang, Lin-chang, and Hui-chang so that they might better understand their Chinese roots, it is along the same vein that Wang hopes to achieve for general readers of Chinese ethnic.

In three parts — history, civilisation and contemporary history-writing — the essays deal with historical topics, focussing on T'ang and Sung dynasties; Chinese attitudes to civilisation, including consideration of social rights and duties, and of the place of the individual throughout the course of Chinese history; and Chinese self-absorption with their past, and that their recent past, no less than their ancient traditions, constitutes the heart of their Chineseness.

It is the onus of modern biographers to assess Chinese rebel-reformers figures in historical context as Wang explained in the essay, "The Rebel-Reformer and Modern Chinese Biography", citing Sun Yat-sen as a prominent example of rebel-turned-"Father of the nation". At the end of the 19th century, the Chinese felt that their civilisation was under threat and were confronted with the need to change, modernise and civilise. The solution then, as explained in the essay, entitled "The Chinese Urge to Civilise: Reflections on Change", was adopting Western learning as the instrument to implement reforms.

The Chinese Way: China's Position in International Relations
Oslo: Scandinavian University Press, 1995

"The analysis of the roots of the problems of Sino-American relations alone make the book worth reading...But above all this slim volume deserves to be read in the PRC as it addresses many of the intellectual issues that should be on the agenda of serious thinkers about the future course of a modernizing China."

— Michael Yahuda
The China Quarterly, no. 147 (September 1996), pp. 973–974

This book presents the text of lectures delivered by Wang Gungwu at the Norwegian Nobel Institute's 1995 Spring Lecture.

Given the remarkable yet uneasy economic development of China since its open door policy in 1978, the rise of China from a century-long slumber to become an imminent great power is a fascinating subject to both academia and common people alike, in and outside of Asia. To foreigners, what may concern them most is how this emerging power will affect them when it assumes an increasingly important role in the international arena and becomes an indispensable factor in other countries' foreign policy. Wang addresses the issue from two broad perspectives: China's divergent economy and its unique political culture.

The term "divergent economies" has a two-tier meaning. First, the Chinese economy is divergent if Taiwan, Hong Kong and Macau are taken into account. This is a legitimate claim since Hong Kong and Macau would soon be handed over to mainland China at the time this lecture was given, whereas Taiwan, in Wang's opinion, will be reunited with the People's Republic of China "sometime in the 21st century". The term "Greater China" is then appropriate in describing the distinctively different economic entities of the Chinese social terrain. The Chinese economy is divergent in another sense, that is, the different, sometimes conflicting, perceptions outsiders have of the Chinese economy. Three images are examined: socialist market economy, developing economy and a universal model of integrating socialist ideals with capitalist means. For each, Wang has provided substantial details. The interaction and tension of these factors determine the trajectory of China's future development and its impact on the world at large.

The second lecture deals with politics and culture. In five sections, Wang traces China's painful and tortuous transformation from a historic empire to a modern nation-state and that from an ancient civilisation to a global power. He outlines the historical background, Chinese traditional ideals, its modern aspirations and critical self-perception, which are essential for China's development and its position in international relations.

China and Southeast Asia: Myths, Threats and Culture
EAI Occasional Paper No. 13
Singapore: World Scientific Publishing Company and Singapore University Press, 1999

China's economic prowess and its rise as a political force have led to critical re-examination of its future role in the Asia-Pacific region. The ubiquitous Chinese presence worldwide whether in terms of economic or social activities has raised the alarm in some countries and the Southeast Asia region as a forewarning

to China's future ambitions to dominate the region. The paranoia has intensified to the point where countries take efforts to guard against China and predict what China and the Chinese will do.

The three essays, delivered as lectures on different occasions, in this volume focus on areas where myths and prejudices have persisted in China's relations with Southeast Asia.

"Confronting Myths" examines and discusses the myths and misconceptions of the Southeast Asian Chinese, overseas Chinese and the formation of "China threat" mentality in Asia about China's capitalism and Chinese entrepreneurship.

"China's Place in the Region" envisions the influence China wields in the region and internationally as a rising power, and addresses the challenges it will face to revive its cultural heritage to meet the new threat projections.

"Culture in State Relations" lends an insight into China's perception of the state-system culture, which is intriguing for China that is commonly associated as a culture-state or civilisation-state. In-depth discussion sheds light on the viewpoint from Asia-Pacific region on state-system and culture-state.

Joining the Modern World: Inside and Outside China
Singapore: Singapore University Press and World Scientific Publishing Company, 2000

"Wang's extensive reading on Chinese history and knowledge about the Chinese on Southeast Asia gives his work a distinctive and valuable perspective."
— Lucian W Pye
The China Journal, no. 47 (January 2002), pp. 199–201

This book is a collection of eight essays addressing the enterprise of modernisation in and outside of China. Seven of the essays were first presented as lectures and seminars on different occasions, each of which offers a small fragment to the whole mosaic of the Chinese enterprise of modernisation.

The first chapter, "Joining the Modern World", was the opening lecture at the "Coping with China" symposium in 2000, organised by the Ethics and Public Policy Center and the Ronald Reagan Foundation in Washington, DC. Wang addresses the question of how far China has succeeded after trying relentlessly for 140 years to join the modern world. Chapter two, "The Chinese Revolution and the Overseas Chinese", was a lecture given at Stanford University in 2000. It was part of a series of lectures organised to commemorate the 50th anniversary of the People's Republic of China. The next essay, "A Single Chinese Diaspora", explores the aptness and the inaptness of the term "diaspora" in describing overseas Chinese, and examines their role in China's modernisation enterprise. "Hong Kong and an Ambivalent Modernity" was a lecture given on Hong Kong's history at the Pacific Rim Forum's meeting on the eve of Hong Kong's return to China, during which Wang admitted that Hong Kong's future was truly unpredictable but neither unknown nor unknowable.

Chapter five, "The Shanghai-Hong Kong Linkage", compares two of the most important stories of international Asia in this age from a historical perspective, where Wang's view well penetrates into their future. Chapter six, "Transforming the Trading Chinese", describes the longer-term development — the reversal in the status of merchants — that is changing the fabric of Asian societies generally, but most particularly in China. Chapter seven, "Chinese Values and Memories of Modern War", is a revised version of the Dunlop AsiaLink Lecture, which Wang gave in Melbourne in 1998, as a study of war memories through the prism of Weary Dunlop's war diaries. The last chapter in this volume — "Modern Work Culture and the Chinese" — discusses about coping with changes in the modern-day work culture, and in particular, how China, a vast agrarian society, adapts to modern work conditions.

Together, the collection of essays in this volume shows the Chinese resilience in guarding the modernisation enterprise, and their strong adaptability to change is reflected in the way they seize opportunity whenever and wherever it arises.

The Chinese Overseas: From Earthbound China to the Quest for Autonomy
Cambridge, Massachusetts: Harvard University Press, 2000

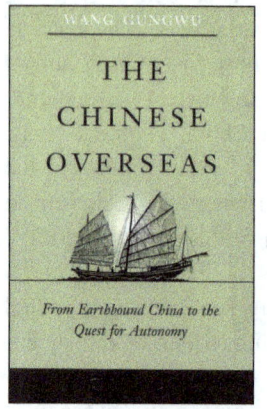

"[...]Wang highlights the transition that Chinese have made from being 'earthbound' and forbidden to leave China, to making up one of the largest diaspora communities in the world... Wang goes on to examine how Chinese overaeas view themselves today, how connected they are to China, and what their relationship is to the countries in which they now reside."

— Amy L Freedman
The Review of Politics, vol. 63, no. 2 (Spring 2001), pp. 380–383

"Autonomy here means being Chinese in a multicultural society, but with China becoming stronger and turning finally seawards, the implications of this for the host societies in the future cannot be fathomed, and Wang Gungwu does not attempt to fathom them."

— Hugh D R Baker
Bulletin of the School of Oriental and African Studies, University of London, vol. 64, no. 1 (2001), pp. 154–155

"[...]Wang implies that the idea of the overseas Chinese as a 'Greater China' is a political myth that comes from seeing the world from a presumed political center, which in this case would be the Chinese government. Wang calls this the land-bound view, a view that for centuries outlawed movement overseas, and then, by 1900, courted emigrants for the wealth they might contribute to China. State policies in the lands where they had settled had at least as much to do with their self-perception."

— David Faure
The Journal of Economic History, vol. 62, no. 2 (June 2002), pp. 603–605

"This short volume introduces the notion of the Chinese diaspora as a significant concept in the study of the Chinese outside of China...[Wang] has elevated the discussion from the Chinese as huaqiao to the Chinese as diasporic in their ambition for autonomy."

— Anthony B Chan
International Migration Review, vol. 37, no. 2 (Summer 2003), pp. 520–521

"Regarding the question of what is Chinese..., Wang celebrates a system in which there are many ways of expressing Chineseness. In such societies, standards of what is Chinese are set by individuals rather than an authoritative community."

— Paul J Bolt
The International History Review, vol. 25, no. 2 (June 2003), pp. 385–386

This book was originally presented as the Edwin O Reischauer Lectures in 1997 at Harvard University, a series set up for East Asia specialists whose scholarship transcends national frontiers. From the perspective of the past two millennia, Wang Gungwu looks into how factors such as the policies of Chinese governments, host governments and the preferences of the Chinese overseas influence the lives and identity of ethnic Chinese venturing abroad. Three lectures are included in the work.

In "Seaward Sweep: the Chinese in Southeast Asia", Wang argues that China's "land-bound and agrarian" characteristic is the reason why the ancient Chinese had not really lived and made their homes outside China despite the fact that China's contact in the Southeast Asian region began as early as the third century BC, whereas in the West, "maritime enterprise" underlines the development of Europe. Wang then examines the various factors that attribute to this "continental mind-set". Eventually, the arrivals of Westerners and colonisation provided the impetus for change — "it was they who started the process that would eventually turn the heads of the Chinese away from the continent to look out toward the sea".

"The Sojourners' Way" explores how Chinese who resided abroad adapted to their environment, and defines the concept of "sojourning" as "temporary residence at a new place of abode (with the intention of returning)". Wang also reveals that Chinese sojourners were initially not accepted by the Chinese governments. It was not until the late 19th century that the term *"huaqiao"* which emphasised devotion to the home country was invented and the long-term sojourners were entitled to the middle-ground position.

"The Multicultural Quest for Autonomy" demonstrates the agonies and compromises the Chinese overseas had been through to find an alternative to either maintaining one's culture or assimilating into the society that acknowledges "multiculturalism" by seeking a form of cultural autonomy. In the process, ethnic Chinese made great efforts to fully participate and create their own Chinese identity in the societies that had offered them acceptance.

Don't Leave Home: Migration and the Chinese
Singapore: Times Academics Press, 2001

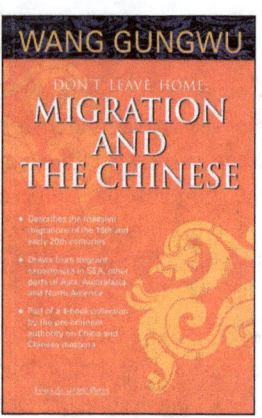

"[T]he subject of migration, Wang argues, naturally lends itself to global history's mission to study linkages between many people over time and space. Another central theme of the collection reevaluates the Chinese migrant experience itself. Wang explores the concept of sojourning as a pattern of migration and in the context of national discourses of migration and historiographies."

— Erika Lee
The Journal of Asian Studies, vol. 62, no. 1 (February 2003), pp. 217–218

"[Wang] draws on a wide body of literature to provide a comparative perspective on the Chinese experience. His insistence that the Chinese experience not be treated as an undifferentiated history, is buttressed by observations on Chinese migrations to North America, Australia, and Latin America, in comparison with his adopted homeland in Southeast Asia."

— Lucie Cheng
International Migration Review, vol. 38, no. 1 (Spring 2004), p. 333

This book is a collection of 15 articles, themed Chinese migration, which have been published previously. The discussion spans from 19th to early 20th century, and the geographical focus covers beyond Southeast Asia to include other parts of Asia, Australasia and North America. The papers collected in *Don't Leave Home* offer a sentimental tug by examining different aspects of the Chinese migrant experiences — bitter and sweet, dilemmas and confrontations, past and future.

"Migration and its Enemies" places the phenomenon of migration in the larger context of global history. Not limited to the modern Chinese movement to Southeast Asia, but drawing from other human experiences and diasporic communities in history, Wang Gungwu posits that migration is "an attack on the nation-state as an institution". In "Patterns of Migration History Revisited", Wang re-examines the Chinese migration history in Southeast Asia from the new perspective of global history as opposed to modern and contemporary world history, thereby discerning the uniqueness of the subject in question. "Sojourning: the Chinese Experience" studies Chinese migration in four distinct stages: transitional states, nation-states, remigration, and globalisation of migration and the various concepts of sojourn. "Migration and the New National Identities" summarises the papers presented at "The Last Half Century of Chinese Overseas: Comparative Perspective" conference held at the University of Hong Kong in December 1994. Wang identifies four major paradoxes in the characteristics of the diasporic communities and groups studied in the conference papers. In "Greater China and the Chinese Overseas", Wang examines the relations between Southeast Asian Chinese and an economically powerful China through his three classifications of overseas Chinese.

The painful experience of Chinese living in a foreign land is chronicled in "Adapting to Non-Chinese Society" in four aspects of trading, working, studying, and living with people in the host country. In "Upgrading the Migrant: Neither *Huaqiao* nor *Huaren*", Wang studies the process of upgrading the status of Chinese migrants by host counties, from North America to Southeast Asia, and brings out the identity crisis confronting most overseas Chinese. "Chinese Trade and Cultural Values", delivered as the keynote lecture at the biannual Meeting of the Asian Studies Association of Australia, traces back the Chinese trading culture to Confucian values and the class of merchants in traditional China. "Chineseness: the Dilemmas of Place and Practice" discusses what it takes to be a Chinese in the societies of Shanghai, Beijing, Singapore and the Chinese communities in San Francisco. "Strategies for a Migrant Entrepreneur" seeks to explore the connection between wealth and culture in Southeast Asia's entrepreneurial history by focussing on the life and career of Tan Kah Kee.

"The Hakka in Migration History" explores the aspects of migration history that the Hakka communities have contributed. In "Southeast Asian Chinese and the Development of China", Wang argues that the surge in overseas Chinese investments, particularly from Southeast Asia, is unique in many ways. "External China" is an overall survey of Chinese outside mainland China, such as Hong Kong, Macao, Southeast Asian countries and other overseas Chinese in general, except Taiwan. "The Future of Overseas Chinese Studies", the keynote speech lecture given at the *Luodi-Shengen* Conference held in San Francisco in 1992, addresses the traditional methods in the field of overseas Chinese studies and some current issues regarding Chinese abroad; Wang also highlights the future trajectory of this academic discipline. The last chapter, "The Early Search for a Base in Southeast Asia", tackles with the historical problem of the Chinese search for a base in *Nanyang* in the 18th century. Wang suggests that the Chinese concept of a "base" was derived from the Europeans, and then borrowed and modified for their own purposes.

王赓武自选集
Selected Works of Wang Gungwu
Shanghai: Shanghai Education Press, 2002

This is a collection of Wang Gungwu's major published pieces on a wide range of topics centred on five themes: Chinese civilisation and its spread; China's external relations; migration and its enemies; Chinese in Southeast Asia; and nationalism and Confucianism.

The pieces themed Chinese civilisation and the diffusion of culture were previously published in *The Use of History* in 1990. Confucius' attitude about approaching history with reverence and sense of importance, as well as subjecting it to critical and objective evaluation is still relevant today.

Papers on China's early contact with the outside world centre on its foreign relations with neighbouring countries during the Sung dynasty and the Five Dynasties. In particular, the voyages of Cheng Ho during the Yung-Lo years marked the climax of Chinese relations with the Nanyang, the territories accessible by sea in Southeast Asia.

The section themed migration and its enemies examines the historical conditions under which people have migrated over great distances and their social status in the host countries. The overseas Chinese in Southeast Asia, including their economic contribution to the region, their identity and their linkages to the development of China are given in-depth treatment in the section themed Chinese in Southeast Asia. A deeper understanding of the Overseas Chinese is gained with the inclusion of chapter that explains the origins of overseas Chinese nationalism and the relationship between the concepts of nationalism and Confucianism.

Bind Us in Time: Nation and Civilisation in Asia
Singapore: Times Academic Press, 2002
Singapore: Eastern Universities Press, 2003

This book — a collection of 20 essays Wang Gungwu wrote over the course of several decades — is a companion volume to *Nation-Building: Five Southeast Asian Histories* edited by him.

Wang looks at the interaction between civilisations and nationalism and seeks to convey how we may be time-bound and how peoples living within state boundaries come to bind with each other as modern nation-states. Amid rapid technological change and global economic development in the 19th and 20th centuries, and the hastening of social and political transformations, historians are well conscious of how the nation-state has come to dominate all civilisations in a fraction of the time, while it takes generations for the world civilisations to develop and evolve.

This collection of essays reflects the author's conviction that although Asians require nation-states to deal with the exigencies of modernisation, the rich heritage of Asian civilisations should not be trivialised but remain vital to the region's total well-being. However, if groups of nations compete to claim superiority of their historic civilisations, they are inclined to espouse the narrower bondage of nationalism, which if goes unchecked, will be a hindrance that mere industrial modernity and scientific advances are unlikely to liberate them.

In the first essay, "Nationalism and Its Historians", Wang asserts his argument that historians played an important role in providing historical scholarship that inspire and shape the various forms of nationalism. The second essay, "Nation and Heritage", puts into context how political heritage — models from the West, including the colonial transition, and the earlier examples of national development in Asia itself — has guided the nation-building task in Southeast Asia. Written during the 1960s and 1970s, the topics in other essays collected in part one range from external pressures on the Southeast Asian region regarding questions of race, religion, and ideology to revival of nationalism in China.

Part two is organised with the larger idea of civilisation. In broad overview, Wang is in search of answers to the three questions that interweave through the essays: first, why various parts of Asia had so readily accepted the universalism of the Western scientific tradition and new approaches to humanistic scholarship, but slow in the uptake of the uses of the social sciences; second, why some countries in Asia have favoured the prospect of a global community sustained by several civilisations; and third, the role of the university as a global institution.

Anglo-Chinese Encounters since 1800: War, Trade, Science and Governance
Cambridge: Cambridge University Press, 2003

"*Another strength lies in the book's comparison of Anglo-American influences (Wang considers America to be the inheritor of Britain's imperial mantle) with those of Japan, Portugal and other countries that interacted with China in the imperial and immediate post-imperial periods.*"

— Peter Gordon
The Asian Review of Books, 3 July 2003, at <http://www.asianreviewofbooks.com/>

"*Challenges Chinese historians to pry open the history of imperial exploitation in China.*"

— Karen M Yuen
Journal of Colonialism and Colonial History, vol. 6, no. 3 (Winter 2005)

As the title suggests, this book deals with the Anglo-Chinese interactions in war, trade, science and governance. Drawn from Arthur Waley's dictum that the British went to China primarily to "convert, trade, rule and fight", Wang reorganises the content in the order of "to fight, to trade, to convert, and to rule". The first two chapters focus on Chinese attitudes towards war and the strategies of entrepreneurs overseas. The last two chapters take on the task of rediscovering China's scientific past, and the Chinese responses to modern statecraft. The book concludes with Wang offering the long view of the Anglo-Chinese phenomenon which certainly stretches beyond Waley's characterisation of their early encounters.

This book is the result of Wang's speeches at the Smuts Commonwealth Lectures. Having spent most of his career in Commonwealth universities and environment, Wang had much to reflect on the Anglo-Chinese connections. The lectures were written from the perspective of how Chinese have fared in their dealings with the British, and what China has made of the encounters with British and their activities in Asia.

The story begins with China's first humiliating defeat by the British in 1842, which chiefly or partly explains why the two peoples never quite get anything right between them thereafter. Trade between the two began much earlier, and is where the Chinese had a better measure of the British. Their mutual assessment of each other became usually more right than wrong over time as they expanded their common enterprises. Waley used the word "convert" in a strictly religious sense, but Wang expands the scope to include both the religious and secular dimensions. Though the missionary enterprise of the British should not be considered a total failure, the real conversion occurred in the non-religious area of education and China's fervent quest for modernity. Needless to say, this "conversion" is only a one-way affair, and even more so in the arena of political governance as discussed in the final section. Such encounters are most vivid in the treaty ports along China's coastline, and in overseas Chinese communities like Hong Kong, Malaya and parts of Borneo.

In conclusion, Wang suggests that the United States' accession to a second phase of Anglo-Chinese encounter had made the larger picture seem continuous and seamless to the present day. Therefore, the four themes discussed in this book remain at the core of their encounters even to this day. The key to the story is that no matter how times have changed, on the most serious matters pertaining to their deeply felt values, the British and the Chinese people remain far apart.

Ideas Won't Keep: The Struggle for China's Future
Singapore: Eastern Universities Press, 2003

"Wang Gungwu's new book Ideas Won't Keep addresses the momentous question of where China is heading today as it emerges from Maoism and isolation to become increasingly integrated into the world economic and political system...Wang's rich and eclectic scholarly background is reflected in the wide range of topics covered by the ten essays...In spite of the dangers and difficulties inherent in the attempt to connect historical dots to link past and present in order to build historical genealogies, Ideas Won't Keep offers extremely informative and stimulating reading for all students of both modern and contemporary China."

— Margherita Zanasi
China Review International, vol. 2, no. 1 (Spring 2005), pp. 260–264

This essay collection, *Ideas Won't Keep*, is the revised edition of *The Chineseness of China — Selected Essays* published in 1991 for the readership of an academic community that had to study China from afar. With China undergoing great transformation since then, *Ideas Won't Keep* provides new insight into the links between old and new ideas and the power that Chinese elites wield today. In the introductory chapter, Wang contemplates on China's future, which may be examined through three prominent themes in its history: the maintenance of regime, morality and the use of Marxism. These are the three pillars of the overarching framework under which China's leaders will be seeking to revitalise China.

The essay "Rights and Duties" interprets how rights relate to duties on the one hand and to power on the other at various periods of Chinese history. The perception that the ancient Chinese only knew of duties and had no notion of rights is challenged and has been re-examined in the context of modern development. The analysis is relevant to the issue of how modern ideas of political, legal, civil, and human rights were introduced into China and how they have influenced China's modernisation.

Wang presents the controversial evaluations of an imperial official Feng Dao, whose firm adherence to Confucianism and loyal service to five different imperial houses and 10 emperors during the Five Dynasties period were discredited by a higher Confucianism of the later period in the essay entitled "Confucian Loyalty". "Rebellious Lives" analyses the traditional and modern biographies about rebels and reformers through Chinese history. Wang highlights that biographical writings in traditional perspective centre chiefly on the individual's contribution to history, whereas modern biographical works focus on providing fresh evaluations and re-assessment of historical figures to create models for the future.

The review of Mao Zedong's lifetime in "Marxist-Leninist and Chinese" offers an understanding of the interaction of power and ideas in Mao's work, which can also be pursued through the study of his Chinese roots. Mao's strong confidence in his Chinese application of Marxist-Leninist theory and his deep Chinese roots had laid foundation for an extensive influence on the policies of Chinese government. "Literati and Intellectuals" focusses on the evolution of literati into intellectuals in China during the 20th century and the conflict that Chinese intellectuals had to confront between cultural heritage and modernisation as an opening-up process to the outside world. "Culture and Revolution" is a comparative study of the May Fourth Movement in 1919 and the Great Proletarian Cultural Revolution between 1966 and 1976.

The reinterpretation of history can be a powerful tool in politics as Wang argues in the essay, "The Past and Politics", examining the modern use of the past and dissecting the impact of one period in the Cultural Revolution of 1966–1976. In "Civilization and Change", Wang highlights the importance of the principle of change in Chinese civilisation, and the urge to civilise in China today is brought about by the transformation of the very nature of modern civilisation itself, no longer by rulers or sages.

Only Connect! Sino-Malay Encounters
Singapore: Eastern Universities Press, 2003

> *"Those who are familiar with Wang's output would undoubtedly agree that the great strength of his scholarship lies in his vision. At his best, although he may not footnote every thought, each paragraph contains the seeds of a PhD dissertation. So, graduate students and Wang*

Gungwu fans take note: at times in this volume, he is indeed at his very best!"

— Liam C Kelley
The Journal of Asian Studies, vol. 63, no. 2 (May 2004), pp. 564–566

"[Wang's] discussion of elites and nationalism is just as salient today as when many of these pieces were written (the 1970s through the 1990s), and the 1998 economic crisis brought to light some of the underlying politics in Malaysia...have created a state-driven economy that benefits a small circle of other elites (a mixed group of Chinese and Malay business leaders)."

— Amy Freedman
Pacific Affairs, vol. 76, no. 4 (Winter 2003/2004), pp. 669–670

This 18-essay collection — which features Wang Gungwu's scholarly output spanning over the past four decades — seeks to trace the history of the economic, cultural and political interactions between ethnic Chinese and native Malays from the 15th to the late 20th centuries. Eleven of the essays in this volume previously appeared in Wang's previous work, entitled *Community and Nation: China, Southeast Asia, and Australia*, now out of print.

The opening of Sino-Malacca relations and Admiral Cheng Ho's first voyage to Malacca in the early 15th century had boosted trading ties and engendered close relationship between the two countries. Analysing various archival records and secondary sources, Wang chronicles the Malacca missions and solves the discrepancies about the first three rulers of Malacca, who established close relations with China. In the chapter "The Melayu in *Hai-Kuo Wen-Chien Lu*", Wang puts into context the earliest use of "Melayu" in Chinese text and the reasons behind the emergent awareness of the term. Delving deep into the constituent elements of Malayan nationalism during the nation-building years enhances the understanding of what these irreconcilable ideas of nationalist sentiment of the Malays, Chinese and Indians are. The 1969 ethnic riots among the main racial groups — Malays, Chinese, and Indians — had laid bare the division of Malaysians between the predominantly Malay political power and the non-Malay economic power, on one hand, and between privileged English-educated elites and underprivileged Malay and Chinese communities, on the other. Wang revisits the topic again in 1986 with further reflections on the Malaysian elites, focussing on patterns of change in the political system.

The introductory essay to Wang's edited volume, entitled *Malaysia: A Survey*, set the theme — which explores the question of the inner political and economic structure of Malaysia — for the 20th-century Malaysia coverage in part two of this book. Articles in this section examine the problems and background leading to the separation of Singapore from the Federation of Malaysia on 9 August 1965; the political change after the 1969 racial riots; and the mixed viewpoint on restoration of political activities.

Part three largely discusses the importance of migration in Malay history, and reinforces the fact that continuities do exist between the modern Southeast Asian countries and their precolonial pasts in terms of their position in the world economy. Wang has systematically corroborated his analysis that Sino-Malay interactions had extended from business into the cultural and political spheres during the 19th and 20th centuries in British Malaya and later in the Malaysian Federation. Despite some serious setbacks in recent decades, the encounters must now be integrated in the nation-building efforts of Malaysia and Singapore.

To Act is to Know: Chinese Dilemmas
Singapore: Eastern Universities Press, 2003

Previously published in the 1970s to 1990s period, the reissue of this collection of 16 essays reflects that China's past and history remain vital in the Chinese mind. A rising China on the global stage has led to a growing interest in the country and in the Chinese coping with rapid changes. Today, the challenge is how the Chinese have struggled to reconcile their past with their present and future. History will always be alive in the Chinese mind as Wang Gungwu revisited his essays that bear testimony to "how the Chinese seem to love the past because they know how to fight with it and use it in their political struggles".

The book is organised into two themes — contemporary China and its ancient past. The chapters that discuss contemporary China take readers through the Chinese struggle with the terminology of revolution and reform, the infamous 1989 Tiananmen incident, revolutionary China, China's integration into the modern international system and China's foreign policy.

Part two attempts to corroborate with evidence how Chinese's obsessive love of history and their ancient past from the era of Qin Shihuang, the "Middle period", Zheng He expedition during the Yongle's reign of the Ming dynasty to the Cultural Revolution has continued to stimulate the Chinese imagination.

移民與興起的中國
Migrants and the Rise of China
Singapore: Global Publishing Company, 2005

This volume is a collection of seven papers previously published in *Southeast Asia and the Chinese*, in 1987, and seven new papers written in recent years to investigate new issues, trends and developments in China and overseas Chinese. Published in 2005, the year marked Cheng Ho's successful expeditions 600 years ago and various events were held in many Southeast Asian countries to commemorate the occasion. This commemorative volume enhances readers' understanding of historical and current issues by exploring the six centuries of "post-Cheng Ho era" (*hou Zheng He shidai*).

Essays on issues and trends in "post-Cheng Ho era" are organised under three broad themes — the history of migrations and foreign relations between China and Southeast Asian region; *huaren*, the origin and definition of the terminology; and the rise of China. The essay "*Liuxue* and *yimin*: from Study to Migranthood" in part one examines the major trends that have led to young Chinese studying overseas and the transition process to migranthood of these Chinese students. The movement of Chinese to overseas during the Ming and Qing dynasties, initially known as "profiteering merchants" and gradually regarded as "migrants", is discussed in detail over five chapters in part one.

Part two studies the changing economic, political, and cultural status and experiences of overseas Chinese, and the definition of *huaqiao*, which loses its relevance today due to ambiguity in the meaning.

China's rise can be envisaged by analysing the military and maritime activities in China's history. The essay "Change in China in the Eyes of the Chinese Abroad" examines, through the lens of overseas China, the four dynamic concept of "modern China" classified by the development phases of China: the later Qing dynasty, the Republic of China (*Min guo*), pre-reform China before 1978, and post-reform China. China's rise in modern-day context is identified as the fourth rise following three previous rises in the third, seventh, and 14th centuries. China's fourth rise has made an impact, bringing earth-shaking changes to the world's political and economic structures.

離鄉別土：境外看中華
China and its Cultures: from the Periphery
Taipei: Institute of History and Philology, Academia Sinica, 2007

The viewpoint from the periphery of mainland China — commonly referred to as the overseas Chinese communities in Southeast Asian region — indeed offers a different perspective of China and the Chinese culture. This book is a compilation of three lectures Wang Gungwu delivered at the Fu Ssu-nien Memorial Lectures at the Institute of History and Philology, Academia Sinica in Taiwan in 2005.

The first lecture, entitled "Layers of Distant Cultures", highlighted the confusion surrounding the concept of nation and culture. Wang pointed out that the Western record of China's history depicts chiefly the lower-level culture of Chinese commoners but very sparsely on the Chinese literati. "Nation" and "nation-state" are essentially Western concepts, which the Chinese had difficulty associating with. The idea of "culture" has been embedded in the Chinese society, but the Chinese did not have a word for it at the time. Gu Hongming (1857–1928), Song Wangxiang

(1871–1941), and Qiu Shuyuan (1874–1941) were three prominent overseas Chinese born in Southeast Asia, and were educated under the Western system, and had lived and worked in mainland China. However, none of them had ever discussed the concept of "nation", and instead the idea of "culture", primarily the literati culture, pervaded their extant written materials.

The second lecture purports to locate the "nation-state" in China after the 1911 republican revolution. Sun Yat-sen brought this idea to China, advocating that it should be the path for China's future. Together with the concept of "nationalism", the idea of nation-state gradually took root both in mainland China and in overseas Chinese communities. It was an irony that culture was seldom talked about, but the idea of "nation" dominated their public discourse.

In the third lecture, entitled "Chinese history and its global future", Wang remarked the increasing parochialism of the concept of "nation-state" in the rapidly globalising world. As time progresses and the world becomes more diverse, the function of Chinese history is not limited within territorial boundaries, which can be effectively transcended. The pertinent questions now are how Chinese culture should adapt itself and how Chinese history should be written in the future.

Divided China: Preparing for Reunification 883–947*
Singapore: World Scientific Publishing Company, 2007

The period of Five dynasties (Wu-tai) is the dark age in-between two glorious eras in Chinese history — the dynasties of Tang and Sung. It is truly a period of anarchy and moral confusion with ever-shifting centres of power and frequent changes in dynastic regimes. Within less than 60 years, five regimes rose to power and then quickly diminished in the rapid currents of history before any one of them was ever stabilised. China was in complete disintegration at the time. Each regime was indeed too short to deserve the title of dynasty. These five dynasties were mostly located in North China and none had ever ruled over more than a third of the

---

*This book is the second edition of *The Structure of Power in North China during the Five Dynasties*, originally Wang's doctoral dissertation at the University of London.

Chinese territory. Concurrently, southern and central China were broken up into the so-called Ten Kingdoms that jostled for dominance.

Yet it is this chaotic period that has always escaped the gaze of historians. It may be due to its short transitional nature, being eclipsed by the two great dynasties that succeeded and preceded it, that it seems to fit perfectly into a preconceived pattern of rise and fall, order and disorder in dynastic history. Its essence can be epitomised as the inevitable chaotic period following centuries of prosperity, and a precondition for reaching another height, beyond which nothing is important or worth examining.

Wang, however, thinks otherwise. He argues in this book that a new form of central government had evolved out of this period. The governmental structure that crystallised in Sung years is not merely a return to the Tang institutions but a new form of power structure incorporating features characteristic of the Wu-tai period. The work begins with the Huang Chao rebellion, the final stage in the decline of the Tang dynasty, to the Khitan invasion in 946–947 when it became clear that foundations for a last push towards unification were in place. It attempts to explain the changes in political institutions and shows that the final central government structure did not reject but had instead incorporated basic features of the *chieh-tu shih* system given that emperors of the Wu-tai period were but powerful *chieh-tu shih* themselves. It shows that by 947, the court had become an enlarged *chieh-tu shih* establishment dominated by the emperor's army (ya-chun) and palace commissioners (*ch'in-li*), and made respectable by the bureaucrats and literati (*p'an-kuan, shu-chi and t'ui-kuan*).

This book is a pioneering work in the history of Five Dynasties. It provides insights into cycles of oneness and division, and is especially illuminating to China's unification enterprise.

His Edited and Co-edited Works

Malaysia: A Survey
Singapore: Donald Moore Books Ltd, 1964
London: Pall Mall Press, 1964
New York: Fredrick A Praeger, 1964
Melbourne: F W Cheshire, 1964

"The volume edited by Professor Wang of the University of Malaya is the sort of encyclopedic volume that is apt to accompany the birth of new countries in our time...Much in this compendium will make it useful as a reference work for some years to come."

— Justus M van der Kroef
Pacific Affairs, vol. 39, no. 1/2 (Spring–Summer 1966), pp. 213–216

"Malaysia: A Survey, most ably edited by Professor Wang Gungwu of the University of Malaya, covers the key features of Malaysia's history, geography, economy and society and particularly its position in the kaleidoscopic world of south-east Asia today. It contains twenty-six studies by different specialists, nearly all of international repute, and is divided into five sections. There are some excellent maps and much useful statistical data."

— M R Ross
Political Studies, vol. 39, no. 1/2 (Spring–Summer 1966), pp. 213–216

"The idea that the formation of Malaysia was an attempt to stake out a wider and stronger claim for democratic institutions in Southeast Asia is one of the most important observations of Professor Wang Gung-wu in his excellent introduction to the volume...The book is notable for two achievements. It provides a single source of information about Malaysia; it sets forth in generally clear terms most of the important problems effecting the viability of the new state."

— J Norman Parmer
The Journal of Asian Studies, vol. 25, no. 4 (August 1966), pp. 804–805

This encyclopedia-like volume was planned to appear soon after the formation of Malaysia as a sovereign state. It was the result of rounds of discussions between Wang and several of his colleagues in the University of Malaya. The volume is divided into five major sections — "Natural and Human Structure", "Historical Background", "Society and Culture", "Economy" and "Politics and Government" — aimed at covering all aspects of this young country. Under each heading, there are several subsections, written by specialists in respective areas, and substantiated by diagrams, maps and tables.

The authors and editor agreed that this book should not cover up-to-date events but concentrate on the basic data for understanding the new country. In the introduction penned by Wang, the name of "Malaysia" is dealt with from both the historical and political perspectives. He put into context the difficulties in perceiving Malaysia geographically, and the challenge of holding it up together as one country. Despite the unanimous consensus that no recent political events pertinent to the formation of Malaysia as a political state should be included in the volume, Wang did discuss, though briefly, the regional responses, mainly oppositions from its neighbouring countries, in his introduction. The crucial drive towards independence — home-grown nationalism — is also touched upon, and future challenges to nation-building are pointed out. This volume, though published half a century ago, is still relevant as a first-hand guide to Malaysia.

Essays on the Sources for Chinese History
Co-edited with Donald D Leslie and Colin Mackerras
Canberra: Australian National University Press, 1973
Columbia, South Carolina: University of South Carolina Press, 1973

> *"[S]cholars around the world [were invited] to write short pieces on a series of topics that do in fact range over the whole chronological span of Chinese studies, from prehistoric archaeology to the new terminology of revolution of the present day...The work will be of use to students and this usefulness has been much enhanced by the provision of extensive bibliographies...More attention has been paid to the periphery then [sic] to the centre, that is, to such subjects as Tibetan, Manchu, Western and Arabic sources, as opposed to traditional Chinese*

Essays on the Sources for Chinese History

Editors
Donald D. Leslie,
Colin Mackerras
& Wang Gungwu

AUSTRALIAN NATIONAL UNIVERSITY PRESS

historical sources themselves. This is a useful book which does credit to its authors and to the scholar [C P FitzGerald] to whom it is dedicated."

— Edwin G Pulleyblank
Pacific Affairs, vol. 49, no. 1 (Spring 1976), pp. 122–124

"Chinese history is endless and endlessly interesting, and C P FitzGerald is a splendid Sinologist, so this collection, occasioned by his 70th birthday, promises a good read. The wide range of contributions includes chapters on oracle bones, wooden documents, local gazetteers, law, Tibetan and Manchu sources, Kuomintang and Republican China..., the Communist Party and overseas Chinese."

— Jonathan Mirsky
The China Quarterly, no. 61 (March 1975), pp. 153–154

This volume, comprising 26 short pieces written by an international array of scholars on Chinese history, is a tribute to Emeritus Professor C P FitzGerald, head of the Department of Far Eastern History, Research School of Pacific Studies of the Australian National University (1954–1968).

The work is a comprehensive reference for research on a wide range of topics of the Chinese history. From oracle bones of the Yin or Shang dynasty, rich wooden documents of the Han period, *Shih-chi* and 24 other works from Han to Sui, and *chi-chuan* (annal-biographies) for the later dynasties, to genealogical sources and archives, readers are treated with brief introductions to archeological studies of China. Records that are geographically localised like *fang-chih*, or *ti-fang chih* (regional gazetteers), *tsung-p'u* (genealogical registers), and *hsing-shu* (books of punishment which are antecedent to written law) provide valuable sources on Chinese society.

Tibetan and Manchu sources as well as *Tao-tsang* (the Great Collection of Taoist Literature), etc., are rich reference on religious and ethnic issues of China. In-depth insight about contemporary China can be drawn from the collection of fine essays on Western Sinology and *Kuomintang* and Communist party sources.

Self and Biography: Essays on the Individual and Society in Asia
Sydney: Sydney University Press for the Australian Academy of the Humanities, 1975

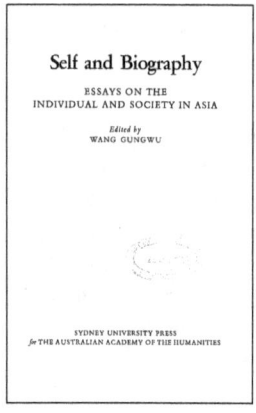

"*Most individuals in both traditional and modern societies operate at the level of low culture: the family rather than the state, liturgy rather than theology: so that one misses the contribution of the demographic historian, the sociologist of religious practice.*"

— S A M Adshead
Australian Journal of Politics and History, vol. 25, no. 2 (1979), pp. 267

"*[...] Wang Gungwu asks why, though biographies have been the staple of historical writing in China since the first century BC, the form has not broken away from subordination to historiographical purposes and developed into the study of the individual personality for its intrinsic interest. An important factor, he argues, has been the very strength of the tradition of celebratory and didactic biography, of biography as the centerpiece of historical writing, leaving precious little room for the 'self-centered biography.'*"

— Ernest P Young
Journal of Asian Studies, vol. 39, no. 1 (November 1979), pp. 121–122

The nine essays in this book were first presented as lectures at a symposium on Asian Studies organised by the Australian Academy of the Humanities at the University of Melbourne, 21 to 23 May 1974. The theme for the symposium, "The Individual in Traditional and Modern Asian Society (as seen through biographies and autobiographies)", allows a broad scope for comparison between past and present, and the East and the West.

This book attempts to explore the biographical treatment of the individual in Asian societies, focussing on three regions: Southeast Asia, South Asia and East Asia.

Three essays by H H E Loofs, A H Johns and J D Legge present the treatment in Southeast Asia, suggesting that the region was very late in developing biography for various reasons. H H E Loofs finds evidence of self-expression in Buddha images of mainland Southeast Asia that were carved with local facial characteristics for the assertion of "national identity". The chapter by A H Johns comments on the challenges in tracing the fragmentary literature and literary works in the Malay world, which is distinguished from the island cultures of the Pacific. Legge's essay offers a dissection of Western scholarship on Sukarno against Sukarno's own autobiography, highlighting what constituted the tradition or a modern construct.

Essays by S A A Rivzi, S N Ray and D A Low represent the South Asian treatment. Rivzi discusses the varied interpretations of the Qu'ran that have offered scope for Muslim scholars to adjust their religion to adapt to the changing circumstances. S N Ray analyses the works of Rabindranath Tagore, who epitomises creative individuality, and puts in the context of the traditional Hindu ethos and the age of Indian Renaissance. D A Low attributes the potential for good biography on Indian nationalist to the availability of rich trove of archival materials and depth of English education the Indians had received.

On East Asia, Harold Bolitho underscores the plethora of possibilities in the materials for biography in Tokugawa Japan that could not have been used in their time as they might be used today. O B van der Sprenkel discusses the six depictions of Confucius the sage, from the "Confucius of the Analects" to the Confucius who comes under the criticism of the communist People's Republic. Wang Gungwu's essay studies the link in China between biography and history-writing, and the future biography, in his prognosis, appears to centre on the type, ranging from the rebel-reformer to the successful conformer.

Hong Kong: Dilemmas of Growth
Co-edited with Leung Chi-keung and J W Cushman
Canberra: Research School of Pacific Studies, Australian National University; Hong Kong: Centre of Asian Studies, University of Hong Kong, 1980

"Of the recently published materials on Hong Kong, this volume offers the most comprehensive and current analyses... Hong Kong: Dilemmas of Growth is a well-organized volume that makes an important contribution to the study of the area. The articles should be of great value to administrators and planners in many third-world cities for

charting economic and urban-planning directions."
— Yuk Lee
The Geographical Review, vol. 73, no. 2 (April 1983), pp. 228–230

"[Hong Kong:] Dilemmas of Growth has a larger scope and framework, with several papers comparing Hong Kong to Singapore or pondering the linkage between Hong Kong and China or the ASEAN countries, thereby giving some substance to the regional/international nature of Hong Kong."
— Ming K Chan
The Journal of Asian Studies, vol. 42, no. 3 (May 1983), pp. 589–598

"The [essay] contributions mainly concern the governing apparatus of Hong Kong; its policies and impact upon the economy, urban growth and development; economic expansion; and selected social issues, including welfare, crime, and community organization."
— Janet W Salaff
Pacific Affairs, vol. 55, no. 1 (Spring 1982), pp. 118–120

This edited volume consists of 29 papers presented in a conference held at the Australian National University in 1979 to identify the post-war achievements and possible future problems in Hong Kong from a multidisciplinary approach, featuring analyses from historians, economists, geographers, planners, political scientists, sociologists, social workers and environmentalists. The changing political institutions, the economy, urban structure and growth, social and ecological issues, and the regional setting of Hong Kong are the five key areas tackled in the volume.

The real dilemma of growth for Hong Kong is the role of government — intervention or non-intervention — in the free market economy. The papers take into account the China factor and influence in the discussion of Hong Kong's political structure, covering issues of policy formulation, administrative growth and change, and institutional response to specific problems such as corruption.

Discussion on Hong Kong's overall economy takes a long-term view on how to maintain growth, how to sustain stability, and how to promote equity.

Hong Kong's urbanisation process is discussed at both the macro and micro levels, thus reflecting problems in the various aspects of urban structure and growth. A closer look at the society reveals a variety of problems related to rising expectation of social welfare benefits, poverty, income inequality, crime and sexual violence, etc.

Hong Kong's identity as a regional bridge between China and the rest of Asia, as an economic player in the region, and a political anomaly are examined in detail in the final section. Wang's concluding paper offers a summary of Hong Kong's dilemmas of growth, and shows that Hong Kong is in a process to fulfill an uncompleted, distinct regional and cultural identity.

Society and the Writer: Essays on Literature in Modern Asia
Co-edited with Milagros Guerrero and David Marr
Canberra: Research School of Pacific Studies, the Australian National University, 1981

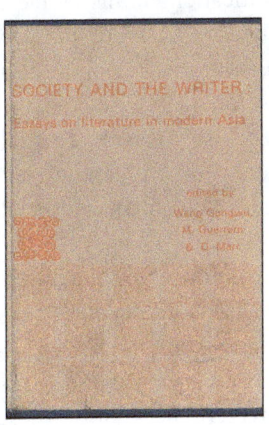

"*Contemporary Asian societies are still divided in ways that reflect their separate roots. One of the most important things they have in common is that almost all of them share some past interlude of colonialization, and thus the influence of alien models is prevalent in their literatures, whether it takes the form of the belated social realism of China or the vernacular adaptations of European popular trash fiction that have appeared in Indonesia or the Philippines.*"

— George Woodcock
Pacific Affairs, vol. 56, no. 1 (Spring 1983), pp. 120–121

"*The present volume is one of those few which attempt to survey trends in modern Asian literature as a whole, facilitating comparisons across such categories as 'Commonwealth' and 'Southeast Asian' literatures... cover[ing] a refreshingly wide spectrum of countries: China, India,*

> *Sri Lanka, the Philippines, Vietnam, Malaysia, [and] Indonesia...The focus is...on the complex responses of writers to the internal processes of their own societies, Westernization being only one among these processes."*
>
> — Indira Viswanathan Peterson
> Journal of the American Oriental Society, vol. 104, no. 3 (July–September 1984)

The book is a collection of 16 essays drawn from the 20 papers presented at a colloquium on "Literature and Social Change in Asia" held at the Australian National University in February 1978. It aims to address the question of how, given Asia's rapid change during the last century, each society demanded its writers and how the writers responded to those demands. Accordingly, the volume assumes a two-part structure: "society's demands on its writers" as part one comprising 10 essays, and "the writer's response" as part two containing 16 papers.

As editor, Wang was confronted with a number of difficulties, of which the criticism of the authors featured in this volume as historians who do not study literature but merely use or exploit it in their research, is the major and most daunting one. To this, Wang responded with valid justifications in his preface. "There is no one way of studying literature. It is not only art; each bit of it is also document." And the authors presented in the volume, with the exception of a few, invariably take mainly modern fiction as their case of study — that is, the type of prose narrative closest to the writing of history. This reveals their social concerns rather than their artistic predilections; they see works of literature not as monumental pieces of artistic mastery but more as hallmarks of social changes.

Each essay collected in this volume approaches the main theme from a different angle; some through language, some through new forms and content conceived while others through probing into the conscious and subconscious struggle experienced by writers. Undeniably, this collection is by no means comprehensive on all genres of literature, or all kinds of social changes, or the whole of Asia. The authors' interests and expertise determine the scope of the book and there are clear omission of Asia countries like Pakistan, Japan, Korea, etc. Yet it nonetheless marks the "beginning of a difficult enterprise". A general consensus looms out of the essays: given the backdrop of a rapidly changing Asia, society's demands always come first, to which writers would respond by "going along with the changes and bring their literary skill with them".

Changing Identities of the Southeast Asian Chinese since World War II
Co-edited with Jennifer Cushman
Hong Kong: Hong Kong University Press, 1988

"The articles...while multi-disciplinary, emphasize a historical perspective on the question of identity and examine primarily Chinese communities in Malaysia, Singapore, Indonesia, and the Philippines...This work is a useful interdisciplinary contribution to the recent scholarship on Chinese communities in Southeast Asia, one which both provides a broad survey of the field and points the way to new research priorities."

— Jean DeBernardi
Journal of Asian Studies, vol. 49, no. 2 (May 1990), pp. 432–433

"Wang comments that ideas about Chinese identities [in Southeast Asia] have changed 'because conditions in China and in the region had changed and the Chinese themselves were changing'...The whole range of identities reveals that modern Southeast Asian Chinese, like most other peoples today, do not have a single identity but tend to assume multiple identities."

— Ng Chin-keong
Journal of Southeast Asian Studies, vol. 20, no. 2 (September 1989), pp. 311–312

"The most enlightening essay is Professor Wang's own Introduction: discerning four types of identity every individual's conduct may be shaped by (national, cultural, class and ethnic), he suggests that to each there corresponds a well-recognized norm of conduct; changing observance of the norms, and changes in balance, could afford a sensible guide for the single investigator into parts of the general subject."

— Dennis Duncanson
The China Quarterly, vol. 119, no. 2 (September 1989), pp. 637

This volume of is the product of a symposium, "Changing Identities of the Southeast Asian Chinese since World War II", held at the Australian National University in Canberra in June 1985. The collection of papers by historians, economists, anthropologists, and political scientists from universities in Australia, North America and Southeast Asia represent some recent thinking about the complex issues of identity faced by Southeast Asian Chinese today and further illustrate the trends, changes and the driving forces behind the changing identities of the Chinese.

Identity being the revolving theme of the symposium could not be more apt as perceptions of self appear to lie at the heart of the present-day Chinese experience in Southeast Asia. It is obvious that there is no single Chinese identity when identity can be moulded by the different political, social, economic or religious circumstances an individual faces at any given time. However, references to the past are still made because it is believed that identity is firmly rooted in individuals' pasts. All of the essays are thus written from a historical perspective with supporting statistical data that will certainly serve as a useful source of case studies, in which much of the writing about the Chinese in Southeast Asia is now cast.

Hong Kong's Transition: A Decade after the Deal
Co-edited with Wong Siu-lun
Hong Kong: Oxford University Press, 1995

Ten years after the British and the Chinese signed the Joint Declaration which will end Hong Kong's British colonial status on 1 July 1997 and return it to Chinese rule, the University of Hong Kong organised a "Hong Kong Lectures" series to assess the rocky path Hong Kong had taken during the past decade. Wang Gungwu was then vice-chancellor of the University of Hong Kong. Instead of the usual format of academic conference, 10 eminent speakers, chosen for their unique experience and expertise in their respective fields, were invited to give an hour-long lecture each, including discussion with audience. The lectures were held between 15 January and 14 April 1994. This book is a collection of these thought-provoking lectures, exploring a wide range of topics.

Hong Kong legislator Sir Sze-yuen Chung looked into the reasons behind the souring of Sino-British relations, especially after the 1989 Tiananmen incident. Louis Cha, founder of the *Ming Pao Daily News* and eminent writer, discussed the challenges facing the media in the transitional period. George Shen, chief editor of the *Hong Kong Economic Journal* highlighted issues for business whereas Justice of Appeal Henry Litton examined the urgent need for legal reform. Finally, Governor Chris Patten provided his own perspective of Hong Kong's transition and its prospects after 1997.

Clearly, each lecture has a focus of its own, but several recurrent common themes shed light on Hong Kong's development during the past decade. First, the June Fourth democratic movement at the Tiananmen Square was a watershed event in the transition; second, the remarkable economic growth of China were addressed by the speakers, moving towards diminishing economic boundaries between mainland China and Hong Kong. That this unanticipated economic growth had contributed to the continuing prosperity of Hong Kong is the third theme that runs through the lectures and lastly, the changing mood within the community in its preparation for 1997 was a concern among all speakers.

Despite the inability to include the Chinese official views due to declined invitation from Chinese officials closely involved in Hong Kong to speak at the lecture series because of time constraints and other reasons, this book is nonetheless one of a kind in presenting a variety of views and perspectives on Hong Kong's transitional period and its future after 1997.

香港史新編 – Volumes 1 and 2
Hong Kong History: New Perspectives
Hong Kong: Joint Publishing (HK) Co Ltd, 1997

The two-volume collection, which offers a whole new, unexplored perspective of Hong Kong, is different from other historical and research references on Hong Kong's past and present. The development of the uniquely different Hong Kong mentality and consciousness culminates in the concept of "Hong Kong people" (*xianggang ren*) in the 1970s, therefore giving rise to this new perspective. Past

histories of Hong Kong were written invariably from the British perspective since the establishment of Hong Kong as a treaty port were recorded and kept by the British. The scope of these historical narratives rarely venture beyond the focus of Hong Kong as a colony, as an economic entity, and as a political entity for bureaucratic management.

The social fabric of Hong Kong gradually changed after World War II. With the influx of mainland Chinese to Hong Kong, the interaction and integration slowly produced a new form of social consciousness that was different and what the Hong Kong people called as their own. This new social ethos by which the Hong Kong people live and work is therefore uniquely Hong Kong's. A reappraisal of previous texts about Hong Kong's history is henceforth imperative, giving justification to the project Wang and other historians undertook.

The essays were authored by historians who were born after the World War II and grew up in the milieu where the new Hong Kong consciousness was in the making and are thus the product of the new social ethos. Coming from different fields, these historians tell a different story about Hong Kong through their own lens and voices. Stories about practically all facets of the city are told — spanning from the past to the present and well into the future, ranging from something as practical as doing business to theatrical drama and musical opera, as well as secular and religious social customs governing the everyday life of Hong Kong people.

Wang's epilogue puts the concept of "Hong Kong people" and their embodied characteristics in a historical and evolutionary context, which serves as a perfect conclusion to the book.

Dynamic Hong Kong: Business and Culture
Co-edited with Wong Siu-lun
Hong Kong: The Centre of Asian Studies, the University of Hong Kong, 1997

This essay collection is the third volume in the series of publications arising from the "Hong Kong Lectures" series initiated and organised by the University of Hong Kong. Entitled "Business and Culture", this series of lectures, held between September and November in 1995, drew inspiration from Hong Kong's economic marvel and its unique position among other Asia-Pacific economies, and probed its success through the varying angles of the speakers.

The speakers hailed from both academia and the business world, speaking from their respective fields of expertise and their years of experience. Most prominent among them is Ying-shih Yu whose lecture provided a historical perspective of relating "business culture" to "Chinese tradition". The main thesis of his talk is that "business culture from the very beginning had been an integral part of Chinese culture as a whole and must not be considered as an isolated phenomenon confined only to the business world".

Gordon Redding, former director of the University of Hong Kong Business School and the Poon Kam Kai Institute of Management, reinforced Yu's point by discussing how Chinese traditions had profoundly influenced Hong Kong's business culture. And Gary G Hamilton, professor of sociology at the University of Washington went a step further to trace how Hong Kong's own brand of capitalism found its way into the expanding global economy around the world.

Linus Cheung, Hari Harilela, David Li and Victor Fund, top executives of major firms in Hong Kong explicated how Hong Kong's business environment is conducive to their operations. John Kamm, managing director of Kamm and Associates Ltd, and chairman of Market Access Ltd, and Elizabeth Sinn, resources officer in the Department of History of the University of Hong Kong, approached the topic from a more humane angle. Kamm softened the pragmatic tone of the business world by addressing the need to acknowledge the importance of promoting respect for human rights in profit-driven environment whereas Sinn explored philanthropy in Hong Kong's business practice based on the case study of the Tung Wah Group of Hospitals.

The volume concludes with a chapter by Wang Siu-lun, the co-editor of the book. His lecture on transplanting Chinese enterprises in Hong Kong dovetailed with Yu's opening chapter on the intertwining nature of business and Chinese culture throughout history for Hong Kong, which welcomes mainland capital and entrepreneur talents with open arms.

Global History and Migrations
Boulder, Colorado: Westview Press, 1997

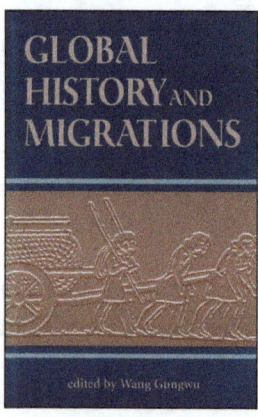

"*Overall, this book is one of the better collections on the ever more salient issue of international migration....in their convergent interest, the contributors to the book manage to synthesize the protean faces and facets of human migration in relation to historical processes and practices (of territorial statist governance, for example) that have engendered the world in which we all seem to be migrants.*"

— Nevzat Soguk
Journal of World History, vol. 10, no. 1 (Spring 1999), pp. 227–230

"*What makes this collection valuable is that a series of experts have distilled the themes of particular time periods and approaches into convincing, accessible chapters...In the end continuity prevails over change...Migration in terms of opportunity, response and conflict, has a permanent place in global and local history.*"

— John Connell
Pacific Affairs, vol. 71, no. 1 (Spring 1998), pp. 83–85

"*The book makes several important contributions to the subject. First, it draws attention to the relationship between migration and global history and to the possibility of using the movement of people to understand the larger patterns of transnational interaction. Second, ...[t]he authors focus on migrations involving Africa, India, China, Japan and Southeast Asia as well as the more traditional areas of Europe and the Americas. And third, its authors provide many insights into such important issues as the relationship between global and world history, the features of globalization, the interactions among migration systems and nation states, and the linkages that tie macro-structures and micro-networks together."*

— Samuel L Baily
Journal of American Ethnic History, vol. 17, no. 2 (Winter 1998), pp. 71–72

"*....[A]lthough Wang does not attempt to differentiate world history from global history, he believes that a broader approach, a global perspective, can help in understanding general migration patterns, as well as local situations and adaptations. His essay ranges over various case studies from the long histories of China and Southeast Asia, showing how the movement of peoples has generated change, as well as how local contexts have influenced immigrant societies.*"

— Craig A Lockard
Journal of World History, vol. 9, no. 2 (Fall 1998), pp. 272–275

Global History and Migrations is a collection of writings about migrations and its role in the global history. The book offers insightful interpretations of contemporary migration issues and their possible influences on future thinking about migration patterns. Wang Gungwu envisions the volume as "a few steps forward in grasping some features of globalisation and apply a global history approach to one of its most important manifestations".

The chapter contributions by scholars are such attempts offering different perspectives. Examining the two "mass migrations" in the 1955–1994 and 1870–1914 periods, Ewa Morawska and Willfried Spohn argue that contemporary population movements occur in the context of the worldwide economic inequalities and can be seen as outcomes and contributors to globalisation processes. Philip D Curtin believes that technological advantage is the primary reason for a variety of migration patterns while other variables like commercial skills, military power, slave trade, political asylum, and individual migrations also played a part. Focussing on the global migration crisis, Myron Weiner suggests that the dual character of creating benefits to countries on one hand and generating conflicts between states on the other has made migration an object of intense national concern, therefore the creation and expansion of international institutions and norms become necessary.

Robin Cohen uses the concept "diaspora" to discuss various migration issues labelled as "globalisation" and briefly explores its connection with global history.

Focussing on the evolution of legal framework in migrant workers history, Yash Ghai examines the interactive mechanism facilitating globalisation: migration, markets and the law. The best way to understand global patterns of population mobility in urbanising Asia over the past 50 years, as Ronald Skeldon suggests, is "to envisage them within a unitary framework of the expansion of a capitalist system". Astri Suhrke looks into the globalisation of the refugee phenomenon from three dimensions: the international refugee regime, its causes, and its impact on globalisation. Mike Featherstone discusses the various modes of hybridity and disorder that happen in contemporary social and cultural life with the intensification of global migration. Aristide R Zolberg notes the contradictory character of historical change — the increased intensity of global human movements has led to the erection of legal and administrative barriers between nation-states to discourage the trend.

Hong Kong in the Asia-Pacific Region: Rising to the New Challenges
Co-edited with Wong Siu-Lun
Hong Kong: Centre of Asian Studies, University of Hong Kong, 1997

This volume is a collection of 10 lectures delivered by prominent speakers at the second "Hong Kong Lecture" series held at the University of Hong Kong from 24 September to 26 November 1994. Hailing from different parts of the Asia-Pacific region, the speakers — chosen for their experience and expertise in their respective fields — offered regional perspective and invaluable insight into Hong Kong's new role in the Asia-Pacific region as a Special Administrative Region (SAR) of China and the accompanying new challenges.

Interwoven through the lectures are four main recurring themes. First, Hong Kong will enjoy prosperity beyond 1997 and continue to play a dynamic role as an active economic player in the Asia-Pacific region. Hong Kong's international renown for its robust financial sector, excellent service as well as information and media openness has firmly anchored its unique position as a gateway to China. As an active investor, or a role model in facilitating Taiwan-mainland ties, or the complicated Sino-British relations, Hong Kong is as important to the region as it is to China.

A major second theme is China's guarantee to Hong Kong's continued political stability by allowing the territory to uphold the existing legal system and observe the rule of law. To sustain its economic dynamism and competitiveness, Hong Kong should actively seek out new opportunities and strengthen ties not only with China but also with the whole region, particularly Southeast Asia. The fourth theme centres on the singular feature of Hong Kong as the home to the Chinese of China's coastal region. These Chinese communities based in Hong Kong have catalysed closer integration of Asian economies and contributed to the invaluable human resources for its success.

China's Political Economy
Co-edited with John Wong
Singapore: Singapore University Press and World Scientific Publishing Company, 1998

"This volume covers a wide range of issues, some of which have seldom been discussed elsewhere. It provides good discussion and analysis, which will benefit both specialists and non-specialists alike. General readers will be able to get a sense of what is going on in China and what kinds of challenges and opportunities it is facing. For China scholars, the volume provides different perspectives on and insights into several crucial aspects of the country's politics and economy."

— Dongping Han
The Journal of Developing Areas, vol. 33, no. 2 (Winter 1999), pp. 309–311

"Most of the papers are general and non-technical; little primary research is contained within the covers of this volume. Nevertheless, the approach of most of the writers is analytical with little description of institutional structures and the key political events: in that sense, the book assumes a considerable knowledge of post-1978 developments in the People's Republic."

— Chris Bramall
The Journal of Development Studies, vol. 35, no. 6 (August 1999), pp. 161

"[Wang] argues that China's history and future developments can be both culturally-historically dependent and also agent-oriented. Thus the impact of both external and internal pressures, as well as historical and contemporary processes, is highlighted. This method is insightful as it suggests a holistic approach to understanding future developments in China."

— Alexius A Pereira
China Information, vol. 14, no. 1 (2000), pp. 245

The turn of 1997 — which marked many momentous happenings and two decades after the 1978 open door policy — was of great significance for China. This edited volume — a collection of 15 public lectures and seminar papers presented at the East Asian Institute of the National University of Singapore by academic visitors and scholars — provides broad and in-depth analyses of China in four dimensions: economic reform, political development, social changes, and external relations.

Essays on economic reform explain why the introduction of market forces into several Chinese economic sectors was relative easy to accomplish and that the reform of large-scale state-owned industrial sector is dependent on the political will of the Chinese top leadership. Implementation of economic reform works in China because of its high saving rate and efficient investment in new resources.

Discussion on political development in China explores the concept of rebuilding the nation-state of China from the historical perspective as well as the concept of democratisation and nationalism. A real assessment of Chinese democracy is imperative to avoid another shock and to develop a "right" China policy.

As part of the social development discussion on the impact of economic growth on Chinese people's daily life, the Chinese concept of *xiao-kang* ("modestly comfortable life") is examined in greater depth. *The xia-gang* ("laid-off") phenomenon caused by the state-owned enterprises reform has created social pressure and the main problem lies in the workers' traditional perception of job.

With the changing international and domestic environments and perceived "China threat", China has made adjustments and shifts in its external relations with neighbouring countries. The analysis on Sino-US bilateral relations in the post-Tiananmen era reveals that there is no reason for Beijing to strain further the relationship. In fact, a stable and secure regional environment is vital for China's modernisation programme.

The Chinese Diaspora: Selected Essays
Volumes I and II
Co-edited with Wang Ling-chi
Singapore: Times Academic Press, 1998

"These companion volumes raise important questions about what it means to be of Chinese ancestry in the 21st century. It contains 35 of the best of the academic papers first presented at a major international conference on overseas Chinese held in California."

— Michael R Godley
The China Journal, no. 44 (July 2000), pp. 232–233

The two-volume collection features a selection of papers presented at *Luodi-shenggen*: an International Conference on Chinese Overseas, organised by the Ethnic Studies Department, University of California at Berkeley, in San Francisco in 1998. The theme of the conference — *luodi shenggen* or the planting of permanent roots in the soils of different countries — represents a significant departure from two existing paradigms to the treatment of the study of overseas Chinese. First, most overseas Chinese today no longer see themselves as sojourners. The era of the *luoye-guigen* paradigm — the inevitability of returning to China has been on the decline in this *fast-globalising* world. Another approach is the *zhancao-chugen* paradigm, or the total elimination of racial identity and cultural heritage. Proponents of this approach regard the process towards assimilation as natural and inevitable. This is, however, contrary to what happened in reality. Increasingly, this approach has been called into question.

The conference was a landmark in the study of the "Chinese Diaspora" after the end of the Cold War, bringing together, for the first time since the end of the Cold War, scholars from all six continents. Scholars could now remove the ideological straitjacket and look at the subject in a fresh light.

There exist many studies of the large Chinese communities in Southeast Asia, and there have been an increasing number of studies focussing on the much smaller and less well-known groups elsewhere in Asia, Europe, the Americas, Australia and the Pacific. The next stage in research, says Wang in his preface, is to encourage and enable systematic comparative studies in the field.

The two-volume compendium consists of 35 essays, which were chosen from nearly 150 papers presented in English at the conference. Many of the papers, presented in Chinese and Spanish at the conference, have been published elsewhere. Papers that explore communities less well known and less studied on were given priority in order to convey a fuller picture of the diaspora worldwide, and stimulate readers and aspiring scholars in Southeast Asia to take on new comparative perspectives of their own experiences.

In general, the volumes cover two broad areas: first, the transnational issues and concerns of the Chinese overseas; and second, regional studies, including those of lesser-known regions. This collection aims to clearly define the emerging field of overseas Chinese studies and provide scholars around the world with the first truly comprehensive treatment of the subject.

China: Two Decades of Reform and Change
Co-edited with John Wong
Singapore: Singapore University Press and World Scientific Publishing Compny, 1999

This volume edited by Wang Gungwu and John Wong is an overview of China's overall development over the span of 20 years since 1978, the watershed year when the unprecedented market economic reform and the open door policy were initiated. The five-essay collection covers developments and transformation in various spheres of the rapid-growing nation: political, legal, social, and economic reforms; and more importantly, highlights China's problems and implications for its next phase of transition.

Since the implementation of the open door policy, China's economic performance between 1978 and 1997 was described as hyper growth. China's dynamic economic growth is attributed to mechanisms and tactics such as input-driven growth and export-oriented strategy, which are discussed in detail in the overall context of the East Asian region and the 1997 Asian financial crisis. Economic changes at breakneck speed have inevitably brought about economic reform and institutional changes. Legal reform has facilitated the transition from direct government intervention in the market to indirect management based on policies and regulations. Chinese lawmakers today face challenges in upholding transparency, compliance and enforcement of law, as well as creating awareness of the human rights law. In terms of political reform, China follows a managed process of institutional adjustments or "political incrementalism" to ensure economic development, political and social stability on one hand, and to accommodate consequent drastic socio-economic changes, on the other.

The expansion of social space varies across different social realms. However, the work unit (*danwei*) system and household registration (*hukou*) system have undergone gradual transformation. Amid increased freedom of domestic and international mobility, new social strata, e.g., the professionals, emerge and take shape. There is also a growing tolerance for media freedom, cultural pluralism, religion affiliation and expanded private space and lifestyle changes. In closing, the volume deals with the delicate *Sino-Taiwanese* bilateral relationship, highlighting the major characteristics of cross-strait political, economic, social and cultural interactions, and the perennial problems and prospects of "reunification".

Hong Kong in China: The Challenges of Transition
Co-edited with John Wong
Singapore: Times Academic Press, 1999

"It is a kind of a 'health check' of Hong Kong a little over a year after its unification with China...Most of the contributors are well-established scholars who have published widely on contemporary Hong Kong, and a majority of them based their contributions on their own previous works...The volume therefore provides a useful survey for general readers and a summary of some of most important events in the first year of the SAR..."

— Steve Tsang
The China Journal, no. 45 (January 2001), pp. 235–236

On 1 July 1997, the handover of Hong Kong to mainland China took place amid much tension and uncertainty at the height of the Asian financial crisis that shook its economic and financial system. The handing over presented a challenge to Hong Kong's legal system which is backed by the Basic Law of the Hong Kong Special Administrative Region (HKSAR), and the Sino-British Joint Declaration which is intrinsically and delicately linked to the principle of "one country, two systems". In addition, the people of Hong Kong confront the predicament of an identity crisis and social problems related to Chinese immigration. These factors compounded Hong Kong's agonising experience as it seeks to find its place in a new political equation.

The volume comprises an introductory chapter and 11 papers that discuss salient post-handover issues covering politics, economics, society, and legal system. Chapters two and three evaluate the institutional implications of "one country, two systems" concept and analyse the political difficulties of the HKSAR government by focussing upon the disunity of political elites.

The next four chapters discuss the economic transformation in greater detail. The sudden decline of the economy became the dominant concern in Hong Kong but that should motivate it to carry out economic restructuring to develop higher value-added sector. The Hong Kong economy needs to maintain a degree of "coherence" in its own structure as the "Manhattanisation" process focussing on services is inconsistent with the "one country, two systems" arrangement. Though controversial, the Hong Kong government intervention in the stock market in the wake of the Asian financial crisis is technically necessary to bolster its position as an international financial centre in the Asia-Pacific. With Hong Kong's growing economic integration with China, Guangdong will still be Hong Kong's main investment destination though it has spread its link beyond Guangdong to Shanghai, Fujian, Zhejiang, etc.

The chapters on social changes in Hong Kong take serious view on the identity crisis in Hong Kong, and the emergence of a new immigrant family structure: the split-family phenomenon. The worsening economic situations have sidelined Hong Kong middle class, and it was the political community, rather than the social classes, that was in conflict. Under mounting economic and political pressures, the middle class will be forced to act collectively to defend their interests.

Hong Kong's legal development in the handover transition is dealt in detail in the final two chapters. The Basic Law, as the principal legal document for the HKSAR, is "not sufficient to protect its autonomy and integrity as a separate system". Various legal implications of this transition are delved into, recognising the shift of Hong Kong's legal system from the English Common Law to the Basic Law.

Reform, Legitimacy and Dilemmas: China's Politics and Society
Co-edited with Zheng Yongnian
Singapore: Singapore University Press and World Scientific Publishing Company, 2000

> *"In terms of its comprehensiveness and its timely focus on the Chinese politics under Jiang Zemin, this book adds to our understanding of the present dilemmas and dynamics of the decades-long Chinese reform. By and large the contributors are appreciative of the efforts China has*

made in political reform while remaining critical of the challenges faced by the current leadership... Most of the essays in the volume seek to highlight this aspect of institution-building as a key freature of China's on-going reform."

— Lei Guang
The Journal of Asian Studies, vol. 60, no. 4 (November 2001), pp. 1177–1179

This volume is essentially a collection of working papers and background briefs written by scholars and academic visitors at the East Asian Institute between 1999 and 2000, addressing the issues of reform, legitimacy and the dilemmas confronting the third generation of Chinese leaders. The first of the three parts in this book examines the political and social changes experienced by China in the post-Deng era, and the leadership's responses to these changes. The second part focusses on the linkages between economic and social reforms, illustrating how crucial social reforms are for the regime's legitimacy. The final part discusses the domestic concerns for external relations, that is, how domestic factors affect China's foreign behaviour.

The introduction, co-written by Wang and Zheng, attempts to answer several key questions by illuminating the major points presented in the papers. The pertinent questions include: What are the new sources of political legitimacy of the new leadership? How have changing social and political environments altered the bases of political legitimacy? What strategies has Jiang Zemin adopted to cope with changing circumstances, and to improve and strengthen his leadership? What challenges have new reform measures generated for the leadership? And how have domestic concerns constrained the leadership's plans in China's foreign relations?

The first part, titled "Party, State and Society", comprises five papers. The issues addressed focus on the politics of power succession and the distinction between rule by law versus the rule of law in China. The second part, entitled "Social Reform and Challenges", consists of four essays dealing with the close linkages between economic and social reforms. Lo Vai Io's paper traces the development of law and surveys in detail the context of law in China. Gu Xin's case study of urban housing reform shows why social reforms have become necessary with the introduction of economic reforms. Yu Wei's case study of urban health insurances points out that the most difficult problem facing the leadership is managing the conflict between societal desire and individual responsibilities. Tong Yanqi's paper deals with one of the most serious consequences resulting from rapid modernisation and industrialisation — environmental degradation.

The four papers collected in the final section — "Domestic Concerns for External Relations" — attempt to spell out the impact of the leadership's domestic concerns for its foreign policy intentions. Lance Gore and Lo Vai Io discuss the politics of human rights in China. John Wong and Zheng Yongnian's paper shows that the complexity of China's nationalism makes it difficult for the Chinese leadership to utilise it in its foreign policymaking. In the paper "China's Strategic Intentions and Demands", Wang Fei-ling discusses more directly the domestic constraints on the leadership's international intentions, having observed that China has taken a relatively conservative and defensive foreign policy since the start of the reform.

王宓文纪念集
Wang Fo-wen, 1903–1972: a Memorial Collection of Poems, Essays and Calligraphy
River Edge, New Jersey: Global Publishing Company, 2002

This volume is a memorial collection of poems, essays, and calligraphy by Mr Wang Fo-Wen (1903–1972), father of Wang Gungwu. Wang edited the book in memory of his father. The rich array of writings that include narratives, opinion pieces and lyric poetry is manifestation of Mr Wang's great literary talent. The noble elegance between the words, the colourful metaphors in his literary work and the subliminal form of artistic expression in his calligraphic works are evocative of a scholarly man with high attainment in Chinese culture and mastery in literature. This volume includes a collection of eulogies written by relatives and friends, whose sincere thoughts and reverence for Mr Wang exude between the lines. The poignant accolades are a tribute to Mr Wang as a well-respected scholar for his commitment to scholarly research and education as well a man of high morals and integrity.

Mr Wang Fo-Wen, alias *Yi Chu*, or *Ti Zhai*, was born in a family of scholars in Taizhou, Jiangsu province. He graduated from Nanjing Higher Normal School and Southeastern University, and later became a schoolteacher and school principal in many Southeast Asian countries. He was promoted to the highest officer rank as inspector in charge of Chinese schools in the ministry of education in Malaya. After his retirement, he continued to serve in education as the principal of Foon Yew High School in Johor Bahru. Mr Wang was worthy of the honour as an educator, and was a paragon of virtue and tireless learning throughout his whole life.

Damage Control: The Chinese Communist Party in the Jiang Zemin Era
Co-edited with Zheng Yongnian
Singapore: Eastern Universities Press, 2003

"Jiang Zemin was the only Chinese Communist leader with no previous Zhongnanhai experience. He had problems everywhere: the Tiananmen Incident, corruption, opposition from Deng, Falun Gong, political reformers. How did he cope? Read this book for thoughtful well-researched answers."

— Ezra Vogel, Henry Ford II Research Professor in the Social Sciences, John F Kennedy School of Government, Harvard University

"Edited by two of the best known China scholars, Damage Control: The Chinese Communist Party in the Jiang Zemin Era, brings together expert analysis on the fate of the Chinese Communist Party. Experts from within China and overseas critically evaluate the Party's decline and its struggle for relevance. There is no more important subject than the fate of CCP for the future of China and indeed the stability of the world. The book suggests quite plausibly that in spite of a rough ride a revitalized Party will continue to manage the affairs of state in China for some time to come."

— John P Burns, University of Hong Kong

"China's Communist Party required ideological 'damage control' after 1989. This book is the best available summary of CCP survival, even as communism collapsed in Europe. Jiang Zemin supplemented police repression with positive policies: age criteria for succession, civilian oversight of military promotions, village elections, anti-corruption drives, recruitment of better-educated cadres, and the admission of 'entrepreneurs' (capitalists) to the Communist Party. The chapters comprehensively assess such reforms and conservative resistance to them. Everyone interested in China's past dozen years must read this book."

— Lynn T White III, Professor of Politics and East Asian Studies, Princeton University

This volume is a joint effort by scholars in the East Asian Institute, National University of Singapore to offer a general overview of the changes that had taken place within the Chinese Communist Party under Jiang Zemin, who stepped down as secretary general in 2002. The essays probe into the direction of the Party, its transforming ideology, and the possible introduction of democracy into the institutions as China undergoes rapid and drastic socio-economic changes. In three broad sections, the papers offer insights into the major areas where the Party had shown decline, the Party's response to control the decay of Party, and the major efforts by the Jiang administration to transform the Party.

The fall of communism can be explained and investigated from ideological and organisational perspectives, with analysis centring on the legitimacy problem in delivering economic welfare to its people and total bureaucratisation.

Damage control to party decay as reflected in Falun Gong, corruption, central-local relations, and rural governance are in place with implementation of measures and changes to the regulations related to recruitment and retirement of Party cadres and government officials, the establishment of age limit in power succession and the admission of private entrepreneurs (capitalists). Other response mechanisms include reforms of cadre management system, judicial system, and institutionalisation of Party-military relations.

Beyond damage control, Jiang had steered the Party away from the Marxist-Leninist tradition by initiating a series of campaigns — such as "talking about politics", learning of the "three represents", crackdown on the opposition party, "rule by virtue, and introducing the newly rising capitalism — to revive the Party ideology.

The Iraq War and its Consequences: Thoughts of Nobel Peace Laureates and Eminent Scholars
Co-edited with Irwin Abrams
Singapore: World Scientific Publishing Company, 2003

"The Iraq War and its Consequences offers an interesting mix of articles short and long, brief and thorough, from big names and lesser-known authors, written shortly before or after the 2003 Iraq war."

— Editorial Review, at
<http:// www.encyclopedia.com>

"The editors deserve our gratitude for putting together these valuable essays in one easily accessible volume."

— Gregory C Chow
Princeton University

"This collection will satisfy both the professional academic and the average reader curious about the impact of the war on daily life ... the editors have put together an intriguing collection of important voices to offer comfort and insight for those seeking to understand what has happened in Iraq and its implications for the future."

— Friends Journal

This is the first and the only collection that brings together 33 Nobel Peace laureates and eminent scholars in various fields to offer opinions, analyses and insights on the Iraq war. They probe into such questions as the origins of the war, its conduct, its aftermath, and the future of the United Nations and human rights. The essays were written at different phases of the war, while some were written specifically for this volume.

The book is organised into three parts. Part I features contributions from Nobel Peace Prize winners like Tenzin Gyatso, the 14th Dalai Lama of Tibet, and Irene Khan, secretary-general of Amnesty International. Part II composes of essays by eminent scholars like Noam Chomsky, Joseph Stiglitz and Lisa L Martin. The editors added a humanistic touch in Part III with the inclusion of two sermons delivered by Bishop Gunnar Stalsett of Oslo, former deputy chairman of the

Norwegian Nobel Committee, on two occasions — on the eve of the Iraq War and at the memorial service for victims of the bombing of the UN headquarters in Baghdad in August 2003.

In putting together the wisdom and sentiments of prominent figures and scholars from our era, the editors hope to achieve the objective of helping our humanity think through the questions raised by the war. Though thinking ahead of the consequences may not be easy while the war is still ongoing, it is certainly not too early to contemplate how such wars can be avoided in the universal quest for peace.

Maritime China in Transition 1750–1850
Co-edited with Ng Chin-keong
Wiesbaden: Harrassowitz Verlag, 2004

This volume is a collection of papers presented at a conference, Maritime China in Transition, organised by the National University of Singapore in 1999. The focus of the conference was to find corroborative evidence whether there was a transition period for maritime China leading up to the First Anglo-Chinese War (1839–1842), the turning point of modern Chinese history. In doing so, scholars attempt to envisage maritime China in terms of change and transition from the 1750s to the 1850s from a variety of perspectives.

The papers are organised in five thematic sections. First, maritime China is scrutinised as a segment of a tributary system created by an agrarian and continental empire to deal with foreign countries reachable by sea. In this sense, the system was presented as a series of concentric circles in hierarchical order, which was subject to overall imperial considerations, and experienced a weakening structure. There was no transition during the 1750–1850 period.

Second, seen from inside, maritime China is studied as the periphery of a continental centre, with the coastal provinces pushing out seaward away from an inward-looking centripetal polity. During the period, some changes but no real transitions took place when some Chinese traders came across alternative value-systems along the coast or offshore.

Third, from an outside perspective, maritime China is perceived as a terminus, which foreign merchants were eager to enter to tap the China market, the eastern end of maritime Asia. The transition was qualitative in terms of Chinese traders' external extensions into the rest of Asia by maintaining "sojourner networking" linked to China.

Fourth, the "whole" maritime China lends a holistic approach, incorporating maritime China as segment, periphery and terminus, the total sum of which lends relative importance in terms of their role in transforming China. Maritime China as a segment is vital to an integrated world view; as a periphery, maritime China gained ground but the structure of continental centre was weakened; and as a terminus, maritime China became more dynamic and important to the overall development of China.

An ideal maritime China in the rhetoric refers to the ideal of a balance in Chinese power and civilisation between which is continental and which is maritime. That said, the ideal serves to support continuity and reduce the need for radical change.

Nation-Building: Five Southeast Asian Histories
Singapore: ISEAS Publications, 2005

"This publication is historic because seven of the nine contributors are senior scholars who have not only witnessed in their lifetimes formative developments in the subject matter, nation-building, but helped to shape the scholarship on it...The nature of the relationship between state and nation is a recurrent theme in the rich and diverse offerings of this book."

— Sumit K Mandal
Pacific Affairs, vol. 79, no. 2, (Summer 2006), pp. 346–347

"...[T]here is clearly a danger of exaggerating western colonial influences [in the nation-building efforts of the five founding member states of the Association of Southeast Asian Nations]. Wang points to equally powerful Asian examples which informed nationalist discourses: from Meiji Japan, Guomindang China and the Indian National Congress, as well as the *often underestimated nationalist message which Showa Japan brought to Southeast Asia...Moreover, into the future, the multi-ethnic models of the United States, Australia, Canada and New Zealand may have far greater significance and relevance for Southeast Asia than inheritances from western Europe."*

— Nicholas J White
Journal of Imperial and Commonwealth History, vol. 34, no. 4, December 2006, pp. 650–652

The essays in this book are the product of a conference, "Nation-Building Histories: Thailand, the Philippines, Indonesia, Malaysia and Singapore", organised by the Institute of Southeast Asian Studies in Singapore in September 2002. Eminent scholars in the field of Southeast Asia history convened at this conference to reflect upon the nation-building process these countries undertook. Participants were invited to express their thoughts on the general question of the historicity of nation-building, especially of countries recently committed to the task, and the issues they encountered while writing the contemporary history of Southeast Asia.

The conference raised a number of critical questions to the writing of nation-building history in the region, all dealt with in different aspects and with varying methods in the 10 essays collected in this volume. Some of the key questions raised include: When did nation-building begin and how did it fit into the writing of contemporary history? How should historians treat the past of each country and nationalism that guided the nation-building task? At which point should political culture come in, especially when dealing with modern challenges of class, secularism and ethnicity? What role does external or regional pressure play during nation-building? When archival sources are not available, how should narrative, social science analyses and personal experience be handled? The 10 essays address some of the questions with specific reference to each of the five founder members of the Association of Southeast Asian Nations (ASEAN) focussed in this conference, and also offer greater insight into the region and the political association of ASEAN.

China and the New International Order
Co-edited with Zheng Yongnian
New York: Routledge, 2008

"*A timely reflection of contemporary Chinese politics and international relations...Rather than providing speculative analyses, this book is rich in the connections between the present and history, between the international and the domestic, and between the empirical and the conceptual...While the transient complexity of the new international order poses problems for many students of international relations, the book has grasped the most significant aspects of this complexity in relation to China...An outstanding feature of this book is that the contributors make their observations from both outside-in and inside-out perspectives...In short, China and the New International Order is a knowledgeable and thoughtful contribution to China studies, and deserves a wide audience interested in China and the contemporary international order.*"

— Yang Jiang
The China Journal, no. 61 (January 2009), pp. 240–242

This book is a collection of contributions from the 2006 International Conference on China in the International Order: Integrating Views from Outside-In and Inside-Out. In this volume, 15 China experts analyse the domestic sources of China's international behaviour in the post-Cold War era. Concepts such as nationalism, sovereignty, and identities, as well as multilateralism, regionalism, international entitlement, and global governance are explored. Analyses of China's past and present international behaviour show that China's relationship with the outside world is highly interactive, and this interaction hinges on its highly interdependent and mutually constitutive domestic and international domains. The notion of whether China can reshape the international order boils down to its ability to manage its domestic developments economically, in tandem with the social and political arenas.

The chapters are organised in four themed sections. To put the discourse in perspective, the first section highlights the key issues in conceptualising China's international behaviour: China's interpretation of the world order, Chinese conception of nationalism and sovereignty, and civil-military relations. In these areas, China's domestic factors are closely associated with its international behaviour.

The discourse in sections two and three advances to studying the impact of external factors, namely globalisation and regionalism, on linking China with the international order. In the age of interdependence, China seeks to integrate itself into the new international order, which however in return imposes constraints on China. Through these interactions, China and the international community are constantly mutually adjusting to and transform each other.

Faced with daunting challenges in understanding China's integration into the mainstream international order, developing a Chinese school of international relations study may be deemed controversial even among Chinese scholars. In reality, the international-relations theory building extends beyond constructing it from the Chinese culture. China's contribution to the international order will be a process of continuous interaction and open dialogue between the Chinese and international academia as well as between the Chinese civilisation and foreign civilisations.

中国的"主义"之争：从"五四运动"到当代
China's Ideological Battles since the May Fourth Movement
Co-edited with Zheng Yongnian
Singapore: Global Publishing Company, 2009

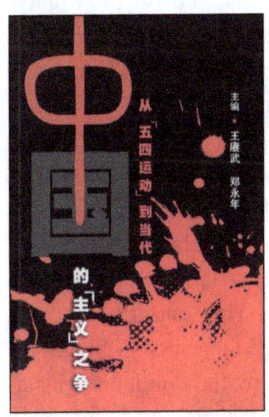

The May Fourth Movement is a watershed event in the history of modern China. Thereafter, virtually all developments in Chinese history are inextricably related to it in one way or another, be it in the cultural and/or political terrain. This is a 14-essay collection published by the East Asian Institute to commemorate the 90th anniversary of the May Fourth Movement as China grapples with the search of its legacy in the now trouble-fraught contemporary society.

In fact, the problems China faces today and the issues that dominate Chinese public discourse are but old issues that contributed to the movement and have never gone away in its aftermath. This volume will provide an invaluable background to May Fourth Movement and establish the movement's linkage with today's China.

Topics such as democracy, freedom, the radicalisation of intellectuals and liberation of thought dominate the study of the May Fourth Movement. Wong Sin Kiong's paper on the Chinese anti-missionary movement during the late imperial China, and the demonisation of the Jesuits and Christianity reflects the intensity of China's xenophobia before the May Fourth Movement.

Wang Gungwu and Zheng Yongnian's papers present an in-depth discussion of the development of "isms" after the May Fourth Movement, focussing particularly on the rise of nationalism and liberalism in contemporary China and their resurrection after the open door reform. The fierce contention among the various "isms", which include liberalism, New Leftist, Marxism, and democratic socialism, have led to theorisation of reform by the Chinese government.

Voice of Malayan Revolution:
The CPM Radio War against Singapore and Malaysia, 1969–1981
Co-edited with Ong Weichong
Singapore: S Rajaratnam School of International Studies, 2009

This edited volume is an invaluable reference for research into the Second Malayan Emergency (1968–1989) — the resurrection of the armed struggle of the Communist Party of Malaya (CPM) — because most other works focus only on the Malayan Emergency (1948–1960) rather than the second round of insurgency.

The collection of full transcripts of the clandestine radio broadcasts of the CPM — transmitted on the airwaves from a Chinese military base in Hunan, China as the "Voice of Malayan Revolution" (VMR) — spans over the first 12 years of the insurgency from 1969 to 1981. The transcripts provide first-hand material for the major events taking place in Malaysia and Singapore during the heyday of the Cold War, and demonstrate how the communist insurgency helped shape the nation-building process of both Malaysia and Singapore.

The volume is also a significant reference source for the analysis of Southeast Asian Cold War dynamics from an Asian perspective.

The ideological struggle of the CPM is examined in five themed chapters. The first chapter collects the key documents related to Marxist-Leninist-Maoist propaganda, including the announcement of constitutions, manifestos, declarations, party programmes and political statements on the key events of the "revolutionary calendar". The second chapter unravels and details the people's revolutionary armed struggles launched by the CPM, whose guerillas were "familiar with the terrain, skilled in jungle warfare, and skilled in hiding and retreating employing Mao Tse-tung's war tactics".

Chapter three is an account of the relationship between the CPM and the Chinese Communist Party (CCP) and Indo-Chinese communist parties in Southeast Asia, bringing "the proletarian internationalist spirit" in full manifestation. Chapter four attempts to explain the schism within the CPM and the influence of propaganda war on unity. The last chapter traces how the CPM's propaganda campaign against "social injustice" that aimed to create a class-conscious proletariat had successfully agitated the masses with issues on "civil rights violations" but finally lost the battlefield with the rapid economic growth in Malaysia and Singapore.

Festschrifts

坦蕩人生，學者情懷：王賡武訪談與言論集
The Life and Sentiment of a Scholar: Anthology of Professor Wang Gungwu's Interviews and Speeches
Edited by Liu Hong
River Edge, New Jersey: Global Publishing Company, 2000

This edited volume is a collection of articles written about and by Wang Gungwu — the renowned scholar and world authority in China studies and Chinese migration. It is hoped that readers will gain a deeper understanding of Wang through his prolific work, his life experiences as a Chinese overseas during the turbulent post-war and postcolonial periods, and of course, his mind and thoughts. A glimpse into Wang's eminent achievements reveals the multiple roles he undertakes as a teacher, a scholar, an educationist, and a social activist, demonstrating at the same time his scholarly interest in and deep concern for social, cultural, and political issues as well as more lofty subjects like philosophy of life. Wang is the epitome of dedication as an academic and an academic administrator — his thoroughness and participatory approach in scholarly research and his ardent push to create a vibrant research culture when he was vice-chancellor of the University of Hong Kong are a testament to his commitment. He also shows his sincere solicitude for social problems, striving to translate scholarship into practical applications for solving issues and problems in the community.

   This volume is divided into three sections. The first section is composed of interviews with Wang conducted by his friends, colleagues, students, journalists, and the editor. These conversations cover a wide range of topics from his family, his personal experiences, his scholarly research, and his academic journey, particularly his tenure at the University of Hong Kong.

   The second section consists of a compilation of the public speeches Wang had given on various occasions, covering topics such as the past, present and future of China, overseas Chinese, Chinese businessmen, and Hong Kong. The third section is a collection of essays written by Wang as foreword and introduction for other publications.

海外华人研究的大视野与新方向
Overseas Chinese Studies: New Horizon and Direction — Collected Essays by Professor Wang Gungwu
Edited by Liu Hong and Huang Jianli
Singapore: Global Publishing Company, 2002

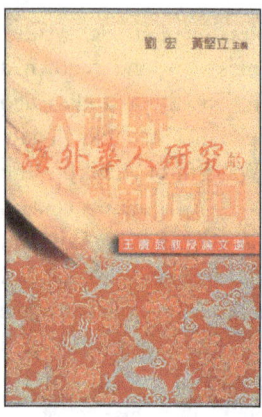

This book is the sister volume of *The Life and Sentiment of a Scholar — Anthology of Professor Wang Gungwu's Interviews and Speeches* also published by Global Publishing in 2000. The earlier work reconstructs Wang's life as a public intellectual, spanning from his childhood, his formative years, his academic pursuit and mission, to his appointment as vice-chancellor of the University of Hong Kong. This volume, however, focusses on Wang's role as an academic and his contribution to the overseas Chinese studies.

This volume is a collection of 20 essays by Wang — undoubtedly the pioneer in the newly established field of overseas Chinese studies — who approaches the diverse and complex subject from different angles and perspectives. For the convenience of readers, and to facilitate further research and development of the discipline, the essays are grouped into four broad categories. The book begins with five essays on theory and methodology that review the current ones and make forecast on new development.

In the section themed "Nationalism", Wang discusses how nationalism among overseas Chinese is different from that in mainland China; the relation of nationalism with Confucianism, the role of ethnicity in the Asia-Pacific region. The section on Global and the Periphery consists of six papers on the ever-evolving relationship between Greater China and the overseas Chinese communities from the early revolutionary years to present-day China as an economic powerhouse in frantic search for alliance and partners in the Pacific region. The fourth section revisits the issue of the construction of the discipline from the angles of research topics and historical material resources. The essays reflect that Wang's global perspective have their roots in local concerns.

Power and Identity in the Chinese World Order: Festschrift in Honour of Professor Wang Gungwu
Edited by Billy K L So, John Fitzgerald, Huang Jianli, James K Chin
Hong Kong: Hong Kong University Press, 2003

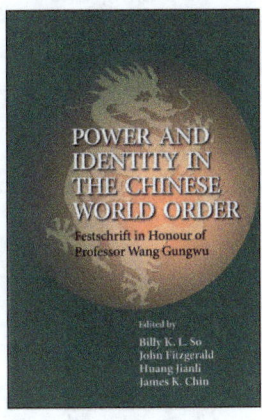

This book is a collection of 14 essays written by former graduate students under the tutelage of Wang Gungwu, who are now distinguished scholars in their various fields in universities across the world. It is a collective effort to honour Wang on the occasion of his 70th birthday in commemoration of his contribution to the study of Chinese history during his academic career and the influence he exerts over the younger generations of historians.

The book begins with a historiographical prologue by Philip A Kuhn who surveys Wang's writings over a span of 50 years, revealing how his thoughts developed in response to the historical events he witnessed, and also the fundamental concerns that he consistently weighed up throughout his lifetime in academia. Echoing the prologue, Lee Guan-kin offers an oral history of Wang's life in the epilogue. The account is based on nine interviews conducted with Wang in 1999, covering every phase of his life from childhood in Ipoh to taking the helm at the East Asian Institute in Singapore. This helps readers tremendously in understanding his scholarship with reference to his family background and life experiences.

The essays by former students of Wang revolve around two major topics — power and identity — which are two fundamental academic concerns of Wang. Grouped into four sections, the first two sections focus on the search for power in modern China, covering topics such as power restructuring, state power, and economy and society. The third and fourth sections — "In Search of Chineseness: Identity of a Nation" and "In Search of Chineseness: Community and Self" — focus on the search for a Chinese identity. In one way or another, the collection of essays reflects the influence Wang has on his remarkable students.

The comprehensive list of Wang's publication from 1957 to 2001, arranged in chronological order as an appendix of the book, opens up a treasure trove of knowledge and anchors him as a prolific author. This book is a celebration of the life, work and impact of Wang Gungwu and the influences he wielded in the academic circle over the past four decades of his scholarly life.

Diasporic Chinese Ventures: The Life and Work of Wang Gungwu
Edited by Gregor Benton and Liu Hong
London and New York: RoutledgeCurzon, 2004

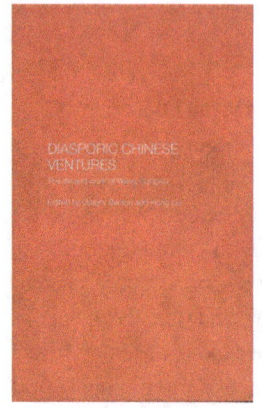

"This attractive compendium, headed by a revealing biographical interview by Hong Liu, brings together hard-to-find articles, lectures and interviews by Wang Gungwu, the premier historian of Chinese overseas migration...The book's main contribution is to make available little-known gems of Wang's historical thought (of which only a sampling can be offered here)."

— Philip A Kuhn
The China Journal, no. 53 (January 2005), pp. 275–276

"The volume is certainly novel in its format and indeed worth reading by those seeking a convenient introduction to diverse aspects of Wang Gungwu — the individual and the scholar. Those working in the area will probably be quite familiar with most of the inclusions, but the translated pieces will be useful for those who do not have access to the Chinese-language versions."

— Geoff Wade
Singapore Journal of Tropical Geography, vol. 27, no. 3 (2006), pp. 345–347

Unifying the biographical and conceptual themes, this is a collection of essays by and about Wang Gungwu. Part one, entitled "Encounters", is a collection of six essays written by different authors on the various stages and defining moments of Wang's life. Liu Hong's essay, an interview with Wang, lends a comprehensive background to Wang's early childhood, his formative years in Malaya and China, and his academic life against the backdrop of turbulent times and geographical settings. Laurent Malvezin's interview with Wang puts the problems with Chinese diaspora into perspective in political and social context. In another essay, Wang relates his reading interests and how reading the *Historical Records (Shiji)* had kindled his passion for history.

Part two and part three, entitled "Reflection: Cultural Concerns" and "Reflections: Chinese Overseas in Historical and Comparative Perspective" respectively, consist of essays authored by Wang. Most of the essays were originally delivered as keynote speeches at meetings and conferences in Asia, Europe and North America, except "Confucius the Sage", which Wang wrote for a high-school publication when he was 16. The essay sets precedent of Wang's fundamental concerns, which include the impact of culture and tradition on the Chinese both in China and abroad, even at such tender age.

The other papers are selected from a wide corpus of his recent scholarly writings. Unlike his earlier research, which was meticulously based on well-researched case studies, his recent writings are more concerned with conceptual formulations, theoretical frameworks, macro-perspectives, and grand patterns. His analyses and dissection of contemporary world are penetrative and insightful, thus lending possible future directions that the field might take. These works, though a small fraction of Wang's entire writings, are a representative body of his scholarship and thought.

PART III
Chronology of Wang Gungwu

University Professor at the National University of Singapore, Faculty of Arts and Social Sciences.

Emeritus Professor of the Australian National University, Canberra.

Born in Surabaya, Indonesia on 9 October 1930, he is an Australian citizen and currently a permanent resident of Singapore.

1930   Surabaya

Born on 9 October in Surabaya, Indonesia, the only child of Wang Fo-wen 王宓文 (1903–1972) and Ting Yien 丁儼 (1905–1993). The Wang ancestral home was in the city of Zhengding, Hebei, for centuries before his great-grandfather moved to Taizhou, Jiangsu in 1869. The Ting ancestral home was in the city of Zhenjiang, south of the Yangtze River before the family became refugees from the Taiping rebels who captured Zhenjiang in 1853; they settled in Dongtai, also in Jiangsu.

Father graduated from Southeastern University, the predecessor of National Central University; recruited to teach in Singapore, Kuala Lumpur and Malacca before being appointed as the first headmaster of Huaqiao School in Surabaya in 1929.

1931   Surabaya • Ipoh

The Great Depression forced his father to leave Surabaya and take up a position as assistant inspector of Chinese schools in the state of Perak. Family moved to Ipoh, British Malaya, at the end of the year.

For full details and a complete list of Wang Gungwu's writings, see *Wang Gungwu, Junzi, Scholar–Gentleman, in conversation with Asad-ul Iqbal Latif*, pp. 204–250; and the Appendix to *Power and Identity in the Chinese World Order: Festschrift in Honour of Professor Wang Gungwu*, pp. 408–427.

1936 Ipoh

Attended Maxwell Primary School for one year before the school was merged into Anderson School, a government English school in Perak.

Visited China in 1936 with parents for three months. Saw grandparents and extended family in Taizhou, and stayed for a few weeks with relatives in Shanghai.

From 1937, accompanied mother on campaigns to raise funds for the war in China. Saw patriotic films. Friends at Anderson School and in Green Town where he lived were Chinese, Indian and Malay boys. Teachers included two British women, three Ceylonese and Indians, a Sikh, a Malay and a Chinese.

1941–1945   Ipoh under Japanese Occupation

Completed Standard 5 before the Japanese invaded in December 1941. Family joined friends in hiding around Kinta Valley in Tanjung Tualang timber camp and the caves at Pasir Puteh. Returned and stayed at the homes of friends in Ipoh town, with a Foochow family, then a Hokkien family, later a Henghua family and finally a Hakka family.

Went to Ming Teh Primary School, a Chinese school where Japanese was also taught.

Left school and joined a class started by his father where children were taught classical Chinese. Read from a library of looted volumes of English classics and popular fiction. The only entertainment came from a few films made in Japanese-occupied Shanghai.

1945   Ipoh

When war ended, returned to Anderson School, and was promoted to Standard 8 (Junior Cambridge Certificate).

1946   Ipoh

Sat for the Cambridge School Certificate examinations.

Wrote an article "Confucius the Sage", which was published in the school magazine, *Anderson School Publication*.

1947   Ipoh • Nanjing

Family moved to Nanjing, China. Sat the entrance examinations to the National Central University (中央大学) in the summer. Accepted into the Department of Foreign Languages. Classes started in October.

Was taught English literature by Lou Guanglai 楼光来, Fan Cunzhong 范存忠, Liu Shimu 刘世沐, Hua Linyi 华林一, Lü Tianshi 吕天石; Chinese literature by You Shou 游寿; Chinese history by Miao Fenglin 缪凤林. Also took courses in French, German and ethics. Took the compulsory course for all freshmen, the Three Principles of the People (三民主义).

1948   Nanjing

Father taught at the University's Secondary School (中大附中) but, because of ill health, returned to Ipoh, Malaya.

Spent summer in Shanghai and experienced the spectacular acceleration of inflation that destroyed the national economy. Began second-year studies in October.

University closed in November. Left Nanjing in December to return to Malaya via Shanghai, Keelung, Amoy, Hong Kong and Singapore.

1949   Ipoh • Singapore

Taught part-time at Anderson School and at St Michael's Institution in Ipoh. Registered as Federal citizen of Malaya.

Enrolled in the newly established University of Malaya, Singapore. Took three subjects for Bachelor of Arts general degree. Was taught English literature by Graham Hough, Ellis Evans, Patrick Anderson and Roy Morrell; history by Brian Harrison, Ian Macgregor and Eric Stokes; and economics by Thomas Silcock, Lim Tay Boh, Paul Sherwood, Charles Gamba and You Poh Seng.

1950   Singapore

Befriended by Beda Lim at the University, who published Wang's book of verse, *Pulse*. Elected as freshman representative to University of Malaya Students' Union (UMSU), then as publications secretary and editor of *The Malayan Undergraduate*, the official organ of UMSU.

Attended the Rockefeller Foundation-sponsored Writers' Conference in Manila. Published his first short story.

1951   Singapore

For first two years, stayed in dormitories around the University Quadrangle. Moved to Dunearn Road Hostels in 1951 and stayed till the middle of 1954.

Elected President of UMSU. Represented UMSU at a students' conference in Colombo. Published poem in *Times of Ceylon*.

Led UMSU delegation to the United Nations Student Conference in Delhi.

Father appointed Federal Inspector of Chinese Schools, family moved to Kuala Lumpur.

1952   Singapore

Elected Chairman of UMSU Council.

Graduated with a Bachelor of Arts general degree. Accepted to do his honours degree in history, taught by C N Parkinson. Went to Hong Kong to collect materials for graduation exercise, on "Chinese Reformists and Revolutionaries in the Straits Settlements, 1900–1911".

1953   Singapore

Graduated with a Bachelor of Arts (Honours) degree. Tutored in the Department of History of the University of Malaya. Embarked on his master's degree. Elected founding president of the University Socialist Club and started publication of its organ, *Fajar*.

Joined archaeological excavations at Johor Lama organised by the director of the National Museums, Federation of Malaya, Lance Sieveking.

Published "Chinese Historiography: the Standard Histories".

1954   Singapore • London

Completed master's thesis before leaving for London in August 1954 on the British Council Scholarship. Sailed to Genoa, then to London by train via Paris. Submitted master's thesis, *The Nanhai Trade: A Study of the Early History of Chinese Trade in the South China Sea*.

Engaged to fellow alumnus of the University of Malaya, Margaret Lim Ping-ting.

Published "Johor Lama: an Introduction to Archaeology".

Applied for PhD research at the School of Oriental and African Studies, University of London. Supervisor was D G E Hall, assisted by Denis Twitchett. Advised by Walter Simon, W G Beasley, C H Philips, C D Cowan and Otto van der Sprenkel. Ronald Dore ran an advanced Japanese reading class for graduate students, including Philip Kuhn. Other contemporaries included Jerome Chen, Romila Thapar and Jitendra Singh Uberoi.

1955 London

Married in London. Margaret obtained her Bachelor of Arts (Honours) in English Literature in 1954, taught senior classes at St Andrew's Secondary School in Singapore in 1954–1955, and then studied at Homerton College, Cambridge (now a constituent college of the University of Cambridge).

Father retired, and arrived in London for private research at the University of London.

T D Ts'ien 钱存典, formerly minister counsellor of the Chinese Embassy and father's schoolmate in Taizhou, China, gave Margaret away at their wedding. The married couple lived in Cambridge for a year.

In Cambridge, advised by Edwin Pulleyblank and Cheng Te-k'un.

In Malaya Hall, London, met Goh Keng Swee, John Eber and Wan A Hamid.

1956 London

Attended International Congress of Jeunes Sinologues in Paris. Met Xia Nai 夏鼐, Jian Bozhan 翦伯赞, Zhou Yiliang 周一良 and Zhang Zhilian 张芝联; also Luo Xianglin 罗香林, He Guangzhong 贺光中; Paul Demiéville, Anthony Hulsewé, Herbert Franke, Benjamin Schwartz.

Parents returned to Singapore.

Review of Bernard S Solomon's translation, *The Veritable Record of the T'ang Emperor Shun-tsung*, in *Journal of the Royal Asiatic Society*.

1957   London • Singapore

Son Shih-chang (Hsin-ming) was born in London.

Submitted PhD thesis, *The Structure of Power in North China during the Five Dynasties*.

Awarded doctorate in Mediaeval History, University of London.

Returned to Singapore by sea, celebrated Malayan independence on board.

Joined the Department of History of University of Malaya as Assistant Lecturer. The head was Professor C N Parkinson. Colleagues included Eunice Thio, K G Tregonning, Alastair Lamb, L K Young.

Lived in flats at MacAlister Road, behind the Medical Faculty.

Published "The *Chiu Wu-Tai Shih* and History-Writing during the Five Dynasties" (Chinese translation published in *Shih-huo yueh-k'an* 《食货月刊》, 1984).

1958   Singapore

University of Malaya established a division in Kuala Lumpur. Lectured in Singapore to second-year students on East Asian History, 1500–1800; for two days every fortnight, lectured in Kuala Lumpur to the freshman class temporarily located at the Technical Institute. Work began on the new campus buildings in Kuala Lumpur.

With Alastair Lamb and students, conducted archaeological excavation at the Bujang Valley, Kedah, in February and again in May.

Fellow of Raffles Hall, University of Malaya, Singapore; moved home to University Road beside College Green, Dunearn Hostels.

Asked to join the Singapore Nanyang Hsueh-hui (South Seas Society) council. Invited to edit the *Nanyang Hsueh-pao* 《南洋学报》.

Broadcast eight talks on the overseas Chinese for Radio Sarawak, entitled "A History of the Nanyang Chinese".

Published "The Nanhai Trade: a Study of the Early History of Chinese Trade in the South China Sea" as a monograph issue of *Journal of Malayan Branch Royal Asiatic Society* (Chinese translation published in 1988);

"The Chinese in Search of a Base in the Nanyang"; and

"Trial and Error in Malayan Poetry", in *Malayan Undergrad*.

Twelve poems published in *Litmus One, Selected University Verse, 1949–1957*.

1959   Singapore • Kuala Lumpur

Promoted to Lecturer at University of Malaya.

Moved to the Kuala Lumpur campus of the University of Malaya as lecturer in the Department of History.

Daughter Lin-chang (Hsin-Mei) was born in Kuala Lumpur.

Published *A Short History of the Nanyang Chinese* (Chinese translation published in 1969; Japanese translation in 1972; and a new Chinese translation in Hong Kong in 1988). Also published "Sun Yat-sen and Singapore".

Review of Karl Wittfogel's *Oriental Despotism: a Comparative Study of Total Power*.

1960   Kuala Lumpur

Spent four months in the United States. Visited the following universities and wrote report for the Asia Foundation on his impressions of Asian studies in the United States:

- University of Hawaii; University of Washington, Seattle. Conducted seminar to graduate students.
- University of California, Berkeley and Stanford University, Palo Alto. Visited the Asia Foundation.
- University of Arizona. Spoke to an undergraduate class on Islam in Southeast Asia; University of Colorado. Gave seminar on the Western impact in Asia; and a lecture on the overseas Chinese. Delivered lecture to graduate students on the history of Malaya.

- Washington University, St Louis. Presented lecture on the 19th century Chinese history; conducted three seminars on Southeast Asian politics; and gave lecture on "Free Thought in China"; University of Chicago. Gave seminar on "New Nations".
- In Washington DC, the School of Advanced International Studies at the Johns Hopkins University, and Howard University.
- Columbia University. Also attended Asian Studies Association Conference in New York. Visited Princeton University, used the Gest Library; Yale University, used the Stirling Memorial Library Southeast Asian Collection; Cornell University. Visited Southeast Asia Library, gave lecture on Ming relations with Southeast Asia.
- Harvard University, Centre of East Asian Studies, used the Harvard-Yenching Institute Library. Gave seminar on Feng Tao 冯道.

In London, visited School of Oriental and African Studies (SOAS) of the University of London. Gave lecture on "Malayan Politics" at the Malaya Hall.

Continued to teach East Asian history at the Singapore campus of the University of Malaya.

External examiner for the History and Geography department at Nanyang University, Singapore.

Published "An Early Chinese Visitor to Kelantan"; and "Memperkembang Bahasa Kebangsaan: Peranan Perseorangan dan Badan Kesusasteraan" (Developing the National Language: the Role of Individuals and Literary Bodies).

Review of Donald E Willmott's *The Chinese of Semarang*; and Lea E Williams' *Overseas Chinese Nationalism*, published in *Journal of Southeast Asian History*.

1961   Kuala Lumpur • London

Promoted to Senior Lecturer at University of Malaya.

Spent a year in England as Rockefeller Fellow at the School of Oriental and African Studies in the University of London. Other fellows from Southeast Asia were O D Corpuz and Nugroho Notosusanto.

Travelled with Margaret and Shih-chang. Lin-chang stayed with parents in Johor Bahru.

Daughter Hui-chang (Hsin-lan) was born in London.

In Europe, visited Universities of Hamburg, Leiden and Munich.

Gave lecture at the Royal Commonwealth Society, "The Chinese in Southeast Asia", published in *Commonwealth Journal*, 1962.

Attended Confucian Personalities Conference in New York and presented a paper on Feng Dao, published as "Feng Tao, an essay on Confucian loyalty" in 1962 (reprinted in *Confucianism and Chinese Civilisation* in 1964; and Chinese translation in 1973).

Attended the First Conference of Southeast Asian Historians in Singapore.

Published "The Emergence of Southeast Asia"; "A Letter to Kuala Pilah, and "Mr Harrison and the 'Western Bias' in the Nanhai Trade".

1962 London • Kuala Lumpur

Elected Dean of the Faculty of Arts at University of Malaya. Also the Acting Head of the new Department of Chinese Studies, invited Cheng Te-k'un from University of Cambridge; succeeded by Ho Peng Yoke as Professor and Head of the department.

Elected Vice-President of the Malayan Branch of Royal Asiatic Society, and editor of its journal (1962–1968).

In London, completed research on Ming relations with Southeast Asia during the reigns of Zhu Yuanzhang and Zhu Di.

Gave lecture at the Royal Central Asian Society, "Malayan Nationalism", published in 1962 (Malay translation in 1973).

Attended the Fourth International Conference on World Politics, Athens.

Planned the volume on *Malaysia: a Survey*, together with colleagues at the University of Malaya.

Invited by Dewan Bahasa dan Pustaka to write for *The Cultural Background of the Peoples of Malaysia* project. Published the volume for

Chinese culture, *Latar Belakang Kebudayaan Pendudok di-Tanah Melayu: Bahagian Kebudayaan China* (Republished in 1978).

Published "Fuhrungsprobleme der Chinesen in Malaya und Singapore" in 1962 (the English original, "Traditional leadership in a New Nation: The Chinese in Malaya and Singapore", published in 1968).

Published "Malacca in 1403"; and "Adaptability: Can the Nanyang Chinese Remould their Lives in Southeast Asia?".

1963   Kuala Lumpur

Promoted to Professor of History and Head of department. Taught new honours degree course, "Theory and Method of History".

For the volume on *Malaysia: A Survey*, visited Brunei, Sabah and Sarawak. When Brunei declined to join Malaysia, several essays had to be revised and this delayed the volume's publication.

Published *The Structure of Power in North China during the Five Dynasties*, University of Malaya Press. (Reprinted in 1968; also published by Stanford University Press in 1967.)

Also published "The Melayu in Hai-kuo Wen-chien Lu" and "The Sino-Turk Alliance in Wu-Tai History".

1964   Kuala Lumpur

Appointed member of the Commission of Inquiry on the Singapore Riots.

Invited to chair the Nanyang University Curriculum Review Committee, report completed in May 1965 and published later that year in September.

Attended the International Association of Historians of Asia (IAHA) Conference in Hong Kong. Elected President of the IAHA for 1964–1968.

Attended the Kuala Lumpur Conference on Development and Cooperation in the South Asia Pacific Region. Presented a paper, "Nation Formation and Regionalism in Southeast Asia", published in *South Asia Pacific Crisis: National Development and the World Community*.

Attended the Association of Asian Studies (AAS) Annual Meeting in Washington DC.

Published the edited volume, *Malaysia: A Survey*.

Also "The Opening of Relations between China and Malacca, 1402–1405", in *Malayan and Indonesian Studies: Festschrift for Richard Winstedt* (Chinese translation in 1986; republished in *Admiral Zheng He and Southeast Asia*, edited by Leo Suryadiniata, 2005).

Published "A Short Introduction to Chinese Writing in Malaya"; "The Teaching of History in a Southeast Asian Context"; and "The Vietnam Issue".

Review of Jerome Ch'en's *Yuan Shih-k'ai, 1859–1916: Brutus Assumes the Purple*, in *Bulletin of the School of Oriental and African Studies, University of London*.

1965 Kuala Lumpur

Invited to be Asia Fellow at the Australian National University (ANU), May to August 1965.

Moved to new home in Petaling Jaya.

Appointed member of the Commission on Traditional Medicine, Kuala Lumpur, 1965–1968.

Edited *Raniri and the Wujudiyyah of 17th Century Acheh*, by Sayyid Muhammad Naguib al-Attas; and *The Civil War in Kelantan in 1839* by Cyril Skinner for the Monograph series of Journal of the Malaysian Branch of the Royal Asiatic Society.

During his Asian Fellowship at ANU, also visited Victoria University of Wellington, University of Adelaide, University of Melbourne and Monash University and University of Sydney.

At ANU, in the Department of Pacific History, supported plan to develop Southeast Asian history. Spent time also in the Department of Far Eastern History. Gave talk to the Oriental Studies Society and two graduate seminars.

Presented a seminar on leadership in Malaysia at University of Adelaide.

At Monash University, conducted a seminar at the Centre of Southeast Asian Studies.

At the University of Sydney, gave a seminar to Oriental Studies students on Chinese history. Presented a public lecture to the Oriental Society of Australia, on early Chinese relations with foreign countries. Published as "Chinese Historians and the Nature of Early Chinese Foreign Relations" in *The Journal of the Oriental Society of Australia* in 1965.

Submitted paper for John K Fairbank's conference on The Chinese World Order but unable to attend. Published as "Early Ming Relations with Southeast Asia — A Background Essay" in 1968 (Chinese translation in 1987).

Malaysia-Singapore separation on 9 August, also his last day in Australia.

At University of Malaya, led the History Department study trip up the Perak River.

Published "The Uniqueness of Europe", in *The Glass Curtain between Europe and Asia,* edited by Raghavan Iyer (German translation in 1968);

"The Concept of Malaysia", "Early Chinese Influence in Southeast Asia", "Political Malaya, 1895–1941", "The Japanese Occupation and Post-war Malaya, 1941–1948", "Malaya: The Road to Independence and Malaysia", in *History of the Malaysian States*, 1965; and

"Introduction" to John Cameron's *Our Tropical Possessions in Malayan India*, Oxford Historical Reprints, 1965.

Review of Wolfram Eberhard's *Social Mobility in Traditional China* in *Journal of Southeast Asian History*.

1966 Kuala Lumpur

Gave inaugural lecture as Professor of History at University of Malaya. Published as *The Use of History* (also published in *Papers in International Studies*, Ohio University, 1968; and in *Syarahan Perdana, 1959–84*, edited by Ungku A Aziz and Shaharil Talib, 1988; Chinese translation in 1990).

Commissioned to write on Asian communist parties that are not in power.

Visited India and then Japan and South Vietnam. Published as "Asian Communism Now", "The Ingenious Infiltrators", "Have the Reds Missed the Boat?", "Vietnam — The Decisive Test", in *The Asia Magazine,*

Hong Kong. (Published in *Journal of the Historical Society*, 1967; also published as "Kommunism di Asia" in Malay translation, *Dewan Masharakat*, 1968.)

Department study trip to the west coast of Perak: Lumut, Pangkor, Bruas, Taiping, Port Weld, Matang, Kuala Selinsing and Kamunting.

Organised History Teachers Association of Malaysia Conference.

Visit to Kota Bahru: opening of the Pasar Wakaf Siku.

Study trip to Sarawak, Sarawak Museum; and visited the Second Division of Sarawak: Simanggang and Engkilili and the Indonesian border.

Attended the International Congress of Maritime History in Beirut. Published "'Public' and 'Private' Overseas Trade in Chinese History", in *Societes et Companies de Commerce en Orient et dans l'Ocean Indien*, 1970.

Published "1874 in Our History" and "Malaysia's Social History", in *Peninjau Sejarah*, 1966; and

"Malayan Nationalism", in *Malaysia: Selected Historical Readings*, edited by John Bastin and Robin W Winks, 1966.

1967 Kuala Lumpur

Accepted invitation to succeed C P FitzGerald as Professor and Head of the Department of Far Eastern History at the ANU.

Appointed Chairman of the Istilah Committee for History, Dewan Bahasa dan Pustaka, Kuala Lumpur, 1967–1968.

Guest of the conference organisers of the XXVII International Congress of Orientalists at the University of Michigan, Ann Arbor, member of a controversial panel with John King Fairbank that debated issues pertaining to China, Taiwan and the Chinese overseas.

Invited as commentator at the China in Crisis Conference at University of Chicago. Published as "Comment on C Martin Wilbur's paper on Warlordism in Modern China", in *China in Crisis*, edited by Ho Ping-ti, University of Chicago Press, 1968.

Invited to South Korea as guest of the Ministry of Education. Visited Seoul National University, Korea University, Yonsei University, Ehwa Women's University, Sungkyunguan University and Sogang University. Met historians Kim Jun-Yop, Koh Byong-ik, Chon Hae-jung, Soon Po-ki, Yi Ki-baek.

Published "Introduction", Isabella Bird, *The Golden Chersonese*, Oxford Historical Reprints, 1967.

Review of Charles O Hucker's *The Censorial System of Ming China*, in *Journal of Southeast Asian History*.

1968   Kuala Lumpur • Canberra

Appointed Professor (1968–1986) and Head (1968–1975, 1980–1986) of the Department of Far Eastern History, and Director of Research School of Pacific Studies (1975–1980), Australian National University, Canberra.

Organised the Department of History at University of Malaya to host the Fourth Conference of the International Association of the Historians of Asia (IAHA) in Kuala Lumpur. The conference attracted over 200 papers and was the largest gathering ever of international scholars of Southeast Asia. It took place at a time when conflict between the Soviet Union and Czechoslovakia over political reforms was reaching a climax and, at the conference, Russian and Czechoslovak scholars openly debated their differences. Later, at a conference in Bangkok that followed soon afterwards, Russian troops marched into Czechoslovakia to stop President Dubcek and his "Prague Spring".

Edited, with S T Alishabana and X S Thaninayagam, *The Cultural Problems of Malaysia in the Context of Southeast Asia*, published by the Malaysian Society of Orientalists, Kuala Lumpur, 1968.

Published "The First Three Rulers of Malacca", *Journal of the Malaysian Branch Royal Asiatic Society* (Chinese translation in 1987; republished in *Admiral Zheng He and Southeast Asia*, edited by Leo Suryadinata, 2005); and "A New Sensation", in *Twenty-two Malaysian Stories: An Anthology of Writing in English*, edited by Lloyd Fernando.

Review of Jonathan Spence's *Ts'ao Yin and the K'ang-hsi Emperor*, in *Journal of Asian Studies*.

1969 Canberra

The research schools at ANU admitted only doctoral candidates. During the period 1968–1986, the department produced over 20 PhD graduates who went on to significant academic and public careers. In Chinese and Japanese history, they include Colin Mackerras, Yen Ching-hwang, Edmund Fung, Leif Littrup, Adrian Chan, Lincoln Li, John Fitzgerald, Beverley Hooper, Antonia Finnane, Jennifer Jay Wei-yen, Richard Rigby, Huang Jianli, Terry Narramore, Pauline Keating, Brian Martin, Theresa Munford, Chou Hung-hsiang, Yeung Ching-kong, Wong Yin-wai, Sally Borthwick and Kenneth Wells.

Began reading the Cultural Revolution Collection at the Menzies Library and the National Library of Australia, in preparation for the volume on contemporary China, *China and the World since 1949*, published in 1977.

Gave lecture at the University of New South Wales Symposium, "Is Australia part of Asia?", published as "Cultural Tensions in Asia".

Delivered lecture to the Australian-Asian Association of Victoria Conference on "The Generational Gap and Australian-Asian Relations", Melbourne, published as "Reflections on the Generational Gap in Asia".

Presented the keynote lecture at the Asian Workshop on Higher Education in the Chinese University of Hong Kong, published as "The University in relation to Traditional Culture".

After the May 13 riots in Malaysia, addressed the Monash University Malaysia-Singapore Students' Association, published as "Malaysia: An Interim View", in *The May Tragedy in Malaysia: A Collection of Essays*.

Published "The Compulsion to Look South: Asian Awareness of Australia".

Review of Howard Boorman and Richard Howard's (editors) *Biographical Dictionary of Republican China*, vol. II Dalai-Ma, in *Pacific Affairs*.

Review of Joseph R Levenson's *Confucian China and its Modern Fate: A Trilogy*, in *Journal of Southeast Asian History*.

1970   Canberra

Established a programme to visit and lecture at universities that were interested in the development of Asian Studies in Australia. A particularly urgent task was to meet the shortage of social scientists linguistically equipped to study the cultural and historical underpinnings of Asian modernisation. This required conscious efforts to build bridges between classical Oriental studies and modern academic disciplines. At the ANU, continued to do research in traditional Chinese political institutions and the early history of China's external relations. At the same time, also taught the history of the Chinese revolution in the history department of the Faculty of Arts, and the study of overseas Chinese communities in Southeast Asia in the Faculty of Asian Studies.

Presented the inaugural Flinders Asian Studies Lecture, Flinders University, Adelaide, published *Scholarship and the History and Politics of Southeast Asia*.

Gave a lecture for the Octagon Lectures series at the University of Western Australia, published as "On the South-Eastern Edge of Asia: an Asian View", in *Everyman in Australia*, edited by G C Bolton, 1972.

Published "Chinese Politics in Malaya", in *The China Quarterly* (Chinese translation in 1987);

"China and Southeast Asia, 1402–1424", in *Social History of China & Southeast Asia* (Chinese translation in *Nankai Shixue*, 1982);

"Political Change in Malaysia", in *Pacific Community*;

"Race, Religion and Nationalism in Asia", in *Tenggara*, Kuala Lumpur (reprinted in *Westerly*, Perth, 1971 and again in *Westerly Looks to Asia*, edited by Bruce Bennett, 1993);

"Malaysia: Contending Elites", in *Current Affairs Bulletin*, Sydney; and

"The Pier", "Moon Thoughts", "Ahmad", "A New Sensation", in *The Flowering Tree: Selected Writings from Singapore/Malaysia*, compiled by Edwin Thumboo, Singapore.

1971   Canberra

Elected Fellow of the Australian Academy of the Humanities.

Member of the organising committee of the 28th International Congress of Orientalists that convened at the Australian National University.

In Singapore, delivered the keynote and closing lectures at the Second Workshop on Higher Education organised by the Association of Southeast Asian Institutions of Higher Learning, published "The University and the Community", 1972.

Published "Die Kulturen Sudostasiens von 1200 bis 1800", in *Saeculum Weltgeschichte* (revised English version published in *Historia: Essays in Commemoration,* 1984);

"Asia and the Western Experience", *Quadrant,* Sydney; and

Review article, "Secret Societies and Overseas Chinese", on Wilfred Blythe's *The Impact of Chinese Secret Societies in Malaya: A Historical Study*, in *The China Quarterly*.

Review of Jerome Ch'en's *Mao Papers: Anthology and Bibliography*; and Edward Wheelwright and Bruce McFarlane's *The Chinese Way to Socialism*, in *Australian Journal of Politics and History*.

Review of Edgar Wickberg's (editor) *Historical Interaction of China and Vietnam: Institutional and Cultural Themes,* in *The Journal of the American Oriental Society*.

Review of John M Steadman's *The Myth of Asia*, in *Australian Outlook*.

1972 Canberra

Senior Visiting Fellowship at SOAS, University of London. Entrusted children with parents in Johor Bahru to attend Foon Yew School.

Father died of heart attack. Returned for funeral.

Worked on contemporary writings on Chinese historiography and translations of Western and Soviet historiographical writings in SOAS Library, published "Juxtaposing Past and Present in China Today", in *The China Quarterly*, 1975.

Invited to the Second Williamsburg Conference in Jogjakarta, the first really close encounter between leading US thinkers and policymakers and their Southeast Asian counterparts. During this visit to the country of his birth, visited Surabaya and made contact with the Chinese who remembered pre-war Netherlands East Indies, including one who had worked in his father's Chinese High School. They ranged from immigrants who had adapted to war and revolution outside China to local-born Peranakan families who had to adjust to postcolonial Indonesian nationalism. Met Charles Coppel's friends, the Go and Oei families of Malang, who had a collection of over 250 Chinese books of the 19th century. No buyer from Australia or Singapore could be found and the collection went to Leiden University where a catalogue was published in 2010.

Invited to the Conference on Southeast Asia in the Modern World, Institut fur Asienkunde, Hamburg, published "Political Chinese: an Aspect of Their Contribution to Modern Southeast Asian History", in *Southeast Asia in Modern World*, edited by Bernard Grossman (Chinese translation in 1994).

Submitted paper at the Quatrième Congrès de l'Association Historique Internationale de l'Océan Indien, held in Mauritius, published as "The Chinese Overseas", in *Mouvements de Populations dans l'Ocean Indien*, 1979. Made contact with the Chinese communities in Mauritius and Reunion, worked with Edouard Lin Fatt of the University of Mauritius and Madeleine Ly-Tio-Fane of the Mauritius Institute.

Published "The Inside and Outside of Chinese History", *The Round Table*, London.

Review of Edward H Schafer's *Shore of Pearls*, in *Pacific Affairs*.

1973 Canberra

After Australia established diplomatic relations with the People's Republic of China, went to China with a delegation of ANU historians of Asia led by Anthony Low. Visited historical sites at Anyang, Zhengzhou, Xi'an, Beijing, Nanjing, Shanghai and Guangzhou. Visited the Chinese Academy of Social Sciences and universities: Peking University, Beijing Normal University, Nanjing University, Northwest University, Fudan University and Sun Yat-sen University.

Attended the 29th International Congress of Orientalists in Paris, the last under that name; thereafter, the International Congress of Human Sciences in Asia and North Africa and then, the International Congress of Asian and

North African Studies (ICANAS). This was a major break between classical scholars and social science research focussing on modern and contemporary Asia, with repercussions for Asia scholarship at the ANU.

Gave a lecture to the New Zealand Institute of International Affairs, Wellington, published as *The Re-emergence of China*.

Edited, with Donald Leslie and Colin Mackerras, *Essays on the Sources for Chinese History,* in honour of C P FitzGerald on his retirement, published by ANU Press and University of South Carolina Press, with essay on "Some Comments on the Later Standard Histories".

Published "The Middle Yangtse in T'ang Politics", in *Perspectives on the T'ang*, edited by Arthur F Wright and Denis Twitchett;

"Nationalism in Asia", in *Nationalism: the Nature & Evolution of an Idea*, edited by Eugene Kamenka;

"Chinese Society and Chinese Foreign Policy", in *International Affairs*.

"Bureacracy in Imperial China", in *Public Administration*, Sydney.

Comments on Soedjatmoko, "The Role of the Medium and Small Nations in the New Asia-Pacific Setting", in *Foreign Policy for Australia: Choices for the Seventies*.

Review of Brian McKnight's *Village and Bureaucracy in Southern Sung China*, in *Australian Journal of Politics and History*.

Review of C M Turnbull's *The Straits Settlements, 1826–67: Indian Presidency to Crown Colony*, in *Bulletin of the School of Oriental and African Studies, University of London*.

1974   Canberra • Oxford

Gave the annual lecture of the Australian Academy of the Humanities, published *The Rebel-Reformer and Modern Chinese Biography*, Sydney University Press (also published in *Self and Biography: Essays on the Individual and Society in Asia*, 1975; and in *Australian Academy of the Humanities Proceedings 1974*, 1975).

Visiting Fellow of All Souls College at University of Oxford, 1974–1975.

Member of the College Seminar conducted by Maurice Freedman, together with Arthur P Wolf and Goran Aijmer, other colleagues at Oxford, and regular visitors from all over the United Kingdom.

Daughters Lin-chang and Hui-chang attended secondary school in Oxford. Son Shih-chang admitted to the Faculty of Medicine at the University of Sydney and returned to Australia earlier.

Drafted a book on history of contemporary China and its relations with the world response to global change.

Invited to the UNESCO Conference on Historical Relations across the Indian Ocean, held in Mauritius. Paper published as "The Chinese and the Countries across the Indian Ocean", in *Historical Relations across the Indian Ocean: Report and Papers of the Meeting of Experts organized by Unesco at Port Louis, Mauritius, from 15 to 19 July 1974*, in 1980.

Invited as guest scholar by the Japan Foundation to visit universities in Tokyo, Kyoto, Osaka, Hiroshima and Nagasaki; delivered a lecture to the International House of Japan, published as "Some Aspects of Southeast Asian Attitudes towards Japan", in *Bulletin of the International House of Japan* (Japanese translation in 1976).

Published "Chinese Civilisation and the Diffusion of Culture", in *Grafton Elliott-Smith: The Man and His Work* (Chinese translation in 1990);

"Auslandschinesen" (Chinese Overseas), in *China Handbuch*, edited by Wolfgang Franke and Brunhild Staiger;

"Burning Books and Burying Scholars Alive: Some Recent Interpretations Concerning Ch'in Shih-huang", in *Papers on Far Eastern History*.

Review of C P FitzGerald's *The Southern Expansion of the Chinese People*, in *Historical Studies*.

1975   Canberra • Oxford

Appointed Director of the Research School of Pacific Studies, 1975–1980. In that capacity, visited colleagues and students doing fieldwork research around the Pacific, notably in Fiji, Samoa, Tonga, Solomon Islands, New Hebrides, New Caledonia, Tahiti, Papua New Guinea and the Northern

Territory of Australia. Visited Chinese communities in all these territories, except in Tonga where there was no such community at the time.

Appointed Adviser to the Culture Learning Institute of the East-West Center in Hawaii, 1975–1980.

Delivered a lecture at the invitation of Alice Tay in the Faculty of Law at the University of Sydney on issues of law and order in traditional China, the Confucian-legalist divides and the emergence of the civilisation-state.

Published "The Limits of Nanyang Chinese Nationalism, 1912–1937", in *Southeast Asian History and Historiography: Essays Presented to D G E Hall*, edited by C D Cowan and O W Wolters (Chinese translation in 1987);

"The Chinese Minority in Southeast Asia", in *Mindanao Journal* (reprinted in Singapore in 1978); and

"The Military Governors and the Decline of the T'ang Dynasty", in *The Making of China: Main Themes in Premodern Chinese History*, edited by Chun-shu Chang.

Review of Frank Kiernan and John K Fairbank's (editors) *Chinese Ways of Warfare*, in *Pacific Affairs*.

1976 Canberra

Appointed Council member of the Asian Studies Association of Australia, 1976–1982. After the International Congress of Orientalists in Canberra in 1971, following long discussions with A R Davies of the University of Sydney and the Orientalists Society of Australia (founded in 1956), joined A L Basham of the ANU and John Legge of Monash University to establish the Association in 1976. This reflected the global divide between the Orientalists and the social science-inclined scholars of Asia that began at the International Congress of Orientalists in Paris in 1973.

Published "'Are Indonesian Chinese Unique?': Some Observations", in *The Chinese in Indonesia*, edited by J A C Mackie;

"Nationalism in China before 1949", in *China: The Impact of Revolution, a Survey of Twentieth Century China*, edited by Colin Mackerras;

Biographies of Chang Fu, Fei Hsin, Hsia Yuan-chi, Huang Fu, Ma Huan, in *Dictionary of Ming Biography*, edited by L Carrington Goodrich and Chao Ying Fang;

"The Origins of Civilisation: an Essay on Chinese Scholarship in Transition", in *Asian Thought and Society: an International Review*; and

"The Question of the 'Overseas Chinese'", in *Southeast Asian Affairs 1976* (Chinese translation in 1994).

Review of Howard J Wechsler's *Mirror to the Son of Heaven: Wei Cheng at the Court of T'ang T'ai-tsung*, in *Pacific Affairs*.

1977   Canberra

Presented a lecture on the impact of European historiography on modern and contemporary history-writing in China, especially the rewriting of Chinese history after the fall of the Qing dynasty and the end of the emperor-state. Questions of identity among the Chinese overseas during recent centuries can be linked to traditional cultural processes used by Chinese literati to encourage sinicization in lands adjacent to, or incorporated into, China. This can demonstrate the strong relationship between past and present in Chinese political culture and social change. It can also connect traditional concepts of state power with current Chinese thinking about international relations.

Submitted a paper at the Fifth Leverhulme conference in Hong Kong, published as "Recent Reinterpretations of History", in *China: Development and Challenge*, edited by Lee Ngok and Leung Chi-keung (Chinese translation in 1979).

Submitted a paper at the Seventh Conference of the International Association of Historians of Asia (IAHA) in Bangkok, published as "The Writing of Pre-modern History in Modern China", in *Proceedings: Seventh Conference of Asian Historians, Bangkok*, 1979.

Daughter Lin-chang admitted to the Australian National University.

Published *China and the World since 1949: The Impact of Independence, Modernity and Revolution* (Spanish translation, Mexico City, 1979).

Published "Mao the Chinese", in *Mao Tse-tung in the Scales of History*, edited by Dick Wilson (the Chinese translation in 1997 did not identify 王賡武, but mistakenly used the name of 王衮吾);

"A Note on the Origins of Hua-ch'iao", in *Masalah-Masalah International Masakini*, edited by Lie Tek Tjeng (also published in *The Chinese*

Diaspora in the Pacific, edited by Anthony Reid, 2008; Chinese translation in 1987).

Review Article on John Wong's "Second Chance for Viceroy Yeh", in *Journal of the Oriental Society of Australia*.

Review of Lawrence D Kessler's *K'ang-hsi and the Consolidation of Ch'ing Rule, 1661–1684*; and John W Haeger's, *Crisis and Prosperity in Sung China*, in *Pacific Affairs*.

Review of Robert B Oxnam's *Ruling from Horseback: Manchu Politics in the Oboi Regency, 1661–1669*; Vitaly Rubin's *Individual and State in Ancient China: Essays on Four Chinese Philosophers*; and J R V Prescott's *Map of Mainland Asia by Treaty*, in *Australian Journal of Politics and History*.

Review of Chan Heng Chee's *The Dynamics of One Party Dominance: The PAP at the Grass-roots*, in *Singapore Book World*.

Review of Ho Ping-ti's *The Cradle of the East: An Inquiry into the Indigenous Origins of Techniques and Ideas of Neolithic and Early Historic China, 5000–1000 BC*, in *The China Quarterly*.

1978 Canberra

Elected President of the Asian Studies Association of Australia, 1978–1980.

Invited to conduct a lecture at the Chinese University of Hong Kong (with Yale-China Association), published as "Change and More Change in Asia: Thoughts on Recent History", in *Public Lectures, 1977–1978*, 1979.

Daughter Hui-chang admitted to the Australian National University.

Published Biographies of Han Tung, Li Ch'ung-chin, Li Yun and P'an Mei, in *Sung Biographies*, edited by Herbert Franke, Wiesbaden: Steiner;

"China-Vietnam: Nostalgia for, Rejection of, the Past", in *The Vietnam-Kampuchea-China Conflicts: Motivations, Background, Significance*, edited by M Salmon.

Review of John Curtis Perry and Bardwell L Smith's (editors) *Essays on T'ang Society: the Interplay of Social, Political and Economic Forces*, in *Pacific Affairs*.

Review of Roxane Witke's *Comrade Chiang Ch'ing*; and Bill Brugger's *Contemporary China*, in *Australian Journal of Politics and History*.

1979   Canberra

Appointed member of an International Advisory Panel of the East-West Center, Honolulu, 1979–1991.

Gave the 40th George Ernest Morrison Lecture in Ethnology in Canberra, published as *Power, Rights and Duties in Chinese History*, 1979 (reprinted in *Australian Journal of Chinese Affairs*, 1980).

Organised conference in Canberra on Hong Kong: Dilemmas of Growth. Edited, with C K Leung and Jennifer Cushman, *Hong Kong: Dilemmas of Growth,* with essay "Some Reflections on Hong Kong's Regional Role and Cultural Identity", 1980.

Son Shih-chang awarded Bachelor of Science (Medicine) by the University of Sydney.

Published "China and the Region in Relation to Chinese Minorities", in *Contemporary Southeast Asia* (Chinese translation in *Singapore Monthly*);

"May Fourth and the GPCR: The Cultural Revolution Remedy", in *Pacific Affairs*, issue in honour of William Holland.

Review of Arif Dirlik's *Revolution and History: the Origins of Marxist Historiography in China, 1919–1937*, in *American Historical Review*.

1980   Canberra

Elected fifth President of the Australian Academy of the Humanities (AAH), 1980–1983. The AAH was established in 1969 on a parallel basis with the Australian Academy of Science and the Social Science Research Council of Australia and provides support for research in the humanities. It is particularly active in fields of languages, literature, history, philosophy, classical and archaeological studies, and the fine arts. During the 1980–1983 period, special attention was paid to completing the *Language Atlas of China* (led by Stephen Wurm) in collaboration with the Institute of Nationalities in China and the Chinese Academy of Social

Sciences, and published in Hong Kong in 1987. Another area of interest, to mark the 600th anniversary of Wat Tyler's Revolt of 1381, was the nature of peasants' revolts in mediaeval Europe and comparable rebellions in traditional Asia.

Published "The Study of the Southeast Asian Past", in *Perceptions of the Past in Southeast Asia*, edited by A J S Reid and D Marr;

"Foreword", in Paul Yun-ming Jiang, *The Search for Mind: Ch'en Pai-sha (1428–1500) Philosopher-Poet*.

Review of Denis Twitchett and John K Fairbank's (editors) *The Cambridge History of China, vol. 3, Sui-T'ang China*, in *Pacific Affairs*.

Review of Fang Hsiu's (translated by Angus W McDonald) *Notes on the History of Malayan Chinese New Literature, 1920–1942*, in *Journal of Asian Studies*.

Review of Jerome Ch'en's *China and the West: Society and Culture 1815–1937*, in *The China Quarterly*.

1981   Canberra • Honolulu

After returning as Head of the Department of Far Eastern History, elected Chairman of the Professorial Board of the Institute of Advanced Studies, ANU. Asked by the Vice-Chancellor to report on the integration of research resources of the two halves of the ANU, the Research Schools of the Institute of Advanced Studies and the Faculties (formerly the School of General Studies). The report was the first step towards the establishment of the ANU Graduate School (in 1989) to coordinate teaching and research across the University.

Appointed John A Burns Distinguished Visiting Professor of History at the University of Hawaii. Gave a series of 10 lectures to the graduate class in Chinese History.

Led delegation of Australian Southeast Asianists to the PRC, visited institutes and centres of Southeast Asian studies at Peking University, Chinese Academy of Social Sciences, Xiamen University, Sun Yat-sen University, Yunnan Academy of Social Sciences and Yunnan University. Conducted lectures at Xiamen and Kunming.

Published *Southeast Asian Studies in China: A Report*, with Anthony Reid and others.

Son Shih-chang awarded MBBS, University of Sydney.

Published *Community and Nation: Essays on Southeast Asia and the Chinese* (selected by Anthony Reid).

Edited, with M Guerrero and David Marr, *Society and the Writer: Essays on Literature in Modern Asia*.

Published "Southeast Asian Hua-ch'iao in Chinese History-Writing", *Journal of Southeast Asian Studies* (Chinese translation in 1987);

"*Guanyu huaqiaoshi de yixie wenti* 关于华侨史的一些问题" (On Some Questions of Overseas Chinese History), *Nanyang wenti — Xiamen daxue liushi zhounian xiaoqing ji jiansuo ershiwu zhounian jinian tekan* 《南洋问题——厦门大学六十周年校庆及建所二十五周年纪念特刊》 *Southeast Asian Problems, Commemorative Volume for the University's 60th Anniversary and the Institute's 25th Anniversary*.

Review of Akira Iriye's (editor) *The Chinese and the Japanese: Essays in Political and Cultural Interactions*, in *Pacific Affairs*.

Review of Ross Terrill's *Mao: A Biography*, in *Australian Journal of History and Politics*.

1982 Canberra

Appointed member of the University and Polytechnic Grants Committee of Hong Kong, 1982–1985. The expansion of higher education on the eve of Hong Kong's return to China was a high priority for the Hong Kong government. This included planning for a third university and for the adoption of the British policy of transforming all polytechnic and specialist colleges into a variety of universities. Meetings were held alternatively in Hong Kong and the UK to compare secondary and tertiary education practices. Most glaring differences were seen in the research facilities in the universities. The key issue was funding for new universities and the urgent need for research development for the existing institutions.

Visiting Professor at National University of Singapore. Gave lectures and seminars in the Department of History. Delivered the Faculty of Arts Public Lecture, published as *The Chinese Intellectual — Past & Present*, 1983.

Appointed member of the Committee on Australia-Japan Relations, 1982–1984, Ministry of Foreign Affairs, Australia.

Conducted research at Xiamen University on changing policies of the PRC towards the Chinese overseas.

Appointed member of the Regional Advisory Council of the Institute of Southeast Asian Studies.

Delivered Presidential Lecture of the Australian Academy of the Humanities, published "The Chinese Urge to Civilize: Reflections on Change", in *Proceedings: Australian Academy of the Humanities, 1982–1983*, in 1984 (reprinted in *Journal of Asian History,* 1984).

Presented paper at conference entitled China among Equals in New York, published as "The Rhetoric of a Lesser Empire: Early Sung Relations with its Neighbours", in *China Among Equals: The Middle Kingdom and its Neighbours, 10th-14th Centuries*, edited by Morris Rossabi.

Invited by the Korean National Academy of Sciences, lecture published as "Human Values, Science and Learning from History", in *Proceedings: The Xth International Symposia*, 1982.

Published "Introduction: The Chineseness of China"; and entries on "External China"; "Five Dynasties and Ten Kingdoms, 907–959; Tangut empire (Xi Xia dynasty); Khitan empire (Liao dynasty)", in *The Cambridge Encyclopaedia of China*, edited by Brian Hook;

"The Interests of Revolutionary China: an Overview", in *International Security in the Southeast Asian and Southwest Pacific Region*, edited by Tom B Millar, University of Queensland Press;

"Interdependence and Moral Order: China's Historical Experience", in *Essays in Commemoration of the Golden Jubilee of the Fung Ping Shan Library (1923–1982)*, edited by Chan Ping-leung *et al.*, Hong Kong University Press;

"Introduction: ASEAN between Tradition and Modernity" in *Understanding ASEAN*, edited by Alison Broinowski.

Review of Simon de Beaufort's *Yellow Earth, Green Jade: Constants in Chinese Political Mores*; and Merle Goldman's *China's Intellectuals: Advise and Dissent*, in *The China Quarterly*.

1983   Canberra • Lawrence, Kansas

Appointed Rose Morgan Visiting Professor of History at the University of Kansas. Conducted lectures and seminars on modern Chinese history. Used the Harry Truman Presidential Archives in Kansas City on Sino-US relations at the last stage of Chinese Civil War, 1946–1949, and American policies during the first years of the Malayan Emergency, 1948–1950.

Presented paper at the conference entitled When Patterns Change at the Hebrew University of Jerusalem, published as "Strong China, Weak China: What Has Changed?", in *When Patterns Change: Turning Points in International Politics*, edited by Nissan Oren, St Martin's Press and the Hebrew University Magnes Press.

Published "China and Southeast Asia: some Recent Developments", in *Collected Essays in Sinology, dedicated to Professor Kim Jun-yop*, Korea University Press.

Review of J K Fairbank and K C Liu's (editors) *The Cambridge History of China, vol. II, Late Ch'ing 1800–1911, Part 2*, in *Harvard Journal of Asiatic Studies*.

Review of Charles Backus's *The Nanchao Kingdom and T'ang China's Southwestern Frontier*, in *American Historical Review*.

1984   Canberra

Appointed Chairman of the Australia-China Council, 1984–1986. Visits to various agencies in China that were dedicated to encourage cultural exchange, from funding of the arts and other cultural organisations to scholarships and fellowships.

Appointed member of the Board of Trustees of Jinan University, Guangzhou.

Visited ancestral home, Zhengding county in Shijiazhuang, Hebei whose party secretary was a young Xi Jinping.

Invited to meet Hu Jintao and learn about the work of the Communist Youth League during his visit to Canberra in his capacity as its First Secretary. It was announced that he was appointed to be First Secretary of Guizhou province.

Delivered the Annual Lecture of the Malaysian Branch of the Royal Asiatic Society, published as "Migration Patterns in History: Malaysia and the Region", in *Journal of the Malaysian Branch of the Royal Asiatic Society*, 1985.

Published "Southeast Asia between the 13th and 18th Centuries: Some Reflections on Political Fragmentation and Cultural Change", in *Historia: Essays in Commemoration*, edited by A B Muhammad, A Kaur and Abdullah Zakaria (German translation published earlier in 1971).

Review of David Wyatt and Alexander Woodside's (editors) *Moral Order and the Question of Change*, in *Pacific Affairs*.

Review of Rosemary Quested's *Sino-Russian Relations: A Short History*, in *Australian Journal of Politics and History*.

Review of John Y Wong's *Anglo-Chinese Relations, 1839–1860: A Calendar of Chinese Documents in the British Foreign Office Records*, in *Journal of the Oriental Society of Australia*.

1985   Canberra

Invited to meet the Council Committee charged to recommend a new Vice-Chancellor for the University of Hong Kong. Visited Hong Kong to meet the Council and Senate members, representatives of the staff and students. Offer of appointment confirmed to succeed Rayson Huang, a scientist and colleague at the University of Malaya in the 1960s, who had served for 14 years and retired in mid-1986.

Organised International Conference on Changing Identities of the Southeast Asian Chinese, in Canberra. Edited, with Jennifer Cushman, *Changing Identities of the Southeast Asian Chinese since World War II*, published in 1988, with an essay, "The Study of Chinese Identities in Southeast Asia", that was translated into Indonesian in 1991 (the first Chinese translation published in Xiamen, 1986; another version in Taipei, 1992).

Delivered public lecture at the Centre of Asian Studies, the University of Sydney, published as *The China-Japan Relationship: Implications for Australia* (reprinted in *Hong Kong and Japan: Growing Cultural and Economic Interactions, 1845–1987*, edited by Yue-him Tam in 1988).

Published "Loving the Ancient in China", in *Who Owns the Past?*, edited by Isabel McBryde;

"External China as a New Policy Area", in *Pacific Affairs*;

"South China Perspectives on Overseas Chinese", in *Australian Journal of Chinese Affairs*;

"Two New Sources of Hokkien Local History", in *Asian Studies Association of Australia Review*;

"Foreword", in *Ideal and Reality: Social and Political Change in Modern China, 1860–1949*, edited by David Pong and Edmund S K Fung;

"Foreword", in Jane Kate Leonard, *Wei Yuan and China's Rediscovery of the Maritime World*; and

"Asia in Australian Education", in *Addresses at the Amalgamation Conference of the Heads of the Independent Schools of Australia*, Canberra, 25–30 August 1985.

1986   Canberra • Hong Kong

Appointed Vice-Chancellor (President) of the University of Hong Kong (HKU), 1986–1995. Focussed on the university's research capacity while the university doubled in size during his tenure, expanded its graduate degree programmes fourfold. Initiated changes to foundation courses for language and critical thinking. Established HKU Endowment Fund. Presided over the 80th anniversary of HKU, and the 100th anniversary of its Medical Faculty. Arranged regular visits to each of the university's academic departments and centres.

Involved the university actively in the Association of Commonwealth Universities, the International Association of Universities, the Association of Southeast Asian Institutions of Higher Learning and the Association of Pacific Rim Universities conferences. With China, initiated closer academic relations with major universities in Beijing, Shanghai, Nanjing, Wuhan and Chengdu, and those in the provinces of Guangdong and Fujian. Gave lectures to graduate course on comparative Asian studies. Supervised two PhD students in Chinese history.

Appointed Administrative Board Member of the Association of Southeast Asian Institutions of Higher Learning, 1986–1988.

Presented paper at the Second International Conference on Sinology organised by Academia Sinica in Taipei, published as "Sung-Yuan-Ming Relations with Southeast Asia: some Comparisons", in 1989.

Published "Reflections on Malaysian Elites", in *Review of Indonesian and Malay Studies*;

"Cultural Interpreters", in *Australian Diplomacy: Challenges and Options*, edited by A C Milner and T Wilson;

"Introduction", in *Southeast Asia in the Ninth to Fourteenth Centuries*, edited by D G Marr and A C Milner;

"Foreword", in Yen Ching-hwang, *A Social History of the Chinese in Singapore and Malaya, 1800–1911*; and in John Y Wong, *The Origins of an Heroic Image: Sun Yatsen in London, 1896–1897*.

Review of Francesca Bray and Joseph Needham's *Science and Civilisation in China, Volume Six, Biology and Biological Technology, Part Two: Agriculture*, in *The Economic History Review*.

1987 Hong Kong

Invited to report to the East-West Center on establishing the Institute of Culture and Communication.

Invited to present paper at the conference on The Rise of Merchant Empires, at the University of Minnesota, published as "Merchants Without Empire: the Hokkien Sojourning Communities", in *The Rise of Merchant Empires: Long-Distance Trade in the Early Modern World, 1350–1750*, edited by James D Tracy, 1990 (Chinese translation in 1993; reprinted in *Merchant Networks in the Early Modern World*, edited by Sanjay Subrahmanyam, 1996).

Presented the keynote lecture to the Royal Asiatic Society, Hong Kong Branch.

Appointed member of Executive Council of the World Wildlife Fund for Nature, Hong Kong, 1987–1995; member of Board of Directors of the East Asian History of Science Foundation, Hong Kong, 1987–1995; Fellow, Honorary Corresponding Member and Chairman of the Hong Kong Chapter of the Royal Society of Arts, London, 1987–1995.

Published *Dongnanya yu Huaren: Wang Gungwu jiaoshou lunwen xuanji*《东南亚与华人：王赓武教授论文选集》*Southeast Asia and the Chinese*, translated by Yao Nan 姚楠;

"Pre-modern History: Some Trends in Writing the History of the Song Dynasty (Tenth-Thirteenth Centuries)", in *New Directions in the Social Sciences and Humanities in China*, edited by Michael B Yahuda; and

"The Scholar in Chinese Society: Historical Background", in *Asian Culture*.

Review of Benjamin Schwartz's *China's Cultural Values*, in *The China Quarterly*.

1988 Hong Kong

After the Association of Commonwealth Universities Conference in Perth, presented the keynote address at the bicentenary conference of the Asian Studies Association of Australia in Canberra, published as *Trade and Cultural Values: Australia and the Four Dragons*, Melbourne; also in *Asian Studies Association of Australia Review*, Sydney (Chinese translation in 1988).

Presented paper at the Australian Academy of the Humanities' conference on migration, published as "The Life of William Liu: Australian and Chinese Perspectives", in *Stories of Australian Migration*, edited by John Hardy.

Delivered the Tan Kah Kee Lectures in Singapore; gave talk at the East-West Center Workshop on social values.

Appointed Emeritus Professor of the Australian National University.

Elected President of the International Association of Historians of Asia, 1988–1991.

Appointed Chairman of the Environment Pollution Advisory Committee (EPCOM); continued as Chairman when EPCOM renamed in 1993 as Advisory Council on the Environment (ACE), 1988–1995.

Published *Nanhai maoyi yu Nanyang Huaren*《南海贸易与南洋华人》*The Nanhai Trade and Southeast Asian Chinese*, translated by Yao Nan 姚楠.

Review of John K Fairbank and Denis Twitchett's (editors) *The Cambridge History of China, vol. 14, The People's Republic, Part 1, 1949–1966*, in *Pacific Affairs*.

Review of Stuart R Schram's (editor) *The Scope of State Power in China*; Lee Chae-Jin's *China and Japan: New Economic Diplomacy;* and Susan L Shirk's *The Challenge of China and Japan: Politics and Development in East Asia*, in *The China Quarterly*.

1989 Hong Kong

Steered HKU through the ramifications of its part in the Tiananmen demonstrations; addressed public meeting of staff and students.

Attended the Inaugural Meeting of Pacific Rim Universities Presidents, Berkeley; second meeting in Bangkok (1990) and the third in Seoul (1991).

Appointed to the Executive Committee of the Association of Commonwealth Universities, 1989 –1993.

Appointed Chairman of the Council for the Performing Arts of Hong Kong, 1989–1994; member of the Independent Commission Against Corruption (ICAC) Complaints Committee, 1989–1995; member of Board of Directors of the Institute of East Asian Philosophies, Singapore, 1989–1997, which was renamed Institute of East Asian Political Economy in 1991.

Delivered the keynote lecture at the International Conference on the Overseas Chinese in Asia between the Two World Wars, the Chinese University of Hong Kong, published as "*Tonghua, guihua yu Huaqiaoshi* 同化, 归化与华侨史" (*Tonghua, guihua* and Overseas Chinese History), in *Overseas Chinese in Asia between the Two World Wars*, edited by N H Ng Lun 吴伦霓霞 and C Y Chang 郑赤琰.

Delivered the Walter E Edge Lecture at the Princeton University, published as "Outside the Chinese Revolution", in *Australian Journal of Chinese Affairs*, 1990 (Chinese translation in 1989; Japanese translation in 1991; revised version in *Chinese Nationalism*, edited by Jonathan Unger, 1996). This volume was published in Spanish translation in 1999.

Delivered the CIL Distinguished Lecture at the University of Toronto-York University Joint Centre for Asia Pacific Studies, published as *The Culture of Chinese Merchants*, 1989.

Delivered the keynote lecture at the Asian Studies Association of Australia Conference in Wellington, on "The Four Little Dragons: the Detached Periphery".

Spoke on Hong Kong at the workshop on China's Crisis, ANU, published as "Hong Kong", in *China's Crisis: the International Implications*, edited by G Klintworth, 1990.

Attended joint conference of the Asian Studies Association of Australia, with the Institute of Southeast Asian Studies, Singapore, and the National University of Singapore, offered comments on "New Directions in Asian Studies".

Published "Lu Xun, Lim Boon Keng and Confucianism", in *Papers on Far Eastern History*, Canberra.

1990 Hong Kong

Appointed Executive Councillor of the Executive Council of the Hong Kong Government, 1990–1992; intense period of negotiations between London and Beijing through Hong Kong, especially over issues of electoral timetables and the new airport at Chek Lap Kok.

Appointed member of the Council of the Asia Society, Hong Kong Centre, 1990–1995; member of the Council of the Asia-Australia Institute, University of New South Wales (1990–1994).

Awarded Honorary Doctorate of the University by Soka University, Tokyo.

Gave the keynote address at conference on "China and Hong Kong at the Crossroads" at Hong Kong Baptist College.

Presented paper at the conference on Cultural China at East-West Center in Honolulu, published as "Among Non-Chinese", in *Daedalus, Journal of the American Academy of Arts and Sciences* (republished as *The Living Tree: the Changing Meaning of Being Chinese Today*, edited by Tu Wei-ming).

Conducted lectures and chaired sessions at Conference on the Chinese of Indonesia at Cornell University, and the Wingspread Conference on the State of Southeast Asian Studies at Racine, Wisconsin; Sixth International

Conference of the History of Science in China; International Congress of Orientalists (International Congress of Asian and North African Studies) at Toronto; Chinese Academy of Social Sciences Conference on Modern Chinese History at Mentougou, Beijing.

Published 《历史的功能》 (*Lishi de gongneng, The Use of History*), translated by Yao Nan 姚楠;

"Patterns of Chinese Migration in Historical Perspective", in *Observing Change in Asia — Essays in Honour of J A C Mackie*, edited by R J May and W J O'Malley (Chinese translation of an earlier version, 1985);

"The Chinese as Immigrants and Settlers", in *Management of Success: the Moulding of Modern Singapore*, edited by K S Sandhu and Paul Wheatley;

"*Wubai nianqian de Zhongguo yu shijie* 五百年前的中国与世界" (China and the World 500 Years Ago), in *Er-shih-yi shih-chi* 《二十一世纪》 (*Twenty-first Century*), Hong Kong; and

"Children in Chinese Migration History", in *Proceedings of the International Symposium on Children and Migration*, Hong Kong.

Review of Ray Huang's *China: a Macro History*, in *Pacific Affairs*.

Review of Ross Garnaut's *Australia and the Northeast Asian Ascendancy* (Report to the Prime Minister and the Minister for Foreign Affairs and Trade, 1989), in *Asian-Pacific Economic Literature*.

1991   Hong Kong

Awarded the Commander of the Order of the British Empire (CBE).

Awarded Honorary Professorship by the University of Hong Kong.

Awarded Honorary Degree of Doctor of Letters (D. Litt.) by the University of Sydney.

Appointed member of Review Panel of Chiang Ching-kuo Foundation, Taipei, 1991–2002; and Committee of Review of the Department of History of University of Queensland.

Presented paper at the International Conference on Conceptualizing Global History at Bellagio, Italy, published as "Migration and Its

Enemies", in *Conceptualizing Global History*, edited by Bruce Mazlish and Ralph Buultjens, 1993 (also published in *The Global History Reader*, edited by Bruce Mazlish and Akira Iriye, 2005).

Commentator at the Centenary Conference on Higher Education, University of Chicago, published "Comments on 'The Traditions of the University' by Walter Ruegg", in *Minerva: a Review of Science, Learning and Policy*, 1992.

Published *China and the Chinese Overseas*, Singapore (republished in 2003; Chinese translation in 1994).

Published *The Chineseness of China: Selected Essays*, Hong Kong, New York.

Published "Ming Foreign Relations: Southeast Asia", "Little Dragons on the Confucian Periphery" and "Education in External China", in *China and the Chinese Overseas*;

"*Haiwai Huaren shehui yu difangzhi wenxian* 海外华人社会与地方志文献", (Local Historical Sources and Chinese Communities Overseas) in *Collected Essays on Local History of the Asian-Pacific Region*, edited by Lin Tien-wei 林天蔚, Hong Kong;

"China: 1989 in Perspective", in *Southeast Asian Affairs 1990*; and

"Foreword", in Chan Kwok Bun, *Smoke and Fire: The Chinese in Montreal*, Hong Kong.

1992   Hong Kong

After Chris Patten succeeded David Wilson as British Governor of Hong Kong, inaugurated the Li Ka-Shing Lecture at the University of Hong Kong: Lecture by Lee Kuan Yew on "A Tale of Two Cities: 20 Years On".

Elected member of the Academia Sinica 中央研究院院士.

Elected member of the Council of the International Institute of Strategic Studies (IISS), London, 1992–2001.

Presented lecture at the Institute of Economic Science, Hong Kong, "The Will to Reform".

Delivered the keynote lecture at the Inaugural International Conference on the Chinese Overseas in San Francisco, published as "The Status of Overseas Chinese Studies", in *Chinese America: History and Perspectives 1994* (reprinted in *The Chinese Diaspora: Selected Essays*, edited with Wang Ling-chi, 1998; Chinese translation in 1993).

Delivered lecture at the First Richard A Harvill Conference on Higher Education at University of Arizona, published as "The University as a Global Institution", in *The Universities of the Future: Roles in the Changing World Order*, 1994.

Gave lectures at Forum on Australia and Asia, University of Western Australia and at The Sydney Institute, published "The Australia Asians Might Not See", and "Australia's Identity in Asia", in *Australia in the World: Perceptions and Possibilities*, edited by Don Grant and Graham Seal in 1994 (also published in *Australian Quarterly*, 1992; and *The Sydney Papers*, 1992, respectively).

Presented lecture at Wolfson College, Oxford, on China after Tiananmen.

Published *Community and Nation: China, Southeast Asia and Australia* (new edition of *Community and Nation: Essays on Southeast Asia and the Chinese*, 1981);

"Universities in Transition in Asia", *Oxford Review of Education*; "Memoir", in *Fairbank Remembered*, compiled by Paul A Cohen and Merle Goldman.

Review of Jon L Saari's *Legacies of Childhood: Growing up Chinese in a Time of Crisis, 1890–1920*, in *The China Quarterly*.

1993   Hong Kong

Mother died on 27 September.

Announced decision to retire in 1995.

Organised HKU's Expo 2001 exhibition to conclude its 80th anniversary celebrations and planned the HKU Foundation for Educational Development and Research.

Official visits to universities in China, and signed graduate students agreements in Beijing, Shanghai, Nanjing and Hefei.

After visit to Shantou University 汕头大学, instituted five-year Li Ka Shing Doctoral Training Scholarships at HKU for its junior academic staff.

Hosted the International Congress of Asian and North African Studies in Hong Kong as Honorary President with Ji Xianlin 季羡林.

Appointed Chairman of the Commission on Remuneration for Members of the Legislative Council, Hong Kong, 1993–1995.

Member of Consultative Council of the Australian National University, reviewed Faculty of Asian Studies and the Research Schools, report completed in 1995.

Elected President of the International Society for the Study of the Chinese Overseas, 1993–2004.

Awarded Honorary Degree of Doctor of Laws (LL.D.) by Monash University.

Presented a paper at the Greater China Conference in Hong Kong, published as "Greater China and the Chinese Overseas", in *The China Quarterly*, 1993 (issue republished as *Greater China*, edited by David Shambaugh).

Presented a lecture at the Second World Chinese Entrepreneurs Convention, Hong Kong, published as "The Chinese Entrepreneur and His Cultural Strategies", 1993 (Chinese translation in 1994).

Invited to edit *Hong Kong History: New Perspectives*, published as 《香港史新编》, published in Hong Kong, two volumes, 1997.

Gave the keynote lecture on "Bridging Cultures: the Challenge to the Universities" at the Hong Kong-America Centre Symposium.

Invited to present paper at the Conference on China in Transformation, published as "To Reform a Revolution: Under the Righteous Mandate", in *Daedalus, Journal of the American Academy of Arts and Sciences*, 1993 (issue republished as *China in Transformation*, edited by Tu Wei-ming).

Presented paper at Nobel Symposium on The Fall of Great Powers, Trumso, Norway, published as "Empires and Anti-empires: Asia in World Politics", in *The Fall of Great Powers — Peace, Stability, and Legitimacy*, edited by Geir Lundestad, 1994.

As International Advisory Panel member, delivered a speech at the Institute of Southeast Asian Studies international conference on "Southeast Asia: Challenges of the 21st Century".

Gave the Annual Asian Studies Lecture, University of Tasmania, published as *The Modern Chinese Experience of Reform*, 1994.

Conducted seminar on "The Future of Hong Kong" at Monash University, Melbourne.

Published "Wealth and Culture: Strategies for a Chinese Entrepreneur", in *A Special Brew: Essays in Honour of Kristof Glamann,* edited by Thomas Riis;

"China's Overseas World during the Reign of Yongle (1402–1424)", in *A Festschrift in Honour of Professor Jao Tsung-i on the Occasion of His 75th Anniversary*;

"C P FitzGerald 1902–1992 — In Memoriam", *Australian Journal of Chinese Affairs*;

"Preface", in Jennifer Wayne Cushman, *Fields from the Sea: Chinese Junk Trade with Siam during the Late Eighteenth and Early Nineteenth Centuries*, Southeast Asia Program, Cornell University; and

"Foreword", in *Tradition and Change: Contemporary Art of Asia and the Pacific*, edited by Caroline Turner, University of Queensland Press.

1994   Hong Kong

New Graduate House was planned to meet the growing residential needs at HKU.

Re-established official relations with National Education Commission in Beijing; visited the Chinese Academy of Sciences and Chinese Academy of Social Sciences and Peking University.

Signed exchange agreements on visits to Wuhan University; Northwest University and Xi'an Jiaotong University in Xi'an; and Sichuan United University in Chengdu.

Organised (together with Wong Siu-lun) the Hong Kong Lectures, 1994–1997, series of 10 lectures per year. Edited, all four volumes with Wong Siu-lun, *Hong Kong's Transition: A Decade after the Deal*, 1995; *Hong Kong in the Asia-Pacific Region: Rising to the New Challenges*, 1997, with lecture published as "Hong Kong as the Home of China Coast Chinese: An Historical Perspective"; *Dynamic Hong Kong: Business and Culture*, 1997; and *Towards a New Millennium: Building on Hong Kong's Strengths*, 1999.

Organised Conference on Migrations and Global History at University of Hong Kong. Edited the volume, *Global History and Migrations*, with "Introduction", "Migration History: Some Patterns Revisited", 1997 (republished in 2004). Revised version published as "Global Development and the Movement of Peoples", in *Culture, Development and Democracy: The Role of the Intellectual*, edited by Selo Soemardjan and Kenneth W Thompson, Tokyo, 1994.

Hosted Second International Conference of the International Society for the Study of the Chinese Overseas at HKU, gave the keynote lecture, "Upgrading the Migrant: Neither *Huaqiao* nor *Huaren*", published in *Chinese America: History and Perspectives 1996*; and in *The Last Half Century of Chinese Overseas,* edited by Elizabeth Sinn, 1998 (Chinese translation in 1995).

Elected Foreign Honorary Member of the American Academy of Arts and Science.

Awarded International Academic Prize of the Fukuoka Asian Cultural Prize, gave speech, published as "Commemorative Lecture", in *The Commemorative Lectures*, Fukuoka Asian Cultural Prizes 1994.

Awarded Honorary Doctorate of the University (D. Univ.) by Griffith University, Brisbane, gave address on the Economic Revolution in Asia.

Appointed Co-Patron of Asialink, University of Melbourne.

Appointed Adviser of the Southeast Asian Area Studies Program, Academia Sinica, 1994–2002.

Invited to give the keynote lecture at the International Conference on Hakka Studies at the Chinese University of Hong Kong, published as "The Hakka in Migration History", in *Kejia yanjiu jikan* 《客家研究季刊》 *Journal of Hakka Studies*; also in *The Proceedings of the International Conference on Hakkaology*, edited by Hsieh Chien and C Y Chang, 1995.

Invited to deliver a lecture to the Institute of International Studies, Ministry of Foreign Affairs, Bangkok; and a seminar at Chiang Mai University.

In Singapore, gave the keynote address at the Conference on Southeast Asian Chinese: Culture, Economy and Society, published as "Southeast Asian Chinese and the Development of China", *Asian Journal of Political Science*, Singapore (also in *Southeast Asian Chinese and China: The Politico-Economic Dimension*, edited by Leo Suryadinata; Chinese translation in 1995).

Invited to comment at Conference on Cultural China, published as "*Guanyu wenhua Zhongguo de sige yiwen* 关于文化中国的四个疑问" (Four Questions about Cultural China), in *Wenhua Zhongguo: linian yu shijian* 《文化中国: 理念与实践》 *Cultural China: the Concept and the Reality*, edited by Chen Chi-nan and Chou Ying-hsiung, Taipei.

Presented the inaugural ALUMNUS (Annual Lecture of University of Malaya and National University of Singapore) at NUS Reunion Day, Singapore; the keynote lecture at the Kanagawa Foundation Conference, published as "East-West Cultural Encounters: Reflections on Conflicts and Convergences", 1995; and the Mansfield Lecture at the University of Montana, Missoula, "The Global Community in Asian Historical Perspective".

Published "Preface", in Wang Tai Peng, *The Origins of Chinese Kongsi*, Pelanduk Publications, 1994; and

"Foreword", in *Reluctant Exiles? Migration from Hong Kong and the New Overseas Chinese*, edited by Ronald Skeldon, 1994.

1995 Hong Kong

Led the HKU delegation on an official visit to Taiwan, signed academic agreement with National Taiwan University; and visited several institutes in Academia Sinica, National Science Council, Ministry of Education, and several offices dealing with mainland and Hong Kong affairs.

Led delegation to meet President Jiang Zemin. Made official visit to Education Commission in Beijing; Peking University agreed to allow HKU establish a Liaison Office on campus; visited Tsinghua University to strengthen links with HKU's Faculty of Engineering. In Shanghai, delivered a speech on the globalisation of higher education at the 90th Anniversary of Fudan University where HKU will also establish a Liaison Office on campus.

Opening of the Meng Wah Complex (Wong Chue Meng Building and Wong Chuang Lai Wah Building), University of Hong Kong.

Lady Kadoorie agreed to a major donation for a building in University of Hong Kong dedicated to the Biological Sciences to commemorate her late husband.

Delivered the Joseph Needham Lecture, East Asian History of Science Foundation, Hong Kong.

Appointed member of Board of Governors of the Chinese Heritage Centre, Singapore, 1995–2001.

Appointed member of Advisory Panel of the Research Centre for Chinese Studies, National University of Singapore, 1995–1998.

Appointed Adviser of the International Confucian Association, Beijing.

Awarded Honorary Professorship by Fudan University, Shanghai; and Peking University, Beijing.

Appointed Adviser to Southern College 南方学院, Johor, Malaysia.

Invited to the World Economic Forum in Davos, and presented session on "One Civilization for All, or a World of Several Civilizations?"

Invited to give the Nobel Institute Spring Lectures in Oslo, published as *The Chinese Way: China's Position in International Relations*, Scandinavian University Press. Also presented a seminar at the University of Bergen.

Gave the keynote lecture to the Conference on Chinese Maritime Trade at Academia Sinica, published as "*Hua-shang wen-hua te yenchiu* 华商文化的研究" (The Study of Chinese Merchant Culture), in *Chung-kuo hai-yang fa-chan shih lun-wen chi*《中国海洋发展史论文集》, 1997.

Presented paper at the Conference on Islam and Confucianism, University of Malaya, published as "The Significance of Confucianism in Chinese Culture: Past and Present", in *Islam and Confucianism: A Civilizational Dialogue*, edited by Osman Bakar and Cheng Gek Nai, 1997.

Published "*Yimin diwei de tisheng:` jibushi huaqiao, yebushi huaren* 移民地位的提升：既不是华侨，也不是华人" (Upgrading the Migration:

Neither *Huaqiao* nor *Huaren*), in *Huaqiao huaren lishi yanjiu*《华侨华人历史研究》*Overseas Chinese History Studies*, Beijing; and

"Foreword", in *Greater China: Law, Society and Trade*, edited by Alice E-S Tay and Conita S C Leung, Sydney.

1996   Singapore

Left Hong Kong on 2 January to take up the position of Executive Chairman of the Institute of East Asian Political Economy (IEAPE), 1996–1997. After it became the East Asian Institute (EAI), an autonomous research centre of the National University of Singapore, re-established links with equivalent research centres and institutes in China. Regular meetings with the heads of various institutions, mainly in Beijing.

Appointed Distinguished Professorial Fellow of the Institute of Southeast Asian Studies (ISEAS), 1996–2002. After his lecture on "Nation-building in Southeast Asia and Theories of Nationalism" at the 14th International Conference on Asian History in Bangkok in 1996, ISEAS agreed to support a series of studies on the history of nation-building in the region since the end of the Second World War.

Appointed member of the National Arts Council, Singapore, 1996–2000.

Appointed Corresponding Director of the East Asian History of Science Foundation, Hong Kong.

Appointed Adviser to Fok Ying Tung Foundation and Chairman of Fok Ying Tung Prize Committee, 1996–2000.

Elected Honorary Research Fellow of the Chinese Academy of Social Sciences.

Elected President of the Tan Kah Kee International Society, 1996–2008.

Awarded Honorary Degree of Doctor of Laws (LL.D.) of the Australian National University.

Awarded Honorary Fellow of the School of Oriental and African Studies, London.

Donated books to start a library for the Chinese Heritage Centre, Singapore.

Gave the Wu Teh-yao Lectures on Chinese Culture, National University of Singapore, published as *Nationalism and Confucianism*, and *Haiwai huaren de minzu zhuyi*《海外华人的民族主义》 *The Nationalism of the Chinese Overseas*, 1997.

Delivered the Ruth Wong Lecture in Education, published as "National Education and the Scientific Tradition", in *The Australian Educational Researcher*, 1997 (reprinted in *Educational Research: Building New Partnerships*, 1997).

Presented the International Institute for Asian Studies (IIAS) Annual Lecture, Leiden University, published as *The Revival of Chinese Nationalism* (Chinese translation in 1998).

Presented the Jennifer Cushman Lecture, Sydney, published as "Sojourning: The Chinese Experience in Southeast Asia", in *Sojourners and Settlers: Histories of Southeast Asia and the Chinese*, edited by Anthony Reid.

Presented the keynote lecture at the Ethnicity and Nationalism in the Asia-Pacific Region Conference, University of Georgia, Athens, published as "Nationalism, Ethnicity and the Asia Pacific", in *Public Policy*, 1998 (Chinese translation in 1999).

Gave the keynote lecture at Xiamen University, published as "*Xin jiu minzu zhuyi yu haiwai huaren* 新旧民族主义与海外华人", in *Shiji zhi jiao de haiwai huaren*《世纪之交的海外华人》, edited by Zhuang Guotu 庄国土, 1998.

Gave the keynote lecture at Sun Yat-sen Anniversary Conference (130th year of his birth) in Kobe, Japan, published as "*Haiwai huaren yu minzu zhuyi* 海外华人与民族主义" (The Nationalism of the Chinese Overseas), in *Sun Wen yu Huaqiao*: jinian Sun Zhongshan danchen 130 zhounian guoji xueshu taolunhui lunwenji,《孙文与华侨: 纪念孙中山诞辰130周年国际学术讨论会论文集》, 1997.

Presented the Australian Economics Society Annual Lecture, published as *National Choice*, in Pacific Economic Papers no. 260, 1996 (reprinted in *Asian Studies Review*, 1996).

Published "A Machiavelli for Our Times", review article on Samuel Huntington's *The Clash of Civilizations*, in *The National Interest*, Washington.

Review of Anthony Milner's *The Invention of Politics in Colonial Malaya: Contesting Nationalism and the Expansion of the Public Space*, in *The Review of Politics*, 1996.

1997 Singapore

After the East Asian Institute (EAI) became part of the National University of Singapore, appointed Director, and also Faculty Professor in the Faculty of Arts and Social Sciences, 1997–2007.

Appointed member of the Human Capital Committee, Social Science Research Council, New York, 1997–2003.

Appointed Chairman of the Asia-Pacific Council, Griffith University, Brisbane, 1997–2000.

Appointed member of National Library Board, Singapore, 1997–2003; and Chairman of the Panel of Advisers of the National Collection on China and the Chinese Diaspora, 1997–2000.

Appointed member of the National Heritage Board, Singapore, 1997–1999.

Appointed Coordinator and General Editor of the History of Nation-building Project for ISEAS.

Appointed member of International Advisory Board of the Institute of Asian Research at the University of British Columbia, 1997–2007.

Awarded Honorary Degree of Doctor of Laws (LL.D.) by the University of Melbourne.

New lecture theatre in the Graduate House at HKU officially opened as Wang Gungwu Lecture Hall.

Guest of the Hong Kong Government at the Handover Ceremony marking the return of Hong Kong to China and the end of 155 years of British rule; followed by the Swearing-in Ceremony of the new Chief Executive.

Conducted lecture at the Pacific Rim Forum, published as "Hong Kong and an Ambivalent Modernity", in *Joining the Modern World: Inside and Outside China*, 2000.

Presented the Edwin O Reischauer Lectures at Harvard University, published as *The Chinese Overseas: From Earthbound China to the Quest for Autonomy*, 2000 (Korean translation in 2003).

Gave the Menzies Oration on Higher Education, University of Melbourne, published as *The Modern University, in Australia and Asia*, 1997.

Presented the 11th Panglaykim Memorial Lecture at the Institute of Strategic and International Studies, Jakarta, published as *China's Place in the Region: the Search for Allies and Friends* (reprinted in *The Indonesian Quarterly*, 1997; Chinese translation in 1999).

Submitted paper at Conference on Hong Kong and the Chinese Diaspora, University of Washington, Seattle, published as "Chineseness: the Dilemmas of Place and Practice", in *Cosmopolitan Capitalists: Hong Kong and the Chinese Diaspora at the end of the 20th Century*, edited by Gary Hamilton, 1999.

Delivered the keynote lecture at the First International Malaysian Studies Conference, University of Malaya, published as "Continuities in Island Southeast Asia", in *Reinventing Malaysia: Reflections on its Past and Future*, edited by Jomo K S Bangi, 2001.

Published "Chinese Civilisation in Historical Perspective", *The Chinese Collections*, Singapore;

"*Tan Xianggang zhengzhi bianqian* 谈香港政治变迁" (Coping with Political Change in Hong Kong), *Er-shih-yi shih-chi*《二十一世纪》*Twenty-first Century*, 1997 (reprinted in *Zhuanhua zhong de Xianggang: shenfen yu zhixu de zaixunqiu*《转化中的香港: 身份与秩序的再寻求》, 1998);

"Thoughts on the Economic Revolution in Asia", in *Financial Reporting in the Pacific Asia Region*, edited by Ronald Ma; and

"*Ajia ni okeru daigaku to toshi no patonashipu* (City and Region: The Role of Universities)", in *Kokusaika suru toshi to daigaku* (*Proceedings of Conference on Universities and Cities*), Fukuoka.

Review of Marilyn A Levine's *The Found Generation: Chinese Communists in Europe during the Twenties*, in *China Review International*.

1998 Singapore

Appointed member of Board of Governors of the Institute of Defence and Strategic Studies (later renamed Rajaratnam School of International Studies) at Nanyang Technological University (NTU).

Appointed Chairman of the Board of the Asia Scholarship Foundation (formerly Asian Studies in Asia Programme, Institute of International Education, New York), Bangkok, 1998–2007.

Appointed member of Advisory Committee of the East Asian Institute of the University of Cambridge, 1998–2007.

Appointed Adviser of the Chinese Overseas Databank, HuayiNet.

Awarded Honorary Degree of Doctor of Letters (D. Litt.) by the University of Hull, UK.

Awarded Honorary Professorship by Jinan University, Guangzhou.

Delivered the keynote lecture at the international conference of the International Study for the Study of Chinese Overseas (ISSCO) in Manila, published as "Ethnic Chinese: The Past in their Future", in *Intercultural Relations, Cultural Transformation, and Identity — The Ethnic Chinese*, edited by Teresita Ang See, 2000 (also published in *Chinese America: History and Perspectives 2000*; and *Yazhou wenhua*《亚洲文化》 *Asian Culture*, 1999; Chinese translation in *Huaqiao huaren lishi yanjiu*《华侨华人历史研究》 *Overseas Chinese History Studies*, Beijing, 1999).

Delivered the Sir Edward Dunlop Lecture at Asialink, University of Melbourne, published as "Chinese Values and Memories of Modern War", in *Joining the Modern World: Inside and Outside China*, 2000.

Delivered the inaugural Sokwanlok Lecture at University of California, San Diego; and the Second Annual East Asia Distinguished Lecture at University of Virginia.

Conducted lecture at the Pacific Rim Forum in Shanghai, published as "The Shanghai-Hong Kong Linkage", in *Joining the Modern World: Inside and Outside China*, 2000.

Gave the keynote lecture at NUS Conference on East-West Studies: Tradition, Transformation and Innovation, published as "China between Progress and Tradition", in *Dongxi wenhua chengchuan yu chuangxing: Zhao Lingyang jiaoshou rongxiu jinian lunwenji*《东西文化承传与创新：赵令扬教授荣休纪念论文集》 *East-West Studies: Tradition, Transformation and Innovation. A Festschrift in Honour of Professor Chiu Ling Yeong on his Retirement*, 2004.

Published revised edition of *The Nanhai Trade: The Early History of Chinese Trade in the South China Sea* (republished in 2003).

Edited, with Wang Ling-chi, *The Chinese Diaspora: Selected Essays*, two volumes (republished in 2003).

Edited, with John Wong, *China's Political Economy*; also published "China's New Paths for National Re-emergence" (first published as *The Chinese Way: China's Position in International Relations* in Oslo in 1995).

Published "Ming Foreign Relations: Southeast Asia", in *The Cambridge History of China, vol. 8: The Ming Dynasty, 1368–1644, Part 2*, edited by Denis Twitchett and Frederick W Mote;

"Introduction"; and "Nationalism among the Overseas Chinese", in *The Encyclopedia of the Chinese Overseas*, edited by Lynn Pan (Chinese translation in 1998, French translation in 2000);

"Commentary on Wolf Lepenies' Paper, in Wolf Lepenies, *The End of the Cultural Westernisation of the World?*, Singapore;

"Allies and Friends: Culture in Asia-Pacific State Relations", in *Asian Journal of Political Science* (French translation in 1998);

"Malaysia-Singapore: Two Kinds of Ethnic Transformations", in *Southeast Asian Journal of Social Science*;

"Foreword", in J Y Wong, *Deadly Dreams: Opium and the Arrow War (1856–1860) in China*; and

"Singapore at the Crossroads of Civilisation", in *Singapore: Re-Engineering Success*, edited by Arun Mahizhnan and Lee Tsao Yuan.

Review of Constance Lever-Tracy, David Ip, and Noel Tracy's *The Chinese Diaspora and Mainland China: An Emerging Economic Synergy*; and of Rajeswary Ampalavanar Brown's (editor) *Chinese Business Enterprise in Asia*, in *The China Quarterly*.

1999 Singapore

Appointed Board Member of the Social Science Research Council, New York, 1999–2006.

Appointed Distinguished Fellow of the Centre of Asian Studies at the University of Hong Kong.

Appointed Adviser of the National Heritage Board, Singapore, 1999–2002.

Gave the keynote lecture at NUS Conference on Maritime China in Transition, published in *Maritime China in Transition, 1750–1850*, edited with Ng Chin-keong, 2004.

Attended Workshop on the History of the Malayan Emergency, with Chin Peng, at the ANU, Canberra, comments published in "Closing Comments and Questions", in *Dialogues with Chin Peng: New Light on the Malayan Communist Party*, edited by C C Chin and Karl Hack, 2004 (Chinese translation in 2006).

Presented the Asa Briggs Lecture at the Commonwealth of Learning Annual Conference, Brunei, published as "Modern Work Cultures and the Chinese", in *Joining the Modern World: Inside and Outside China*, 2000.

Presented paper at the Conference on Southeast Asia's Changing Landscape, Bangkok, published as "ASEAN and the Three Powers of the Asia-Pacific", in *Southeast Asia's Changing Landscape: Implications for US-Japan Relations on the Eve of the Twenty-First Century*, edited by Gerrit W Gong (Chinese translation in 2000).

Delivered the opening lecture at the Inaugural Meeting of the Centre for the Study of the Chinese Southern Diaspora, Australian National University, published as "A Single Chinese Diaspora? Some Historical Reflections", in *Imagining the Chinese Diaspora: Two Australian Perspectives*, 1999 (Chinese translation in 2000).

Delivered the Distinguished Scholars Lecture at Lingnan University, Hong Kong, published as "*Huaren yimin bianqian shi* 华人移民变迁史" (Changes in Chinese Migration History), in *Yishi E'e — Huang Shihua xiansheng "Ba-yi" rongshou zhengwen ji*《一士谔谔 ：黄石华先生八一荣寿征文集》, edited by Rao Meijiao, Guo Yiyao and Zheng Cheyan, 2000.

Presented the J Earl Moreland Asian Lecture at Randolph-Macon College, Virginia, on "Keeping People In or Sending People Out: China's Historical Dilemma".

Gave plenary lecture at the Conference on Chinese Diaspora in Latin America, in Havana, Cuba.

Submitted paper for the Panel on Diasporas at the Annual Conference of the American Historical Association, Washington DC.

Chaired the opening session of the 80th Anniversary Conference on the May Fourth Movement, in Peking University.

Conducted lecture to NUS' Department of Chinese Studies on Chinese ideas of identity, published as "*Zailun haiwai Huaren de shenfen rentong* 再论海外华人的身份认同" (Chinese Identity Revisited), in *Hanxue zongheng* 《汉学纵横》 *Excursions in Sinology*, edited by Li Zhuoran, Hong Kong, 2002.

Published *China and Southeast Asia: Myths, Threats, and Culture*, Singapore; and

"Qiaoxiang Ties: 'Cultural Capitalism' in South China (Preface)", in *Qiaoxiang Ties: Interdisciplinary Approaches to "Cultural Capitalism" in South China*, edited by Leo Douw, Cen Huang and Michael R Godley.

Edited, with John Wong, *Hong Kong in China: The Challenges of Transition*, published "Introduction" (with John Wong); and *China: Two Decades of Reform and Change*, Singapore, published "Introduction" (with John Wong).

Edited, with Wong Siu-lun, *Towards a New Millennium: Building on Hong Kong's Strengths*, Hong Kong.

Presented the NUS Faculty of Arts and Social Sciences Lecture, published as *Shifting Paradigms and Asian Perspectives: Implications for Research and Teaching* (reprinted in *Reflections on Alternative Discourses from Southeast Asia,* edited by Syed Farid Alatas, 2001).

2000 Singapore

Appointed member of the National University of Singapore (NUS) Council, 2000–2004.

Appointed member of the Management Board of Asia Research Institute, NUS.

Appointed member of the Multidisciplinary Assessment Committee, Canadian Foundation for Innovation, Ottawa, 2000–2002.

Appointed Chairman of the Advisory Panel for Chinese Library Services, National Library Board, Singapore, 2000–2003.

Asked by NUS President to plan a university institute for Asia research.

Presented the Smuts Commonwealth Lectures at the University of Cambridge, four lectures published as *Anglo-Chinese Encounters since 1800: War, Trade, Science and Governance*, Cambridge, 2003.

Gave lecture at Stanford University on the 50th anniversary of the establishment of the PRC, published as "The Chinese Revolution and the Overseas Chinese", in *Joining the Modern World: Inside and Outside China* (Chinese translation in 2001).

Presented the keynote lecture at the 16th Conference of the International Association of Historians of Asia at Kota Kinabulu, published as "The Search for Asian National Histories", in *IAHA 2000: Proceedings of the 16th Conference of the International Association of Historians of Asia*, 2004 (also published in *Yazhou wenhua*《亚洲文化》*Asian Culture*.

Presented lecture at the Wissenschaftkolleg Symposium in Berlin, on Creativity in the Social Sciences.

Gave the opening plenary lecture to Conference on Immigrant Societies and Modern Education at NUS, published as "Social Bonding and Freedom: Problems of Choice in Immigrant Societies", in *Asian Migrants and Education: the Tensions of Education in Immigrant Societies and among Migrant Groups*, 2003 (Chinese translation in 2001).

Presented the Annual Lecture of the Malaysian Branch of the Royal Asiatic Society, published as "Political Heritage and Nation Building", in *Journal of the Malaysian Branch of the Royal Asiatic Society*, 2000.

Presented the opening lecture to the Symposium on "Coping with China" in Washington DC, published as "Joining the Modern World", in *Joining the Modern World: Inside and Outside China*; and published as "China's Struggle with Modernity", in *American Purpose*, 2001.

Gave the keynote lecture to the Anthropology Division of the Third International Conference on Sinology held in Taipei, published as

"Questions of Identity during the Ch'ing Dynasty", in *Proceedings of the Third International Sinology Conference: Anthropology*, 2003.

Presented the keynote lecture on Cross-cultural Historiography at Institute of China Studies Conference at Sariska, India.

Presented paper on "Cultural Centres for the Chinese Overseas", published in *Chinese and Indian Diasporas: Comparative Perspectives*, edited by Wong Siu-lun and Melissa Curley, 2004.

Published *Joining the Modern World: Inside and Outside China*; published "Joining the Modern World", "The Chinese Revolution and the Overseas Chinese", "A Single Chinese Diaspora?", "Hong Kong and an Ambivalent Modernity", "The Shanghai-Hong Kong Linkage", "Transforming the Trading Chinese", "Chinese Values and Memories of Modern War" and "Modern Work Cultures and the Chinese".

Papers collected and published in *Tandang rensheng, xuezhe qinghuai: Wang Gengwu fangtan yu yanlunji*《坦荡人生，学者情怀：王赓武访谈与言论集》*The Life and Sentiment of a Scholar: Anthology of Professor Wang Gungwu's Interviews and Speeches*, edited by Liu Hong.

Edited, with Zheng Yongnian, *Reform, Legitimacy and Dilemmas: China's Politics and Society*.

Published "Memories of War: World War II in Asia, in *War and Memory in Malaysia and Singapore*, edited by P Lim Pui Huen and Diana Wong;

"*Ershi nianqian de yiduan wangshi — Wang Gengwu tan "Nanda shijian* 二十年前的一段往事—王赓武校长谈'南大事件'", in *Tandang rensheng, xuezhe qinghuai: Wang Gengwu fangtan yu yanlunji*《坦荡人生，学者情怀：王赓武访谈与言论集》*The Life and Sentiment of a Scholar: Anthology of Professor Wang Gungwu's Interviews and Speeches*, edited by Liu Hong (first published in 1986); and

"Preface", in Liu Hong 刘宏, *Zhongguo-Dongnanya xue: lilun jiangou, hudong moshi, gean fenxi* 《中国－东南亚学：理论建构，互动模式，个案分析》 *Sino-Southeast Asian Studies: Theoretical Frameworks, Interaction Patterns, Case Analyses*, Beijing: *Zhongguo shehui kexue* (China Social Science Publishing House).

Review of Lu Hanchao's *Beyond the Neon Lights: Everyday Shanghai in the Early Twentieth Century*; and Ng Wing Chung's *The Chinese in Vancouver, 1945–1980: the Pursuit of Identity and Power*, in *Pacific Affairs*.

2001 Singapore

Member of delegation led by then Minister of Trade and Industry George Yeo to Xinjiang and Xi'an.

Appointed Vice-Chairman of the Board of Governors of Chinese Heritage Centre.

Appointed Chairman of International Advisory Group for the NUS Public Policy Programme, 2001–2004.

Appointed Secretary of the Social Science Research Council, New York, 2001–2006.

Appointed member of the Advisory Board of the Southeast Asia Research Centre at the City University of Hong Kong, 2001–2007.

Awarded Honorary Professorship by Nanjing University, China; gave public lecture on Recent Emigrations from China.

Submitted paper at the Conference on Locating Southeast Asia at Amsterdam, published as "Two Perspectives of Southeast Asian Studies: Singapore and China", in *Locating Southeast Asia: Genealogies of Knowledge and Politics of Space*, edited by Paul H Kratoska, Remco Rabin and Henk Schulte Nordholt, 2005 (Chinese translation in 2004).

Presented the keynote lecture at the International Society for the Study of Chinese Overseas (ISSCO) conference in Taipei, published as "New Migrants: How new? Why new?", in *Hai-wai hua-tsu yen-chiu lun-ji* 《海外华族研究论集》 *Essays on Ethnic Chinese Abroad*, Three Volumes, 2002 (Chinese translation in 2001).

Presented the keynote lecture to Asian Scholarship Foundation scholars, published as "Reflections on Networks and Structures in Asia", in *Asianizing Asia: Reflexivity, History and Identity*, Bangkok.

Gave the keynote lecture at the Joint Conference of International Convention of Asia Scholars (ICAS) and Association for Asian Studies

(AAS), in Berlin on "Divergence and Dominance: Challenges of Asian Studies".

Presented the opening lecture on Southeast Asian Studies in China, at the launch of the Southeast Asian Research Centre of the City University of Hong Kong.

Gave concluding comments at the Conference on Decolonization held at the NUS, published as "The Limits of Decolonization", in *The Transformation of Southeast Asia: International Perspectives on Decolonization*, 2003.

Published *Only Connect! Sino-Malay Encounters* (republished in 2003); *Don't Leave Home: Migration and the Chinese* (republished in 2003).

Published "The Future of Secular Values", in Social Science Research Council's "After September 11" 2001 Online Essay Forum, at <http://www.ssrc.org/sept11/essays/wang.htm>;

"Europe's Heritage in Asia", in *Asia-Europe on the Eve of the 21st Century,* Bangkok, 2001;

"*Zhongguo renkou qianyi: guoqu yu xianzai* 中国人口迁移过去与现在" (People Movement in China, Past and Present), in *Ershiyi shiji: wenhua zijue yu kuawenhua duihua*《二十一世纪:文化自觉与跨文化对话》(*21st Century: Cultural Self-consciousness and Cross-cultural Dialogue*), edited by Ma Rong and Zhou Xing, Beijing;

"Diaspora, a Much Abused Word" (interview conducted with Wang by editor of *Asian Affairs*), *Asian Affairs*, Hong Kong;

"Foreword", in Shen Yuanfang, *Dragon Seed in the Antipodes: Chinese-Australian Autobiographies*, Melbourne;

"Transforming the Trading World of Southeast Asia" , in e-journal, *The Asianists' Asia*, Centre de Recherche sur les Etudes Asiatiques, Paris; and

"*Xu* 序 (Preface)", in Lee Guan Kin, *Dongxi wenhua de chuangji yu Xinhua zhishifenzhi de sanzhong huiying: Qiu Shuyuan, Lin Wenqing, Song Wangxiang de bijiao yanjiu*《东西文化的撞击与新华知识分子的三种回应:丘菽园, 林文庆, 宋旺相的比较研究》*Responding to Eastern and Western Cultures in Singapore: A Comparative Study of Khoo Seok Wan, Lim Boon Keng and Song Ong Siang.*

2002 Singapore

Appointed Chairman of the Board of Trustees of the Institute of Southeast Asian Studies, Singapore.

Appointed Chairman of International Advisory Board of Universiti Tunku Abdul Rahman (UTAR), Malaysia.

Appointed Adviser of the Center for Overseas Chinese Research at Chinese Academy of Social Sciences, Beijing.

Appointed Adviser of Asia-Pacific Studies Program, Academia Sinica.

Appointed Chairman of Advisory Committee on Chinese Programmes (ACCESS), MediaCorp, Singapore, 2002–2005.

Appointed member of National Brains Trust on Education, Malaysia, 2002–2004.

Appointed member of International Advisory Board of the Department of Chinese Studies at Nanyang Technological University.

Awarded Honorary Degree of Doctor of Letters (D. Litt.) by the University of Hong Kong.

Organised Workshop on the History of Nation-building in Southeast Asia, edited volume of essays, *Nation-building: Five Southeast Asian Histories*, published by Institute of Southeast Asian Studies, 2005.

Delivered the Giri Deshingkar Memorial Lecture in New Delhi, published as "Secular China", *China Report*, 2003.

Presented paper at Universiti Kebangsaan Malaysia (UKM) Conference, Bangi, published as "Chinese Political Culture and Scholarship about the Malay World", in *Chinese Scholarship on the Malay World: a Revaluation of a Scholarly Tradition*, edited by Ding Choo Ming, 2003 (Chinese translation in 2004).

Delivered the keynote lecture at Conference on Modern China and Public Intellectuals (*Xiandai Zhongguo yu gonggong zhishi fenzi* 现代中国与公共知识分子) at East China Normal University, published as "*Haiwai huaren yanzhongdi Zhongguo bianqian* 海外华人眼中的中国变迁" (Change in China in the Eyes of the Chinese Abroad), in *Liwa hepan lun sixiang — Huadong shifan daxue siyuwen jiangzuo yanjianglu* 《丽娃河畔论思想-华东师范大学思与文讲座演讲录》 *Discussing Ideas by the*

Liwa River: Lectures on Thought and Literature at East China Normal University, edited by Xu Jilin and Liu Qing, 2005.

Delivered the keynote lecture at Singapore Society of Asian Studies Conference, published as "Chinese Ethnicity in New Southeast Asian Nations", in *Ethnic Relations and Nation-building in Southeast Asia: The Case of the Ethnic Chinese*, edited by Leo Suryadinata, 2004 (Chinese translation in 2006).

Presented the inaugural Australian Broadcasting Corporation (ABC) Asia Lecture, "The Emergence of China".

Delivered three lectures in Copenhagen as guest of Danish Institute for International Studies, University of Copenhagen and Copenhagen Business School.

Presented the Tan Kah Kee Foundation 20th Anniversary Lecture, published as "Who Should Pay for Universities?", in *The Tan Kah Kee Spirit Today*, 2003.

Published *To Act is to Know: Chinese Dilemmas* (republished in 2003); *Bind Us in Time: Nation and Civilisation in Asia* (republished in 2003);

Haiwai huaren yanjiu de dashiye yu xinfangxiang: Wang Gengwu jiaoshou lunwen ji《海外华人研究的大视野与新方向: 王赓武教授论文集》 (*Broad Views and New Directions for Overseas Chinese Studies: Selected Essays of Professor Wang Gungwu*), edited by Liu Hong and Huang Jianli;

Wang Gengwu zixuanji《王赓武自选集》*Selected Works of Wang Gungwu*, Shanghai.

Edited *Wang Fo-wen jinianji*《王宓文纪念集》*Memorial Collection of Poems, Essays and Calligraphy by Wang Fo-wen, 1903–1972*, Global Publishing.

Published "State and Faith: Secular Values in Asia and the West", in *Critical Views of September 11: Analyses from around the World*, edited by Eric Herschberg and Kevin W Moore, New York;

"Local and National: a Dialogue between Tradition and Modernity", in *Ethnic Chinese in Singapore and Malaysia: A Dialogue between Tradition and Modernity*, edited by Leo Suryadinata, Singapore (Chinese translation in 2002);

"City, and Citadel, on the Hill", (in One Year On: Power, Purpose and Strategy in American Foreign Policy), in *The National Interest*;

"China and Southeast Asia: Collision or Co-operation?", *Trends in Southeast Asia*, Singapore;

"*Haiwai huaren de wenhua zhongxin* 海外华人的文化中心" in *Haiwai huaren lunji*《海外华人论集》*Essays on Chinese Overseas*, edited by Hao Shiyuan, Chinese Academy of Social Sciences Press;

"*Haiwai huaren yu zuowei Zhongguo ren* 海外华人与作为中国人" (Overseas Chinese and Being Chinese), *Huaqiao huaren baike quanshu*《华侨华人百科全书》*Encyclopedia of Chinese Overseas*, edited by Zhou Nanjing, in 12 volumes, Beijing;

"Globalization and Human Civilization", in《南京大学学报告会》(自然科学) *Journal of Nanjing University (Natural Sciences)*, 2002;

"Introduction", in Cheah Boon Kheng, *Malaysia: the Making of a Nation*, Singapore;

"Foreword", in Patricia Lim Pui Huen, *Wong Ah Fook: Immigrant, Builder and Entrepreneur*;

"Foreword", in Wong Sin Kiong, *China's Anti-American Boycott Movement in 1905: a Study in Urban Protest*.

Review of Josephine M T Khu's (editor), *Cultural Curiosity: Thirteen Stories about the Search for Chinese Roots*, in *The China Journal*.

Review of Michael R Godley and Grayson J Lloyd's (editors), *Perspectives on the Chinese Indonesians*, in *Bulletin of Indonesian Economic Studies*.

2003 Singapore

Chinese Heritage Centre resource collection is named Wang Gungwu Library; it began with his donation of books to the Centre in 1996.

Elected President of World Congress of Libraries and Institutes for Chinese Overseas Studies.

Appointed member of Singapore Documentary History Committee, 2003–2006.

Appointed member of Editorial Board of the *Dictionary of Hong Kong Biography*, 2003–2011.

Appointed Adviser of Asia-Pacific Research Centre at Academia Sinica, Taipei.

Gave the keynote lecture at a conference at Chinese University of Hong Kong, published as "Mixing Memory and Desire: Tracking the Migrant Cycles", in *Chinese Overseas: Migration, Research and Documentation*, edited by Tan Chee-Beng, Colin Storey and Julia Zimmerman, 2007 (Chinese translation in 2003).

Presented paper to Conference on China and Asia's New Dynamics, organised by George Washington University, published as "China and Southeast Asia", in *Power Shift: China and Asia's New Dynamics*, edited by David Shambaugh, Berkeley: University of California Press, 2005.

Presented the Sasakawa Peace Foundation Lecture in Washington DC, published as "What Asia Understands of US Grand Strategy", in *Asian Voices Series*, Washington DC, 2003.

Presented lecture at the Japan Center for International Exchange Conference in Kunming, published as "The Cultural Implications of the Rise of China for the Region", in *The Rise of China and a Changing East Asian Order*, edited by Kokubun Ryosei and Wang Jisi, 2004.

Presented lecture at HKU on "Chinese Political Culture and the Impact of Revolution", in commemoration of Sun Yat-sen's visit to HKU in 1923.

Gave lecture at the University of Oregon, "Cultures in Eastern Asia"; and at the Stanley Foundation Conference on ASEAN and the United States, at Warrenton, Virginia.

Opened conference on Paradigms and Perspectives in Hong Kong Studies, at HKU, published as "One Country, Two Cultures", in *Rethinking Hong Kong: New Paradigms, New Perspectives*, 2009.

Presented paper at conference organised by the Centre for Defence and Strategic Studies, Australian Defence College, Canberra, published as "Perspectives of United States Grand Strategy in a Changing Southeast Asia", in *Yazhou wenhua* 《亚洲文化》 *Asian Culture*, 2004.

Power and Identity in the Chinese World Order: Festschrift in Honour of Professor Wang Gungwu was published. This was edited by Billy K L So, John FitzGerald, Huang Jianli and James K Chin, with essays by some of his students, Lee Kam-keung, So Wai-chor, Huang Jianli, Jane Lee, Ho Hon-wai, Terry Narramore, Edmund S K Fung, Ng Chin-keong, Adrian Chan, James Chin, Jennifer W Jay, Antonia Finnane, John FitzGerald, with an Introduction by Billy K L So and "An Oral History" by Lee Guan Kin. Philip A Kuhn, a fellow student at SOAS London in 1955, contributed the opening essay, "Wang Gungwu: The Historian in His Times".

Published *Ideas Won't Keep: the Struggle for China's Future*.

Edited, with Zheng Yongnian, *Damage Control: The Chinese Communist Party in the Era of Jiang Zeming*, Singapore.

Edited, with Rafe de Crespigny and Igor de Rachewiltz, *Sino-Asiatica: Papers Dedicated to Professor Liu Ts'un-yan on the Occasion of His Eighty-fifth Birthday*, Canberra, published "The Travails of National Confucianism".

Edited, with Irwin Abrams, *The Iraq War and its Consequences: Thoughts of Nobel Laureates and Eminent Scholars*.

Edited, with Gong Shaopeng 宫少鹏, *Yizhan qishilu*《伊战启示录》*Iraq: an Unveiling*, Global Publishing.

Published "Reflections on Networks and Structures in Asia", in *China and Southeast Asia: Changing Social-cultural Interactions*, edited by Melissa G Curley and Liu Hong, Hong Kong;

Minzu zhuyi yu Rujia xueshuo "民族主义与儒家学说" (Nationalism and Confucianism), in *Ruxue yu shijie wenming: guoji xueshu huiyi lunwen xuanji*《儒学与世界文明：国际学术会议论文选集》*Confucianism and World Civilisation*, edited by Chen Rongzhao, two volumes;

"China Rising: Prospects and Implications for Asia Pacific", in *Asia Pacific Security: Uncertainty in a Changing World Order*, edited by Elina Noor and Mohamed Jawhar Hassan, Kuala Lumpur: Institute of Strategic and International Studies;

"Prospects for Pacific Asia Integration" (with Jesus P Estanislao), in *Global Governance: Enhancing Trilateral Cooperation*, Seoul: The Trilateral Commission;

"Overseas Chinese & Ethnic Chinese Studies: Methodologies" (with Shiba Yoshinobu, Hamashita Takeshi, Chen Tianxi and Takahashi Goro), *China 21*, vol. 17;

"Wong Lin Ken (1931–1983)", in *Wong Lin Ken, The Trade of Singapore, 1819–1869*, reprint no. 23, Kuala Lumpur: Malaysian Branch of the Royal Asiatic Society;

"Foreword", in *An Impossible Dream: Hong Kong University from Foundation to Re-establishment, 1910–1950*, edited by Chan Lau Kitching and Peter Cunich, Hong Kong;

"Foreword", in *Chew Boon Lay: A Family Traces its History*, compiled by Ong Chwee Lim, Singapore; and

"Foreword", in *Legacies of White Australia*, edited by Laksiri Jayasuria, Jan Gothard and David Walker, University of Western Australia Press.

Review of T N Harper's *The End of Empire and the Making of Malaya*, 1999, in *Modern Asian Studies*.

2004 Singapore

Awarded Public Service Medal by the Government of Singapore.

Appointed Coordinator for Singapore of the Network of East Asian Think-tanks (NEAT).

Appointed Chairman of the Educations Services Accreditation Council, Ministry of Education, 2004–2006, and member of China Studies Syllabus Committee, 2004–2005.

Appointed member of International Adviser, Singapore History Museum, 2004–2008.

Awarded Honorary Professorhip by Tsinghua University, Beijing.

Diasporic Chinese Ventures: The Life and Work of Wang Gungwu was published, edited by Gregor Benton and Liu Hong, London; with "Looking Forward, Looking Back: an Interview with Wang Gungwu", by Liu Hong and translated by Gregor Benton.

Study by Liu Hong, "*Cong Xinjiapo kan huaren shijie: Wang Gengwu jiaoshou yu haiwai huaren yanjiu* 从新加坡看华人世界：王赓武教授与海外华人研究" (The Chinese World from Singapore: Professor Wang Gungwu and Research on the Chinese Overseas) published as appendix in Liu Hong, *Zhanhou Xinjiapo huarenshehui di shanbian: bentu qinghuai, quyu wangluo, quanqiu shiye* 《战后新加坡华人社会的嬗变：本土情怀，区域网络，全球视野》 *The Transformation of Chinese Society in Post-War Singapore: Localising Process, Regional Networking and Global Perspective*, Xiamen University Press.

Presented the keynote lecture at the 18th Conference of International Association of Historians of Asia (IAHA), held in Taipei, published as "The Age of New Paradigms", in *Asia-Pacific Forum*, Taipei, 2005 (also published in *International Sociological Association E-Bulletin*, 2007).

Gave plenary lecture at the international conference of the International Society for the Study of the Chinese Overseas (ISSCO) in Copenhagen, published as "*Liuxue* 留学 and *yimin* 移民: From Study to Migranthood", in *Beyond Chinatown: New Chinese Migration and the Global Expansion of China*, edited by Mette Thuno, Copenhagen: NIAS Press, 2007.

Presented the opening lecture at the workshop on Local Scholarship and the Study of Southeast Asia: Bridging the Past and the Present, published as "Post-imperial Knowledge and Pre-Social Science in Southeast Asia", in *Decentring and Diversifying Southeast Asian Studies: Perspectives from the Region*, edited by Goh Beng-Lan, 2011.

Delivered lecture to Contemporary History Institute of Ohio University, Athens on "Systems and Cultures: Hong Kong and China".

Gave lecture at the conference on China's Changing Position in the International Community, 1840–2000, at the University of Vienna, on "The Narrowing and the Widening of the Idea of History".

Delivered the keynote lecture at the 10th Anniversary Conference of the Centre for Chinese Language and Culture at Nanyang Technological University, published as "*Nanqiao qiuxueji: butong de shidai, zou butong de lu* 南侨求学记：不同的时代，走不同的路" (In Search of Learning: Different Times, Different Roads), in *Kuayue jiangjie yu wenhua tiaoshi*《跨越疆界与文化调适》*Crossing Borders and Cultural Adjustments*, edited by Lee Guan Kin, 2008.

Presented the second annual Herb Feith Lecture at Monash University, Melbourne, on "Divisive Modernity: Thoughts on Southeast Asian History", at <http://groups.yahoo.com/group/melb-disc/message/9984>.

Presented lecture at Singapore Management University on "Chinese Overseas as Knowledge Brokers".

Gave the keynote lecture at the conference organised by the Asia Research Centre of Chulalongkorn University, "The Uses of Ethnic Knowlege".

Delivered lecture at Sun Yat-sen University, "*Haiwai huaren yu Zhongguo de xingqi* 海外华人与中国的兴起" (Chinese Overseas and China's Rise).

Presented public lecture at the Chinese Heritage Centre, Singapore, published as "*Xiandai wenhua yu Huaren chuantong* 现代文化与华人传统" (Cultures Today and the Chinese Heritage), *Huayiguan tongxun*《华裔馆通讯》*CHC Bulletin*.

Delivered the Daisaku Ikeda Annual Lecture, published as *The Universal and the Historical: My Faith in History*, Singapore (Chinese translation, "*Lishi yu zhishi: zhongxi fenlei de chayi* 历史与知识：中西分类的差异" (History and Knowledge: Different Library Classifications in China and the West), in *Nanshan lunxueji: Qian Cunxun xiansheng jiuwu shengri jinian*《南山论学集：钱存训先生九五生日纪念》, Beijing, 2006).

Gave the keynote lecture at National Sun Yat-sen University, Kaohsiung, published as "China and Southeast Asia: Changes in Strategic Perceptions", in *China and Southeast Asia: Global Changes and Regional Challenges*, edited by Ho Khai Leong and Samuel C Y Ku, 2005.

Presented lecture on Diaspora and Identity at Peking University, published as "*Wuyi jietuo di kunjing*? 无以解脱的困境?" (Writing as *Haiwai Huaren*: Dilemma without Relief?), *Dushu*《读书》, Beijing.

Gave the keynote lecture at the inaugural international conference on Southeast Asia since 1945, at Universiti Sains Malaysia Conference, Penang, published as "Party and Nation in Southeast Asia", in *Millennial Asia*, Delhi, 2010.

Published "China's Long Road to Sovereignty", in *Law and Legal Culture*, edited by G Doeker-Mach and K A Ziegert, Stuttgart;

"The Uses of Dynastic Ideology: Confucianism in Contemporary Business", in *Asia's New Crisis: Renewal through Total Ethical Management*, edited by Frank-Jurgen Richter and Pamela C M Mar, Singapore (Chinese translation in 2005);

"2003 in Review", *Singapore Yearbook 2004*, Singapore: National Archives of Singapore;

"An American Education — the Right End of a Seesaw", *Harvard China Review*, Spring 2004;

"The Fourth Rise of China: Cultural Implications", in *China: An International Journal*;

"Changing China — Views of a Scholar", an interview with Professor Wang Gungwu, published on Malaysiakini website, at <http://www.malaysiakini.com/opinions/22715> and <http://www.malaysiakini.com/opinions/22716 >;

"Wang Gengwu jiaoshou fangtan lu 王赓武教授访谈录" (Interviews with Professor Wang Gungwu), edited by Xie Shijian 谢诗坚, *Hanjiang xuebao* 《韩江学报》 *Journal of Han Chiang College*, Penang;

"Foreword", in Goh Keng Swee, *Wealth of East Asian Nations*, edited by Linda Low, Singapore.

Review of Ariel Heryanto and Sumit K Mandal's (editors) *Challenging Authoritarianism in Southeast Asia: comparing Indonesia and Malaysia*, in *Contemporary Southeast Asia*.

2005 Singapore

Appointed Chairman of Governing Board of the Lee Kuan Yew School of Public Policy, NUS.

Appointed member of Management Board of Institute of South Asian Studies, NUS.

Awarded Distinguished Service Award by National University of Singapore.

Established the Annual Wang Gungwu Prizes for the Best Doctoral Theses at National University of Singapore.

Presented the Ishizaka Lectures in Tokyo, published as *Chuka Bunmei to Chugoku no yukue*《中華文明と中国のゆくえ》 *Chinese Civilization and China's Position*, (translated into Japanese by Kato Mikio, Iwanami Shoten, 2007).

Gave the Fu Ssu-nien Memorial Lectures at Academia Sinica, published as *Lixiang bietu: jingwai kanzhonghua*《离乡别土：境外看中华》 *China and its Cultures: From the Periphery*, Taipei: Institute of History and Philology, Academia Sinica, 2007.

Delivered the inaugural lecture at the Institute of Humanities, Nanjing University, on "*Jinri de Zhonghua wenhua* 今日的中华文化" (Chinese Culture Today).

Gave HKU Library Lecture, Review of Chang Jung, *Mao: the Unknown Story*, published as eVideo at <http://library.hku.hk/record=b3567597>; summary by 文灼非 Man Cheuk-fei, in *Xinbao yuekan*《信报月刊》 *Hong Kong Economic Journal*, no. 346, 2007.

Published essay collection, *Yimin ji xingqi de Zhongguo*《移民及兴起的中国》 *Essays on Migrants and China's Rise*, Global Publishing;

"Introduction" and "Conclusion", in *UNESCO History of Humanity: Scientific and Cultural Development. Volume VI: The Nineteenth Century*, edited by P Mathias and N Todorov, UNESCO and Routledge;

"Within and Without: Chinese Writers Overseas", *Journal of Chinese Overseas* (Chinese translation in 2008);

"Preface", in, *Kinta Valley: Pioneering Malaysia's Modern Development*, edited by Khoo Salma Nasution and Abdur-Razzaq Lubis, Ipoh: Perak Academy;

"Foreword", in Ming Govaars, *Dutch Colonial Education: The Chinese Experience in Indonesia, 1900–1942* (translated from Dutch by Lorre Lynn Trytten), Singapore;

"Foreword", in Suchen Christine Lim, *Stories of the Chinese Overseas*, Singapore and San Francisco; and

"Xu (Preface)", in Cheng Xi 程希, *Qiaowu yu waijiao guanxi yanjiu: Zhongguo fangqi "shuangchong guoji" de huigu yu fansi*《侨务与外交关系研究:中国放弃"双重国籍"的回顾与反思》*Overseas Chinese Affairs and Diplomatic Relations: Retrospect on China Abandoning its "Dual Nationality" Policy*, Beijing.

2006 Singapore

Appointed Chairman of Expert Panel for Singapore Ministry of Education Academic Research Fund.

Appointed member of a United Kingdom 2008 Research Assessment Panel, 2006–2009.

Awarded Honorary Professorship by Xi'an Jiaotong University.

Organised the Nalanda University Symposium at the National University of Singapore.

Presented the inaugural Tsai Lecture at Harvard University, on "*Tianxia* and Empire: External Chinese Perspectives", at <http://www.fas.harvard.edu/~asiactr/Archive%20Files/Tsai%20Lect.Harvard.05.06.doc>.

Delivered lecture at the international conference on Southeast Asia: Past, Present and Future at University of Auckland, published as "Southeast Asia: Imperial Themes", *New Zealand Journal of Asian Studies*, 2009.

Delivered the keynote lecture at the University of Nottingham Conference, "China and the International Order: some Historical Perspectives", published in *China and the New International Order*, edited by Wang Gungwu and Zheng Yongnian, 2008.

Presented lecture at Xi'an Jiaotong University, translated and published as "*Zhongguo wenhua haiwaiguan* 中国文化海外观" (Chinese Culture from Outside China), in *Xi'an Jiaotong daxue xuebao (shehui kexue ban)*《西安交通大学学报（社会科学版）》*Journal of Xi'an Jiaotong University (Social Sciences)*, 2007.

Gave the 10th Annual Gaston Sigur Memorial Lecture at George Washington University, Washington DC, on "Empires and their Shadows over Asia".

Delivered the 2006 Foundation Lecture at the University of Manchester, "The Chinese Pursuit of Higher Education".

Gave the opening plenary lecture at the Asian Migrations Conference, organised by University of Binghamton, on "Comings and Goings: Issues in Chinese Migration Studies".

Presented lecture at Cornell University, "Traditions of Empire: China and Southeast Asia".

Delivered the keynote lecture at the conference on Rationalizing China's Place in Asia, 1800–2005, published as "Family and Friends: China in Changing Asia", in *Negotiating Asymmetry: China's Place in Asia*, edited by Anthony Reid and Zheng Yangwen, 2009.

Gave talk at the Australian National University Strategic and Defence Studies Centre's 40th Anniversary, published as "The Rise of China: History as Policy", in *History as Policy: Framing the Debate on the Future of Australia's Defence Policy*, Canberra, 2007, at <http://epress.anu.edu.au>.

Delivered the East Asian Lecture at University of Delaware, on "Nation-states in East and Southeast Asia".

Presented the keynote lecture at the International Society for the Study of Chinese Overseas (ISSCO) Conference in Pretoria, on "Heritage and Communication: Education, Chinese Overseas, and China's Soft Power".

Presented paper on "*Dalu tianxia guan* 大陆天下观" (A Continental Worldview) at the panel of the Beijing Forum.

Presented comments and closing remarks at the commemorative conference for Benjamin Schwartz at East China Normal University, Shanghai.

Gave lecture on comparative histories at the Inaugural Conference of the Northeast Asian History Foundation, Seoul.

Delivered the keynote lecture at the 20th Century China Historians Conference, at National University of Singapore, on "Imperial State and the Nation Agenda: Changing Perspectives of Political China".

Gave the William Willetts Lecture for the Southeast Asian Ceramics Society, Singapore, on "Trade and Tribute: Ming Dynasty".

Published "Inception, Origins, Contemplations: a Personal Perspective", in *Imagination, Openness and Courage: The National University of*

Singapore at 100; "Foreword"; "Patterns of Chinese Migration in Historical Perspective"; "The Study of Chinese Minorities in Southeast Asia"; "Greater China and the Chinese Overseas"; "Political Chinese: Their Contribution to Modern Southeast Asian History", in *The Chinese Overseas*, edited by Liu Hong, Routledge Library of Modern China, four volumes;

"Preface and Introduction", in second edition of *The Encyclopedia of the Chinese Overseas*, edited by Lynn Pan;

"Some Remarks on Singapore and Asia in this Era of Globalisation", in *Going Glocal: Being Singaporean in a Globalised World (Singapore Perspectives 2006)*, edited by Lai Ah Eng, Singapore;

"People and the Coombs Effect", in *The Coombs: A House of Memories*, edited by Brij Lal and Allison Ley, Canberra;

"Introduction" to "In their Own Words: Personal Reflections as History. Autobiographical Writings when Japan Ruled the Pacific", *Journal of Colonialism and Colonial History*.

"Introduction: Dissent and Affirmation, the Chinese in Singapore", in *Tongmenghui, Sun Yat-sen and the Chinese in Southeast Asia*, edited by Leo Suryadinata, Singapore;

"Foreword: Surface Tensions and Deep Structures", in *Asia and Europe in Globalization: Continents, Regions and Nations*, edited by Goran Therborn and Habibul Haque Khondker, Leiden: Brill;

"Foreword", in *Essays on the Chinese Diaspora in the Caribbean*, edited by Walton Look Lai, St Augustine, Trinidad & Tobago: University of the West Indies;

"Foreword", in Lim Boon Keng, *The Chinese Crisis from Within* (reprint of Wen Ching, *The Chinese Crisis from Within*, published in 1901), Singapore;

"Foreword", in *Malays/Muslims in Singapore: Selected Readings in History, 1819–1965*, edited by Khoo Kay Kim, Elinah Abdullah and Wan Meng Hao, Subang Jaya.

Review of Edward L Dreyer's *Zheng He: China and the Oceans in the Early Ming Dynasty, 1405–1433*, in *International Journal of Maritime History*.

2007 Singapore

Retired as Director of the East Asian Institute and appointed Chairman of its Management Board. Organised the EAI's 10th Anniversary International Conferences, in Chinese and in English.

Appointed University Professor of the National University of Singapore.

Appointed Council Member of the Toyo Bunko Governing Board, Tokyo, 2007–2011.

Appointed member of the White Rose East Asia Centre International Advisory Board, Universities of Leeds and Sheffield, UK, 2007–2011.

Appointed alternate member of the Nalanda Mentor Group, Delhi, 2007–2010.

Awarded Honorary Degree of Doctor of Letters (D. Litt.) of the Open University of Hong Kong.

Donated more of his book collection to the Chinese Heritage Centre Library.

Gave lecture at the Conference on the East Asian Mediterranean, published as "The China Seas: Becoming an Enlarged Mediterranean", in *The East Asian "Mediterranean": Maritime Crossroads of Culture, Commerce and Human Migration*, edited by Angela Schottenhammer, Wiesbaden.

Organised the section on the China Seas for the Conference in Washington DC, on Connecting Seas and Connected Ocean Rims, published "Linkpoints in a Half-Ocean: Introduction to The Worlds of East and Southeast Asian Seas", in *Connecting Seas and Connected Ocean Rims: Indian, Atlantic, and Pacific Oceans and China Seas Migrations from the 1830s to the 1930s*, edited by Donna R Gabaccia and Dirk Hoerder, Leiden: Brill, 2011.

Presented the keynote lecture at the University of Hong Kong, published as *Hong Kong Challenge: Leaning In and Facing Out*, 2009.

Delivered lecture at the Australia Strategic Policy Institute Third International Conference in Canberra, published as "The Great Powers in Asia: a View from Singapore", in *Global Forces 2007*, two volumes, Canberra.

Gave lecture on "Trade, Community and Security in East Asia", at the international conference organised by Waseda University Institute of Asia-Pacific Studies, published in *Towards an East Asian Community: Beyond Cross-Cultural Diversity: Inter-cultural, Inter-societal, Inter-faith Dialogue,* edited by Yasushi Kikuchi, 2008.

Delivered lecture at the University of Kolkata, on "East Asian Regionalism and the Idea of Community".

In conjunction with the official opening of the National University of Singapore Bukit Timah Campus, gave a public lecture on "New University, Three Generations: China, Malaya, Singapore 1949–2007", published in *s/pores: New Directions in Singapore Studies,* at <http://s-pores.com/2008/02/generations/>.

Presented the keynote lecture at the ISSCO Conference in Beijing on "Changes in Focus in the Study of the Chinese Overseas".

Interviews on history and the social sciences, "Rethinking Chinese History in a Global Age: an Interview with Wang Gungwu" by Alan Baumler, in *The Chinese Historical Review;* "In Conversation with Wang Gungwu" by Vineeta Sinha, in *ISA (International Sociological Association) E-Bulletin,* no. 6 (both interviews reprinted in *Wang Gungwu, Junzi Scholar-Gentleman,* 2010);

"*Wang Gengwu jiaoshou de huaqiao huarenshi yanjiu* 王赓武教授的华侨华人史研究" (Professor Wang Gungwu's Overseas Chinese and Chinese People History Studies) by 胡再德 Hu Zaide and 曹云飞 Cao Yunfei, in *Zhongbei daxue xuebao (shehui kexue ban)* 《中北大学学报（社会科学版）》 *Journal of North China Institute of Technology (Social Sciences).*

Published *Divided China: Preparing for Reunification, 883–947,* revised edition of *The Structure of Power in North China during the Five Dynasties*;

"The First Decade: Historical Perspectives", in *The First Decade: The Hong Kong SAR in Retrospective and Introspective Perspectives,* edited by Yeung Yue-man, Hong Kong;

"Trading Order and Polity Structures in Asia", in *The Inclusive Regionalist: A Festschrift dedicated to Jusuf Wanandi,* edited by Hadi Soesastro and Clara Joewono, Jakarta;

"The Pull of Southeast Asia", in *Historians and Their Disciplines: the Call of Southeast Asian History*, edited by Nicholas Tarling;

"*Zouxiang xin de xiandaixing: Xianggang huigui de lishi shijiao*走向新的现代性：香港回归的历史视角" (Towards New Modernity: The Return of Hong Kong from a Historical Perspective), *Er-shih-yi shih-chi*《二十一世纪》*Twenty-First Century*, no. 101;

"China: Economic Strength and Structural Weaknesses?", in *7th Asian-European Editors' Forum*, edited by Werner vom Busch and Tobias Rettig, Singapore;

"Preface", in Gregor Benton, *Chinese Migrants and Internationalism: Forgotten Histories, 1917–1945*, London and New York;

"Preface", in *Chinese Diaspora since Admiral Zheng He, with Special Reference to Maritime Asia*, edited by Leo Suryadinata, Singapore;

"Foreword", in Tan Siok Sun, *Goh Keng Swee: a Portrait*, Singapore.

"Foreword", "The Nanhai Trade: A Study of the Early History of Chinese Trade in the South China Sea" and "The First Three Rulers of Malacca", in Geoff Wade, *Southeast Asia-China Interactions: Reprint of Articles from Journal of the Malaysian Branch of the Royal Asiatic Society*;

"*Zongxu* 总序" Preface to *Nanyang daxuexueshu luncong*《南洋大学学术论丛》(*Nanyang University Research Series*), edited by 陈剑 Chen Jian, 10 volumes, Singapore: The Youth Book Co.

"Opening Remarks", in *World War II: Transient and Enduring Legacies for East and Southeast Asia 60 Years On*, edited by David Koh, Singapore Review of Alexander Woodside's *Lost Modernities: China, Vietnam, Korea, and the Hazards of World History*, in *Pacific Affairs*.

2008   Singapore

Received his second Public Service Medal from the Government of Singapore.

Appointed Corresponding Research Fellow of the Institute of Modern History, Academia Sinica.

Member of the Harvard-Berkeley Research Group on Higher Education in China, 2008–2010.

Invited to be General Editor of Brill Series on Chinese Overseas: History, Literature, Society.

Presented the second Yu Ying-shih Lectures in History at the New Asia College, Chinese University of Hong Kong.

Presented the keynote lecture at the Conference on China and India in Singapore, on "China and India: Different Historical Trajectories".

Gave the opening lecture at the Conference on Chineseness Unbound, organised by Asia Research Institute, NUS, published as "Chinese History Paradigms" in *Asian Ethnicity*, 2009.

Presented lecture at the History of Chinese High Schools Exhibition, organised by the Chinese High School, Singapore, on "*Shixue yu xiandai Zhongguo*史学与现代中国" (Chinese Historiography and Modern China).

Gave the inaugural Lim Boon Keng Memorial Lecture, organised by the China Society, Singapore, published as "The Model Transnational" (excerpts from the lecture), in *The Straits Times*, 9 April 2008.

Delivered the opening lecture at the International Conference on University Education at the Universiti Kebangsaan Malaysia, Bangi, on "Universities and Modernity for Asia".

Presented lecture at the Carter Center, Atlanta on "China's Relations with Southeast Asia".

Presented lecture on "Re-imagining Asia" at the Symposium on New Asian Imaginations at the Nanyang Academy of Fine Arts, Singapore.

Edited, with Zheng Yongnian, *China and the New International Order*, Routledge, 2008.

Published "Flag, Flame and Embers: Diaspora Cultures", in *The Cambridge Companion to Modern Chinese Cultures*, edited by Kam Louie, Cambridge;

"*Nei yu wai de jiexi — lun haiwai Huaren zuojia*内与外的解析－论海外华人作家" (Translation of "Within and Without: Chinese Writers Overseas"), *Shijie Huaqiao Huaren yanjiu*《世界华侨华人研究》 *Overseas Chinese Studies*, vol. 1, 2008;

"India and Indians in East Asia: an Overview", in *Rising India and Indian Communities in East Asia*, edited by K Kesavapany, A Mani, P Ramasamy, Singapore;

"*Qian suo weiyou de ganjue* 前所未有的感觉" (A New Sensation), by Awang Kedua, in *Huidao Malaiya: Huama xiaoshuo qishinian*《回到马来亚：华马小说七十年》*Return to Malaya: Stories by Chinese Malaysian Writers, 1937–2007*, edited by Tee Kim Tong 张锦忠, Ng Kim Chew 黄锦树, Chong Fah Hing 庄华兴, Singapore;

Reminiscences: "Learning Me Your Language", "Trial and Error in Malayan Poetry", and "An Interview with Wang Gungwu by Robert Yeo from the mid-1980s", in *s/pores: New Directions in Singapore Studies*, at <http://s-pores.com/2008/01/learningme/>; <http://s-pores.com/2008/01/malayanpoetry/>; and <http://s-pores.com/2008/02/interview/>);

"Introduction", in Edwin Lee, *Singapore: The Unexpected Nation*, Singapore: Institute of Southeast Asian Studies; and

"Foreword", in H Ly Tio Fane-Pineo and Edouard Lim Fat, *From Alien to Citizen: the Integration of the Chinese in Mauritius*, Rose-Hill, Mauritius: Editions de L'Ocean Indien.

2009 Singapore

Awarded Honorary Degree of Doctor of Letters (D. Litt.) by the University of Cambridge.

Appointed Distinguished Fellow of the Institute of Humanities and Social Sciences at University of Hong Kong.

Appointed Honorary Fellow of the Wolfson College, Cambridge.

In honour of his 80th birthday, East Asian Institute, NUS, organised Conference on China Studies and International Relations, published as *China and International Relations: The Chinese View and the Contribution of Wang Gungwu*, edited by Zheng Yongnian, London: Routledge, 2010.

Delivered the keynote lecture at the Conference for the 100th Anniversary of the 1911 Revolution "九十年来家国: 1919, 1949, 2009", organised by the Academia Sinica, published as "*Dangguo minzhu: sandai haiwai Huaren de jin yu tui* 黨國民主：三代海外華人的進與退" (Party-state

Democracy: Three Generations of Chinese Overseas between Enthusiasm and Skepticism), *Zhongyang yanjiuyuan jindaishi yanjiusuo jikan* 《中央研究院近代史研究所集刊》 *Bulletin of Institute of Modern History, Academia Sinica*, no. 67, 2010.

Presented inaugural lecture, "Changing Images of the Global", in the series Beyond the Headlines, China and the Global Future at University of California, Los Angeles, podcast from UCLA Center for Chinese Studies, at <http://www.international.ucla.edu/china/podcasts/article.asp?parentid=105436>.

Presented the 13th Space for Thought Lecture at London School of Economics, "The State between Migration and Sojourning: The China Difference, at <http://richmedia.lse.ac.uk/publicLecturesAndEvents/2009-0428_1830_theStateBetweenMigrationAndSojourningTheChinaDifference.mp4>.

Gave the keynote lecture at the Fourth International Conference of Institutes and Libraries for Chinese Overseas Studies, organised by Jinan University, on "Migrants Old and New: Perspectives of National Histories".

Presented public lecture at Jinan University, "*Zhonghua wenmin zhiwai* 中华文明之外" (Beyond the Chinese Civilisation).

Delivered the keynote lecture at the international conference, Peranakan Chinese in a Globalizing Southeast Asia: The Cases of Singapore, Malaysia and Indonesia, organised by the Chinese Heritage Centre and NUS Museum/Baba House, published as "The Peranakan Phenomenon: Pre-national, Marginal, and Transnational", in *Peranakan Chinese in a Globalizing Southeast Asia*, edited by Leo Suryadinata (French translation in 2010).

Presented the keynote lecture in Bali, at the Conference on Water in Religious Life: the Impact on South and Southeast Asian History, on "The Openness of the Nusantara World".

Presented the keynote lecture at the Festival of Ideas, Melbourne, "China and the West: the Puzzling Past/The Uneasy Present", Video Podcast, Live@Melbourne, 18 June 2009.

Gave lectures for the Humanities Program at Zhejiang University.

Delivered the opening speech at the conference on Ethnicity, History and Culture (*Zuqun lishi yu wenhua* 族群、历史与文化), organised by the

Department of Chinese Studies, NUS, published as "*Daixu* 代序" ("Preface") in *Zuqun lishi yu wenhua: kuayu yanjiu dongnanya he Dongya — qingzhu Wang Gengwu jiaoshou bashi jinyi huadan zuanji*《族群、历史与文化：跨域研究东南亚和东亚－庆祝王赓武教授八秩晋一华诞专集》 *Ethnicity, History and Culture: Trans-regional and Cross-disciplinary Studies on Southeast Asia and East Asia — In Honour of Professor Wang Gungwu on His 81st Birthday*, two volumes, edited by 黄贤强 Wong Sin Kiong, 2011.

Edited, with Zheng Yongnian, *Zhongguo de "zhuyi" zhi zheng — cong "wusiyundong" dao dangdai*《中国的"主义"之争 — 从"五四运动"到当代》 *China's Ideological Battles since the May Fourth Movement*, Singapore: Global Publishing.

Edited, with Ong Weichong, *Voice of Malayan Revolution: The CPM Radio War against Singapore and Malaysia, 1960–1981*, Singapore.

Published "The Fifty Years Before", in *1959–2009: Chronicle of Singapore: Fifty Years of Headline News*, edited by Peter H L Lim, Singapore;

"One Country, Two Cultures: An Alternative View of Hong Kong", in *Rethinking Hong Kong: New Paradigms, New Perspectives*, edited by Elizabeth Sinn, Wong Siu-lun and Chan Wing-hoi, Hong Kong;

"Introduction", in Taufik Abdullah, *Indonesia: Towards Democracy*, Singapore: Institute of Southeast Asian Studies;

"*Yueyang xunqiu kongjian: Zhongguo de yimin* 越洋寻求空间：中国的移民" (Seeking Their Own Space: China's Migrants), in *Huaren yanjiu guoji xuebao*《华人研究国际学报》 *International Journal of Diasporic Chinese Studies*, 2009; and

"Plus One", "Three Faces of Night" and "A New Sensation", in *Writing Singapore: A Historical Anthology of Singapore Literature*, edited by Angelia Poon, Philip Holden and Shirley Geok-lin Lim, Singapore.

Review of John Lagerway's (editor) *Religion and Chinese Society*, Hong Kong and Paris: The Chinese University Press and Ecole francaise d'Extreme-Orient, Hong Kong and Paris, 2006, two volumes, in *International Sociology of Books*.

Review of Wm. Theodore de Bary's (editor) *Sources of East Asian Tradition Vol. 1, Premodern Asia; Vol. 2, The Modern Period*, New York:

Columbia University Press, two volumes, in *East Asia: an International Quarterly.*

2010 Singapore

Conferred the title Darjah Dato' Paduka Mahkota Perak (DPMP) by the Sultan of Perak, Malaysia.

Appointed member of Nalanda University Governing Council.

Appointed Rector of Cinnamon College of National University of Singapore, home to University Scholars Programme, and focussed on regular meetings with groups of students.

Appointed member of Advisory Board of the European Consortium Project for Integrating and Developing European Asian Studies (IDEAS).

Elected one of seven "Andersonians of the Century" at the 100th Anniversary of Anderson School, Ipoh.

Official opening of the Wang Gungwu Library at the Chinese Heritage Centre as a library open to staff and students of the Nanyang Technological University.

In honour of his 80th birthday, the Institute of Southeast Asian Studies (ISEAS) published *Wang Gungwu, Junzi, Scholar-Gentleman, in conversation with Asad-ul Iqbal Latif.*

Invited by the Indian Council of Cultural Relations to visit India, gave lecture on Chinese history in Delhi, and on Rabindranath Tagore in Kolkata.

Conducted review and assessment of Institute of Malaysian and Indonesian and Studies (IKMAS) at Universiti Kebangsaan Malaysia.

Presented the fourth Fei Xiaotong Memorial Lecture at Peking University, published as *"Zhongguo qingjie: huahua tonghua yu yihua* 中国情结：华化、同化与异化" (Chinese Ties: Sinicisation, Assimilation and Alienation), in *Beijing daxue xuebao*《北京大学学报》*Journal of Peking University*, 2011.

Delivered the NUS Asia Research Institute Public Lecture 2010, "China's Century of Revolutions", NUS-ARI YouTube <http://www.ari.nus.edu.sg/publication_details.asp?pubid=1635&pubtypeid=VI>.

Gave the keynote lecture at Kunming Conference on the Southeast Asian Region, published as "*Guoji jinrong weiji yu Yatai guoji guanxi* 国际金融危机与亚太国际关系" (Global Financial Crisis and International Relations of Asia-Pacific), *Sixiang zhanxian (Kunming)* 《思想战线（昆明）》 *The Ideological Front (Kunming)*, 2010.

Gave concluding remarks at the Asia Research Workshop on Empire, Civilisation and the Anthropology of China, published as "Thoughts on Four Subversive Words", in *The Asia-Pacific Journal of Anthropology*, 2012.

Presented the keynote lecture at the International Conference on Sun Yat-sen, Nanyang and and the 1911 Chinese Revolution, organised by the Institute of Southeast Asian Studies and Chinese Heritage Centre, published as "Sun Yat-sen and the Origins of Modern Chinese Politics", in *Sun Yat-sen: Nanyang and the 1911 Revolution,* edited by Lee Lai To and Lee Hock Guan, 2011 (Chinese translation in 2011).

Presented the keynote lecture at the Hong Kong Central Policy Unit Conference, on "Hong Kong in the Asia-Pacific Region".

Presented the Bridges to the Future Lecture at University of Denver, on "China's Quest: A New Cultural Identity", at <http://blogs.du.edu/today/news/chinese-scholar-sees-a-nation-in-flux-rooted-in-history-with-an-eye-to-the-future>.

Delivered the keynote lecture at the conference on Malaysia-China Relations since 1974, on "Reflections on an Historical Relationship".

Delivered the keynote address at the conference on Towards Building an Inclusive Malaysian Chinese Society, organised by the Centre for Malaysian Chinese Studies, published as "Malaysian Chinese and Regional Developments", in *Malaysian Chinese: an Inclusive Society*, 2011.

Presented the annual lecture to the University of Hong Kong Museum Society, on "Art, History and Revolution: Some Reflections".

Gave the opening address to the 21st Conference of the International Association of Historians of Asia (IAHA) in Singapore, on "Rising Asia: How does the Historian's Role Change?", at <http://www.fas.nus.edu.sg/hist/iaha/index.htm>.

Gave the inaugural Penang Story Lecture, Penang, on "Comparing Sun Yat-sen of Hong Kong and Ku Hung-ming of Penang".

Gave lecture to the Singapore Academy of Law Expert Series, "China as No. 2?"

Published "Introduction: Ships in the Nanyang", in *Shipwrecked: Tang Treasures and Monsoon Winds*, edited by Regina Krahl, John Guy, J Keith Wilson and Julian Raby, Washington DC and Singapore;

"Preface", in *A Scholar's Path, an Anthology of Classical Chinese Poems of Chen Qing Shan: A Pioneer of Malayan-Singapore Chinese Literature*, English Translation and Appreciation by Peter Chen and Michael Tan (Chinese edition in 2010);

"Foreword", in Joergen Orstrom Moller, *How Asia Can Shape the World: from the Era of Plenty to the Era of Scarcity*, Singapore: Institute of Southeast Asian Studies;

"*Xuyan* 序言" (Preface), in *You yangguang de difang jiuyou huaren*《有阳光的地方就有华人》*Where the Sun Shines, There Are Chinese*, edited by 崔贵强 Choi Kwai Keong, three volumes, Singapore.

Interview by Chinese Academy of Social Sciences, published in "*Zhonghua wenmin yu haiwai huaren — fang Xinjiapo guoli daxue teji jiaoshou Wang Gengwu* 中华文明与海外华人－访新加坡国立大学特级教授王赓武" (Chinese Civilisation and Chinese Overseas — An Interview with University Professor Wang Gungwu of the National University of Singapore), in *Zhongguo shehui kexuebao* 《中国社会科学报》 *Chinese Social Sciences Today*, no. 148, 16 Dec. 2010.

2011 Singapore

Deposited parts of his private papers and books to the Institute of Southeast Asian Studies (ISEAS).

Celebrated the 100th Anniversary of the University of Hong Kong at the HKU 100 Gala Dinner.

Presented three lectures on *Wenhua, minzu, guojia: lishi de changhe*文化、民族、国家：历史的长河 at the Chen Yinke 陈寅恪 Lectures at Sun Yat-sen University: the first on "*Wan Tang: tianxia wenhua* 晚唐：天

下文化"; the second on "*Ming Qing zhiji: wenhua minzu* 明清之际：文化民族"; the third on "*Xinhai yihou: minzu guojia, guojia wenhua* 辛亥以后：民族国家、国家文化".

Delivered the China Changing Lecture at the Lowy Institute in Sydney, on "The US and China: Respect and Equality", at <http://www.themonthly.com.au/china-changing-lecture-2011-wang-gungwu-3162>.

Delivered the keynote lecture at the Conference on Hong Kong in the Global Setting, on "*Ershi shiji de Xianggang yu quanqiuhua — jiantan bainian gangda de jueshe* 二十世纪的香港与全球化 — 兼谈百年港大的角色" (On the Edges of Globalization?: Hong Kong's 20th Century), *Xinbao caijing yuekan*《信报财经月刊》*Hong Kong Economic Journal*, no. 411.

Presented the keynote lecture at Lien Fung's Colloquium on Ancient Silk Routes: Cross-Cultural Exchange and Legacy in Southeast Asia.

Gave lecture on "Education as a Mode of Production" at the Hong Kong Institute of Education's Second Asian Roundtable of Presidents of Universities of Education.

Presented the inaugural lecture, on "Possible Dreams: HKU and a Changing Asia" at the University of Hong Kong Libraries Centenary Book Talk Series.

Gave lecture on "Sino-Korean Relationships in History" at the Northeast Asia History Foundation in Seoul.

Published "Secularism Makes a Stand", *10 Years after September 11*, Social Science Research Council (SSRC) Essay Forum.

2012   Singapore

Awarded Honorary Degree of Doctor of Laws (LL.D.) by Wawasan Open University, Malaysia.

Conducted review of the Sun Yat-sen Institute of Humanities and Social Science, Academia Sinica.

Commentator at the Integrating and Developing European Asian Studies (IDEAS) International Conference, at the Chinese University of Hong Kong.

Presented the plenary lecture on "Power and Faith in China, Past and Present" at Faith and Power Symposium at Universiti Sains Malaysia, Penang.

Presented lecture on "Who are the Chinese Overseas Today?" at University of Malaya, Kuala Lumpur.

Gave lecture on "The China Effect in Anxious Europe" at the Symposium on Rising Asia at the University of Copenhagen.

Delivered lectures on "*Song Yuan Ming sanchao Zhongguo yu Dongnanya guanxi* 宋元明三朝中国与东南亚关系" and "*Qingchao de Dongnanya huaqiao shehui* 清朝的东南亚华侨社会" at Zhejiang University, Hangzhou.

Roundtable presentation on "China in Asia, Then and Now", HKU-SSRC Workshop on Inter-Asian Connections, Institute of Humanities and Social Sciences, Hong Kong.

Delivered the keynote lecture, "Autonomy for Overseas Chinese?", at the Conference on Trajectories of Chinese Communities in Southeast Asia, at the Singapore Management University, Singapore.

Gave the keynote lecture, "Imperial China and its Southern Neighbours", at International Conference on Imperial China and its Southern Neighbours, Nalanda Srivijaya Centre, ISEAS, Singapore.

Presented lecture on "The Call for Malaysia: 50 Years On" at the 17th James C Jackson Memorial Lecture to the Malaysia and Singapore Society of Australia at the Asian Studies Association of Australia Conference in Sydney.

Published "A Two-Ocean Mediterranean", in *Anthony Reid and the Study of the Southeast Asian Past*, edited by Geoff Wade and Li Tana, Singapore;

"Thoughts on Four Subversive Words", in *The Asia-Pacific Journal of Anthropology*;

"*Wang Gengwu fangtanlu — zai quanqiuhua shidai fansi Zhongguo lishi* 王赓武访谈录—在全球化时代反思中国历史" (Rethinking Chinese History in a Global Age: an interview with Wang Gungwu), in *Zhongguo renleixue pinglun*《中国人类学评论》*Chinese Review of Anthropology* (translation of Alan Baumler's "Rethinking Chinese History in a Global Age: an interview with Wang Gungwu" first published in *The Chinese Historical Review*, 2007).

"China's Historical Place Reclaimed", review article of Henry Kissinger's *On China*, New York: The Penguin Press, 2011; and Martin Jacques's *When China Rules the World: the End of the Western World and the Birth of a New World Order*, New York: The Penguin Press, 2009, in *Australian Journal of International Affairs*.

Index

academic elitism, 170
American model,
    funding for universities, 51–52, 55–56, 185
    Japanese skepticism about, 91
Anglo-American standards, 180
Anglo-Chinese, 229–232
anti-missionary movement, 306
Arts and Social Sciences, 77, 132, 175–176
Asia-Europe Meeting (ASEM), 155, 157
Asia-Pacific, vii, 29, 92
    English as an international language, 95
    institutions of higher education in, 96–97
    that includes the United States, 28
    universalism in education, 76, 87, 89
    what regionalism means in, 84–86
Asia-Pacific Economic Cooperation (APEC), 79, 92, 95–97
Asian renaissance, 72, 74
Asian studies, 221–223
Asian universities,
    basic operation structures of, 12–15
    comparative survey of, 64
    layers of relationship with the community, 8–9
    paradigmatic shift, 131–133
    revival of new kinds of European studies, 157
    tackling the problem of social science, 114–117
    the first, 49
assimilation, 135–136
    "melting pot" ideal, 136
    "nation-state" ideal, 136

Association of Commonwealth
Universities (ACU), 77, 90,
215–216
Association of Southeast Asian
Institutions of Higher Learning
(ASAIHL), 3, 17, 80–81, 92–93
Commonwealth university
values, 214
First Asian Workshop on Higher
Education, 6
Second Asian Workshop on
Higher Education, 3, 17
Association of Southeast Asian
Nations (ASEAN), 79
intra-regional exchange, 81
linguistic variety, 227
regional identity, 93–94
Australia,
establish diplomatic ties with
China, viii
referred to as the West, 84,
105–106
Australian National University (ANU),
Commonwealth model, 160
director of Research School of
Pacific Studies, vii
Emeritus Professor, 317
professor and head of
Department of Far Eastern
History, vii,
tenure from 1968 to 1986, 53

Bahasa Indonesia, 93, 226, 229
Bahasa Malaysia, 226, 229
Barisan Socialis, Singapore, 205
Beijing,
4 May 1919, 209, 211
after 1949, 40
missionary institutions, 187
pre-handover negotiation
between London and, ix

successful transplantation of
modern secular university
in, 87
the idea of a modern university
started in, 46
bilingual education,
in advancing science and
technology, 232
Book of History, The, 140
borderless world paradigm, the,
122, 134–136
Britain,
polytechnics converted to
universities, 54
see also United Kingdom
British,
first clear and lasting
breakthrough in Asia, 111
control the largest maritime
empire, 164
universities in former territories,
88
British colonies, 156, 198, 218
Singapore, 163–164
British Commonwealth,
education system, 72, 172
British Empire, vi
British excellence, 90
British government, vi, 46
British India, 71
the educated elites in, 218
the first universities in, 87, 148
British Malaya, 165, 173, 198–201,
267
see also Malaya
British model, 77, 175
early rejection in Burma, 90
British power, 166, 176
British Protected Persons, 200
British rule, 166, 174–175
British superiority, 156

British universities,
  the oldest, 146
British vulnerability, 167
Buddhism, 10, 106, 140, 222
Buddhist,
  priesthood of high ranks, 184
  scriptures, 141
  value system, 76, 89
Bukit Timah campus, NUS, viii, 159, 197, 206
Burma,
  early rejection of British model in universities, 90
business (schools/studies), 60
  in Britain, 146
  in Singapore, 170–171

Cai Yuanpei, 185
capitalism, 28, 40, 78, 121, 134, 140–141, 146
Cardinal Newman,
  idea of university, 60, 89
Carr-Saunders Commission, 168
Carr-Saunders Report, 162
Catholic Church, 48, 51
  Asia's earliest colleges, 49, 112, 147
  separation of church and state, 48
Chen Cheng-i, 40
Chen Duxiu, 37, 210
Chen Li-fu,
  Sheng chih yuan-li (The Philosophy of Life), 38
Cheng Ho expedition, 222
Chiang Kai-shek, 73
China,
  education being a private affair in, 47
  elitist roots of education in, 184–185
  emigrants to the United States, 230
  ensure no threat from external power, 194
  its earlier scientific discoveries, 39, 66–67
  its first foreign language, 230–231
  major foreign language of higher education, 230
  the changing education culture during wartime, 186–187
  see also People's Republic of China
China Presence, the, 198–202, 206
Chinese civilisation,
  knowledge transmission, 38
  no less scientific than the West, 33–34
Chinese Communist Party, 37
  preserving loyalty of, 190
  transformation of higher education 30 years after victory of, 186–187
Chinese coolies, 231
Chinese diaspora, viii, 247
Chinese entrepreneur,
  today, 142–143
  traditional, 142
Chinese entrepreneurship, 142
Chinese mandarinate, 190
  the best tradition of, 188
  see also mandarins
Chinese medium schools, 199
Chinese-medium students, 199
Chinese migration, viii, 248–250, 258–259
Chinese Nobel laureates, 148
Chinese Orientalism, 222
Chinese re-migrants, 230

Chinese scientists,
  rediscover a scientific tradition for China, 33
Chinese University of Hong Kong, 214–215
Christianity,
  in 20-century China, 112
Chulalongkorn University, 88, 92–93
cities,
  universalist education, 75–78, 85–86, 89
clash of civilisations, 28, 84, 124, 134–135
Cold War,
  ideological divide, impact of, 77, 90–92
  new world order defined, the end of, 28, 84
colonial universities, 48
colonisation,
  in the Philippines, second round of, 112
Commander of the Order of the British Empire, ix
Commonwealth (higher education),
  model, 160
  system, 56, 161
  universities, 77, 90, 175–176, 198, 213–216
community,
  the concept of, 9–10
"Confucian" civilisation,
  in response to scientific method, 33
  may end Western dominance, 28, 84
Confucian values, 76, 89, 170
  mandarinate, 140, 170, 184
Confucianism, 10, 222
  Lim Boon Keng, 36
  rejection of, 209
  indirect contribution to entrepreneurship, 140–141
cultural pluralism, 136
Cultural Revolution, 182, 188, 191

decolonisation, 80, 88, 114, 130, 156, 163, 166, 175, 191, 198, 213
democracy, 28, 37, 119, 211, 219
democratisation,
  the Chinese, 193
Deng Xiaoping, 73
  his published works, times have changed, 141
  resume formal nationwide examination, 188
  radical reforms, 191

East Asia,
  English language and national languages, 227
East Asian Institute (EAI), NUS,
  chairman, vi, vii
  director, vii
Eastern Europe,
  state paid for education, 53
  turning away from Marxist science, 116, 132
economics,
  shifting paradigm, 133
  Wang's subject at University of Malaya, vi
educational excellence, 29, 76, 88
  a shared sense of, 77
  regionalism approach to, 85–86
  the measures/ standards/ ideals of, 89–97
educational expansion, 88, 102, 127
  in Australia, 88
  in Hong Kong, 215
  in NUS, 174
educational regionalism, 92–94
elite excellence, 28, 83

emigration, 135
"end-of-history" school of thought, 28, 120–121, 134
engineering (fields/ studies),
    famous engineering universities in China, 182
    in Britain, 146, 165
    in China, 187–188
    in Singapore, 170–171
    modernisation as goal, 148
    take prominent place in Asian society, 126–127
English (language), 225–227, 229–232
    as an international language, 95
English-language schools in Malaya, 166–167, 198–202, 204
English literature,
    Wang's subject at University of Malaya, vi
Enlightenment, 48, 76, 88, 122, 135
European Continental system, 56
European studies, 157
European Union, 79, 157, 225

Fa-hsien, 222
Faculty of Arts and Social Sciences, NUS,
    faculty professor, vii
Federation of Malaya, 160–161, 168, 200
Feng Dao, 265
Four Books, 140
France, 112, 148, 156–157
    Catholic missions, 46, 88
    language nationalists in, 225
French,
    Cohin-China, 72
French colonials, 156
French empire, 73–74
French language, 226
French missionaries, 46, 185, 187

French model, 64
French Revolution, 48, 86
Fudan University, 186
Fukuyama, Francis, 118, 123, 127
    "end of history" thought, 120–121, 134

German,
    missionary institutions, Tongji, 187
    Lutheran missions, 46
German universities, 48–49
gewu, 34
global institution, 64–69, 108
globalisation, 68, 85, 105, 122, 135–136, 149
Goh Keng Swee, vii
Great Depression, vi, 50, 317
Great Leap Forward, 194
Gu Hongming, 35
Guangzhou,
    missionary colleges, 46, 187
    Sun Yat-sen University, 187
Guha, Ranajit, 118, 120, 123, 127
    creative application of concepts of Marxist social philosophy, 119
guiqiao (returned overseas Chinese), 231
Gurney, Henry, 204

Hanlinyuan (Collage of Letters), 47
higher education,
    Chinese imperial government, 46–47
    Chinese pursuit of, 181–195
    state responsibility for, 48
    region and universalism in, 83–97
history,
    Wang's subject at University of Malaya, vi

historian,
    Wang, as a, vi, 38, 111, 129, 145
Hong Kong,
    get out of the Commonwealth mould, 215
    major sources of Anglo-Chinese, 230–232
    new universities during the "Commonwealth" phase, 214
Hong Kong University of Science and Technology, 214–215
Hu Shih, 37, 73, 210
humanities,
    classical traditions of knowledge, 109–111
    commonalities and comparisons with social sciences in Asia, 110–117
    less mass appeal in Singapore, 170–171
    major source of cultural enrichment, 151, 150–152
    relevance and awareness of change, 25
    resistance to new paradigms, 131
Huntington, Samuel
    clash of civilisations, 28, 124, 134–135

imperial examinations, 47, 183, 185
imperial government, Qing dynasty,
    taking up the idea of modern university, 46–47
imperial universities,
    Japan, 49, 87
Industrial Revolution, 34, 40, 76, 86, 146
Institute of East Asian Political Economy,
    chairman, vii
Institute of Southeast Asian Studies,
    chairman, vi

international metropolitanism, 75, 86
internationalisation, 174
    in Japan, 77, 91
    in Universitas 21, 103

Japan,
    adopt German model, 49
    as Western extensions, 28, 84
    calls for internationalisation, 77, 91
    economic miracle of, 88, 139
    education in, 73, 87
    first Asian universities completely supported by state, 49
    long history of studying China as its Other, 223
    rapid economic development, 49
    Tokugawa, 227
Japanese atrocities, 238
Japanese,
    Asian language, 226–227
    educational criteria to remain unique, 91
    learn technologies of the West, 112
    look to the West, 148
    national renaissance, 73
    share Classical Chinese and doctrinal texts of Confucius, 140
    studies of Chinese Buddhism, 222
Japanese Occupation,
    Ipoh under, 318
Japanese war, 186, 201
Jingshi Daxuetang (the Metropolitan University), 46
jinshi (advanced scholars), 47
June Fourth, 210
jus sanguine (the law of descent), 200

Kang Youwei, 47, 73
Keio University, 87, 148
Kent Ridge campus, NUS, viii, 159, 161, 174, 197, 205
King Edward VII College of Medicine, 160, 165, 173–174
knowledge-driven creativity, 125
knowledge-driven shifts, 133–135
    "borderless world" paradigm, 135
    "clash of civilisations", 135
    "end of history", 134–135
    from unisex (male) analysis to gender studies, 134
    Orientalism, 134
    postcolonial, postmodernism paradigms, 133–134
Korean War, 201
Kuala Lumpur,
    University of Malaya in, 46, 199, 204, 214
Kuomintang (KMT), 181, 185, 200, 214–215

Labour Party, Australia, 53–54
Labour Party, Singapore, 205
Lao Zi, 140, 142
Lee Kuan Yew, 15, 72
Lee Kuan Yew School of Public Policy,
    chairman, vi
"Let the Hundred Flowers Bloom" campaign, 188
Li Ka-shing, 44
Liang Qichao, 35, 73
liberal social science, 115–116, 131
Lim Boon Keng, 36, 50–51
literati, Chinese, 183–185, 190
Lu Xun (Hsun), 36, 73, 250

Malacca, 200
Malay nationalism, 161, 203–204

Malay States, 164–166, 198, 200, 218
Malaya,
    at tail end of imperial expansion, 164
    Emergency, 168–169, 175–176, 201–202
    independence, 176–200
    see also British Malaya
Malaya Dream, the, 198–199, 202–205
Malayan Communist Party, vi, 176, 201, 306–307
Malaysian Malaysia, 169, 205
mandarins, 47, 100, 183–184, 190
    see also Chinese mandarinate
Mao Zedong, 73, 169, 188, 193–194, 199
Marshall, David, 205
Marxist-Leninist,
    value of writings of, 141
Marxist paradigm, 116, 132
Marxist science, 115–116, 131–133
May Fourth Movement, 186, 211
    70th anniversary in 1989, 210
    80th anniversary in 1999, 210
    demonstrations in 1919, 209
    learning science, after 1920, 34–35
mediaeval history,
    Wang's PhD in, vi, 322
medicine,
    field of study, 30–31, 33, 60, 77, 91, 111, 117, 126–127, 148, 165, 182
    King Edward VII College of Medicine, 160
Melayu Raya, 167, 202
meritocracy, 102
    in Asian universities, 23
    in Chinese bureaucracy, 184
    in education, 66

NUS founding concept, 179
of the mandarinate, 170
metropolitan powers, 79, 90
missionary colleges, 46–47, 50,
  64–65, 88, 112, 148, 185, 187, 202,
  230–231
modern university/universities,
  63–64, 76, 108, 145, 151, 163, 177
  decisive break from the past, 193
  established after 1945 in Asia,
    147
  in China, 46
  in Japan, 50
  the heritage of, 99–101
  the universalism phenomenon in,
    86–88
modernity, 145–153
  values of, 145–146

Nanjing, vi, viii, 44–46, 87, 181–182
Nanyang Technological University,
  214
Nanyang University (Nantah), 169,
  201
  demographics of students, 199
  Commonwealth phase, 214
  Curriculum Revision Committee,
    161
  merge with University of
    Singapore, 161, 205
nation, concept of, 10
nation-building, 14, 100, 168, 179,
  189
nation-state, 86
  China neither a conventional
    empire nor a mere, 194
  ideal, 136
  shift to borderless world, 135
  Singapore, 168
nation-statism,
  the resurgence of nationalism,
    86

National Central University, vi, viii,
  44–45, 181, 186
national education
  in Singapore, 32
  in the context of promodern
    scientific traditions, 41
national identity,
  China, 35
  Malaya, 203–204
  Singapore, 179
  Thai, 73
National Taiwan University, 148
National University of Singapore
  (NUS), 159–180
  centennial celebrations in 2005,
    vii
  in Universitas 21, 103
  merger of Nanyang University
    and the University of
    Singapore, 161, 205
  Bukit Timah campus of, 197
  contributing to the leadership of
    professional classes and
    national community, 178
  plural society model, 164–166,
    168–169, 174, 178–180
nationalism, 179, 227
  Chinese, 191
  Chinese revolutionary, 200
  communal, 168
  Indian, 119
  Malay, 161, 203–204
nationalist awakening, 209–210
natural sciences,
  as key criteria of excellence, 150
  commonality with humanities,
    123–124
  comparisons with social
    sciences, 117–119, 151
  dominance of scientific
    knowledge, 110–113, 126–127
  in University of Berlin, 146

intertwining creativity with
social sciences, 125
its advent in Europe, 109
main penetration in universities,
77, 91
new opportunities in, 187
Needham, Joseph,
*Science and Civilisation in
China*, 39, 66
neo-Confucian,
ideas and practices, 35
neo-Marxist, 116, 132
Network of East Asian Think-Tanks
(NEAT), ix
nong-gong-shang (peasant-artisan-
merchant), 191
North American model,
funding for universities, 51–52,
55–57, 185
Japanese skepticism about,
91
see also American model
North Korea, 77, 91

Occidentals,
the Other, 221–223
Ohmae, Kenichi (Ken, Kenneth), 123,
127, 135
"the borderless world", "the end
of the nation state" paradigm,
121–122
one world paradigm, 122, 135
Orientalism, 134, 221
Chinese, 222
imperial, 222
Said, Edward, 120
overseas Chinese, viii, 35, 142

paradigms,
meaning of, 129–130, 137
Parkinson, C N, vi
Peking University, 46

contribute to China's historical
transformation, 185–186,
209–211
People's Action Party, 169, 205
People's Republic of China,
law of descent, 200
side with the Soviet Union, 201
see also China
Philippines, the, 72, 77, 80, 88, 91,
113, 148, 156
Spanish universities, first Western
type in Asia, 49, 64, 112
Phua Kok Khoo, v, xii
politicisation of science, 37
polytechnics,
in Britain, 54
in Singapore, 170
private universities, 54–55, 57
in China, 44–45, 51, 56–57, 88,
183
in Japan, 49, 87
in the United States, 51–52, 57,
126
University of Melbourne, 54
Xiamen University, 43–45, 50
provincialism,
English-language, 217
imperial, 218
Public Service Medal, Singapore, ix
public universities, 45, 57, 197
American, 51–52, 126
Chinese, 45, 57, 64, 87, 185

Qian Wenyuan, 39
Qing dynasty, 40, 46, 142, 155

Raffles College, 159–160, 165,
173–174
Record of the Buddhistic Kingdoms,
222
regionalism,
in higher education, 85–86

postcolonial, 90
the ASAIHL in Southeast Asia,
   92–94
Reid, Anthony, 223
Republic of China (Taiwan), 200
   see also Taiwan
revisionism, 116, 132, 211
   anti-colonial, 114, 130
Romance of the Three Kingdoms, 140

Said, Edward, 118, 123, 127
   Orientalism, 120
School of Oriental and African
   Studies,
   as Rockefeller Fellow, 324
   awarded Honorary Fellow of,
      359
   graduate study in, vi, 46, 321
Science Society, 37
scientific tradition,
   12th to 15th centuries, 31
   17th century, 31
   early traditions, 30
   in China during the 20th century,
      33
   the Muslims and the Christians,
      30
scientism, 37
Scottish renaissance, 71, 73–74, 217
Scottish education, 71
   Gu Hongming, 35
secular education, 86, 157, 231
secular university, 87–89
Sen, Amartya, 120–123
   first Asian to receive a Nobel
      prize in economics, 113
   creativity from layers of
      economic and social theory,
      117–119
separation of Singapore from
   Malaysia, 161, 199
Shandong, 209

Shanghai, 226, 229, 232
   missionaries colleges, 46, 187
   the most cosmopolitan city in
      Asia, 73
   universities in, 87, 182,
      186–187
Shantou University, 44
Sima Qian, 140
Singapore,
   a British colony, 164
   Chinese in, 249–250
   comparison with the United
      States, 52
   education scene in, 32
   first world country, 163,
      170–171
   major sources of Anglo-Chinese,
      230–232
   remaking of, 198, 205–206
   separation from Malaysia,
      199
   the first Singapore, before the
      Second World War, 164–166
   the second Singapore, 166–170
   the third Singapore, 170–172
   who should pay for universities,
      51–56
Sino-Japanese war, 201
situational change, 114, 117, 130
situational shifts, 130–133
   from classical/traditional to
      modern/Western, 131
   from colonial to the anti-colonial
      (decolonisation), 130–131
   from culturalist to anti-
      culturalist, 133
   from liberal social science to
      Marxist "science", 131–132
social sciences, 77, 91, 129, 155,
   175–176, 188
   Asian studies, 222
   challenges of, 126–128

commonalities and comparisons
  with humanities in Asia,
  110–117
in quest for modernity, 152–153
its position between humanities
  and natural science, 110–113
less mass appeal in Singapore,
  170–171
rapid rise of, 150
shifting paradigms, 131–133,
  137
the use of, 151
work within value system,
  152
Yan Fu, 35
Son of Heaven, 184
South Asia,
  earliest modern universities in,
  72
  quality of English language in,
  227
South Asia's renaissance, 72
South Korea, 77, 88, 91, 132
  four tigers of East Asia, 139
Southeast Asia,
  competing cultural values, 89
  developments of scientific
    knowledge, 112–113
  educational regionalism, 92–94
  solution to its linguistic variety,
  203
Soviet model, 88
Soviet Union, 84, 156–157
  after the fall of, 134–135
  free education, 53, 56
  Marxist paradigms, 116, 132
Straits Chinese, 165, 199
Straits Settlements, 71, 164, 198, 218
Sukarno, 72
Sun Yat-sen, 73, 191, 210
Sun Yat-sen University, 187
Surabaya, vi, 317

Taiwan, 40, 73, 77, 91, 116, 139,
  141, 148, 187, 200, 230, 232
  see also Republic of China
Tan Kah Kee, 43–46, 50–51, 58
Tang poems, 140
Taoism, 10, 140
Thailand, 156
  Chulalongkorn University, 88
three rejections,
  in modern Chinese history, 192
Tiananmen Square/incident,
  pro-democracy demonstrations,
  210–211
Tianjin, 46
Toynbee, Arnold, 124
traditional society, 47
Tsinghua University, 186

ummat, 10, 115
United Kingdom,
  burden of financing higher
    education, 55
  model of proven excellence and
    universal validity, 90
  see also Britain
United Nations,
  future of, 300
United Southwestern University, 186
United States,
  as a superpower, 219
  at top third of pyramid, 28, 84
  balance of power in the, 90, 91
  model in education, 51–52,
    56–57
  see also American model
universal academy,
  concepts of, 66, 102
universalism, 85
  in education, 76, 86, 94–97
  of knowledge, 87, 90
Universitas 21, 103
Universiti Brunei Darussalam, 214

Universiti Kebangsaan Malaysia, 214
Universiti Putra Malaysia, 214
Universiti Sains Malaysia, 214
Universiti Teknoloji Malaysia, 214
Universiti Utara Malaysia, 214
universities
    as bureaucratic structures, 13
    as non-political mixed structures, 12–13
    as political structures, 13
    Chinese policies of, 46–47
    Commonwealth phase, 214
    Empire phase, 213–214
    European, 6, 48, 56, 100
    first introduced on the peripheries of ancient civilisations, 64
    in Asia, 101
    international English-speaking phase, 214
    post-1950, 214
    the image of, 6
    under totalitarian systems, 14
    what being political means, 12
university,
    an ivory tower, 7, 104
    as a global institution, 64–69, 108, 262
    definition of, 102
    the image of, 6
University of Berlin,
    the first university that fits modern criteria, 146–147
University of Bombay, 48, 64, 72, 87, 111, 148, 165
University of Calcutta, 48, 64, 72, 87, 111, 148, 165
University of Cambridge, 48–49, 146, 160
University of Hong Kong,
    bridging the East and the West, 64
    Commonwealth universities, 213
    educational regionalism, 92
    in Universitas 21, 103
    vice-chancellor of, vii-viii, 346
University of Indonesia, 92–93
University of Kyoto, 48–49, 87, 148
University of London,
    municipal responsibility towards, 49
    the direct model in British India, 148
    Wang did graduate research at, 160
    Wang's PhD research at, 321–322
University of Madras, 48, 64, 72, 87, 111, 148, 165
University of Malaya (MU),
    a member of ASAIHL, 92–93
    elitism, 170, 174
    English-language university in a Malay world, 198
    in Bukit Timah campus, 159, 197
    in the new Federation of Malaya, 160, 168, 213–214
    Malaya under Emergency rule in 1948, 175, 199–202
    merging of two colleges in Singapore, 161–162, 166–167
    nation-building, 179
    study and return to teach in, vi, 45–46, 181, 319–325, 328, 330
University of Melbourne,
    initiative in Universitas 21, 103
    modern university in Australia, 100, 103–104
    setting up a private university, 54
University of Rangoon, 88, 213–214
University of Santo Tomas, 49, 147
University of Singapore, 161, 169, 204–205
University of Tokyo, 49–50, 64, 87, 148

Versailles conference, 209
Vietnam,
    French-speaking, foreign
        language status, 90, 226
    Marxist paradigm, 116, 132
Visva Bharati University,
    merge Indian and European ideas
        and values, 148
von Humbodlt, Wilhelm, 146

Wang Gungwu, v-ix, 315–396
Wang Gungwu,
    his authored works, 235–271
    (in alphabetical order)
    *A Short History of the Nanyang
        Chinese* 南洋華人簡史,
        237–238
    *Anglo-Chinese Encounters since
        1800: War, Trade, Science and
        Governance*, 262–263
    *Bind Us in Time: Nation and
        Civilisation in Asia*, 261–262
    離鄉別土：境外看中華 *China
        and its Cultures: from the
        Periphery*, 269–270
    *China and Southeast Asia: Myths,
        Threats and Culture*, 253–254
    China and the Chinese Overseas,
        249–251
    *China and the World since 1949:
        The Impact of Independence,
        Modernity and Revolution*,
        242–244
    *Community and Nation: Essays
        on Southeast Asia and the
        Chinese*, 244–246
    *Community and Nation: China,
        Southeast Asia and Australia*
        (New Edition), 244–246
    *Divided China: Preparing for
        Reunification 883–947*,
        270–271
    *Don't Leave Home: Migration
        and the Chinese*, 258–260
    *Ideas Won't Keep: The Struggle
        for China's Future*, 264–265
    *Joining the Modern World:
        Inside and Outside China*,
        254–255
    移民與興起的中國 *Migrants
        and the Rise of China*,
        268–269
    *Only Connect! Sino-Malay
        Encounters*, 265–267
    王賡武自选集 *Selected Works of
        Wang Gungwu*, 260–261
    東南亞與華人：王賡武教授論
        文選集 *Southeast Asia and the
        Chinese*, 246–248
    *The Chinese Overseas: From
        Earthbound China to the
        Quest for Autonomy*,
        256–258
    *The Chinese Way: China's
        Position in International
        Relations*, 252–253
    *The Chineseness of
        China — Selected Essays*,
        251–252
    *The Nanhai Trade: The Early
        History of Chinese Trade in
        the South China Sea* 南海貿易
        與南洋華人, 236–237
    *The Structure of Power in North
        China during the Five
        Dynasties*, 239–241
    歷史的功能 *The Use of History*,
        248–249
    *To Act is to Know: Chinese
        Dilemmas*, 267–268
Wang Gungwu,
    his edited and co-edited works,
        272–309
    (in alphabetical order)

Changing Identities of the Southeast Asian Chinese since World War II, 281–282

China and the New International Order, 304–305

China: Two Decades of Reform and Change, 293–294

中国的"主义"之争：从"五四运动"到当代 *China's Ideological Battles since the May Fourth Movement*, 305–306

China's Political Economy, 289–291

Damage Control: The Chinese Communist Party in the Jiang Zemin Era, 298–299

Dynamic Hong Kong: Business and Culture, 285–286

Essays on the Sources for Chinese History, 274–275

Global History and Migrations, 286–288

Hong Kong: Dilemmas of Growth, 277–279

香港史新編 — Volumes 1 and 2 *Hong Kong History: New Perspectives*, 283–284

Hong Kong in China: The Challenges of Transition, 294–295

Hong Kong in the Asia-Pacific Region: Rising to the New Challenges, 288–289

Hong Kong's Transition: A Decade after the Deal, 282–283

Malaysia: A Survey, 273–274

Maritime China in Transition 1750–1850, 301–302

Nation-Building: Five Southeast Asian Histories, 302–303

Reform, Legitimacy and Dilemmas: China's Politics and Society, 295–297

Self and Biography: Essays on the Individual and Society in Asia, 276–277

Society and the Writer: Essays on Literature in Modern Asia, 279–280

The Chinese Diaspora: Selected Essays Volumes I and II, 291–292

The Iraq War and its Consequences: Thoughts of Nobel Peace Laureates and Eminent Scholars, 300–301

Voice of Malayan Revolution: The CPM Radio War against Singapore and Malaysia, 1969–1981, 306–307

王宓文纪念集 *Wang Fo-wen, 1903–1972: a Memorial Collection of Poems, Essays and Calligraphy*, 297–298

Wang Gungwu, Festschrifts, 308–313

(in alphabetical order)

Diasporic Chinese Ventures: The Life and Work of Wang Gungwu, 312–313

海外华人研究的大视野与新方向 *Overseas Chinese Studies: New Horizon and Direction — Collected Essays by Professor Wang Gungwu*, 310

Power and Identity in the Chinese World Order: Festschrift in Honour of Professor Wang Gungwu, 311

坦蕩人生，學者情懷：王賡武訪談與言論集 *The Life and*

Sentiment of a Scholar: Anthology of Professor Wang Gungwu's Interviews and Speeches, 309
Waseda University, 87, 148
Western civilisation,
  breakthrough into the East, 87
  complex nature of, 150
  doubt about its supremacy, 124
  universalist approach, 29
Whitlam, Gough, 53
Wilson, David, ix
Wong Lin Ken, 161
Workers' Party, Singapore, 205
world, the
  as a pyramid, 28, 84

  as a universal civilisation, 29, 85, 87
Wu Lien-teh, 36

Xi'an Jiaotong University, 182
Xiamen (Amoy) University, 36, 43–45, 50, 58
Xin Zhongguo, 202
Xuan Zang,
  qu jing (to bring back the sutras), 194–195

Yangtze River, 44, 317
Yan Fu, 35

Zheng Yongnian, v, xi
Zhou Enlai, 73
Zhuang Zi, 140, 142

www.ingramcontent.com/pod-product-compliance
Lightning Source LLC
Chambersburg PA
CBHW070306230426
43664CB00015B/2648